Louis Armstrong, Duke Ellington, and Miles Davis

D1287466

Louis Armstrong, Duke Ellington, and Miles Davis

A Twentieth-Century Transnational Biography

Aaron Lefkovitz

LEXINGTON BOOKS
Lanham • Boulder • New York • London

Published by Lexington Books
An imprint of The Rowman & Littlefield Publishing Group, Inc.
4501 Forbes Boulevard, Suite 200, Lanham, Maryland 20706
www.rowman.com

Unit A, Whitacre Mews, 26-34 Stannary Street, London SE11 4AB

Copyright © 2018 by The Rowman & Littlefield Publishing Group, Inc.

All rights reserved. No part of this book may be reproduced in any form or by any electronic or mechanical means, including information storage and retrieval systems, without written permission from the publisher, except by a reviewer who may quote passages in a review.

British Library Cataloguing in Publication Information Available

Library of Congress Cataloging-in-Publication Data

Names: Lefkovitz, Aaron E., author.
Title: Louis Armstrong, Duke Ellington, and Miles Davis : a twentieth-century transnational biography / Aaron Lefkovitz.
Description: Lanham : Lexington Books, 2018. | Includes bibliographical references and index.
Identifiers: LCCN 2018017569 (print) | LCCN 2018020696 (ebook) | ISBN 9781498567527 (Electronic) | ISBN 9781498567510 (cloth) | ISBN 9781498567534 (pbk.) Subjects: LCSH: Jazz--History and criticism. | Music and transnationalism. | Armstrong, Louis, 1901-1971. | Ellington, Duke, 1899-1974. | Davis, Miles. | Jazz musicians. | Music and race.
Classification: LCC ML3506 (ebook) | LCC ML3506 .L417 2018 (print) | DDC 781.65092/2--dc23
LC record available at https://lccn.loc.gov/2018017569

Table of Contents

Introduction

Jazz's racial, gender, sexual, ethnic, class, national, and transnational dimensions were the intersecting modalities in which African-American virtuoso trumpeter, vocalist, composer, actor, and "jazz ambassador" Louis Armstrong (1901–1971), Duke Ellington (1899–1974), one of the most internationally acclaimed African-American jazz composers, songwriters, bandleaders, arrangers, pianists, and cultural diplomats, and legendary, eclectic, and controversial jazz trumpeter Miles Davis (1926–1991) negotiated their insider/outsider status in US and transnational popular cultures. Illuminating jazz as a political-cultural force central to US and international cultural histories, used to confirm US exceptionalist claims and the concept of the free-spifrited, convention-defying "musical genius" as the ultimate construction of the bourgeois subject, in their lives and music, Armstrong, Ellington, and Davis challenged myths of US jazz exceptionalism by living and performing jazz's transnational character. Each accentuates jazz's evolution, from its roots in Africa and the southern United States to the myriad styles heard around the world, confounding claims that this supposedly quintessential and uniquely "American music" should be confined to the United States's borders and used to buttress claims of US distinctiveness and superiority.

Armstrong, Ellington, and Davis highlight jazz's innovations, the importance of improvisation in the musical culture, jazz's privileged place in US self-perceptions, and how jazz has long been part of the political-cultural heritage of musicians and audiences of various races, gender, sexualities, classes, and nations. Each notes jazz as a source of inspiration for rock, pop, and hip hop, links between the jazz soloist's rise and US myths of individualism, and ways a work of art's content and form gains adherence from how well it agrees with fashionable political-cultural trends and ideologies.[1] Armstrong, Ellington, and Davis illuminate jazz's transformations from a distinct, turn-of-the-twentieth-century musical style and its emergence out of ragtime during an era of the growth of cities and industries through the 1930s swing-era and post–World War II anti-assimilationist bebop experimentations.[2]

In their unique compositions and politically implicated styles, Armstrong, Ellington, and Davis serve as examples of ways popular music was influenced by and influenced US political-cultural movements, operating as a marker for the emergent 1920s youth culture while impacting the 1920s and 1930s Harlem Renaissance,[3] the countercultural rebellion that grew around jazz in the 1940s and 1950s, and jazz's role as a source of African-American self-assertion, autonomy, and emancipation during the 1950s, 1960s, and 1970s Black Power, Black Arts, and Civil Rights Movements.[4]

Even as Armstrong, Ellington, and Davis offer evidence that jazz did not solely remain within US borders, each illuminates ways jazz swept through US culture and affected painting, photography (with photographers devoting their careers to documenting jazz performers and their music), filmmaking, and visual culture more broadly.[5] Historically associated with visual culture, the "jazz image" includes fashion, slang, drug use, relationships between performative demeanors and musical meanings, and ways postures and attitudes of such pianists as Bill Evans[6] and Keith Jarrett influence their perceptions as serious artists.

Numerous US films center on jazz, such as *The Jazz Singer* (1927),[7] *Strike Up the Band* (1940), *Blues in the Night* (1941), *Orchestra Wives* (1942), *Jazz on a Summer's Day* (1959), *The Cotton Club* (1984), *'Round Midnight* (1986), *Bird* (1988), *Mo' Better Blues* (1990), and *Kansas City* (1996). As jazz confounded high and low cultural distinctions, it crossed racial, gender, sexual, ethnic, class, and national borders, echoing cinematic transgressions of revered but under-documented marquee names, major and minor filmmakers, and auteurs at the edge of the high/low cultural divide. This includes sexual melodramas of Weimer German cinema, films of directors Tod Browning, Pier Pasolini, and Peter Watkins, and the film exhibition industry's niche market of sexual melodramas, cult films, and documentaries.[8]

Jazz's improvisational pluralism, games of color and space, rhythms, and sudden changes influenced such artists as US painter Jackson Pollock.[9] Dancing to jazz as he painted, Pollock was a leading exponent of Abstract Expressionism, an art movement characterized by free-associative gestures in paint, referred to as "action painting." Jazz had an effect on Stuart Davis, US abstract artist whose idiosyncratic Cubist paintings of urban settings predated 1960s Pop artists' use of commercial art and advertising, Dutch painter Piet Mondrian, leader in the development of modern abstract art and a major exponent of the Dutch abstract art movement known as *De Stijl* ("The Style"), and Archibald Motley, known for his paintings of urban black life and realistic portraits of refined "New Negro" imagery.[10]

Throughout the twentieth century, jazz appeared in multiple eras and varied cultural spheres. It became a political, aesthetic, and racialized model incorporated by such composers as George Gershwin and Aaron Copland[11] and influenced popular song, classical music, architecture, fiction, poetry, and such writers as James Baldwin, Eudora Welty, John Clellon Holmes, Toni Morrison,[12] Jack Kerouac, Vachel Lindsay, Richard Wright,[13] and Harlem Renaissance writers Langston Hughes, Claude McKay, and Zora Neale Hurston.[14] "Lost Generation" writers Malcolm Cowley, F. Scott Fitzgerald, and Gertrude Stein[15] celebrated jazz as an expression of African-American culture and symbol of rebellion against bourgeois, conformist, capitalist, white supremacist, and hetero-sexist US culture. Jazz influenced US poets William Carlos Williams, Carl Sandburg, Percy Johnson, and African-American painter Romare Bearden, whose collages of photographs and painted paper on canvas depict aspects of black culture in a style derived from Cubism, and his stage and costume designs for Alvin Ailey and Dianne McIntyre.[16]

Jazz's impact on the US can be understood in the observation of Ralph Ellison (1914–1994), African-American writer who gained prominence through his novel *Invisible Man* (1952),[17] that US culture has been "jazz-based." Critics noted relationships between skyscrapers and swing-era music, basketball's jazz/dance-like Afro-American reinventions, and jazz's articulation of the US's multi-cultural hues and grooves. An integral strand in the US cultural fabric and claimed to be the United States's great gift to the world, jazz can be understood as analogue, influence, and model for the US Constitution, New York City's skyline, and Mark Twain's humorous monologues. Jazz's "wildness" and boundary-breaking expressions reflected breathless, energetic, and hyper-active times in the US nation, even as its transnational routes belie any claim of national distinctiveness.

JAZZ'S HETERO-PATRIARCHAL HISTORIES

Visually represented as hyper-masculine symbols within and beyond the jazz world, emphasizing hetero-patriarchal dominance among early jazz pioneers and later iconic jazz figures, Armstrong, Ellington, and Davis embody links between jazz and hetero-patriarchy and jazz's masculine and hetero-normative histories. With additional jazz "founding father" cornetist Buddy Bolden,[18] Armstrong was noted as a "father figure" of jazz. Armstrong was linked to bandleader Paul Whiteman (1890–1967), called the "King of Jazz" for popularizing a musical style introducing jazz to mainstream audiences during the 1920s and 1930s and aiming to "make a lady" of jazz, giving it symphonic gloss with string sections and commissions from popular composers. While Armstrong was described as the "father of jazz trumpeters," if not jazz phrasing itself, Ellington, the "father of the US songbook," personifies jazz as a woman in his autobiography *Music Is My Mistress* (1973). While Ellington demonstrates the feminization of jazz as an object to control and tame, Davis achieved the status of jazz "patriarch" and his relationships with women, sometimes physically abusive, tarnished his reputation.

Similar to other popular music genres, women have been central to jazz's development. Jazz's global gender histories include singer Sarah Vaughan, vocalist and pianist known for her rich voice, with an unusually wide range, and improvisations displaying an inventiveness and virtuosity,[19] pianist, composer, and arranger Mary Lou Williams, pianists Emma Barrett and Lil Hardin Armstrong (Armstrong's second wife),[20] and such all-female bands as the International Sweethearts of Rhythm. Subverting hetero-normative chauvinism and balancing life on the road with love, marriage, and motherhood, twentieth- and twenty-first-century jazz women faced personal and professional tradeoffs. Female musicians emerged in jazz, transitioning from novelty acts to respected professionals, made strides in the male-dominated jazz world, and performed in Hollywood films.[21] Reflecting global gender and sexual attitudes, stereotypes of female musicians focused on their attractiveness and physical attributes and myths circulated that women lacked the physical strength to play certain instruments.[22]

JAZZ AS HIGH AND LOW CULTURE

Comparisons of jazz to high art, juxtaposed with descriptions of jazz emerging out of turn-of-the-twentieth-century New Orleans brothels, then performed by the century's end in the world's most respected concert halls[23] note ways Armstrong, Ellington, and Davis uniquely demonstrate jazz's crisscrossing of high and low cultural borders and jazz's ability to transverse multiple US cultural and transnational domains. Unlike literature and classical music, before 1945 jazz enjoyed no such high-artistic standing. Dependent on and responsive to its audience, with bebop's post–World War II advent, the relationship reversed and avant-garde jazz was perceived as inaccessible. Davis and others played with their backs to the audience and bebop scat singers, such as Ward Swingle and the Swingle Singers, applied scat techniques to the classical repertoire, stemming from a desire to find new *solfège* (vocal exercises sung to the solmization syllables of do, re, mi, etc.) exercises for classically trained singers.

As jazz writing moved toward high art, comparisons were made between jazz and avant-garde and more traditional art. This led to jazz's canonization in such venues as Lincoln Center and mainstream film and television. Jazz's high/low cultural border crossings encompassed multiple musical strands, with European classical influences sharing aspects of folk, popular, and art music. Early white jazz musicians, from the European-American musical tradition, were not as acquainted with heterophony (textures resulting from simultaneous performances of melodic variants of the same tune) and gave their music a formal shape that was closer to concert music than African-American jazzmen.

Jazz reiterated histories of four centuries of European music, moving from the heterophonic polyphony of the early New Orleans style to 1930s big-band romanticism, bebop chromaticism, and post-1960 free-form experimentations. Pendulations occurred in jazz between formal "European" modes and spontaneous "African" approaches. Jazz transversed from its bohemian, underground, African, creole,[24] and New Orleans beginnings to multiple manifestations in the entertainment business to widespread acceptance by US and transnational popular cultures as a form of serious, high art, all the while retaining its low cultural character. Although jazz began to be taught in colleges and universities in the same ways that literature and painting were and presented in formal concert settings, it retained one foot in a high art milieu while maintaining its low-cultural identities.

In contrast with turn-of-the-twentierth-century, harmonious, complex, and exclusive Eurocentric cultural hierarchies, racialized jazz was denounced as discordant, uncivilized, too accessible, and subversive to reason and order.[25] This corresponded to broader high/low cultural distinctions, including Shakespearean drama, opera, orchestral music, painting, sculpture, the writings of such authors as Charles Dickens and Henry Wadsworth Longfellow, the Marx Brothers, and vaudeville. Jazz demonstrated how variable and dynamic cultural boundaries could be and the fragility of recent cultural categories accepted as natural and eternal.

For most of the nineteenth century, a wide variety of expressive forms simultaneously enjoyed high cultural status and mass popularity. In the nineteenth century, Americans shared a public culture less hierarchically organized and fragmented into rigid groupings than their descendants were to experience. By the twentieth century, this cultural eclecticism and openness became rare. Cultural space was more sharply defined and less flexible. The theater, once a microcosm of the United States, housing the spectrum of the population and range of entertainment, such as tragedy, farce, juggling, ballet, opera, and minstrelsy, fragmented into discrete spaces catering to distinct audiences and separate genres. Similar transitions occurred in concert halls, opera houses, and museums. A growing chasm between "serious" and "popular" and "high" and "low" culture dominated US expressive arts. Americans were separated from contact to such creators as Shakespeare, Beethoven, and Verdi, whom they enjoyed for much of the nineteenth century. Rigid cultural categories made it difficult to understand popular art forms' importance. Those considering themselves educated and cultured lost their ability to discriminate and understand that because a form of expressive culture was ac-

cessible and popular it was not devoid of redeeming value and artistic mer-
it.[26]

Though jazz once shared the stage with tawdry elements, it ultimately
shed these connections to become an art worthy of the European classical
tradition. It did so largely through Louis Armstrong's efforts.[27] Throughout
his career, Armstrong was able to synthesize high and low cultures for a
broad audience with sensitivity, technique, and capacity to express emotion.
As Armstrong ensured the survival of jazz, he led its development into a fine,
"high" art Ellington and others expanded. Early jazz practitioners, such as
Armstrong, demonstrated the power and decline of symphonic jazz,[28] an
additional example of jazz's high/low cultural border crossing.

From the early 1930s, such African-American composers as Ellington
and James P. Johnson (1894–1955), a highly influential African-American
jazz pianist who also wrote popular songs and composed classical works,
was a founder of the stride piano idiom, and a crucial figure in the transition
from ragtime to jazz,[29] engaged with concert jazz to create what they put
forward as "authentic" adaptations of jazz and ragtime into classical forms.
Ellington and Johnson's compositions transverse borders between jazz and
concert music. Such works as Ellington's *Creole Rhapsody* (1931) and Johnson's *Harlem Symphony* (1937) have been called extended jazz compositions
to distinguish them from the "inauthentic" symphonic jazz of white composers. A racialized barrier, based on racial authenticity politics,[30] between
black and white composers' concert jazz emerged in critical and scholarly
accounts of these traditions. However, cross-fertilization meant no clear and
consistent divisions existed between black and white composers' output.

Ellington influenced concert jazz by African-American musicians, such
as Mary Lou Williams and John Lewis, pianist and composer-arranger who
was an influential member of the Modern Jazz Quartet, one of jazz's longest-
lived and best-received groups. Ellington and Johnson were part of a close-
knit community of generations of Harlem musicians. Such older figures as
James Reese Europe, Will Marion Cook, Will Vodery, and W. C. Handy
were members of the generation of black musicians that initially crossed
New York City entertainment racial barriers in the twentieth century's first
two decades.[31] By the 1920s, Cook, Vodery, and Handy were mentors to
Harlem's younger musicians. This generational connection became key to
understanding Ellington and Johnson's ambitions to use the success of Harlem's white-oriented entertainment trade as a springboard for establishing a
black concert musical tradition based on Harlem jazz and popular sounds.

A symphonic jazz pioneer, Ellington composed for the ballet and theater.
Following Ellington in this respect were such jazz musicians as Thelonious
Monk (1917–1982), pianist and composer who was among the first creators
of modern jazz,[32] Charles Mingus (1922–1979), composer, bassist, bandleader, and pianist who integrated loosely composed passages with impro-

vised solos and shaped and went beyond mid-twentieth-century jazz trends,[33] and Gil Evans (1912–1988), Canadian-born composer and arranger who was one of jazz's greatest orchestrators and remains best known for his collaborations with Miles Davis.[34] Ellington combined jazz and symphonic forms in his compositions and drew on his orchestra members for ideas. His recording of "Black and Tan Fantasy" (1927) was regarded as an indication that jazz was to be taken seriously.

Throughout his long career, Ellington's music was offered as evidence that jazz should be treated as an art. As the Modern Jazz Quartet's Baroque- and classically-influenced chamber jazz (from 1952) appealed to an audience behavior associated with the concert hall, Ellington proselytized jazz as an art. The swing era brought jazz additional respectability, moving into US ballrooms a music that until that time was associated with New Orleans brothels and Prohibition-era[35] Chicago gin mills.

Ellington integrated African-American folk music with European art music. In the 1930s, he became intrigued with possibilities of composing jazz within classical forms. *Black, Brown and Beige* (1943), introduced by Ellington at Carnegie Hall as a "parallel to the history of the Negro in America," was the first in a series of suites Ellington composed, usually consisting of pieces linked by subject matter. This was followed by *Liberian Suite* (1947), commissioned from the government of the African nation to celebrate the 100th anniversary of its founding by freed US slaves and acting as the first formal manifestation of a process by which Ellington would become a musical ambassador to the world, *A Drum Is A Woman* (1956), created for a television production, impressions of Shakespeare's scenes and characters, called *Such Sweet Thunder* (1957), and a recomposed, reorchestrated version of *Nutcracker Suite* (1960). Ellington's "A Rhapsody of Negro Life" was the basis for the film short *Symphony in Black: A Rhapsody of Negro Life* (1935) featuring Billie Holiday, whose scene in this film features her rendition of "Big City Blues," or "The Saddest Tale," performed on the street, where a former lover shoved her and continuing Holiday's "tragic mulatto," mysterious, victim, abusive, and torch singer[36] stereotypes.

Among Miles Davis's final projects was his synthesizing of jazz and hip hop.[37] Davis's last official studio album, *Doo-Bop* (1992), was posthumously released and features hip hop and R&B record producer Easy Mo Bee as co-producer. In his combination of jazz and hip hop, Davis emphasized each musical culture's relationships to African-American and broader black-transnational histories. Each popular musical style negates jingoistic claims that jazz, like the rap music that succeeded it, can be exclusively defined as indigenous US folk music.

Both jazz and hip hop confronted conflicting demands of art and commerce and struggled to maintain their artistic and political integrity despite marketplace pressures. Though Davis attempted to shift jazz to more experimental grounds, the music fell into the hands of musical neo-conservatives and contemporary jazz superstars, such as Wynton Marsalis. With Marsalis's creation of a conservative jazz canon at Lincoln Center came the establishment of a cultural legitimacy for brittle, heartless, and neo-classical jazz and narrow and nationalistic visions of jazz histories. Debates surrounding Jazz at Lincoln Center under Marsalis's direction note ways a musical style avoiding institutionalization has nonetheless been contained. Davis and Marsalis's differences indicated larger political-cultural conflicts with regard to racial and musical essentialism and authenticity.

The bridge Davis and other jazz musicians provided between jazz and hip hop highlights musical transformations of preexisting material to new ends, heard in jazz's references to previous styles and compositions and a fundamental element of hip hop culture, heard in the sampling practice of sounds taken from a recorded medium and transposed onto a new recording. From taking an old dance move for a breakdancing battle, quoting from a famous speech, such as John F. Kennedy's 1961 Inaugural Address, and sampling numerous musical styles, jazz and hip hop aesthetics involve borrowing from the past.[38] By appropriating and re-appropriating cultural artifacts, fragments become transformed into something new and different. Musical borrowing in hip hop includes digital sampling and a web of references and quotations within and beyond hip hop culture, from Nas to Jay-Z, A Tribe Called Quest, and Eminem.[39] Though many musical genres adapt preexisting material, hip hop flaunts its "open source" culture, as sampling and other types of borrowing become a framework with which to analyze hip hop and broader cultural trends.

Louis Armstrong, Duke Ellington, and Miles Davis provide a panoptic, transnational understanding of jazz's twentieth-century histories, struggles over its nationalistic definitions, its relations to hetero-patriarchy and US exceptionalism, and merging of high and low cultures. As a constellation of unique and distinct jazz performers and iconic, globally routed, and heteronormative male African-American figures, Armstrong, Ellington, and Davis highlight non-white musicians' negotiations as they transversed US and transnational formations of race, gender, sexuality, ethnicity, class, and nation within shifting US and transnational cultural terrain. Though Armstrong, Ellington, and Davis are exploited as proof of jazz's authentic, exclusive, and exceptional US character, each proves jazz has been too rich and varied for one country to claim, define, and contain. Armstrong, Ellington, and Davis uniquely took jazz back to its transnational routes and utilized multiple international sounds and influences in their body of work.

NOTES

1. James Lincoln Collier. *Jazz: The American Theme Song*. New York: Oxford University Press, 1993.

2. Francis Davis. *Bebop and Nothingness: Jazz and Pop at the End of the Century*. New York: Schirmer Books, 1996; Scott Knowles DeVeaux. *The Birth of Bebop: A Social and Musical History*. Berkeley: University of California Press, 1997; Leonard Feather. *Inside Bebop*. New York: J. J. Robbins, 1949; Jacqueline Foertsch. *American Culture in the 1940s*. Edinburgh: Edinburgh University Press, 2008; Frank Foster. *In Defense of Be-Bop*. Scarsdale, NY: Frank Foster Music, 1979; Eddie S. Meadows. *Bebop to Cool: Context, Ideology, and Musical Identity*. Westport, CT: Greenwood Press, 2003; Donald Megill and Richard S. Demory. *Introduction to Jazz History*. Englewood Cliffs, NJ: Prentice-Hall, 1984; Dave Oliphant, et al. *The Bebop Revolution in Words and Music*. Austin, TX: Harry Ransom Humanities Research Center, University of Texas at Austin, 1994; Thomas Owens. *Bebop: The Music and Its Players*. New York: Oxford University Press, 1995; Guthrie P. Ramsey. *The Amazing Bud Powell: Black Genius, Jazz History, and the Challenge of Bebop*. Berkeley; Chicago: University of California Press, 2013; Peter Rutkoff and William Scott. "Bebop: Modern New York Jazz." *The Kenyon Review*, New Series 18.2 (Spring 1996): 91–121; Arnold Shaw. *Black Popular Music in America: The Singers, Songwriters, and Musicians Who Pioneered the Sounds of American Music*. New York: Schirmer Books, 1986; A. B. Spellman. *Four Lives in the Bebop Business*. [London]: Macgibbon & Kee, 1967.

3. Paul Allen Anderson. *Deep River: Music and Memory in Harlem Renaissance Thought*. Durham: Duke University Press, 2001; Geneviève Fabre and Michel Feith. *Temples for Tomorrow: Looking Back at the Harlem Renaissance*. Bloomington: Indiana University Press, 2001; Jean C. Griffith. "'Lita Is—Jazz': The Harlem Renaissance, Cabaret Culture, and Racial Amalgamation in Edith Wharton's 'Twilight Sleep.'" *Studies in the Novel* 38.1 (Spring 2006): 74–94; George Hutchinson. *The Cambridge Companion to the Harlem Renaissance*. New York: Cambridge University Press, 2007; Meta DuEwa Jones. *The Muse Is Music: Jazz Poetry from the Harlem Renaissance to Spoken Word*. Urbana: University of Illinois Press, 2011; A. B. Christa Schwarz. *Gay Voices of the Harlem Renaissance*. Bloomington: Indiana University Press, 2003; Saadi Simawe. *Black Orpheus: Music in African American Fiction from the Harlem Renaissance to Toni Morrison*. New York: Garland Pub., 2000; Wallace Thurman, Amritjit Singh, and Daniel M. Scott. *The Collected Writings of Wallace Thurman: A Harlem Renaissance Reader*. New Brunswick, NJ: Rutgers University Press, 2003; Cheryl A. Wall. *Women of the Harlem Renaissance*. Bloomington: Indiana University Press, 1995; James F. Wilson. *Bulldaggers, Pansies, and Chocolate Babies: Performance, Race, and Sexuality in the Harlem Renaissance*. Ann Arbor: University of Michigan Press, 2010.

4. Jack M. Bloom. *Class, Race, and the Civil Rights Movement*. Bloomington: Indiana University Press, 1987; Dennis Chong. *Collective Action and the Civil Rights Movement*. Chicago: University of Chicago Press, 1991; Lance E. Hill. *The Deacons for Defense: Armed Resistance and the Civil Rights Movement*. Chapel Hill: University of North Carolina Press, 2004; Larry Isaac and Lars Christiansen. "How the Civil Rights Movement Revitalized Labor Militancy." *American Sociological Review* 67.5 (October 2002): 722–746; Peter J. Ling and Sharon Monteith. *Gender and the Civil Rights Movement*. New Brunswick, NJ: Rutgers University Press, 2004; Anne Marie Mingo and Gwendolyn Zoharah Simmons. "Expanding the Narrative: Exploring New Aspects of the Civil Rights Movement Fifty Years Later." *Fire!!!*, 2.2, (2013): 1–4; Mark R. Schneider. *We Return Fighting: The Civil Rights Movement in the Jazz Age*. Boston: Northeastern University Press, 2002; Debra L. Schultz. *Going South: Jewish Women in the Civil Rights Movement*. New York: New York University Press, 2001.

5. Benjamin Cawthra. *Blue Notes in Black and White: Photography and Jazz*. Chicago; London: University of Chicago Press, 2011; Jessica Ferber and Marc Myers. *Rebirth of the Cool: Discovering the Art of Robert James Campbell*. Brooklyn, NY: powerHouse Books, 2015; Herman Leonard and Philippe Carles. *The Eye of Jazz*. London; New York: Viking, 1989; Herman Leonard, David Wallace Houston, and Jenny Bagert. *Jazz, Giants, and Journeys: The Photography of Herman Leonard*. London: Scala; Easthampton, MA: Distributed in USA by Antique Collectors' Club, 2006; Graham Marsh, Glyn Callingham, and Felix Cromey.

Blue Note: The Album Cover Art. San Francisco: Chronicle Books, 1991; K. Heather Pinson. *The Jazz Image: Seeing Music Through Herman Leonard's Photography.* Jackson: University Press of Mississippi, 2010; Henry Pleasants. "Jazz and the Movies / Jazz et Cinéma / Jazz und Film." *The World of Music* 10.3 (1968): 38–47; Duncan P. Schiedt. *Jazz in Black & White: The Photographs of Duncan Schiedt.* Bloomington, IN: Indiana University Press, 2004; Peter Stanfield. *Body and Soul: Jazz and Blues in American Film, 1927–63.* Urbana: University of Illinois Press, 2005; W. Royal Stokes, Charles Peterson, and Don Peterson. *Swing Era New York: The Jazz Photographs of Charles Peterson.* Philadelphia: Temple University Press, 1994; Francis Wolff, Michael Cuscuna, Charlie Lourie, Oscar Schnider, and Blue Note (Firm). *The Blue Note Years: The Jazz Photography of Francis Wolff.* New York: Rizzoli, 1995; Scott Yanow. *Jazz on Film: The Complete Story of the Musicians & Music Onscreen.* San Francisco, CA: Backbeat Books, 2004.

6. Chuck Israels. "Bill Evans (1929–1980): A Musical Memoir." *The Musical Quarterly* 71.2 (1985): 109–115; Steve Larson. "Musical Forces, Melodic Expectation, and Jazz Melody." *Music Perception: An Interdisciplinary Journal* 19.3 (Spring 2002): 351–385; _____. "Composition versus Improvisation?" *Journal of Music Theory* 49.2 (Fall 2005): 241–275; Peter Pettinger. *Bill Evans: How My Heart Sings.* New Haven: Yale University Press, 1998; Jack Reilly. *The Harmony of Bill Evans.* Brooklyn, NY: Unichrom; Milwaukee, WI: H. Leonard [distributor], 1993; David Schroeder. "Four Approaches to Jazz Improvisation Instruction." *Philosophy of Music Education Review* 10.1 (Spring 2002): 36–40; Keith Shadwick. *Bill Evans: Everything Happens to Me, A Musical Biography.* San Francisco, CA: Backbeat Books, 2002.

7. Michael Alexander. *Jazz Age Jews.* Princeton, NJ: Princeton University Press, 2001; Monta Bell. "Movies and Talkies." *The North American Review* 226.4 (October 1928): 429–435; Robert L. Carringer, Alfred A. Cohn, and Samson Raphaelson. *The Jazz Singer.* Madison: Published for the Wisconsin Center for Film and Theater Research by the University of Wisconsin Press, 1979; C. Scott Combs. "The Jazz Singer or the Corpse: Al Jolson, Diegetic Music, and the Moment of Death." *Music and the Moving Image* 5.3 (Fall 2012): 46–55; Linda Dittmar. "Immigration Filmography for Educators." *The Radical Teacher* 84, Teaching and Immigration (Spring 2009): 61–67; Ron Hutchinson. "The Vitaphone Project. Answering Harry Warner's Question: 'Who the Hell Wants to Hear Actors Talk?'" *Film History* 14.1, Film/Music (2002): 40–46; Jeffrey Knapp. "Sacred Songs Popular Prices: Secularization in The Jazz Singer," *Critical Inquiry* 34.2 (Winter 2008): 313–335; Charles Musser. "Why Did Negroes Love Al Jolson and The Jazz Singer?: Melodrama, Blackface and Cosmopolitan Theatrical Culture." *Film History* 23.2, Black Representations (2011): 196–222; Michael Rogin. "Blackface, White Noise: The Jewish Jazz Singer Finds His Voice." *Critical Inquiry* 18.3 (Spring 1992): 417–453; _____. "Making America Home: Racial Masquerade and Ethnic Assimilation in the Transition to Talking Pictures." *The Journal of American History* 79.3, Discovering America: A Special Issue (December 1992): 1050–1077; _____. "'Democracy and Burnt Cork': The End of Blackface, the Beginning of Civil Rights." *Representations* 46 (Spring 1994): 1–34; _____. *Blackface, White Noise: Jewish Immigrants in the Hollywood Melting Pot.* Berkeley: University of California Press, 1996; Joel Rosenberg. "What You Ain't Heard Yet: The Languages of The Jazz Singer." *Prooftexts* 22.1–2, Special Issue: The Cinema of Jewish Experience (Winter/Spring 2002): 11–54; Jonathan D. Tankel. "The Impact of *The Jazz Singer* on the Conversion to Sound." *Journal of the University Film Association* 30.1, Topics in American Film History (Winter 1978): 21–25.

8. John Cline and Robert G. Weiner. *From the Arthouse to the Grindhouse: Highbrow and Lowbrow Transgression in Cinema's First Century.* Lanham: Scarecrow Press, 2010.

9. Elisabeth Hodermarsky. "The Abstractionist as Regionalist: A Young Jackson Pollock's 'Stacking Hay.' *Yale University Art Gallery Bulletin, Recent Acquisitions* (2014): 42–46; Barbara Jaffee. "Jackson Pollock's Industrial Expressionism." *Art Journal* 63.4 (Winter 2004): 68–79; Catherine M. Soussloff. "Jackson Pollock's Post-Ritual Performance: Memories Arrested in Space." *TDR* (1988–) 48.1 (Spring 2004): 60–78.

10. Donna Cassidy. *Painting the Musical City: Jazz and Cultural Identity in American Art, 1910–1940.* Washington, D.C.: Smithsonian Institution Press, 1997; Michael D. Harris. *Colored Pictures: Race and Visual Representation.* Chapel Hill: University of North Carolina

Press, 2003; Carmenita Higginbotham. "At the Savoy: Reginald Marsh and the Art of Slumming." *Bulletin of the Detroit Institute of Arts* 82.1/2 (2008): 16–29; Theresa A. Leininger-Miller. *New Negro Artists in Paris: African American Painters and Sculptors in the City of Light, 1922–1934*. New Brunswick, NJ: Rutgers University Press, 2001; Amy M. Mooney. "Representing Race: Disjunctures in the Work of Archibald J. Motley, Jr." *Art Institute of Chicago Museum Studies* 24.2, African Americans in Art: Selections from The Art Institute of Chicago (1999): 162–179+262–265; Archibald John Motley, Jr., Richard J. Powell, Nasher Museum of Art at Duke University, Amon Carter Museum of American Art, Los Angeles County Museum of Art, Chicago Cultural Center, and Whitney Museum of American Art. *Archibald Motley: Jazz Age Modernist*. Durham, NC: Nasher Museum of Art at Duke University, 2014; Kymberly N. Pinder. "'Our Father, God; our Brother, Christ; or are We Bastard Kin?': Images of Christ in African American Painting." *African American Review* 31.2 (Summer 1997): 223–233; Phoebe Wolfskill. "Caricature and the New Negro in the Work of Archibald Motley Jr. and Palmer Hayden." *The Art Bulletin* 91.3 (September 2009): 343–365.

11. Aaron Copland. *Music and Imagination*. Cambridge, MA: Harvard University Press, 1952; Aaron Copland, Elizabeth Bergman Crist, and Wayne D. Shirley. *The Selected Correspondence of Aaron Copland*. New Haven: Yale University Press, 2006; Aaron Copland, Richard Kostelanetz, and Steven Silverstein. *Aaron Copland: A Reader: Selected Writings 1923–1972*. New York: Routledge, 2004; Elizabeth Bergman Crist. *Music for the Common Man: Aaron Copland During the Depression and War*. Oxford; New York: Oxford University Press, 2005; Arnold Dobrin. *Aaron Copland, His Life and Times*. New York: Thomas Y. Crowell Co., 1967; David Metzer. "'Spurned Love': Eroticism and Abstraction in the Early Works of Aaron Copland." *The Journal of Musicology* 15.4 (Autumn 1997): 417–443; Carol J. Oja and Judith Tick. *Aaron Copland and His World*. Princeton, NJ; Woodstock, Oxfordshire: Princeton University Press, 2005; Howard Pollack. *Aaron Copland: The Life and Work of an Uncommon Man*. New York: Henry Holt, 1999.

12. Toni Morrison. *Jazz*. London: Vintage Digital, 2014; Sherrie Tucker. "'Where the Blues and the Truth Lay Hiding': Rememory of Jazz in Black Women's Fiction." *Frontiers: A Journal of Women Studies* 13.2 (1993): 26–44.

13. Robert Bone. *Richard Wright*. Minneapolis: University of Minnesota Press, 1969; Michel Fabre. *The Unfinished Quest of Richard Wright*. New York: Morrow, 1973; _____. *The World of Richard Wright*. Jackson: University Press of Mississippi, 1985; Henry Louis Gates and Anthony Appiah. *Richard Wright: Critical Perspectives, Past and Present*. New York: Amistad, 1993; Keneth Kinnamon. *Richard Wright: An Annotated Bibliography of Criticism and Commentary, 1983–2003*. Jefferson, NC: McFarland & Co., 2006; Richard Macksey and Frank E. Moorer. *Richard Wright, A Collection of Critical Essays*. Englewood Cliffs, NJ: Prentice-Hall, 1984; Edward Margolies. *The Art of Richard Wright*. Carbondale: Southern Illinois University Press, 1969; Arnold Rampersad. *Richard Wright: A Collection of Critical Essays*. Englewood Cliffs, NJ: Prentice Hall, 1995; Hazel Rowley. *Richard Wright: The Life and Times*. New York: Henry Holt and Co., 2001; Jennifer Jensen Wallach. *Richard Wright: From Black Boy to World Citizen*. Chicago: Ivan R. Dee, 2010; Constance Webb. *Richard Wright; a Biography*. New York: Putnam, 1968; Richard Wright and Earle V. Bryant. *Byline, Richard Wright: Articles from the Daily Worker and New Masses*. Columbia: University of Missouri Press, 2015; Richard Wright, Keneth Kinnamon, and Michel Fabre. *Conversations with Richard Wright*. Jackson: University Press of Mississippi, 1993; Richard Wright, Ellen Wright, and Michel Fabre. *Richard Wright Reader*. New York: Harper & Row, 1978.

14. Paul de Barros. "'The Loud Music of Life': Representations of Jazz in the Novels of Claude McKay." *The Antioch Review* 57.3, Jazz (Summer 1999): 306–317; Gary Edward Holcomb. *Claude McKay, Code Name Sasha: Queer Black Marxism and the Harlem Renaissance*. Gainesville: University Press of Florida, 2007; _____. "The Sun Also Rises in Queer Black Harlem: Hemingway and McKay's Modernist Intertext." *Journal of Modern Literature* 30.4 (Summer 2007): 61–81; Langston Hughes, Evelyn Louise Crawford, and MaryLouise Patterson. *Letters from Langston: from the Harlem Renaissance to the Red Scare and Beyond*. Oakland, CA: University of California Press, 2016; Langston Hughes and Susan Duffy. *The Political Plays of Langston Hughes*. Carbondale: Southern Illinois University Press, 2000; Zora Neale Hurston, Jean Lee Cole, and Charles Mitchell. *Zora Neale Hurston: Collected Plays*.

New Brunswick, NJ: Rutgers University Press, 2008; Zora Neale Hurston and Carla Kaplan. *Zora Neale Hurston: A Life in Letters*. New York: Doubleday, 2002; Zora Neale Hurston and Alice Walker. *I Love Myself When I Am Laughing . . . And Then Again When I Am Looking Mean and Impressive: A Zora Neale Hurston Reader*. Old Westbury, NY: Feminist Press, 1979; Jonathan Scott. "Advanced, Repressed, and Popular: Langston Hughes during the Cold War." *College Literature* 33.2 (Spring 2006): 30–51; W. S. Tkweme. "Blues in Stereo: The Texts of Langston Hughes in Jazz Music Ellison's Hemingways." *African American Review* 42.3/4 (Fall–Winter 2008): 503–512.

15. Malcolm Cowley. *A Second Flowering: Works and Days of the Lost Generation*. New York: Viking Press, 1973; Malcolm Cowley and Hans Bak. *The Long Voyage: Selected Letters of Malcolm Cowley, 1915–1987*. Cambridge, MA: Harvard University Press, 2014; Malcolm Cowley and Robert Cowley. *Fitzgerald and the Jazz Age*. New York: Charles Scribner's Sons, 1966; Marc Dolan. *Modern Lives: A Cultural Re-Reading of "The Lost Generation."* West Lafayette, IN: Purdue University Press, 1996; Noel Riley Fitch. *Sylvia Beach and The Lost Generation: A History of Literary Paris in the Twenties and Thirties*. New York: Norton, 1983; F. Scott Fitzgerald, Jackson R. Bryer, Alan Margolies, and Ruth Prigozy. *F. Scott Fitzgerald: New Perspectives*. Athens, GA: University of Georgia Press, 2000; Craig Monk. *Writing the Lost Generation: Expatriate Autobiography and American Modernism*. Iowa City: University of Iowa Press, 2008; Gertrude Stein, F. W. Dupee, and Carl Van Vechten. *Selected Writings of Gertrude Stein*. New York: Modern Library, 1962; Michael Zielenziger. *Shutting Out the Sun: How Japan Created Its Own Lost Generation*. New York: Nan A. Talese, 2006.

16. Romare Bearden, Mary Schmidt Campbell, Sharon F. Patton, and Studio Museum in Harlem. *Memory and Metaphor: The Art of Romare Bearden, 1940–1987*. New York: Studio Museum in Harlem: Oxford University Press, 1991; Romare Bearden, Ruth Fine, Mary Lee Corlett, and National Gallery of Art (US). *The Art of Romare Bearden*. Washington: National Gallery of Art, 2003; Romare Bearden, Carla M. Hanzal, Ruth Fine, and Mint Museum (Charlotte, NC). *Romare Bearden: Southern Recollections*. Charlotte, NC: Mint Museum, 2011; Romare Bearden and M. Bunch Washington. *The Art of Romare Bearden: The Prevalence of Ritual*. New York: Abrams, 1973; Avital H. Bloch and Lauri Umansky. *Impossible to Hold: Women and Culture in the 1960s*. New York: New York University Press, 2005; Dianne L. Common. "Teacher Power and Settings for Innovation: A Response to Brown and McIntyre's 'Influences upon Teachers' Attitudes to Different Types of Innovation.'" *Curriculum Inquiry* 13.4 (Winter 1983): 435–446; Ralph Ellison. "The Art of Romare Bearden." *The Massachusetts Review* 18.4 (Winter 1977): 673–680; Ruth Fine. "Expanding the Mainstream: Romare Bearden Revisited." *Proceedings of the American Philosophical Society* 149.1 (March 2005): 40–55; Lee Stephens Glazer. "Signifying Identity: Art and Race in Romare Bearden's Projections." *The Art Bulletin* 76.3 (September 1994): 411–426; Sally Price, Richard Price, and Romare Bearden. *Romare Bearden: The Caribbean Dimension*. Philadelphia: University of Pennsylvania Press, 2006; Matthew S. Witkovsky. "Experience vs. Theory: Romare Bearden and Abstract Expressionism." *Black American Literature Forum* 23.2, Fiction Issue (Summer 1989): 257–282.

17. Ralph Ellison and John F. Callahan. *The Collected Essays of Ralph Ellison*. New York: Modern Library, 1995; Ralph Ellison, Maryemma Graham, and Amritjit Singh. *Conversations with Ralph Ellison*. Jackson: University Press of Mississippi, 1995; Ralph Ellison and Robert G. O'Meally. *Living with Music: Ralph Ellison's Jazz Writings*. New York: Modern Library, 2001; Alan Nadel. *Invisible Criticism: Ralph Ellison and the American Canon*. Iowa City: University of Iowa Press, 1988; Horace A. Porter. *Jazz Country: Ralph Ellison in America*. Iowa City: University of Iowa Press, 2001; Arnold Rampersad. *Ralph Ellison: A Biography*. New York: Alfred A. Knopf, 2007; John S. Wright. *Shadowing Ralph Ellison*. Jackson: University Press of Mississippi, 2006.

18. Danny Barker and Alyn Shipton. *Buddy Bolden and the Last Days of Storyville*. London; New York: Continuum, 2001; Stefan Berg. *Let That Bad Air Out: Buddy Bolden's Last Parade*. Erin, ON: Porcupine's Quill, 2007; Ray Bisso. *Buddy Bolden of New Orleans: A Jazz Poem*. Santa Barbara, CA: Fithian Press, 1998; Daniel Hardie. *The Loudest Trumpet: Buddy Bolden and the Early History of Jazz*. San José: ToExcel, 2001; Donald M. Marquis. *In Search of Buddy Bolden: First Man of Jazz*. Baton Rouge: Louisiana State University Press, 1978.

19. Leslie Gourse. *Sassy: The Life of Sarah Vaughan.* New York: C. Scribner's Sons; Toronto: Collier Macmillan Canada; New York: Maxwell Macmillan International, 1993.

20. Lil Hardin Armstrong. "Satchmo and Me." *American Music* 25.1 (Spring 2007): 106–118; Bicknell. "Just a Song? Exploring the Aesthetics of Popular Song Performance." *The Journal of Aesthetics and Art Criticism* 63.3 (Summer 2005): 261–270; James Dickerson. *Just for a Thrill: Lil Hardin Armstrong, First Lady of Jazz.* New York: Cooper Square Press; [Lanham, MD]: Distributed by National Book Network, 2002; Leslie Gourse. "Playing for Keeps: Women Jazz Musicians Break the Glass Ceiling." *The Women's Review of Books* 18.3 (December 2000): 7–8.

21. Farah Jasmine Griffin. *Harlem Nocturne: Women Artists and Progressive Politics During World War II.* New York: Basic Civitas Books, 2013; D. Antoinette Handy and Piney Woods School. *The International Sweethearts of Rhythm: The Ladies Jazz Band From Piney Woods Country Life School.* Rev. ed. Lanham, MD: Scarecrow Press, 1998; Marilyn Nelson and Jerry Pinkney. *Sweethearts of Rhythm: The Story of the Greatest All-Girl Swing Band in the World.* New York: Dial Books, 2009; Lewis Porter. "'You Can't Get up There Timidly': Jazzwomen: Part II." *Music Educators Journal* 71.2 (October 1984): 42–51.

22. Linda Dahl. *Stormy Weather: The Music and Lives of a Century of Jazzwomen.* New York: Pantheon Books, 1984; Paul De Barros. *Shall We Play That One Together?: The Life and Art of Jazz Piano Legend Marian McPartland.* New York: St. Martin's Press, 2012; Frank Driggs. *Women in Jazz: A Survey.* Brooklyn, NY: Stash Record Inc., 1977; Wayne Enstice and Janis Stockhouse. *Jazzwomen: Conversations with Twenty-One Musicians.* Bloomington: Indiana University Press, 2004; Will Friedwald. *Jazz Singing: America's Great Voices from Bessie Smith to Bebop and Beyond.* New York: C. Scribner's Sons, 1990; Leslie Gourse. *Madame Jazz: Contemporary Women Instrumentalists.* New York: Oxford University Press, 1995; D. Antoinette Handy. *Black Women in American Bands and Orchestras.* 2nd ed. Lanham, MD: Scarecrow Press, 1998; Kristin A. McGee. *Some Liked It Hot: Jazz Women in Film and Television, 1928–1959.* Middletown, CT: Wesleyan University Press, 2009; Sally Placksin. *American Women in Jazz: 1900 to the Present: Their Words, Lives, and Music.* New York: Wideview Books, 1982; Nichole T. Rustin and Sherrie Tucker. *Big Ears: Listening for Gender in Jazz Studies.* Durham: Duke University Press, 2008; Sherrie Tucker. "Telling Performances: Jazz History Remembered and Remade by the Women in the Band." *The Oral History Review* 26.1 (1999): 67–84; _____. *Swing Shift: "All-Girl" Bands of the 1940s.* Durham: Duke University Press, 2000.

23. William Howland Kenney III. "Jazz and the Concert Halls: The Eddie Condon Concerts, 1942–48." *American Music* 1.2 (Summer 1983): 60–72.

24. Gwendolyn Midlo Hall. *Africans in Colonial Louisiana: The Development of Afro-Creole Culture in the Eighteenth Century.* Baton Rouge: Louisiana State University Press, 1992; Arnold R. Hirsch and Joseph Logsdon. *Creole New Orleans: Race and Americanization.* Baton Rouge: Louisiana State University Press, 1992; Shirley Elizabeth Thompson. *Exiles At Home: The Struggle to Become American in Creole New Orleans.* Cambridge, MA: Harvard University Press, 2009.

25. Lawrence W. Levine. "Jazz and American Culture." *The Journal of American Folklore* 102.403 (January–March 1989): 6–22.

26. _____. *Highbrow/Lowbrow: The Emergence of Cultural Hierarchy in America.* Cambridge, MA: Harvard University Press, 1988.

27. Brian Harker. "Louis Armstrong, Eccentric Dance, and the Evolution of Jazz on the Eve of Swing." *Journal of the American Musicological Society* 61.1 (Spring 2008): 67–121.

28. Kenneth Dommett. "Jazz and the Composer." *Proceedings of the Royal Musical Association, 91st Sess.* (1964–1965): 11–20; John Howland. "'The Blues Get Glorified': Harlem Entertainment, Negro Nuances, and Black Symphonic Jazz." *The Musical Quarterly* 90.3/4 (Fall–Winter 2007): 319–370; Neil Leonard. "The Worlds of Andre Hodeir." *American Quarterly* 15.2, Part 1 (Summer 1963): 210–213; Paul Lopes. "Diffusion and Syncretism: The Modern Jazz Tradition." *The Annals of the American Academy of Political and Social Science* 566, The Social Diffusion of Ideas and Things (November 1999): 25–36.

29. Scott E. Brown and Robert Hilbert. *James P. Johnson: A Case of Mistaken Identity.* Metuchen, NJ: Scarecrow Press and the Institute of Jazz Studies, Rutgers University, 1986;

John Howland. "Jazz Rhapsodies in Black and White: James P. Johnson's 'Yamekraw.'" *American Music* 24.4 (Winter 2006): 445–509, Henry Martin. "Balancing Composition and Improvisation in James P. Johnson's 'Carolina Shout.'" *Journal of Music Theory* 49.2 (Fall 2005): 277–299; _____. *"Ellington Uptown": Duke Ellington, James P. Johnson, and The Birth of Concert Jazz.* Ann Arbor: University of Michigan Press, 2009.
    30. Stephanie Brown. "Bourgeois Blackness and Autobiographical Authenticity in Ellen Tarry's 'The Third Door.'" *African American Review* 41.3 (Fall 2007): 557–570; Stanley Crouch. *The Artificial White Man: Essays on Authenticity.* New York: Basic Civitas Books, 2004; Shelly Eversley. *The Real Negro: The Question of Authenticity in Twentieth-Century African American Literature.* New York: Routledge, 2004; John L. Jackson, Jr., *Real Black: Adventures in Racial Sincerity.* Chicago: University of Chicago Press, 2005; Martin Japtok and Rafiki Jenkins. *Authentic Blackness/"Real" Blackness: Essays on the Meaning of Blackness in Literature and Culture.* New York: Peter Lang, 2011; Gene Jarrett. "Entirely Black Verse From Him Would Succeed." *Nineteenth-Century Literature* 59.4 (March 2005): 494–525; Candice M. Jenkins. "Decoding Essentialism: Cultural Authenticity and the Black Bourgeoisie in Nella Larsen's Passing." *Melus* 30.3, Personal and Political (Fall 2005): 129–154; Charlton D. McIlwain and Stephen M. Caliendo. "Black Messages, White Messages: The Differential Use of Racial Appeals by Black and White Candidates." *Journal of Black Studies* 39.5 (May 2009): 732–743; Sonnet Retman. "Langston Hughes's 'Rejuvenation Through Joy': Passing, Racial Performance, and the Marketplace." *African American Review* 45.4 (Winter 2012): 593–602; Sharon Stockton. "'Blacks vs. Browns': Questioning the White Ground." *College English* 57.2 (February 1995): 166–181; Antonio T. Tiongson. *Filipinos Represent: DJs, Racial Authenticity, and the Hip-Hop Nation.* Minneapolis: University of Minnesota Press, 2013; Judith Weisenfeld. "'On Not Being Jewish . . . and Other Lies': Reflections on Racial Fever." *Soundings: An Interdisciplinary Journal* 96.1 (2013): 3–11.
    31. Reid Badger. *A Life in Ragtime: A Biography of James Reese Europe.* New York: Oxford University Press, 1995; Marva Griffin Carter. "Removing the 'Minstrel Mask' in the Musicals of Will Marion Cook." *The Musical Quarterly* 84.2 (Summer 2000): 206–220; _____. *Swing Along: The Musical Life of Will Marion Cook.* New York: Oxford University Press, 2008; Adam Gussow. "'Make My Getaway': The Blues Lives of Black Minstrels in W. C. Handy's Father of the Blues." *African American Review* 35.1 (Spring 2001): 5–28; W. C. (William Christopher) Handy, Abbe Niles, Elliott S. Hurwitt, and Miguel Covarrubias. *W. C. Handy's Blues: An Anthology: Complete Words and Music of 70 Great Songs and Instrumentals.* Mineola, NY: Dover Publications, 2012; Stephen L. Harris. *Harlem's Hell Fighters: The African-American 369th Infantry in World War I.* Washington, D.C.: Brassey's, Inc., 2003; Peter C. Muir. *Long Lost Blues: Popular Blues in America, 1850–1920.* Urbana: University of Illinois Press, 2010; David Robertson. *W. C. Handy: The Life and Times of the Man Who Made the Blues.* New York: Alfred A. Knopf, 2009; Howard Rye and Jeffrey Green. "Black Musical Internationalism in England in the 1920s." *Black Music Research Journal* 15.1 (Spring 1995): 93–107; Karen Sotiropoulos. *Staging Race: Black Performers in Turn of the Century America.* Cambridge, MA; London: Harvard University Press, 2008; Mark Tucker. "In Search of Will Vodery." *Black Music Research Journal* 16.1 (Spring 1996): 123–182.
    32. Thomas Fitterling. *Thelonious Monk: His Life and Music.* Berkeley, CA: Berkeley Hills Books, 1997; Leslie Gourse. *Straight, No Chaser: The Life and Genius of Thelonious Monk.* New York: Schirmer Books: Prentice Hall International, 1997; Robin D. G. Kelley. *Thelonious Monk: The Life and Times of an American Original.* New York: Free Press, 2009; Ingrid Monson. "Monk Meets SNCC." *Black Music Research Journal* 19.2, New Perspectives on Thelonious Monk (Autumn 1999): 187–200; Gabriel Solis. *Monk's Music: Thelonious Monk and Jazz History in the Making.* Berkeley: University of California Press, 2008; _____. *Thelonious Monk Quartet Featuring John Coltrane at Carnegie Hall.* New York: Oxford University Press, 2014; Daniel Stein. "Hearing, Seeing, and Writing Thelonious Monk: Toward a Theory of Changing Iconotexts." *Amerikastudien / American Studies* 50.4 (2005): 603–627.
    33. Holly Farrington. "'I Improvised Behind Him . . . Ahead of Time': Charles Mingus, Kenneth Patchen and Jazz/Poetry Fusion Art." *Journal of American Studies* 41.2 (August 2007): 365–374; Krin Gabbard. *Better Git It In Your Soul: An Interpretive Biography of Charles Mingus.* Oakland, CA: University of California Press, 2016; Charles Mingus. *Beneath*

the *Underdog; His World as Composed by Mingus*. New York, Knopf, 1971; Brian Priestley. *Mingus, A Critical Biography*. London; New York: Quartet Books, 1982; Gene Santoro. "Myself When I Am Real: The Life and Music of Charles Mingus." New York; Oxford: Oxford University Press, 2001; Scott Saul. "Outrageous Freedom: Charles Mingus and the Invention of the Jazz Workshop." *American Quarterly* 53.3 (September 2001): 387–419.

34. Stephanie Stein Crease. *Out of the Cool: The Life and Music of Gil Evans*. Chicago: A cappella, 2001; _____. *Gil Evans: Out of the Cool: His Life and Music*. Chicago: A cappella, 2002; Larry Hicock. *Castles Made of Sound: The Story of Gil Evans*. Cambridge, MA: Da Capo Press, 2002; Steve Lajoie. *Gil Evans & Miles Davis: Historic Collaborations: An Analysis of Selected Gil Evans Works, 1957–1962*. [Rottenburg am Neckar]: Advance Music, 2003.

35. Edward Behr. *Prohibition: Thirteen Years That Changed America*. New York: Arcade Pub.; [Boston]: Distributed by Little, Brown and Co., 1996; Thomas M. Coffey. *The Long Thirst: Prohibition in America, 1920–1933*. New York: Norton, 1975; Joe L. Coker. *Liquor in the Land of the Lost Cause: Southern White Evangelicals and the Prohibition Movement*. Lexington: University Press of Kentucky, 2007; Kathleen Drowne. "'Theah's Life Anywheres Theah's Booze and Jazz': Home to Harlem and Gingertown in the Context of National Prohibition." *Callaloo* 34.3 (Summer 2011): 928–942; Daniel Okrent. *Last Call: The Rise and Fall of Prohibition*. New York: Scribner, 2010; Garrett Peck. *The Prohibition Hangover: Alcohol in America from Demon Rum to Cult Cabernet*. New Brunswick, NJ: Rutgers University Press, 2009.

36. Stacy Linn Holman Jones. *Torch Singing: Performing Resistance and Desire from Billie Holiday to Edith Piaf*. Lanham: AltaMira Press, 2007; John Moore. "'The Hieroglyphics of Love': The Torch Singers and Interpretation." *Popular Music* 8.1, *Performance* (January 1989): 31–58; Larry David Smith. *Elvis Costello, Joni Mitchell, and the Torch Song Tradition*. Westport, CT: Praeger, 2004.

37. James L. Conyers. *African American Jazz and Rap: Social and Philosophical Examinations of Black Expressive Behavior*. Jefferson, NC: McFarland, 2001; Tom Perchard. "Hip Hop Samples Jazz: Dynamics of Cultural Memory and Musical Tradition in the African American 1990s." *American Music* 29.3 (Fall 2011): 277–307; Justin A. Williams. *Rhymin' and Stealin': Musical Borrowing in Hip-Hop*. Ann Arbor: The University of Michigan Press, 2014.

38. "The Search for 'Reason and Experience' Under the Funk Doctrine." *The University of Chicago Law Review* 17.3 (Spring 1950): 525–532; Tony Bolden. *The Funk Era and Beyond: New Perspectives on Black Popular Culture*. New York: Palgrave Macmillan, 2008; _____. "Groove Theory: A Vamp on the Epistemology of Funk." *American Studies* 52.4, The Funk Issue (2013): 9–34; Scot Brown. "The Blues/Funk Futurism of Roger Troutman." *American Studies* 52.4, The Funk Issue (2013): 119–123; Daylanne K. English and Alvin Kim. "Now We Want Our Funk Cut: Janelle Monáe's Neo-Afrofuturism." *American Studies* 52.4, The Funk Issue (2013): 217–230; Tammy L. Kernodle. "Diggin' You Like Those Ol' Soul Records: Meshell Ndegeocello and the Expanding Definition of Funk in Postsoul America." *American Studies* 52.4, The Funk Issue (2013): 181–204; Kesha M. Morant. "Language in Action: Funk Music as the Critical Voice of a Post-Civil Rights Movement Counterculture." *Journal of Black Studies* 42.1 (January 2011): 71–82; Elmo Morgan. "Noise/Funk: Fo' Real Black Theatre on 'Da Great White Way.'" *African American Review* 31.4, Contemporary Theater Issue (Winter 1997): 677–686; Howard Rambsy II. "Beyond Keeping It Real: OutKast, the Funk Connection, and Afrofuturism." *American Studies* 52.4, The Funk Issue (2013): 205–216; Paul Sneed. "Bandidos de Cristo: Representations of the Power of Criminal Factions in Rio's Proibidão Funk." *Latin American Music Review / Revista de Música Latinoamericana* 28.2 (Autumn–Winter, 2007): 220–241; _____. "Favela Utopias: The 'Bailes Funk' in Rio's Crisis of Social Exclusion and Violence." *Latin American Research Review* 43.2 (2008): 57–79; Dan Sicko. *Techno Rebels: The Renegades of Electronic Funk*. Detroit, MI: Wayne State University Press, 2010; Paul Sneed. "Bandidos de Cristo: Representations of the Power of Criminal Factions in Rio's Proibidão Funk." *Latin American Music Review/Revista de Música Latinoamericana* 28.2 (Autumn–Winter 2007): 220–241; Rickey Vincent. *Funk: The Music, The People, and the Rhythm of the One*. New York: St. Martin's Griffin, 1996; Amy Nathan Wright. "Exploring the Funkadelic Aesthetic: Intertextuality and Cosmic Philosophizing in Funkadelic's Album Covers and Liner Notes." *American Studies* 52.4, The Funk Issue (2013): 141–169.

39. Michael Eric Dyson and Sohail Daulatzai. *Born to Use Mics: Reading Nas's Illmatic*. New York: Basic Civitas Books, 2010; Marvin J. Gladney. "The Black Arts Movement and Hip-Hop." *African American Review* 29.2, Special Issue on The Music (Summer 1995): 291–301; Jeff Greenwald. "Hip-Hop Drumming: The Rhyme May Define, but the Groove Makes You Move." *Black Music Research Journal* 22.2 (Autumn 2002): 259–271; Sarah Hankins. "So Contagious: Hybridity and Subcultural Exchange in Hip-Hop's Use of Indian Samples." *Black Music Research Journal* 31.2 (Fall 2011): 193–208; Vincent Stephens. "Pop Goes the Rapper: A Close Reading of Eminem's Genderphobia." *Popular Music* 24.1 (January 2005): 21–36; Shawn Taylor. *Tribe Called Quest's People's Instinctive Travels and the Paths of Rhythm*. London: Continuum International Pub., 2007; Tom Waldman. *We All Want to Change the World: Rock and Politics from Elvis to Eminem*. Lanham, MD: Taylor Trade Pub., 2003; Justin A. Williams. *Rhymin' and Stealin': Musical Borrowing in Hip-Hop Music*. Ann Arbor: University of Michigan Press, 2013.

Chapter One

Louis Armstrong

Exuberant Jazz Legend and Complex Cultural Diplomat

Born in turn-of-the-twentieth-century New Orleans's poorest quarter, in a syncretized "melting pot" of overlapping political and musical histories,[1] to the sixteen-year-old daughter of a slave, Louis Armstrong grew up among New Orleans's prostitutes, pimps, and "rag-and-bone" merchants in an area known as "the battlefield," where Armstrong's family earned a living in unconventional ways, such as prostitution and gambling.[2] Throughout the twentieth century and into the twenty-first, multiple meanings surrounded Armstrong's histories, with various agendas interested in detaining the jazz legend to subservient racialized, gendered, sexualized, and nationalistic positions.

Armstrong's varied roles include racial accommodationist, anti-racist, mythical jazz stalwart, and US jingoistic symbol, while challenging attempts to confine jazz to the United States's borders. One of the most studied figures in popular music, Armstrong has been considered a "mysterious" enigma signifying New Orleans, the city of his birth, and an internationally routed, State Department "jazz ambassador" exporting US ideals of democracy and racial equality, despite the conclusive realities disproving these utopian sentiments. Known as Dippermouth, Papa Dip, Pops, "Reverend Satchelmouth," and ol' Satchmo (a truncation of "Satchel Mouth"), Armstrong transformed early jazz, a regional folk music, into a transnational art form through the virtuosity of his playing as the first great jazz soloist and force of his charismatic personality. Armstrong denounced pretension in an apparent (racial and personal) authenticity, simplicity, and innocence belying his contradictory personality, complex life, and the myriad cultural politics surrounding his career and image, while confirming US self-perceptions and mythologies.

1

Transversing from abject, almost Medieval poverty to playing in famous cafes, cabarets, and saloons of Storyville, New Orleans's African-American area and red-light district, considered jazz's mythic birthplace,[3] from his big break in 1922 with his boyhood idol King Oliver, the leading New Orleans cornetist, to his heyday in Chicago, New York, Hollywood films, transnational tours, and last days in Queens, New York, Armstrong crossed multiple musical, racial, gender, sexual, class, and national borders, navigating US cultural doublespeak and upheavals with an apparent grace, quickness, and sureness. Performing at such "low cultural" New Orleans venues as the Brick House, a honky-tonk where levee workers congregated on Saturday nights, "trading" with women strolling up and down the floor, drinking, fighting, and throwing bottles over the bandstand, Armstrong's early New Orleans days resulted in his 1922 departure to Chicago at twenty-one to play with King Oliver, New York City as the Jazz Age transitioned into the Great Depression, numerous transnational locales, and jazz immortality.

Armstrong's supposed July 4, 1900 birth date contributed to his mythical status, tying him to US nationalistic legends as a quintessential symbol of its imagined community. Daniel Walker, Armstrong's paternal great-great-grandfather, was a third-generation slave brought from Tidewater, Virginia, for sale in 1818 New Orleans. Mary Albert (1885–1927), Armstrong's mother, was a recent arrival to New Orleans from rural Boutte, Louisiana. Albert lived with relatives "back o' town" in New Orleans when she met Armstrong's father William (1880–1933), abandoning his family after Armstrong's birth. Armstrong lived with his paternal grandmother, Josephine, while his mother worked as a domestic and part-time prostitute.

Around the age of five, Armstrong joined his mother, sister, and a multitude of "step-fathers" at a run-down tenement on Perdido Street in New Orleans's red-light district. Armstrong sold newspapers, delivered coal, and picked through garbage barrels for half-spoiled food to sell to restaurants while singing with a quartet on the street at night. On New Year's Eve 1912, at age eleven, Armstrong was arrested for publicly firing his "step-father's" pistol. A repeat offender, Armstrong was sent to the Colored Waif's Home on New Orleans's edge. A military reform school for boys run by an ex-cavalry officer, the Colored Waif's Home provided Armstrong with a daily routine, regular meals, and cornet instruction. As the school band's leader, Armstrong paraded around New Orleans and obtained his first job as a professional musician, playing blues for pimps and prostitutes at a local tavern. Armstrong "second-lined"[4] in ubiquitous New Orleans marching bands, providing music for parties, dances, parades, and, famously, funerals. In "New Orleans Function" (1950), Armstrong and his All Stars recreate an old-time New Orleans jazz funeral, with Earl Hines, bandleader and composer whose unique playing style made him one of jazz's most influential musicians,[5] on piano and Jack Teagarden on trombone.

As jazz spread from New Orleans, the first jazz musicians to leave the city were those joining African-American vaudeville minstrel shows[6] as they passed through the "Big Easy." Other jazz musicians, such as Jelly Roll Morton (1890–1941), composer and pianist pioneering the use of prearranged, semi-orchestrated effects in jazz bands,[7] traveled along the Gulf Coast. After 1930, little New Orleans jazz was recorded, until it was revived in the 1940s. Exposed to "spasm bands," or groups playing Dixieland (referred to as hot or traditional jazz and based on turn-of-the-twentieth-century New Orleans jazz),[8] jug band, skiffle music, and ragtime as it evolved into the blues and then to jazz, Armstrong became one of early jazz's leading performers.[9]

A dark-skinned, poor child, Armstrong grew up under low expectations, Jim Crow–era legislation,[10] Southern vigilante terrorism, and part of a legacy of black-transnational vernacular traditions. Armstrong heard the pre-jazz mixture of ragtime and the blues in New Orleans honky-tonks, brothels, and saloons. He learned street musicians' blues, the plantation tradition of "ragging" a tune, blues music of "rags-bottles-and-bones" men who played on three-foot-long tin horns, and the ecstatic music and heterophonic singing of his mother's Sanctified Church.

As he saw "chicks would get way down" and "shake everything" in Storyville's famous Funky Butt Hall, Armstrong, immersed in black-transnational vernacular culture, was shaped by overlapping early twentieth-century economic, political, and cultural forces, from Jim Crow oppression to persistent US economic inequalities. *Fin-de-siècle* New Orleans had a musical culture of great depth, thanks to its mixed, white, French, and Spanish heritage, creoles of color, a pool of artisan-class musicians trained in European techniques, and an influx of African-based music, contributed by the ex-slave segment of the population. Jim Crow codes forced creoles' associations with previously disdained darker blacks, proving helpful to musicians' technical finishing and those looking for performance opportunities.

Armstrong idolized King Oliver, who reciprocated by giving Armstrong lessons and recommending him for gigs. Oliver left New Orleans for early 1919 Chicago, leaving his place in the highly regarded band of trombonist and composer Kid Ory (1886–1973), to his protégé. That summer, Armstrong joined pianist and bandleader Fate Marable's riverboat band, performing with Marable through 1921 and taking odd jobs in New Orleans in the off season. Armstrong claimed to have met and was influenced by Bix Beiderbecke (1903–1931), 1920s cornetist, improviser, composer, and the first major white jazz soloist,[11] on a trip upriver to Davenport, Iowa, from St. Louis, the riverboats' summer hub.

Armstrong's "apprenticeship" in New Orleans's honky-tonks highlights the power of music to define a place and ways jazz has been a culture identified with a sense of place. New Orleans's centrality to Armstrong's early histories emphasizes the power of this particular place to determine jazz's subcultural, regional, and national definitions and attributes. Disturbing the monolithic, hegemonic boasting of jazz as "America's classical music," Armstrong, the poster-boy for US jazz exceptionalism, serves as a prime example of jazz's refusal to be confined by the nation-state's borders, veering off in multiple transnational directions and participating in various global flows.

Armstrong and other leading jazz figures' political-cultural contexts include the many famous venues where they performed. Daily realities and rhythmic and broader contingencies of musicians' unique places transformed into musical sounds.[12] In the disturbance of racially pure geographies, musicians crossed borders from African American to white, (US and Global) South to North, and rural to urban while finding expressions for these transnational movements in their music. Armstrong's New Orleans, Chicago, New York City, and transnational routes highlight jazz's role in shaping experiences of race, place, and historical epoch.[13]

Offered as an example of conservative, Horatio Alger, and "rags-to-riches" US mythologies, Armstrong negotiated historical, musical, and racial continuities and contingencies. Maneuvering through desperate poverty and persistent US white supremacy, Armstrong was a man of great gifts who became a celebrity escaping New Orleans's racial hierarchy and economic asymmetry that would last into the twenty-first century and made glaringly explicit for transnational audiences by Hurricane Katrina, a tropical cyclone that struck the southeastern United States in late August 2005. The hurricane and its aftermath claimed more than 1,800 lives and ranked as US history's costliest natural disaster.[14]

Armstrong refined his craft in New Orleans brothels and on Mississippi River steamboats. Called to Chicago to play in the Creole Jazz Band, Armstrong's fame spread so that he would become one of the globe's most identifiable jazz musicians and African American figures, performing a distinctively restless form of popular music merging the vagrancies of everyday existence with the technological, industrial, and cultural exigencies of urban life and hustle, bustle, and "optimism" associated with US culture. Those emulating Armstrong included top trumpeters, saxophonists, and singers, such as Billie Holiday, impacted by Armstrong's vocal style's swing and rhythmic flexibility. The swing era's dominant influence, performers attempted to emulate Armstrong's swing-style, dramatic structure, melody, and technical virtuosity. This includes jazz trumpeter and bandleader Max Kaminsky, Lionel Hampton, jazz musician and bandleader known for his rhythmic vitality and showmanship, best known for his work on the vibraphone, and a skilled drummer, pianist, and singer,[15] and Coleman Hawkins, one of the first great jazz tenor saxophone soloists and jazz musicians to expatriate himself to Europe for a significant period, committed to a vision in which African-American jazz musicians would find a place in the jazz world commensurate with their skills.[16] As trombonists adopted Armstrong's phrasing, saxophonists, from Hawkins to Bud Freeman, who, with Hawkins, was one of the first jazz tenor saxophonists, modeled their styles on Armstrong.

Armstrong's trumpet playing, intonation, and lyrical and dynamic performances created exciting and memorable music. While his most creative years were in the 1920s and early 1930s, when he helped create the swing style, in his teens, Armstrong learned music by listening to pioneering jazz artists, such as King Oliver. Armstrong toured the United States and Europe as a soloist accompanied by big bands and replaced his earlier years' blues-based material for popular songs by Duke Ellington, Hoagy Carmichael,[17] the composer, singer, self-taught pianist, and actor, writing several of the United States's most highly regarded popular standards, and Irving Berlin, playing a leading role in popular songs' evolution, from the early ragtime and jazz eras to musicals' "golden age."[18] Armstrong's tone and bravura solos with high-note climaxes led to such compositions as "Body and Soul" (1930) and "Stardust" (1931), featuring Armstrong rewriting the lyrics of this familiar Carmichael ballad. Though he sang such amusing songs as "Hobo, You Can't Ride This Train" (1936), Armstrong also sang standard songs. After 1932, Armstrong's performance style evolved little and his repertoire was limited to popular hits. In his unusual, gravelly, and instantly identifiable voice, Armstrong's memorable renditions include the hits "Blueberry Hill" (1949), "Mack the Knife" (1955), "Hello Dolly" (1964) (displacing The Beatles[19] as number one on the pop charts), and "What A Wonderful World" (1967).

By the mid-1950s, Armstrong was featured by the prestigious Newport Jazz Festival,[20] Royal Philharmonic in London, the New York Philharmonic and Leonard Bernstein (1918–1990), US conductor, composer, and pianist known for his classical and popular music, flamboyant conducting style, and pedagogic flair,[21] and CBS as the subject of *Satchmo The Great* (1957), an autobiographical documentary. Additional accomplishments included being the first jazz musician to appear on the cover of *Time* magazine (1949) and first honoree in *DownBeat Magazine*'s Jazz Hall of Fame (1952).

In his last years, sickness reduced Armstrong's trumpet playing, but he continued as a singer. After several bouts of heart disease, Armstrong died at his home in Corona, Queens. Posthumous recognitions include a 1972 Grammy Lifetime Achievement Award, a statue unveiled in 1980 in New Orleans's Louis Armstrong Park and naming of Louis Armstrong New Orleans International Airport, issuance of a 1995 commemorative stamp, and identification in 1999 as one of *Variety*'s Top 100 20th Century Entertainers. Armstrong recorded approximately 1,500 tracks in studios and at live concerts and at least an equal number of tracks on air checks, film soundtracks, and television performances, marking his visual cultural and popular musical ubiquity.

Armstrong's earliest recordings were with King Oliver, whose thirty-five sides in 1923 represent the first significant body of African-American recorded jazz. In 1924–1925, Armstrong recorded with Fletcher "Smack" Henderson (1897–1952), arranger, bandleader, and pianist who was a leading pioneer in the sound, style, and instrumentation of big band jazz.[22] Equated with late nineteenth- and early twentieth-century German Romantic composer Richard Strauss,[23] Henderson was among the most influential 1930s swing arrangers.

Armstrong also recorded with Clarence Williams's Blue Five, the Red Onion Jazz Babies, and blues singers, including the iconic, queer African-American vocalist Bessie Smith. Deemed the "Empress of the Blues," Smith was the most popular female blues singer of the 1920s and 1930s.[24] Armstrong's 1925 accompaniment of Smith on "St. Louis Blues" was a classic interpretation of the best-known composition of W. C. Handy, arranger, bandleader, composer, cornetist, guitarist, lyricist, publisher, and vocalist deemed "father of the blues" and "America's Greatest Song Writer."

In 1937, Armstrong became the first African American to host a national radio program. During World War II, Armstrong performed on military bases and cut V-discs during the 1942–1944 American Federation of Musicians' recording ban. The mid-1940s big-band era decline dramatically transformed Armstrong's career. Leonard Feather, jazz journalist, producer, and songwriter whose advocacy and standard reference work, *The Encyclopedia of Jazz* (1956), placed him among the most influential jazz critics,[25] arranged for Armstrong to appear with Edmond Hall's New Orleans revivalist band at Carnegie Hall in early 1947. This led to a legendary Town Hall concert in May with a select group of performers, billed as the All Stars. From then to just before his death, Armstrong was on the road with this band, known as Louis Armstrong's All Stars.[26] Producing his highest-charting hits, during the last third of his career, in addition to his All Stars recordings, Armstrong performed famed collaborations with Ellington and jazz singer Ella Fitzgerald.[27]

Armstrong's alleged musical decline produced his greatest jazz albums. His role in the film *New Orleans* (1947), in which a New Orleans gambling hall owner entertains his patrons with hot jazz by Armstrong, Billie Holiday, and Woody Herman (1913–1987), clarinetist, saxophonist, bandleader, and singer who was best known as the front man for a succession of bands he dubbed "herds,"[28] also inspired the All Stars' formation. Armstrong transnationally toured with changing All Stars sextets and produced hit recordings and exceptional albums, including tributes to W. C. Handy and Fats Waller (1904–1943), pianist and composer who was one of the few jazz musicians to win wide commercial fame, though this was achieved at a cost of concealing his musical talents under a façade of broad, blackface minstrel-like comedy.[29] All Stars' concerts and recordings included opening with "Indiana" (1917), continuing with a string of Dixieland, New Orleans, and pop favorites, and closing with "When It's Sleepy Time Down South" (1931). Armstrong's theme song, "When It's Sleepy Time Down South," was reminiscent of his "Stars Fell on Alabama" (1956) duet with Ella Fitzgerald, evoking similar feelings of nostalgia, innocence, and sentimentality for an imagined "Old South." Reminiscent of such films as *The Birth of a Nation* (1915) and *Gone with the Wind* (1939), these musical celebrations of a racially neutral, Disney-like South, seen in such films as *Song of the South* (1946) and *The Princess and the Frog* (2009), continued Armstrong's strategic positioning in US color-blind and "post-racial" myths forecasting Obama-era denials of racial realities, blinding the general public to racial hierarchy's continuation.

CONTESTED RACIAL REPRESENTATIONS

Armstrong's shifting racial representations were a consistent theme running throughout his life and influencing his contemporary legacies, meanings, and interpretations. Perceived as old-fashioned and dismissed as buffoonish, for his grinning and eye-rolling antics Armstrong was labeled an "Uncle Tom,"[30] a racialized insult stemming from the eponymous, desexualized, and pious protagonist of abolitionist Harriet Beecher Stowe's anti-slavery, religious-themed novel *Uncle Tom's Cabin* (1852), represented as a dutiful, long-suffering servant faithful to his white master. Continuing to influence racial visual cultural representations in early twenty-first-century film and television, the "black-on-black" "Uncle Tom" insult denotes African Americans' subservience to whites and betrayal of other African Americans.

Primarily interested in his audience's comfort and a suitable, de-politicized symbol for dominant US culture's desire to hide its racial injustice, even as he was used by the State Department to prove US racial equality abroad, Armstrong's stage persona was regarded as vaudevillian. Some jazz musicians, such as Dizzy Gillespie (1917–1993), trumpeter, composer, and bandleader who was one of bebop's seminal figures, accused Armstrong of "Uncle Tom"–like acquiescence. In addition to Gillespie, Armstrong was dismissed by younger African-American musicians as out-of-touch and a sell-out. African-American singer, dancer, and entertainer Sammy Davis, Jr.[31] and others called out Armstrong for his silence on civil rights issues and performances for segregated audiences. Miles Davis respected Armstrong's playing but hated his "clowning," while claiming jazz itself was an "Uncle Tom" word.

For critics, Armstrong's final decades were a collapse into nineteenth-century blackface minstrelsy, with some regarding Armstrong's wide, signature, and "megawatt" grin as an accommodation to the white world and in contrast to his pre–World War II experimentations at the vanguard of US popular music.[32] In public statements, Armstrong claimed his audience came first and his purpose was to "serve" his audience, responding to criticisms of his "Tomming" by falling back on US cultural notions of simplicity, happiness, and fun. A seemingly pre-political entertainer, accommodating US cultural desires for racial harmony, closure, and rose-colored optimism, Armstrong's innocent racial representations may have been due to financial pressures, career ambitions, or political apathy. Faced with the racial realities of his twentieth-century time and US cultural place, Armstrong was not immune to his era's racial realities. Responding to racial injustice with a determination to overcome that did not include outward bitterness, endearing him to dominant US culture while alienating him from more explicitly countercultural black-transnational artists, Armstrong was aware of and only briefly publicly addressed US racism. This came in the form of a protest against Republican president Dwight D. Eisenhower's reaction to the 1957 Little Rock, Arkansas, school desegregation crisis.[33]

Escorted by the National Guard to Little Rock Central High School, the Little Rock Nine was the name given to the group of African-American high school students at the center of the struggle to desegregate US public schools. The Little Rock Nine's efforts to enroll were supported by the US Supreme Court's *Brown v. Board of Education* (1954) decision, declaring segregated schooling to be unconstitutional. Warned by the Little Rock Board of Education not to attend the first day of school, the Little Rock Nine arrived on the second day accompanied by a small, inter-racial group of ministers. They encountered a white mob in front of the school shouting, throwing stones, and threatening to kill the students. Arkansas National Guard soldiers, sent by segregationist Arkansas governor Orval Eugene Faubus, blocked the school's entrance, as Faubus declared his opposition to integration and intention to defy a federal court order mandating desegregation.

As each lynching and nationally televised spectacle centering on US white supremacy harmed US foreign policy objectives and the nation's image and standing in the world, the "Negro problem" became a central issue in every presidential administration from Harry Truman to Lyndon Johnson.[34] The Little Rock Nine confrontation drew transnational attention to the United States's racial hierarchy and sparked debates concerning US racism, US allies' major concern, central Soviet propaganda theme, obstacle to US foreign policy goals in Africa, Asia, and Latin America, and related to communist containment policy and the economic, geo-political, military, covert, and cultural Cold War.

A musical legend taking a stand against injustice before Bob Dylan, John Lennon, and other rock legends,[35] Armstrong could not contain his outrage during the "Little Rock Nine" incident, provoking him to write Eisenhower a heated letter denouncing the treatment of "his people" and cancel a scheduled government-sponsored Soviet Union tour. Temporarily renouncing his State Department "Jazz Ambassador" role, Armstrong suspended, if only briefly, his racial accommodationist demeanor. In his telegram to Eisenhower, Armstrong offered to take "those little Negro children personally into Central High School" and criticized the conservative president for failing to enforce Southern desegregation. One of the few celebrities who could be so outspoken without suffering substantial backlash and before the 1964 Civil Rights Act's passage,[36] Armstrong's indignation extended to his home state of Louisiana, where he refused to perform with his All Stars because the state prohibited integrated bands.

An outspoken bebop opponent, preferring the assimilationist sounds and style of swing and popular standards, Armstrong was representative of an earlier, more innocent, and traditional form of jazz, a "moldy fig" in radical contrast to the dissonant, anti-assimilationist modern jazz idiom of bebop. Armstrong was everything his bebop successors despised: melodic, harmonious, and apolitical. At Chicago's Sunset Café, a black-and-tan dance hall staging elaborate floor shows, Armstrong sharpened his entertainment skills by adding mugging, dancing, and singing to his repertoire, though he was discouraged from doing so with King Oliver and Fletcher Henderson and contributing to accusations of Armstrong's complicity in the continuation of blackface minstrelsy.

Armstrong's "minstrel mask" connects to W. E. B. Du Bois (1868–1963), sociologist who was the most important black protest leader in the United States during the first half of the twentieth century, shared in the creation of the National Association for the Advancement of Colored People (NAACP) in 1909, and later became identified with communist causes, and his notion of "double consciousness,"[37] or the sense that African Americans' identities have been divided into conflicting parts, at once part of the United States while separated from it.[38] Critics argued that Armstrong's "Tomming," instead of denigrating his race, celebrated black-transnational vernacular legacies by "signifying" upon racism in a reworking of racist conventions, simultaneously perpetuating them while offering a "knowing wink" back at his audience as he understood the absurdity and necessity of their repetition. Others contend Armstrong challenged dominant US culture and attacked its racial hierarchies as he pursued a carnivalesque celebration of bodily pleasures at the expense of US Protestant work and propriety ethics.[39]

Though in some ways he acquiesced to US racial codes and conventions, Armstrong struggled against US racial hierarchy. This was particularly evident in the music industry, as Armstrong's allies cringed when the trumpeter ceded his autonomy to a mob-affiliated white manager extorting him out of millions of dollars. From 1935 to the end of his life, Armstrong's career was managed by Joe Glaser, the tough, notorious former manager of Chicago's

Sunset Café, hiring Armstrong's bands and guiding his film career and radio appearances. Settled by a handshake, the agreement of a 50–50 split of Armstrong's revenues with Glaser lasted for life and made them both millionaires. Sending Armstrong on the road fronting a big band at profitable venues and constantly scheduling Armstrong in the recording studio, Glaser arranged for articles in *Vanity Fair* magazine and negotiated Armstrong's appearance in the film *Pennies from Heaven* (1936). This began a long personal and professional relationship between Armstrong and the film's star, heteronormative crooner extraordinaire Bing Crosby,[40] also performing with Bob Hope in the Orientalist films *Road to Singapore* (1940), *Road to Morocco* (1942), and *Road to Bali* (1952).

ON TO CHICAGO

In 1922, King Oliver sent for Armstrong to come to Chicago to play second cornet in his Creole Jazz Band. Oliver's Creole Jazz Band members, leading practitioners of early contrapuntal (two or more independent melodic lines) New Orleans ensemble style, included such musicians as the brothers Johnny[41] and Baby Dodds and Lillian (Lil) Hardin (1898–1971), the Creole Band's pianist who married Armstrong in 1924. Becoming popular through his ensemble lead, second cornet lines, and cornet duet passages (called "breaks") with Oliver, Armstrong recorded his first solos as a member of Oliver's band in such pieces as "Chimes Blues" (1923) and "Tears" (1923), which Armstrong and Lil composed. The two choruses of "Chimes Blues," Armstrong's first recorded solo, contain Armstrong's stylistic trademarks and full, rich tone. In "Tears," each pair of breaks forms a "call-and-response" pattern in which the second "answers" the first with motivic correspondences.

Though Armstrong began composing in New Orleans, with Oliver in Chicago, Armstrong and Lil composed five to six songs a day, which they sold to the OKeh Record Company.[42] "Weather Bird Rag," "Where Did You Stay Last Night?," and "Tears" were recorded by the Creole Jazz Band. "Yes! I'm in the Barrel" and "Cornet Chop Suey" were recorded by the early Hot Five and "Coal Cart Blues" was recorded by Armstrong with Clarence Williams's Blue Five. Armstrong's most recorded compositions after the 1920s are "Back 'O Town Blues" (with Luis Russell), "Pretty Little Missy" (with Billy Kyle), "Velma's Blues" (with Velma Middleton), and "Swing That Music" (with Horace Gerlach), appearing in tandem with Armstrong's autobiography *Swing That Music* (1936).[43]

The first jazz musician to publish an autobiography, *Satchmo: My Life in New Orleans* (1954) also classifies as Armstrong's autobiography. A jazz literary milestone, Armstrong wrote most of *Swing That Music*'s biographical material, of a different style and scope than his later autobiography, and covering in intimate detail Armstrong's life, documenting his early days on Chicago's South Side with King Oliver, courtship and marriage to Lil Hardin, 1929 New York City move, formation of his own band, European tours, and additional transnational movements. A justification for the style of music then called "swing" but more broadly referred to as "jazz" and one of the earliest attempts to trace jazz's development, *Swing That Music* can be considered a biography, history, and form of entertainment. Advertised as the first standard book in English on the "new swing music," Armstrong's partly ghostwritten *Swing That Music* anticipated *Lady Sings the Blues* (1956), Billie Holiday's ghostwritten autobiography exploiting her "tragic" mulatto, abusive, mysterious, victim, and torch singer myths. [44]

Armstrong's musical migration from New Orleans to Chicago was common, as he and other Southern musicians entered a city dominated by criminal gangs, with few restrictions, and many cabarets and dance halls requiring jazz's hot music. Entering Chicago under the guidance of King Oliver, by 1920, Oliver's Creole Jazz Band, a successor of the Original Creole Band, [45] formed by Bill Johnson (considered the father of the "slap" style of double bass playing), was performing in Chicago's mainly African-American and "black-and-tan" clubs. In 1923, the Creole Jazz Band made seminal recordings, forming the first substantial body of African-American recorded jazz. In 1918, Oliver went to Chicago and formed his band there by 1920. In late summer 1922, Oliver summoned Armstrong to join his Creole Jazz Band at Chicago's Royal Gardens cabaret. There, Armstrong played second to Oliver's lead, intriguing audiences and musicians with his harmony on improvised duet breaks. Armstrong began doubling with violinist and bandleader Erskine Tate's Orchestra, playing for silent films at the Vendome Theater a few blocks from the Dreamland Café. Armstrong's high-register playing and dramatic solos on operatic numbers with Tate enticed crowds and gained the attention of Alpha Smith (1907–1943), Armstrong's third wife. When the Dreamland closed in 1926 for liquor violations, Armstrong doubled from the Vendome to the Sunset Café.

Armstrong became part of broader Chicago jazz histories, of which the Great Migration of millions of African-Americans from the agricultural and rural South to the industrial and urban North, and especially Chicago, [46] played a dominant role. Creating a large audience for African-American music, especially the blues, recent Southern arrivals gathered in Chicago's South Side area, known as the "Black Belt." [47] African American migration from the South to Chicago during and after World War I was crucial to Chicago's jazz development. The South Side, home to a large part of the racial inequalities and segregation giving Chicago its reputation, was, through much of the 1920s, where influential New Orleans jazz musicians performed. Armstrong played at the Sunset and Savoy, King Oliver at Lin-

coln Gardens, the Pekin, and Plantation, and Earl Hines at the Nest and
Apex. In an area of a few blocks, these clubs and dance halls were mostly
"black and tans," attracting audiences that were largely African American on
weeknights, but approximately 75 percent white on weekends. Such young
white jazz musicians as Bix Beiderbecke, Benny Goodman, and Gene Krupa,[48] one of the most popular swing-era percussionists, heard New Orleans
style music. Through much of the 1920s, the "Western" bands of Chicago
were seen as more developed than those in New York and elsewhere. Chicago bands' music was mostly the classic New Orleans polyphonic jazz,
though elements of heterophony remained. Mostly an ensemble music with
few solos, Chicago jazz depended on swing and a thick texture for its effects.
It was not necessarily improvised, as performers generally worked from set
parts, memorized rather than notated, which musicians enriched and varied,
and with solos tending to be similar each performance.

Starting in New Orleans's red-hot clubs, jazz made its way north and
settled in Chicago. The city became a focal point for musicians and many
jazz legends made names for themselves there, such as Armstrong, Oliver,
and Jelly Roll Morton. As jazz grew in popularity, Chicago became a jazz
hub. Benny Goodman (1909–1986), bandleader and renowned clarinet virtuoso dubbed the "King of Swing,"[49] and cornetists Jimmy McPartland and
Muggsy Spanier were a few of the artists benefiting from the arrival of talent
into their hometown. Chicago's influential jazz havens were home to celebrated musicians and the musical phenomenon they created. As Chicago's
downtown had its golden age, world-famous theaters lined State Street, hot
jazz clubs made the South Side a musical Mecca, and jazz had far-reaching
effects on the city's North and West Sides.[50] A "toddlin' town" of dance
halls, cabarets, Prohibition, and segregation, Chicago jazz grew into the musical statement of an era as the city became the major "Roaring Twenties"
jazz center in one of the musical culture's most vital and exciting periods.

Chicago jazz was a bold musical style defining the city's material, racial,
and cultural divides. Black-and-tan cabarets, dance halls, inter-racial dancing's popularity, and the Savoy Ballroom, Friars Inn, and Austin High constituted elements of the jazz scene. Musical entertainment's hustle, bustle,
sounds, and styles permeated the city. From the South Side came legendary
African-American musicians, as Chicago jazz responded to the city's racial
tensions and rise in status.[51] Distressed neighborhoods became the backdrop
of 1960s and '70s Chicago jazz, with the famous Velvet Lounge[52] one of the
city's longest-running clubs. Such avant-garde[53] Chicago jazz musicians as
tenor saxophonist Fred Anderson, pianist and composer Andrew Hill, and
Roscoe Mitchell, composer, instrumentalist, educator, and saxophonist, built
a bridge from the traditional view of jazz to the world of contemporary
innovators. In racially divided Chicago, legendary jazz clubs, the famed
Maxwell Street market, and "L" (short for "elevated") rapid transit system

noted the crossroads of Chicago jazz's racial, gender, sexual, ethnic, class, and transnational tensions and border crossings.[54]

Chicago's peak as the center of US jazz was short. In 1928, a reformist government removed the illegal cabarets and dance halls. By 1929, musicians began to look to New York City. The migration out of Chicago removed the old New Orleans style of what little viability it had. While jazz continued in Chicago nightlife for a decade, it was infrequently played in other cities, especially New York, and to dancers there it sounded dated and unfamiliar. By the end of 1927, Chicago's Sunset Café closed, and Armstrong's attempts to operate a dance hall with Earl Hines and drummer Zutty Singleton failed. Having earlier left the Vendome, Armstrong returned as the "feature man" in a movie theater orchestra. Armstrong spent most of his last two years in Chicago fronting the reunited Sunset Café Band at the new Savoy Ballroom. The Savoy's financial difficulties in 1929 prompted Armstrong to take the band to New York City, where he found work in Harlem substituting for the house band at Connie's Inn, whose band was then on Broadway playing with Fats Waller.

IN NEW YORK

Armstrong became jazz's first great soloist when he moved from King Oliver's Creole Jazz Band in Chicago to Fletcher Henderson's band in New York City in 1924. While with King Oliver, Armstrong married Lil, who encouraged him to establish his own career with Fletcher Henderson in New York City. As Armstrong joined Fletcher Henderson's orchestra in New York as a jazz specialist, he was given solo space on recordings and in performances at the segregated Roseland Ballroom, the band's principal venue. Appreciated as a performer with special, even unusual gifts, Armstrong distinguished himself with his tone and virtuoso technique, melodic invention, ability to "swing," presence, and transparent jubilance. Those in Henderson's band attempted to imitate Armstrong, as did other African American and white musicians, copying his solos on trumpet and other instruments.

As Armstrong played for a year in New York in Fletcher Henderson's band as its "hot" soloist, by 1924, Henderson recognized that audiences wanted a hotter version of dance music than Paul Whiteman, dance bandleader Paul Specht, and others were offering. That fall, Armstrong helped to show the Henderson men and other New York musicians what his hot music was. Not constrained by the eight- or sixteen-bar solos with Henderson, Armstrong's New York small-group sides note a more relaxed, capacious, and virtuosic style, heard on "Cold in Hand Blues" (1925) with Bessie Smith, "Railroad Blues" (1925) with Trixie Smith, "I Ain't Gonna Play No Second

Fiddle" (1925) with Perry Bradford's Jazz Phools, and "Cake Walking Babies from Home" (1925) with Sidney Bechet in Clarence Williams's Blue Five.

Armstrong's participation in the New York City jazz scene predated the mid-1930s and late 1940s, when the center of the jazz world was a two-block stretch of 52nd Street in Midtown Manhattan. Dozens of crowded basement clubs between Fifth and Seventh Avenues hosted Charlie Parker and other jazz legends. A composer and bandleader, Parker has been considered the greatest jazz saxophonist, principal bebop performer, and, with Armstrong, one of jazz's most revolutionary artists.

On 52nd Street, musicians and their audiences crossed racial borders and the traditional line separating serious art from commercial entertainment. 52nd Street became home to some of New York City's first nightclubs to allow racially integrated bands and audiences. Part of New York City's thriving jazz scene, 52nd Street jazz histories complicate simplistic distinctions between musical styles, such as Dixieland, swing and big bands, and small-group bebop, defined along racial lines. The multiplicity of musical genres challenged twentieth century US racial hierarchies as 52nd Street's vibrancy generated inter-racial and musical border crossings. [55]

At the intersection of racial, gender, sexual, ethnic, class, national, transnational, and jazz formations, since the 1930s, "The Street" became jazz's epicenter for two decades. In its rich musical milieu, the United States's fascination with race and money shaped musical styles and the culture industry. A significant chapter in jazz histories, where the respect musicians had for each other was tangible, 52nd Street offered a glimpse into the jazz world during an era of multiple transformations. As New York City became jazz's capital, musicians, jazz lovers, bachelors, college students, and businessmen knew 52nd Street was "The Street that Never Slept" and where every night was New Year's Eve. Walking through jazz histories, hot jazz was born and raised on The Street, as were 1930s big swing bands and 1940s "cool" modern jazz combos. Comics like Alan King and Joey Adams got their start on The Street, along with Erroll Garner, pianist and composer known for his swing playing and ballads, trombonist Jack Teagarden, and tenor saxophonist Coleman Hawkins. Bessie Smith performed on The Street, as did Sarah Vaughan, Dizzy Gillespie, big-band leaders Tommy and Jimmy Dorsey, pianist Art Tatum, [56] pianist and big-band leader Count Basie, and 1930s and 1940s clarinetist and bandleader Artie Shaw. [57] On the "street of jazz," some of the music's greatest artists performed in the late 1950s and early 1960s, such as Miles Davis, John Coltrane, Charles Mingus, and Thelonious Monk. 52nd Street's histories include its birth in Prohibition-era speakeasies, where musicians jammed for gin, post-Repeal development as the center of the jazz universe, lined up and down on both sides with tiny, smoke-filled rooms where African-American and white musicians performed for capacity crowds, and the Street's post–World War II decline as it became a tenderloin of strip and clip joints.

Armstrong's first Broadway opportunity disappointed but his second was a success. Armstrong held the position of lead trumpet in the pit orchestra for Vincent Youman's *Great Day* (1929), a Broadway musical-comedy set in a plantation near New Orleans. Demoted to second trumpet and then fired for "not being adaptable to show business," during previews in Philadelphia, Armstrong returned to New York. There, he appeared in African-American poet, composer, and lyricist Andy Razaf's theater review *Hot Chocolates* (1929). Armstrong's cameo performance of "Ain't Misbehavin'" caused a sensation. The response to Armstrong's "Ain't Misbehavin'" showstopper earned him a larger role on stage and sent him to the studio to record the show's hits. By the end of *Hot Chocolates'* six-month run, Armstrong, already famous among African Americans, became a star among whites.

Additional theatrical endeavors met with less commendation. Armstrong's role in *Swingin' the Dream, A Jazz Midsummer Night's Dream* (1939) lasted only thirteen performances on Broadway, and, in 1961, pianist Dave Brubeck (1920–2012)[58] and his *The Real Ambassadors*, a jazz oratorio (an extended composition with a dramatic text for solo voices, chorus, and orchestra and performed without action, costume, or scenery) concerning US race relations and democracy, featured Armstrong, yet yielded only one live performance. Fired from Connie's Inn in early 1930 after *Hot Chocolates'* close, Armstrong broke up his band, briefly reconciled with Lil, and traveled with her to Los Angeles, where he was hired to front Sebastian's New Cotton Club Orchestra, featuring vibraphonist and bandleader Lionel Hampton. A recording with country singer Jimmie Rodgers[59] earned Armstrong and Lil crossover credit.

Making the West Coast his new home, Armstrong was arrested for smoking marijuana, a drug he used for the rest of his life. After serving minimal jail time in March 1931, Armstrong moved back to the Midwest, where his new manager, Johnny Collins, booked him into a Chicago club. When a fight appeared to threaten Armstrong's safety, Collins found Armstrong a summer residency in New Orleans at the white Suburban Gardens dance hall. On his first trip to New Orleans since leaving nine years earlier, African Americans in the city, carrying Armstrong on their shoulders, greeted "Little Louie" with a hot jazz band. While a large crowd gathered at the Suburban Gardens for Armstrong's first performance, a white radio announcer could not bring himself to announce Armstrong.[60] Unaffected, Armstrong took the microphone and introduced himself, something unprecedented in Jim Crow–era New Orleans. As dancers packed the Suburban Gardens dance hall nightly, Armstrong enjoyed his three-month stay in the Crescent City, paying well-publicized visits to relatives, old haunts, and the Colored Waif's Home. Jim Crow–era codes provoked the cancellation of a farewell concert for Armstrong's African-American fans and caused the band's arrest and temporary imprisonment in Memphis during their Southern tour.

In mid-1932, Armstrong went on a four-month tour of England, where his exuberant onstage demeanor and *altissimo* (very high) playing shocked and fascinated audiences. A year later, Armstrong was greeted by crowds on an eighteen-month European tour, though he had to limit his performances due to lip problems. Armstrong's imperfect technique included a shortcoming in his embouchure, or mouth placement, straining his "chops" to bursting. In the last two decades of his career, Armstrong's ravaged lip prohibited incursions into the trumpet's high register, encouraging him to showcase his inimitable voice on live and recorded music.

HOT FIVES, SEVENS, AND BLACK-TRANSNATIONAL SCAT SINGING

In his early period, Armstrong paraphrased the original melodic line. Gaining confidence, he abandoned the melody and ventured into flights of invention, built on songs' harmonies rather than developed around their melodies. Armstrong's simplified style included melodic paraphrases, variations, and chord change–based improvisations. His trumpet range expanded, heard in his repertoire's high-note showpieces. Armstrong demonstrated his abilities in counterpoint (the combination of simultaneously sounding lines), harmony, and a powerful sense of swing in a combination of uneven eighth notes, pervasive syncopation (accents shifted to weak beats), irregular phrasing, and playing around instead of on top of the beat. This expressed a sense of forward motion characterizing Armstrong's approach to rhythm that would become the swing era's model. Capable of improvising unique solos on different takes of the same composition, such as "Stomp Off, Let's Go" (1926), multiple listenings of Armstrong's recordings highlight ways he refined his ideas from one take to the next rather than rethinking each one. Armstrong's improvisational approach consisted of melodic paraphrase fluctuating from the literal (a duplication of the melody) to the abstract (a new melody based on features of the old).

The pressures of making a living in a competitive atmosphere coalesced Armstrong's gifts, with influences ranging from tap dancing, classical music, New Orleans clarinet style, and Guy Lombardo (1902–1977), a dance band leader whose New Year's Eve radio and television broadcasts with his Royal Canadians became a US tradition for forty-eight years. Mocked by critics as the "king of corn," Lombardo gained long-lasting popularity by conducting what was billed as "the sweetest music this side of heaven."

For Armstrong, 1927 was a year of professional and personal instability. However, the publication of Armstrong's transcribed "hot choruses" and jazz breaks in the middle of that year spoke to his growing popularity. Armstrong began recording a historic series of small-group sides, known as the Hot Fives and Hot Sevens, extending through 1928. One of these recordings, the highly successful "Heebie Jeebies" (1926), established Armstrong's reputation as a jazz singer and was an example of Armstrong's performance of scat singing's most celebrated early instances. A precursor to hip hop cultural beatboxing and rapping and additional black-transnational wordplay traditions of boasting, toasting (talking or chanting, usually in a monotone melody, over a rhythm or beat by a deejay), "playing the dozens" (a game of spoken words between two contestants, where participants insult each other until one gives up), and West-African ritualistic verbal contests, Armstrong's scat singing further distanced him, and jazz more broadly, from any reduction of this musical culture as exclusively American by privileging Armstrong, jazz, and African-American cultural practices in a network of forced and unforced economic, political, and cultural exchanges crisscrossing the Atlantic and beyond.[61]

As rhythm characterizes his usually minimalistic vocals, and speech-like distillations of the melody combine with melodic interpolations between phrases, for Armstrong, lyrics' meanings were second to words' timbral (sounds' character and quality) possibilities, to which Armstrong applied bends, elisions, and smears and replaced with scat singing. These techniques premiered on the early Hot Fives and continued in 1931 on "All of Me," "Lazy River," and other vocal solos. Armstrong began to sing on most of his recordings, varying melodies, and decorating his performances with scat phrases. In a break from his mainstream demeanor, as Armstrong reconfigured standard English in ways jazz and hip hop practitioners would do throughout the twentieth and early twenty-first centuries, he subtly subverted dominant cultural practices.

A technique of jazz singing in which onomatopoeic or nonsense syllables are sung to improvised melodies, some writers traced scat singing to the practice, common in West-African music, of translating percussive patterns into vocal lines by assigning syllables to rhythms. The earliest recorded examples of scat singing involved the free invention of rhythm, melody, and syllables. Scat singing began as singers imitated jazz instrumentalists' sounds. One of early New Orleans jazz's novelty devices, scat singing was heard in undeveloped form on early blues and washboard-band recordings. Armstrong's early scat solos rival his trumpet improvisations in virtuosity, range of feeling, and variety of attacks and timbres. On the Hot Seven track "Hotter Than That" (1927), Armstrong imitates a trumpet's "rip" in his wordless vocal.

Armstrong's scat singing continued with such singers as Cab Calloway (1907–1994), [62] the racially exoticized bandleader and all-around entertainer known for his exuberant style, leading one of the most highly regarded swing-era big bands, and whose 1930s scat solos served as a model for the "urban" black music of Sportin' Life in George Gershwin's "folk opera" *Porgy and Bess* (1935). As jazz improvisation grew more complex, scat singing followed, with the result that later scat singers improvised in the complex bebop idiom. Ella Fitzgerald was known for imitating various jazz instruments and soloists, expanding the range of timbres and attacks in scat singing, and challenging mainstream, wholesome, and non-threatening images of Fitzgerald as the darling of the US and transnational popular cultural establishment. Bebop scat singers include Eddie Jefferson (1918–1979), celebrated vocalist and lyricist credited as an innovator of vocalese, a style in which lyrics are set to an instrumental composition or solo, and Betty Carter (1930–1998), jazz singer best remembered for the scat and other complex interpretations showcasing her vocal flexibility. Anita O'Day (1919–2006) was among the most admired of all jazz singers for her lilting, rhythmically provocative manner and rose to fame as a swinging, good-humored stylist.[63] Joe "Bebop" Carroll (1919–1981), jazz vocalist known for his work with Dizzy Gillespie between 1949 and 1953 and for an upbeat, energetic comedic style, employed scat singing and vocalese. Carmen McRae (1920–1994) was a jazz vocalist and pianist who, from an early emulation of vocalist Billie Holiday, grew to become a distinctive stylist known for her smoky voice, melodic variations on jazz standards, and innovative, complex, and elegant scat improvisations. Additional performers include Babs Gonzales (1919–1980), bebop-era jazz vocalist, and Jon Hendricks (1921–), the "Poet Laureate of Jazz," "James Joyce of Jive," and a jazz lyricist and singer considered one of the originators of vocalese, adding lyrics to instrumental songs, replacing instruments with vocalists, such as Duke Ellington and Count Basie's big-band arrangements, and one of scat singing's most admired practitioners.

Similar to jazz instrumentalists, such as trumpeter Clark Terry's[64] distinctive "mumbling" technique and Dizzy Gillespie's trumpet smear imitations, scat singers, as vocal jazz soloists, adopted a unique, recognizable timbre and delivery and developed a personal stock of syllables and vocal devices. The usefulness of bebop scat singing for teaching jazz was discovered, especially by New York–based jazz pianist Lennie Tristano,[65] a major figure of cool jazz and influential teacher. A large number of scat singing manuals were published, becoming primers in jazz improvisation and ear training. With the mid-1970s bebop revival came renewed interest in bebop scat singing, leading to comebacks for such singers as Betty Carter and Eddie Jefferson. Young scat singers thought of themselves as belonging to the classic bop tradition. Among the best was Al Jarreau, adept at creating vocal equivalents of complex jazz-rock[66] rhythms, and jazz vocalist and conductor Bobby McFerrin,[67] whose wide range and mobility are evident in his unaccompanied solo performances. The 1960s free-jazz movement[68] saw an expansion of the timbres and resources available to scat singers. As scat singing trans-nationally spread to other types of music, Chicago singer Leon Thomas incorporated Central African pygmy yodeling techniques into his singing, while such scat singers as Karin Krog from Norway, Urszula Dudziak from Poland, and Flora Purim from Brazil once again reintroduced jazz to its international routes. The extension of vocal improvisation to include sounds regarded as non-musical, such as cries, screams, sobbing, and laughter, was one of the main innovations of this period and brought jazz singing close to avant-garde art music, heard in the work of Cleo Laine in Britain and Lauren Newton in Vienna and West Germany. Preceding the possibilities of elec-tronic manipulation and vocal distortions, scat singers showed how this vocal art crossed aesthetic and transnational borders.

Upon his 1925 return to Chicago, Armstrong began to make the sixty or so recordings of the "Hot Five" series, bringing him greater exposure. By 1928, when this series was completed, Armstrong's name was becoming more familiar and he was recognized in the jazz world as its leading figure and first great jazz soloist. Although the early recordings by the Hot Five were in the old New Orleans style, record producers pushed Armstrong for-ward as a trumpeter and singer by exploiting his commercial appeal and unconventional voice. By the end of the series, as they became his vehicles, Armstrong created the Hot Five and Hot Seven recordings of 1925–1928. Though the New Orleans ensemble style allowed few solo opportunities and could not contain his creativity, Armstrong held remnants of the style in such compositions as 1927's "Hotter Than That," "Wild Man Blues," and "Potato Head Blues." Armstrong mostly abandoned New Orleans ensemble style when accompanied by pianist Earl Hines on "West End Blues" (1928) and "Weather Bird" (1928), whose dialogue between the piano (Hines) and trum-pet became one of recorded jazz's masterworks.[69] "West End Blues," one of Armstrong's most renowned recordings, notes ways Armstrong drove his instrument into clarinet-like upper ranges without sacrificing ease and clar-ity. The opening cadenza to "West End Blues" became Armstrong's most renowned solo.

As a trumpeter, Armstrong's superior technique dwarfed his competitors. Although his band's members (except for Lil) and its repertoire hailed from New Orleans, the innovative harmony, melody, and form of "Savoy Blues" (1927), the final number recorded by the group, leaves "Big Easy" blues behind. Armstrong's sophisticated, daring sense of harmony, mobile, expres-sive attack, timbre, inflections, gift for creating vital melodies, dramatic, complex solos, and energy made the Hot Five and Hot Seven recordings major jazz innovations. They mark a revolution in jazz, though few traces of this upheaval can be found in the late 1920s historical record, when African-American newspapers covered Armstrong as just one musician among many.

The Hot Five and Hot Seven recordings became Armstrong's most influential body of work. Consolidating what was known and creating something new and fresh, Armstrong's playing on six famous sides recorded between 1926 and 1928 shaped deeper appreciation and understanding of the jazz great. Typifying the transition from an emphasis on the ensemble, represented by King Oliver's Creole Jazz Band, to the soloist, Armstrong's early Hot Fives have been regarded as a key moment in jazz histories.[70] In his band's thirty-three recordings from November 1925 to December 1927, Armstrong can be heard with his solo-like lead, increasing the number of instrumental and vocal solos. The relaxed tempo of "Savoy Blues" allows Armstrong to melodically expand with glides in fluid eighth notes, blurring phrase beginnings and endings with expanded pick-ups and extensions, supplementing his harmonic vocabulary. As a soloist, Armstrong attempted to integrate break-like passages and melodic paraphrasing into a unified style. This can be heard in early Hot Fives, especially "Big Butter and Egg Man" (1926), combining melodic and rhythmic ideas. The correlated choruses of "Yes! I'm in the Barrel" (1925), motivic relationships of "Skid-Dat-De-Dat" (1926) and "Put 'Em Down Blues" (1927), merging of melodic and harmonic improvisations in "Struttin' with Some Barbecue" (1927), and proportions of "King of the Zulus" (1926), "Once in a While" (1927), and "Cornet Chop Suey" (1936) emphasize Armstrong's interest with musical form, leading to "genius" characterizations and complicating caricatures of Armstrong as a simple-minded black man who naturally, even magically possessed God-given musical gifts, inherited due to his poor African-American background.

The early Hot Fives confirm Armstrong's unique ability to internalize a song's harmonic and melodic possibilities, coupled with imaginative phrasing, rhythmic mastery, avoidance of stock figures, and the capacity to conceive of the work as a whole. Additional pre-1940s small-group recordings were made with members of Carroll Dickerson's Orchestra under the names Hot Five, Savoy Ballroom Five, and Louis Armstrong's Orchestra. For the next two decades, Armstrong toured the United States with big bands, playing dance and pop music for largely white crowds.

Armstrong recorded with big bands from mid-1929 to mid-1947. Some of these groups already existed, such as those of Luis Russell, Les Hite, and Chick Webb (1905?–1939), jazz drummer who led one of the swing era's dominant big bands and whose swing, precision, and popularity made it the standard of excellence to which other big bands aspired.[71] Others, like jazz trumpeter and music educator Zilner Randolph's, formed to back up Armstrong, recording some of his best sides, such as "I Can't Give You Anything But Love" (1929), "Sweethearts on Parade" (1930), "Stardust" (1931), "Between the Devil and the Blue Sea" (1932), "Basin Street Blues" (1933), "I've Got My Fingers Crossed" (1935), and "Jubilee" (1938). Refining the synthesis of melodic paraphrase with elements of rhythm and harmony achieved on early Hot Fives, Armstrong abandoned the original tune and extended coherence over multiple choruses by means of recurring rhythmic and melodic motives, combined with a heightening of register. Announced by rip and *glissando* (a gliding effect), climaxes on final or "shout" choruses highlighted a lengthy held note, heard on "Mahogany Hall Stomp" (1929 and 1933), and rhythmically varied repeated pitches, heard on "Swing That Music" (1936).

VISUAL-CULTURAL REPRESENTATIONS

Transversing multiple performative domains, Armstrong's roles in feature, short, foreign, documentary, and European concert films, cartoons, "soundies" for coin-operated viewing machines, and television shows further consolidated his US and transnational popular cultural dominance. In his film, television, and radio appearances, Armstrong performed the role of a good-humored entertainer,[72] playing versions of himself in small parts, infrequently interacting with the main characters, having little to do with the plot, and caricatured according to twentieth-century US racial codes.

In *A Rhapsody in Black and Blue* (1932), a husband who listens to jazz instead of cleaning the floor is hit with a mop by his wife. As he becomes King of Jazzmania, a land of soapsuds and racial cinematic stereotypes,[73] Armstrong performs "Shine" (1910) and "I'll Be Glad When You're Dead You Rascal You" (1950), one of his standards. Though some argue Armstrong "transcended" his era's racial cinematic stereotypes, in *A Rhapsody in Black and Blue*, draped in leopard skin, continuing links between non-white people and animals and evoking the "authentic" jungle of Africa and elsewhere, Armstrong acquiesces to prevailing white supremacist conventions. Despite the strong US cultural desire to freeze Armstrong as an ambassador of goodwill, symbol of innocence, and nostalgic icon for a type of jazz representing various thrills, vivacious escapes, and uniquely American character, in his animalistic, exotic, and "jungle style" performance, Armstrong enters a cinematic subgenre centering Africa as a "dark" continent detained in a timeless colonial past. In addition to *A Rhapsody in Black and Blue*, this can be seen in such films as *Trader Horn* (1931), *The African Queen* (1951), *The Snows of Kilimanjaro* (1952), *Jungle Drums of Africa* (1953), *Out of Africa* (1985), *Coming to America* (1988), *Gorillas in the Mist* (1988), *The Lion King* (1994), *I Dreamed of Africa* (2000), *Tears of the Sun* (2003), *Blood Diamond* (2006), and *Captain Phillips* (2013).[74]

In *Going Places* (1938), Armstrong continues to be associated with racialized animalistic cinematic stereotypes as he serenades a racehorse and performs "Jeepers Creepers" (1939), a song by Johnny Mercer,[75] US lyricist, vocalist, and composer contributing to multiple Broadway productions and

Hollywood films. Armstrong performs alongside future president of the United States Ronald Reagan[76] in *Dr. Rhythm* (1938) and acts in the all-black film musical *Cabin in the Sky* (1943), starring Lena Horne (1917–2010), a light-skinned singer and actress caricatured as a "tragic mulatto" and first coming to fame in the 1940s,[77] and Ethel Waters (1896/1900–1977), blues and jazz singer and actress whose blues-based singing featured her full-bodied voice, wide range, and slow *vibrato* (a pulsating effect, produced by the rapid reiteration of emphasis on a tone).[78]

One of Armstrong's most memorable cinematic performances can be seen in *New Orleans* (1947). Costarring anti-racist protest singer Billie Holiday as a docile and stereotypical African-American Southern maid, in *New Orleans* Armstrong leads a small band of Crescent City jazz legends. Like *The Flame of New Orleans* (1941), *Night in New Orleans* (1942), *The Toast of New Orleans* (1950), the James Bond Blaxploitation[79] film *Live and Let Die* (1973), *New Orleans, Mon Amour* (2008), *Treme* (2010), and *Fat City, New Orleans* (2011), *New Orleans* continues the visual-cultural caricatures of that creole city with distinct Caribbean and broader transnational routes. One *New Orleans* scene, featuring Holiday and evicted Storyville residents singing "Farewell to Storyville," depicts Holiday leading a mass exodus, echoing the Great Migration and 1917 closing of Storyville, a signal to many jazz greats to move north and west in search of new homes for their music, in such places as New York City, Chicago, and San Francisco. Due to pressures to act in more stereotypical ways and an acting coach's instruction that Holiday perform with more "authentic," "Uncle Tom" feeling, on the *New Orleans* set, Holiday broke down and Armstrong comforted her. Holiday's scenes were cut, she injected heroin, and McCarthy-era[80] film censors dictated to *New Orleans*'s producers that they diminish Holiday and Armstrong's screen time.

In *A Song Is Born* (1948), Armstrong performs with Tommy Dorsey, who led some of the most popular swing-era big bands and was a highly respected and influential trombonist. In *Glory Alley* (1952), Armstrong performs with trombonist Jack Teagarden. *A Man Called Adam* (1966) features Sammy Davis, Jr., Frank Sinatra, iconic African-American actor Ossie Davis,[81] and Armstrong as a washed-up jazz trumpeter,[82] unable to cope with problems of everyday life. Affording him his largest scope as an actor, in *A Man Called Adam* Armstrong gained second billing on the marquee.

PARISIAN JAZZ

Armstrong's transnational cinematic performances include the Danish film *Kærlighedens Melodi* (1959) (Love Songs), the West German television film *Berlin-Melodie* (1963), and *Paris Blues* (1961). Centering US jazz musicians living in Paris, in *Paris Blues* Armstrong performs alongside Paul Newman and Sidney Poitier,[83] the Bahamian-American actor, director, and producer who broke the US film industry's color line and was the first African American to win an Academy Award for best actor (for *Lilies of the Field* in 1963). By performing in *Paris Blues*, along with his multiple European tours, Armstrong participates in over a century of French jazz histories, influencing such European jazz musicians as world-renowned gypsy, jazz guitarist, bandleader, and composer Django Reinhardt (1910–1953) and his partner violinist Stéphane Grappelli, and highlighting racial hierarchical contrasts between the United States and France and ways Paris afforded African-American jazz musicians and others a less violent racial atmosphere.

Though US jazz's assimilation into French culture began in the World War I era,[84] throughout the twentieth century and into the twenty-first, in France, popular music acted as an explicit reflection of political-cultural transformations. This occurred in conjunction with France's questioning of traditional ways of understanding politics and culture before and after May 1968, when a student revolt in a Parisian suburb was joined by a strike involving approximately 10 million workers, putting the rest of France at a standstill.[85] As music became part of burgeoning media activities, press, radio, and television developed free from the state information dominance of Charles de Gaulle, the French soldier, writer, statesman, and architect of France's Fifth Republic. Political activism shifted to the use of regional languages and cultures, including the safeguard of traditional popular music against the Republican state's centralizing tendencies. French-language music became a highly visible example of desires to maintain French cultural "exceptionalism"[86] in the face of US economic, political, and cultural imperialism. Laws were passed instituting minimum quotas of French-language music. As the French tried to claim jazz as their own, ethnocentrism and paternalism were rarely absent from what they wrote. Jazz became a proxy in debates over "authentic" national culture, as the French saw in jazz a foreign, racialized, and dangerous threat to the nation's most cherished civilizational, "universalist,"[87] republican, and national regeneration myths.[88]

While the "Jazz Age" evokes images of Armstrong at Chicago's Sunset Café, Ellington in Harlem's Cotton Club,[89] and Ma Rainey (1886–1939), the queer "Mother of the Blues" and recognized as the first great black professional blues vocalist,[90] this period was as much a Parisian phenomenon as it was a US scene. French jazz histories illuminate politics of race, gender, sexuality, ethnicity, class, nation, black-transnational icons, early jazz and its reinventions, black musical theater, white show bands, and wartime swing. While African-American jazz musicians had reasons for living in France due to US white supremacy, French jazz practices and receptions note complexities and pleasures of transnational musical exchanges, the ongoing importance of African-American popular culture in France and Europe more broadly, and discursive networks shaping French jazz's production and consumption.[91]

In the interwar years, Paris welcomed glamorous US expatriates, sensational performers, and jazz, a dynamic musical style emerging out of New Orleans with multiple transnational routes. Transversing cabarets, music halls, and dance clubs, jazz's upbeat, syncopated rhythms added to Paris's appeal as a center of international nightlife and popular culture. A controversial, racialized, and low-cultural art that was reified, fetishized, and degraded, jazz was widely performed in 1920s and 1930s Paris. While the French regarded jazz as alien because of its associations with the United States and "primitive" Africa, some celebrated jazz's vitality and racial "exoticism," part of a broader primitivistic trend seen in Picasso's paintings and performances by Josephine Baker (1906–1975), US-born French dancer, film actress, and singer dancing half naked in a banana skirt as a French-colonial symbol, part of the *vogue nègre* taking interwar Paris by storm.[92]

By the 1930s, French fans, critics, and musicians incorporated jazz into the French entertainment tradition, so that by the twenty-first century jazz became an integral part of French musical culture, along with Prince,[93] Michael Jackson, Kool and the Gang, and hip hop.[94] French jazz can be understood through the prism of the nation's ideas about blackness, Americanization cultural processes, and economic, political, and cultural forces moving across and beyond the Black Atlantic.[95] As jazz shifted from posing a foreign threat, met with resistance by French traditionalists to a naturalized, if continually contested, component of the nation's sense of itself, it became part of ongoing European debates concerning transnational economic, political, and cultural influences versus desires for economic, political, and cultural homogeneity and purity.[96]

In Paris, a small yet dynamic subculture of African-American jazz musicians created a vibrant expatriate scene and introduced the French to jazz. While the Harlem Renaissance occurred across the Atlantic, entertainers in Montmartre, the epicenter of the Parisian jazz scene, contributed to a culture flourishing for two decades, until the June 18, 1940, Nazi occupation. As they escaped US racism to pursue their art in bohemian Europe, contrasts developed between African-American jazz musicians' experiences in Harlem versus Montmartre. While some opened clubs, underwrote loans, and contributed their talents, others played critical roles in shaping the Montmartre jazz scene, such as Ada "Bricktop" Smith, dancer, jazz singer, vaudevillian, and owner of the nightclub Chez Bricktop in Paris from 1924 to 1961,[97] and Sidney Bechet, a clarinetist and master of the soprano saxophone who became legendary in New Orleans as a teenager and by 1917 was attracting attention as a soloist as he toured Northern cities and spent much of the 1920s coming and going to Europe. In 1919, Bechet was engaged by African-American composer and violinist Will Marion Cook (1869–1944) to play in Europe as a featured soloist. Although Bechet was not yet widely known, musicians knew his work as he demonstrated the jazz solo's possibilities.

The Parisian jazz scene played a crucial role in legitimizing jazz in Europe and the United States, while disturbing jingoistic definitions of jazz as exclusively American. A fruitful period in jazz's development, the French subculture of jazz musicians and audiences allowed for the cross-fertilization of jazz with overtly European influences. African-American musicians found the level of support inviting enough to move to Paris and used the city as a base of operations while performing throughout the Continent. Early twentieth-century Paris was one of the first and most important foreign capitals swept by jazz. An expatriate African-American subculture of jazz musicians thrived in the Montmartre district of 1920s and 1930s Paris and helped turn the city into a major jazz capital. A facilitator of this transformation was James Reese Europe, bandleader, arranger, composer, major figure in the transition from ragtime to jazz, and leader of the "Harlem Hellfighters" troop regiment in the US Expeditionary Force during World War I. Despite indignities inflicted by the US military, soldiers and musicians impressed Europeans with their jazz concerts. The Hellfighters became the US Army's most decorated unit. After the war, many stayed in France, lacking US segregationist laws and customs. French citizens welcomed African-American soldiers, targets of discrimination on the front and back home.

Twentieth-century African Americans' affection for Paris includes jazz musicians, such as trumpeters Miles Davis and Bill Coleman, saxophonist Charlie Parker, and Kenny Clarke,[98] a drummer and major advocate of 1940s bebop. Literary figures include Richard Wright (1908–1960), novelist and short story writer who was among the first African-American writers to protest US white supremacy in his novel *Native Son* (1940) and autobiography *Black Boy* (1945) and who inaugurated the protest tradition explored by other post–World War II African-American writers, Harlem Renaissance–era writers Langston Hughes and Claude McKay, detective novelist Chester Himes, and James Baldwin, African-American essayist, novelist, and playwright whose insights and eloquence regarding US white supremacy made him an important voice, especially in the late 1950s and early 1960s United States and throughout Western Europe.[99]

In Paris, Himes and Baldwin, political exiles from a racist US, fit into a vibrant Left Bank subculture, maintaining close ties with French novelist, essayist, and playwright Albert Camus (1913–1960), French poet, librettist, novelist, actor, film director, and painter Jean Cocteau (1889–1963), and Simone de Beauvoir (1908–1986), French Existentialist philosopher and feminist, known for her treatise *Le Deuxième Sexe, 2 vol.* (1949; *The Second Sex*), a feminist classic and plea for the abolition of the "eternal feminine" myth, idealizing a fixed concept of "woman" and one component of gender essentialism, the belief that men and women have different core "essences" that cannot be altered by time or place. [100]

As African-American expatriate writers, artists, musicians, and intellectuals dwelled in Paris since 1914, they became attracted by the myth of a color-blind France and drew inspiration from Paris. The 1960s and 1970s saw the arrival of African-American scientists, photographers, restaurant owners, and taxi drivers, diversifying a black-transnational subculture living amid a certain openness while facing French white supremacy. Expatriates pioneered a type of cosmopolitan blackness, [101] achieving a level of success and freedom denied to them in the United States and exploring multiple black-transnational political-cultural expressions. [102]

Strategically negotiating twentieth-century US and transnational racial hierarchies, with an innocent smile and crowd-pleasing music, Louis Armstrong navigated multiple, Cold War–era upheavals in divergent roles as jazz ambassador and outspoken, anti-racist advocate. Even as he became embroiled in internal US racial disputes, Armstrong's transnational image as "ambassador with a horn" continued his "post-racial," innocent, and optimistic performative demeanor as a stalwart diplomat on behalf of US Cold War interests. Part of the merging of US domestic and transnational racial cultural politics, Armstrong joined State Department–sponsored trips, designed to enhance US standing among non-aligned, "Third World" nations. As the State Department offered Armstrong tours abroad, it enabled "Ambassador Satch" to return jazz to its transnational routes and disentangle the iconic trumpeter from US jazz exceptionalist claims.

CULTURAL COLD WARRIOR

At the height of the Cold War, from 1956 to the late 1970s, the State Department unleashed the unexpected tool of jazz in its anti-communist battle, situating jazz in the struggle for civil rights, growth of the popular music industry, and emergence of the United States as a transnational power whose most effective diplomatic cultural weapon was African-American music. "Jazz ambassadors," such as Armstrong, Duke Ellington, Dizzy Gillespie, Benny Goodman, and Ornette Coleman (1930–2015), saxophonist, composer, and bandleader who was the principal initiator and leading exponent of late 1950s free jazz, [103] reconfigured their roles as cultural ambassadors and articulated and performed intersecting formations of race, gender, sexuality, ethnicity, class, nation, representation, popular music, activism, and jazz diplomacy's potential.

When the United States dispatched its most celebrated jazz musicians from Iraq to India, the Congo, and communist Soviet Union, it aimed to win the hearts and minds of the "Third World" and counter perceptions of US racism. Part of the propaganda war against the Soviet Union, federally funded tours of African-American jazz musicians were deployed around the world. Backstage and onstage, "jazz ambassadors" spread their music and ideas further than the State Department desired. In countercultural ways, under officials' radar, in concerts and after hours, through political statements and romantic liaisons, musicians defied the State Department's dominant "post-racial" narrative that all was well with US race relations by providing transnational audiences a heretofore undisclosed portrait of what life was like for African Americans, famous and forgotten. Alliances developed between jazz musicians and formerly colonized peoples of Africa, Asia, and the Middle East, inspiring racial pride and structures of feeling. Though intended as a "color-blind" celebration of US democracy, the State Department's cultural Cold War strategy unintentionally highlighted the contested racial cultural politics surrounding jazz since its New Orleans "birth." Conflicts developed between the State Department and artists' progressive agendas in the struggle to project an inclusive, integrated, and tolerant United States on a transnational stage even as the "jazz ambassadors" faced governmental exploitation. Jazz musicians transformed US efforts to win the cultural Cold War into something much more subversive.

Transnational audiences living under oppressive political systems went to jazz concerts and clandestinely taped Voice of America[104] jazz programs. They saw in jazz a language of self-expression, a fluid, cosmopolitan art expressing possibilities for freedom and democracy. As they took on a musical and political life of their own, despite the cultural Cold War purposes they served, jazz tours exposed the paradox of using a marginalized people as symbols of the triumph of "post-racial" US democracy, sent abroad to sing the praises of the Jim Crow nation marginalizing them, creating an impression of a nation where racism did not exist, while performing a transnational music claimed as "uniquely American." Abroad, jazz musicians frankly spoke about US racial realities and ventured beyond the elite audiences organized for their concerts. The "Jazz Ambassadors" program was consequential as the early Civil Rights Movement was gaining momentum and during the emergence of forty newly independent African and Asian nation-states, convened at the 1955 Bandung, Indonesia Conference of twenty-nine African and Asian countries.[105]

EXTRA-MUSICAL GIFTS

In addition to being a masterful musician, Armstrong was a memoirist and seasoned writer of letters. One of the most copious writers among the jazz greats and a prolific diarist and correspondent, Armstrong's writings expose a side of the iconic musician not widely known. Presenting thoughts on his life and career, Armstrong wrote in an individualized, vivid, and candid style, featuring an idiosyncratic use of language and punctuation. Armstrong's unique usage of quotation marks, commas, dashes, and underscoring gives his writing a sense of rhythm, warmth, and inventive phrasing, echoing his music.[106]

Prolific in coining colorful expressions entering the lexicon, Armstrong wrote imaginative prose pieces about his experiences. Touring with a typewriter on his transnational tours and using it for his journals, Armstrong wrote hundreds of reminiscences and letters to friends and strangers, composed autobiographical pieces, magazine articles, and essays, and supplied reporters with material about his life. From his earliest surviving letter, dated 1922, to his final sketches from 1969, Armstrong left behind an array of writings. Armstrong revealed his early musical influences, rise to fame, life on the road, and Civil Rights Movement role. He recorded portraits of his era, offered controversial opinions about racism, bebop, other jazz artists, such as Jelly Roll Morton and Coleman Hawkins, and passions for music, marijuana, and laxatives. Armstrong's writings provide a portrait of his life as a jazz musician, legendary entertainer, activist, and transnational popular cultural icon.

In addition, Armstrong created more than 100 collages, using photos and clippings as he composed on hundreds of boxes of reel-to-reel recording tape. These provide a window into Armstrong's life through his scrapbooks and artworks. Armstrong made hundreds of collages using photographs capturing archetypal scenes in the life of a jazz musician.[107] Part of the pantheon of US visual artists, whose art was not exposed to the general public, between sets, Armstrong snipped words and images from ads and greeting cards, letters, telegraphs, and photos of friends and fans and pasted them into colorful collages. Richly detailed color photographs depict Armstrong's tape box collages, compared to the art of painter Romare Bearden.

CONCLUSION

One of the greatest and most legendary jazz trailblazers, Louis Armstrong's post–World War II popular singing concluded his celebrity as it had begun in seedy, early twentieth-century New Orleans. Armstrong shifted roles as trumpeter, bandleader, film star, comedian, all-around entertainer, and symbol of US racial harmony, innocence, simplicity, and optimism. A cultural ambassador and one of the world's most widely known and best-loved personalities, Armstrong was more than a great trumpeter. Dominating the popular market and enchanting transnational audiences, Armstrong was a crossover artist from the "authentic" world of jazz. One of the few jazz musicians most in the United States could identify, so familiar at first sight and hearing that he required no last name, Armstrong impacted the evolution of jazz, which, when he began his career, was considered no more than a novelty. Leaving the jazz club grotto, Armstrong's transnational fame was coupled with touring 300 nights a year and film, television, and radio appearances. His popularity held against him by jazz purists, Armstrong enraged jazz aficionados by becoming popular.

A grinning court jester derided as an "Uncle Tom" and de-odorized black-transnational symbol in the vein of Dr. Martin Luther King, Jr., Rosa Parks, and other heroic figures often stripped of their countercultural identities, Armstrong navigated twentieth-century transnational racial politics as an often-silent critic. A major-key, harmonious, and consonant artist, part of a black-transnational legacy negotiating dissonance and the catastrophic, Armstrong conveyed a sense of US rose-colored, blue-sky cheerfulness even as US racial realities disproved his performative demeanor. As his "children" include jazz greats Dizzy Gillespie, Cab Calloway, and vocalist Maxine Sullivan, Armstrong's naïve disposition cloaked his musical sophistication and inventiveness.

A consummate entertainer, Armstrong walked the tightrope between toeing the official government line, appeasing the dominant culture, and staying true to issues of racial justice. Playing into racial stereotypes while challenging racist indifference, Armstrong was representative of an imagined, "postracial," and color-blind US racial democracy, admired the world over for his personal charms and musicianship. A black man born in New Orleans's poorest quarter, performing in an era when he and his bandmates could not count on food or a friendly face in their travels across the United States, and performing derogatory racial cinematic stereotypes, by the end of his life Armstrong was known and loved around the world.

Using his fame to call attention to Eisenhower's racial apathy in Little Rock while assimilating into dominant US culture as de facto and de jure white supremacy persisted, Armstrong leaves behind a complicated racial and popular musical legacy. Artistically holding himself back yet with a capacity for renewal, Armstrong's love of music and people was clear, even as he had frequent feuds with fellow musicians, a need for approval, jealous streak, explosive temper, larger-than-life personality that was tougher and more sharp-edged than his image reveals, and had a complicated love life, marrying four times and engaging in romantic liaisons in and around his marriages. With an enchanting, carefree stage presence yet introspective and unexpectedly complex, Armstrong's popular musical interpretations and personal reinventions can be traced through World War I, Prohibition, the Roaring Twenties, Jazz Age, Great Depression, World War II, Cold War, and Civil Rights Movement, from Storyville's bordellos and honky-tonks to Chicago, New York City, Hollywood's upscale nightclubs, and transnational tours, from his ascent to stardom to his 1930 marijuana arrest, life-threatening run-in with Chicago gangsters, and triumphant Broadway and Hollywood debuts.

A pioneering artist impacting US and transnational popular culture, Armstrong has been characterized as a spiritual guru, the single greatest creative artist in jazz and US popular music, one of the twentieth century's most influential artists, one of the most important twentieth-century African-American figures, one of the twentieth century's greatest musical innovators, and a pillar of twentieth-century US culture. A trumpet virtuoso, seductive crooner, and consummate entertainer, Armstrong performed his role as patriotic symbol even as he struggled against racist US ideologies, laws, and practices. Armstrong's negotiations, achievements, and career illuminate how twentieth-century black-transnational performers' lives intersected with categories of race, gender, sexuality, ethnicity, class, and nation and the various ways performers adapted and struggled with these categories' contingencies and consistencies. One of the most celebrated and beloved jazz musicians, Armstrong had hit recordings for fifty years, appeared in more than thirty films, and performed around the world. His balancing act between dominant cultural approval and the need to speak out on issues of racial justice provide a model and cautionary tale for contemporary popular cultural figures.

NOTES

1. Bruce E. Baker and Barbara Hahn. *The Cotton Kings: Capitalism and Corruption in Turn-of-the-Century New York and New Orleans.* Oxford; New York: Oxford University Press, 2016; Kodi A. Roberts. *Voodoo and Power: The Politics of Religion in New Orleans, 1881–1940.* Baton Rouge: Louisiana State University Press, 2015.

2. Thomas David Brothers. *Louis Armstrong's New Orleans.* New York: W. W. Norton, 2006.

3. Pamela D. Arceneaux. "Guidebooks to Sin: The Blue Books of Storyville." *Louisiana History: The Journal of the Louisiana Historical Association* 28.4 (Autumn 1987): 397–405; Lois Battle. *Storyville.* New York: Viking, 1993; John Chilton. *Who's Who of Jazz! Storyville to Swing Street.* Philadelphia: Chilton Book Co., 1972; Ernest James Bellocq, Lee Friedlander, and John Szarkowski. *Storyville Portraits: Photographs from the New Orleans Red-Light District, circa 1912.* New York: Museum of Modern Art, cop. 1970; Craig L. Foster. "Tarnished Angels: Prostitution in Storyville, New Orleans, 1900–1910." *Louisiana History: The Journal of the Louisiana Historical Association* 31.4 (Winter 1990): 387–397; David Griffiths. *Hot Jazz: From Harlem to Storyville.* Lanham, MD: Scarecrow Press, 1998; Emily Epstein Landau. *Spectacular Wickedness: Sex, Race, and Memory in Storyville, New Orleans.* Baton Rouge: Louisiana State University Press, 2013; Stephen Longstreet. *Storyville to Harlem: Fifty Years in the Jazz Scene.* New Brunswick: Rutgers University Press, 1986; Alecia P. Long. *The Great Southern Babylon: Sex, Race, and Respectability in New Orleans, 1865–1920.* Baton Rouge: LSU Press, 2005; _____. "Poverty Is the New Prostitution: Race, Poverty, and Public Housing in Post-Katrina New Orleans." *The Journal of American History* 94.3, Through the Eye of Katrina: The Past as Prologue? (December 2007): 795–803; Charles Nanry. *American Music: From Storyville to Woodstock.* New Brunswick, NJ, Transaction Books; distributed by E. P. Dutton, 1972; Dale Peterson. *Storyville, USA.* Athens: University of Georgia Press, 1999; Eric A. Powell. "Tales from Storyville." *Archaeology* 55.6 (November/December 2002): 26–31; Al Rose. *Storyville, New Orleans, Being an Authentic, Illustrated Account of the Notorious Red-*

light District. Tuscaloosa, AL: University of Alabama Press, 1974; Anne Key Simpson. "Those Everlasting Blues: The Best of Clarence Williams." *Louisiana History: The Journal of the Louisiana Historical Association* 40.2 (Spring 1999): 179–195; Richard Wang. "Researching the New Orleans-Chicago Jazz Connection: Tools and Methods." *Black Music Research Journal* 8.1 (1988): 101–112.

4. Helen A. Regis. "Second Lines, Minstrelsy, and the Contested Landscapes of New Orleans Afro-Creole Festivals." *Cultural Anthropology* 14.4 (November 1999): 472–504; Michael P. Smith. "Behind the Lines: The Black Mardi Gras Indians and the New Orleans Second Line." *Black Music Research Journal* 14.1 (Spring 1994): 43–73; Richard Brent Turner. *Jazz Religion, the Second Line, and Black New Orleans.* Bloomington: Indiana University Press, 2009.

5. Stanley Dance. *The World of Earl Hines.* New York: Scribner, 1977; Jeffrey Taylor. "Louis Armstrong, Earl Hines, and 'Weather Bird.'" *The Musical Quarterly* 82.1 (Spring 1998): 1–40; Jeffrey J. Taylor. "Earl Hines's Piano Style in the 1920s: A Historical and Analytical Perspective." *Black Music Research Journal* 12.1 (Spring 1992): 57–77.

6. Ray B. Browne. "Shakespeare in American Vaudeville and Negro Minstrelsy." *American Quarterly* 12.3 (Autumn 1960): 374–391; _____. "Wellerisms in Negro Minstrelsy and Vaudeville." *Western Folklore* 20.3 (July 1961): 201–202; Richard Butsch. *The Making of American Audiences: From Stage to Television, 1750–1990.* Cambridge; New York: Cambridge University Press, 2000; Krystyn R. Moon. *Yellowface: Creating the Chinese in American Popular Music and Performance, 1850s–1920s.* New Brunswick, NJ: Rutgers University Press, 2005.

7. Whitney Balliett. *Jelly Roll, Jabbo, and Fats: Nineteen Portraits in Jazz.* New York: Oxford University Press, 1983; Stacy Brown and Todd Barmann. *Jelly Roll Morton: New Orleans Style! Chicago Style! Kansas City Style! It's all Jelly Roll Style!* New York: Select; Lancaster: Gazelle [distributor], 2011; Lawrence Gushee. "A Preliminary Chronology of the Early Career of Ferd 'Jelly Roll' Morton." *American Music* 3.4 (Winter 1985): 389–412; Alan Lomax. *Mister Jelly Roll: The Fortunes of Jelly Roll Morton, New Orleans Creole and "Inventor of Jazz."* Berkeley: University of California Press, 2001; Jelly Roll Morton and James Dapogny. *Ferdinand "Jelly Roll" Morton: The Collected Piano Music.* Washington, D.C.: Smithsonian Institution, 1982; Philip Pastras. *Dead Man Blues: Jelly Roll Morton Way Out West.* Berkeley: University of California Press; [Chicago]: Center for Black Music Research, Columbia College Chicago, IL, 2001; Howard Reich and William Gaines. *Jelly's Blues: The Life, Music, and Redemption of Jelly Roll Morton.* Cambridge, MA: Da Capo, 2003; Bill Russell. *"Oh, Mister Jelly": A Jelly Roll Morton Scrapbook.* Copenhagen: JazzMedia, 1999.

8. Alan C. Turley. "The Ecological and Social Determinants of the Production of Dixieland Jazz in New Orleans." *International Review of the Aesthetics and Sociology of Music* 26.1 (June 1995): 107–121.

9. Thomas David Brothers. *Louis Armstrong, Master of Modernism.* New York: W. W. Norton and Company, 2014; David Stricklin. *Louis Armstrong: The Soundtrack of the American Experience.* Chicago: Ivan R. Dee, 2010.

10. Catherine A. Barnes. *Journey from Jim Crow: The Desegregation of Southern Transit.* New York: Columbia University Press, 1983; James C. Cobb. *The Brown Decision, Jim Crow, and Southern Identity.* Athens: University of Georgia Press, 2005; Davison M. Douglas. *Jim Crow Moves North: The Battle Over Northern School Segregation, 1865–1954.* New York: Cambridge University Press, 2005; Stanley J. Folmsbee. "The Origin of the First 'Jim Crow' Law." *The Journal of Southern History* 15.2 (May 1949): 235–247; Michael J. Klarman. *From Jim Crow to Civil Rights: The Supreme Court and the Struggle for Racial Equality.* Oxford; New York: Oxford University Press, 2004; John F. Marszalek. *A Black Congressman in the Age of Jim Crow: South Carolina's George Washington Murray.* Gainesville: University Press of Florida, 2006; Leslie Vincent Tischauser. *Jim Crow Laws.* Santa Barbara, CA: Greenwood, 2012; C. Vann Woodward. *The Strange Career of Jim Crow.* New York: Oxford University Press, 1974.

11. Ralph Berton. *Remembering Bix; A Memoir of the Jazz Age.* New York, Harper & Row, 1974; Rick Kennedy and Ted Gioia. *Jelly Roll, Bix, and Hoagy: Gennett Records and the Rise of America's Musical Grassroots.* Bloomington; Indianapolis: Indiana University Press, 2013;

Jean Pierre Lion. *Bix: The Definitive Biography of a Jazz Legend: Leon "Bix" Beiderbecke (1903–1931)*. New York: Continuum, 2005; Richard M. Sudhalter and Philip R. Evans. *Bix: Man & Legend*. New Rochelle, NY: Arlington House 1974.

12. Kofi Agawu. *African Rhythm: A Northern Ewe Perspective*. Cambridge; New York: Cambridge University Press, 1995.

13. Andrew S. Berish. *Lonesome Roads and Streets of Dreams: Place, Mobility, and Race in Jazz of the 1930s and '40s*. Chicago: London: The University of Chicago Press, 2012.

14. Vincanne Adams. *Markets of Sorrow, Labors of Faith: New Orleans in the Wake of Katrina*. Durham: Duke University Press, 2013; Ryan Ashley Caldwell. *Fallgirls: Gender and the Framing of Torture at Abu Ghraib*. Farnham, Surrey; Burlington, VT: Ashgate, 2012; Michael Eric Dyson. *Come Hell or High Water: Hurricane Katrina and the Color of Disaster*. New York: Basic Civitas Books, 2006; Karen J. Greenberg and Joshua L. Dratel. *The Torture Papers: The Road to Abu Ghraib*. New York: Cambridge University Press, 2005; Seymour M. Hersh and Rogers D. Spotswood Collection. *Chain of Command: The Road from 9/11 to Abu Ghraib*. New York: HarperCollins, 2004; Jed Horne. *Breach of Faith: Hurricane Katrina and the Near Death of a Great American City*. New York: Random House, 2006; Romain Huret and Randy J. Sparks. *Hurricane Katrina in Transatlantic Perspective*. Baton Rouge: Louisiana State University Press, 2014; Jeremy I. Levitt and Matthew C. Whitaker. *Hurricane Katrina: America's Unnatural Disaster*. Lincoln: University of Nebraska Press, 2009; Bruce Lincoln. *Religion, Empire, and Torture: The Case of Achaemenian Persia, With a Postscript on Abu Ghraib*. Chicago: University of Chicago Press, 2007; Shadi Mokhtari. *After Abu Ghraib: Exploring Human Rights in America and the Middle East*. Cambridge [UK]; New York: Cambridge University Press, 2009.

15. Robert Gottlieb. *Reading Jazz: A Gathering of Autobiography, Reportage, and Criticism from 1919 to Now*. New York: Pantheon Books, 1996; Lionel Hampton, James Haskins, and Vincent Pelote. *Hamp: An Autobiography*. New York: Amistad: Distributed by Penguin USA, 1993.

16. John Chilton. *The Song of the Hawk: The Life and Recordings of Coleman Hawkins*. Ann Arbor: University of Michigan Press, 1990; Gary Giddins. "Coleman Hawkins, Patriarch." *The Antioch Review* 56.2, Nine Days (Spring 1998): 164–176.

17. Hoagy Carmichael and Stephen Longstreet. *Sometimes I Wonder: The Story of Hoagy Carmichael*. New York: Farrar, Straus and Giroux, 1965; John Edward Hasse and Indiana Historical Society. *The Classic Hoagy Carmichael*. Indianapolis: Indiana Historical Society; Washington, D.C.: Smithsonian Collection of Recordings, 1988; Roger Hewitt. "Black Through White: Hoagy Carmichael and the Cultural Reproduction of Racism." *Popular Music* 3, Producers and Markets (1983): 33–50; Richard M. Sudhalter. *Stardust Melody: The Life and Music of Hoagy Carmichael*. Oxford; New York: Oxford University Press, 2002.

18. Laurence Bergreen. *As Thousands Cheer: The Life of Irving Berlin*. New York: Viking, 1990; David Carson Berry. "Dynamic Introductions: The Affective Role of Melodic Ascent and Other Linear Devices in Selected Song Verses of Irving Berlin." *Intégral* 13 (1999): 1–62; _____. "Gambling with Chromaticism? Extra-Diatonic Melodic Expression in the Songs of Irving Berlin." *Theory and Practice* 26 (2001): 21–85; Philip Furia and Graham Wood. *Irving Berlin: A Life in Song*. New York: Schirmer Books, 1998; Charlotte Greenspan. *Irving Berlin in Hollywood: The Art of Plugging a Song in Film*. *American Music* 22.1 (Spring 2004): 40–49; Charles Hamm. *Irving Berlin's Early Songs as Biographical Documents*. *The Musical Quarterly* 77.1 (Spring 1993): 10–34; _____. "Genre, Performance and Ideology in the Early Songs of Irving Berlin." *Popular Music* 13.2, Mellers at 80 (May 1994): 143–150; _____. *Irving Berlin: Songs from the Melting Pot: The Formative Years, 1907–1914*. New York: Oxford University Press, 1997; Edward Jablonski. *Irving Berlin: American Troubadour*. New York: Henry Holt, 1999; Jeffrey Magee. "Irving Berlin's 'Blue Skies': Ethnic Affiliations and Musical Transformations." *The Musical Quarterly* 84.4 (Winter 2000): 537–580; _____. "'Everybody Step': Irving Berlin, Jazz, and Broadway in the 1920s." *Journal of the American Musicological Society* 59.3 (Fall 2006): 697–732; Benjamin Sears. *The Irving Berlin Reader*. New York: Oxford University Press, 2012; John Shaw. *This Land That I Love: Irving Berlin, Woody Guthrie, and the Story of Two American Anthems*. New York: PublicAffairs, 2013; Ian Whitcomb. *Irving Berlin and Ragtime America*. New York: Limelight Editions, 1987.

19. Michael R. Frontani. *The Beatles: Image and the Media.* Jackson: University Press of Mississippi, 2007; Robert Gauldin. "Beethoven, Tristan, and the Beatles." *College Music Symposium* 30.1 (Spring 1990): 142–152; Jonathan Gould. *Can't Buy Me Love: The Beatles, Britain, and America.* New York: Harmony Books, 2007; Oded Heilbronner. "'Helter-Skelter'?: The Beatles, the British New Left, and the Question of Hegemony." *Interdisciplinary Literary Studies* 13.1/2 (Fall 2011): 87–107; Ian Inglis. "Ideology, Trajectory & Stardom: Elvis Presley & The Beatles." *International Review of the Aesthetics and Sociology of Music* 27.1 (June 1996): 53–78; Devin McKinney. *Magic Circles: The Beatles in Dream and History.* Cambridge, MA: Harvard University Press, 2003; Terence J. O'Grady. "The Ballad Style in the Early Music of the Beatles." *College Music Symposium* 19.1 (Spring 1979): 221–230; _____. *The Beatles: A Musical Evolution.* Boston: Twayne, 1983; Bob Spitz. *The Beatles: The Biography.* New York: Little, Brown, 2005; Charles Gower Price. "Sources of American Styles in the Music of the Beatles." *American Music* 15.2 (Summer 1997): 208–232; Michael Roberts. "A Working-Class Hero Is Something to Be: The American Musicians' Union's Attempt to Ban the Beatles, 1964." *Popular Music* 29.1 (January 2010): 1–16; Naphtali Wagner. "'Domestication' of Blue Notes in the Beatles' Songs." *Music Theory Spectrum*, 25.2 (Fall 2003): 353–365; Kenneth Womack. "Authorship and the Beatles." *College Literature* 34.3 (Summer 2007): 161–182.

20. Anthony J. Agostinelli. *The Newport Jazz Festival, Rhode Island, 1954–1971: A Bibliography, Discography, and Filmography.* Providence, RI: Agostinelli, 1977; African Jazz Pioneers. *The African Jazz Pioneers: Live at the Montreux Jazz Festival.* South Africa: Gallo Music Productions, 1991; Patricia Anne Boisvert and Adrienne Lepore. *Jazz in Newport.* Providence, RI: New Press, 1977; Dizzy Gillespie. *Dizzy Gillespie at Newport.* New York: Verve Records, 1992; Burt Goldblatt. *Newport Jazz Festival: The Illustrated History.* New York: Dial Press, 1977; Alex Kandelhart. *Montreux Jazz Festival Portraits - Live at Montreux.* Hamburg: Edel Germany GmbH, cop. 2012; Carolyn Livingston and Dawn Elizabeth Smith. *Rhode Island's Musical Heritage: An Exploration.* Sterling Heights, MI: Harmonie Park Press, 2008; John Fass Morton. *Backstory in Blue: Ellington at Newport '56.* New Brunswick, NJ: Rutgers University Press, 2008; Sabine Nicole and S. T. Wagner. *On Stage, Backstage: Montreux Jazz Festival.* Lausanne: Editions Illustré, 1986; Claude Nobs and Perry Richardson. *Live from Montreux: "Unbeveevable": 40 Years of Music from the Montreux Jazz Festival.* London; New York: A Publishing Company Limited, 2007; Machie Sakai. *The Newport Jazz Festival Story, 1953–1960: A Profile of the Newport Jazz Festival Founder, Elaine Lorillard.* Larchmont, NY: Machie Sakai, 1998.

21. Leonard Bernstein. *The Unanswered Question: Six Talks at Harvard.* Cambridge, MA: Harvard University Press, 1976; Leonard Bernstein and Nigel Simeone. *The Leonard Bernstein Letters.* New Haven: Yale University Press, 2013; John Briggs. *Leonard Bernstein: The Man, His Work, and His World.* Cleveland; New York: World Pub. Co.; Popular Library, 1961; Meryle Secrest. *Leonard Bernstein: A Life.* New York: A. A. Knopf, 1994; Barry Seldes. *Leonard Bernstein: The Political Life of an American Musician.* Berkeley; London: University of California Press, 2009.

22. Fletcher Henderson and Jeffrey Magee. "Revisiting Fletcher Henderson's 'Copenhagen.'" *Journal of the American Musicological Society* 48.1 (Spring 1995): 42–66; Jeffrey Magee "Fletcher Henderson, Composer: A Counter-Entry to the 'International Dictionary of Black Composers.'" *Black Music Research Journal* 19.1 (Spring 1999): 61–70; _____. "Before Louis: When Fletcher Henderson Was the 'Paul Whiteman of the Race.'" *American Music* 18.4 (Winter 2000): 391–425; _____. *The Uncrowned King of Swing: Fletcher Henderson and Big Band Jazz.* Oxford: Oxford University Press, 2010; Christopher Meeder. *Jazz: The Basics.* New York: Routledge, 2008; Gunther Schuller. *Early Jazz: Its Roots and Musical Development.* New York: Oxford University Press, 1968.

23. Matthew Boyden. *Richard Strauss.* Boston: Northeastern University Press, 1999; Norman Del Mar. *Richard Strauss; A Critical Commentary on His Life and Works.* Philadelphia, Chilton Book Co., 1962; Bryan Randolph Gilliam. *Richard Strauss and His World.* Princeton, NJ: Princeton University Press, 1992; _____. *The Life of Richard Strauss.* Cambridge, UK; New York: Cambridge University Press, 1999; Michael Kennedy. *Richard Strauss: Man, Musician, Enigma.* Cambridge, UK; New York: Cambridge University Press, 1999; George R.

Marek. *Richard Strauss: The Life of a Non-Hero*. New York: Simon & Schuster, 1967; Derrick Puffett. *Richard Strauss, Elektra*. Cambridge [Cambridgeshire]; New York: Cambridge University Press, 1989; Mark-Daniel Schmid. *The Richard Strauss Companion*. Westport, CT: Praeger, 2003; Richard Strauss and Beaumont Glass. *Richard Strauss' Complete Song Texts: In One Volume Containing All Solo Songs Including Those Not Published During the Composer's Lifetime*. Mt. Morris, NY: Leyerle, 2004; Richard Strauss and Stefan Zweig. *A Confidential Matter: The Letters of Richard Strauss and Stefan Zweig, 1931–1935*. Berkeley: University of California Press, 1977.

24. Chris Albertson. *Bessie*. New Haven, CT: Yale University Press, 2003; Chris Albertson, George N. Terry, Clifford Richter, and Gunther Schuller. *Bessie Smith: Empress of Blues*. New York: Collier Macmillan, 1975; Melanie E. Bratcher. *Words and Songs of Bessie Smith, Billie Holiday, and Nina Simone: Sound Motion, Blues Spirit, and African Memory*. New York: Routledge, 2007; Edward Brooks. *The Bessie Smith Companion: A Critical and Detailed Appreciation of the Recordings*. Wheathampstead, Herts, UK: Cavendish Pub. Co.; New York: Da Capo Press, 1982; Thomas F. Marvin. "'Preachin' the Blues': Bessie Smith's Secular Religion and Alice Walker's The Color Purple." *African American Review* 28.3 (Autumn 1994): 411–421; Alona Sagee. "Bessie Smith: 'Down Hearted Blues' and 'Gulf Coast Blues' Revisited." *Popular Music* 26.1, Special Issue on the Blues in Honour of Paul Oliver (January 2007): 117–127; Michelle R. Scott. *Blues Empress in Black Chattanooga: Bessie Smith and the Emerging Urban South*. Urbana: University of Illinois Press, 2008.

25. Leonard Feather. *The Encyclopedia of Jazz*. New York: Horizon Press, 1960; _____. *From Satchmo to Miles*. New York: Stein and Day, 1972; _____. *The Pleasures of Jazz: Leading Performers on Their Lives, Their Music, Their Contemporaries*. New York: Horizon Press, 1976; _____. *Inside Jazz*. New York: Da Capo Press, 1977; _____. *The Jazz Years: Earwitness to an Era*. New York: Da Capo Press, 1987.

26. Ricky Riccardi. *What a Wonderful World: The Magic of Louis Armstrong's Later Years*. New York: Pantheon Books, 2011; Dempsey J. Travis. *The Louis Armstrong Odyssey: From Jane Alley to America's Jazz Ambassador*. Chicago: Urban Research Press, 1997.

27. Sid Colin. *Ella: The Life and Times of Ella Fitzgerald*. London: Hamish Hamilton, 1986; Geoffrey Mark Fidelman. *First Lady of Song: Ella Fitzgerald for the Record*. Secaucus, NJ: Carol Pub. Group, 1994; Leslie, Gourse, ed. *The Ella Fitzgerald Companion: Seven Decades of Commentary*. London: Schirmer Books, 1998; Stuart Nicholson. *Ella Fitzgerald: A Biography of the First Lady of Jazz*. New York: Da Capo Press, 1995.

28. Woody Herman. *The Woodchopper's Ball: The Autobiography of Woody Herman*. New York: Limelight 1994; Gene Lees. *Leader of the Band: The Life of Woody Herman*. Bridgewater, NJ: Replica Books, 2000; Dexter Morrill. *Woody Herman: A Guide to the Big Band Recordings, 1936–1987*. New York; London: Greenwood, 1991.

29. Ed Kirkeby, Duncan P. Schiedt, and Sinclair Traill. *Ain't Misbehavin'; The Story of Fats Waller*. New York, Dodd, Mead, 1966; Paul S. Machlin. *Stride, The Music of Fats Waller*. Boston, MA: Twayne Publishers, 1985; Alyn Shipton. *Fats Waller: The Cheerful Little Earful*. London; New York: Continuum, 2002; Stephen Taylor. *Fats Waller on the Air: The Radio Broadcasts and Discography*. Lanham, MD: Scarecrow Press, 2006; Maurice Waller and Anthony Calabrese. *Fats Waller*. New York: Schirmer Books, 1977.

30. Joy Jordan-Lake. *Whitewashing Uncle Tom's Cabin: Nineteenth-Century Women Novelists Respond to Stowe*. Nashville, TN: Vanderbilt University Press, 2005; Jo-Ann Morgan. *Uncle Tom's Cabin as Visual Culture*. Columbia: University of Missouri Press, 2007; Jason Richards. "Imitation Nation: Blackface Minstrelsy and the Making of African American Selfhood in 'Uncle Tom's Cabin.'" *Novel: A Forum on Fiction* 39.2, Postcolonial Disjunctions (Spring 2006): 204–220; Linda Williams. *Playing the Race Card: Melodramas of Black and White from Uncle Tom to O.J. Simpson*. Princeton, NJ: Princeton University Press, 2001.

31. Matt Birkbeck. *Deconstructing Sammy: Music, Money, Madness, and the Mob*. New York: Amistad, 2008; Sammy Davis, Jr. *The Sammy Davis, Jr. Songbook: A Musical Tribute to the World's Greatest Entertainer*. Port Chester, NY: Cherry Lane / IMP, 1992; Sammy Davis, Jr., Jane Boyar, and Burt Boyar. *Yes I Can; [The Story of Sammy Davis, Jr.]*. New York: Farrar, Straus and Giroux, 1965; Gerald Lyn Early. *The Sammy Davis, Jr. Reader*. New York: Farrar, Straus and Giroux, 2001; _____. *This Is Where I Came In: Black America in the*

1960s. Lincoln: University of Nebraska Press, 2003; Wil Haygood. *In Black and White: The Life of Sammy Davis, Jr*. New York: A. A. Knopf: Distributed by Random House, 2003.

32. Annemarie Bean, James V. Hatch, Brooks McNamara, and Mel Watkins. *Inside the Minstrel Mask: Readings in Nineteenth-Century Blackface Minstrelsy*. Middletown, CT: Wesleyan University Press, 1996; Dale Cockrell. *Demons of Disorder: Early Blackface Minstrels and Their World*. Cambridge; New York: Cambridge University Press, 1997; Washington Dobbins. *A History of Blackfaced Minstrelsy in America from 1828 to 1898*. Parker, CO: Outskirts Press, 2011; Alexander Saxton. "Blackface Minstrelsy and Jacksonian Ideology." *American Quarterly* 27.1 (March 1975): 3–28.

33. Diane Andrews Henningfeld. *Little Rock Nine*. Detroit: Greenhaven Press, a part of Gale, Cengage Learning, 2014; Elizabeth Jacoway and C. Fred Williams. *Understanding the Little Rock Crisis: An Exercise in Remembrance and Reconciliation*. Fayetteville: University of Arkansas Press, 1999; Carlotta Walls LaNier and Lisa Frazier Page. *A Mighty Long Way: My Journey to Justice at Little Rock Central High School*. New York: One World Trade Paperbacks, 2010; David Margolick. *Elizabeth and Hazel: Two Women of Little Rock*. New Haven: Yale University Press, 2011; Kasey S. Pipes. *Ike's Final Battle: The Road to Little Rock and the Challenge of Equality*. Los Angeles: World Ahead Pub., 2007.

34. Mary L. Dudziak. *Cold War Civil Rights: Race and the Image of American Democracy*. Princeton, NJ: Princeton University Press, 2000.

35. Wayne Hampton. *Guerrilla Minstrels: John Lennon, Joe Hill, Woody Guthrie, Bob Dylan*. Knoxville: University of Tennessee Press, 1986.

36. Bernard Grofman. *Legacies of the 1964 Civil Rights Act*. Charlottesville, VA: University Press of Virginia, 2000; Stephen C. Halpern. *On the Limits of the Law: The Ironic Legacy of Title VI of the 1964 Civil Rights Act*. Baltimore: Johns Hopkins University Press, 1995; Robert D. Loevy. *To End All Segregation: The Politics of the Passage of the Civil Rights Act of 1964*. Lanham: University Press of America, 1990; _____. *The Civil Rights Act of 1964: The Passage of the Law That Ended Racial Segregation*. Albany, NY: State University of New York Press, 1997; Todd S. Purdum. *An Idea Whose Time Has Come: Two Presidents, Two Parties, and the Battle for the Civil Rights Act of 1964*. New York: Henry Holt and Company, 2014; Clay Risen. *The Bill of the Century: The Epic Battle for the Civil Rights Act*. New York: Bloomsbury Press, 2014; Charles W. Whalen and Barbara Whalen. *The Longest Debate: A Legislative History of the 1964 Civil Rights Act*. Cabin John, MD; Washington, D.C.: Seven Locks Press, 1985.

37. James Lorand Matory. *Black Atlantic Religion: Tradition, Transnationalism, and Matriarchy in the Afro-Brazilian Candomblé*. Princeton, NJ: Princeton University Press, 2005; Alan J. Rice. *Creating Memorials, Building Identities: The Politics of Memory in the Black Atlantic*. Liverpool: Liverpool University Press, 2010; James Sidbury. *Becoming African in America: Race and Nation in the Early Black Atlantic*. Oxford; New York: Oxford University Press, 2007.

38. Edward J. Blum and Jason R. Young. *The Souls of W.E.B. Du Bois: New Essays and Reflections*. Macon, GA: Mercer University Press, 2009; George Bornstein. "W. E. B. Du Bois and the Jews: Ethics, Editing, and The Souls of Black Folk." *Textual Cultures* 1.1 (Spring 2006): 64–74; Stanley Brodwin. "The Veil Transcended: Form and Meaning in W. E. B. DuBois' 'The Souls of Black Folk.'" *Journal of Black Studies* 2.3 (March 1972): 303–321; W. E. B. Du Bois. *The Souls of Black Folk: Essays and Sketches*. Charlottesville, VA: University of Virginia Library, 1996; Chester Fontenot, Jr., Mary Alice Morgan, and Sarah Gardner, eds. "W. E. B. DuBois and Race: Essays Celebrating the Centennial Publication of The Souls of Black Folk." *South Atlantic Review: The Publication of the South Atlantic Modern Language Association* 67, Part 4 (2002): 135–136; Jay Parini. "'The Souls of Black Folk': A Book That Changed America." *The Journal of Blacks in Higher Education* 62 (Winter 2008/2009): 72–80; Alexander Weheliye. "In the Mix: Hearing the Souls of Black Folk." *Amerikastudien / American Studies* 45.4, Time and the African-American Experience (2000): 535–554; E. Victor Wolfenstein. *A Gift of the Spirit: Reading The Souls of Black Folk*. Ithaca, NY: Cornell University Press, 2007; Ellicott Wright. "The Souls of Black Folk and My Larger Education." *The Journal of Negro Education* 30.4 (Autumn 1961): 440–444; Linda T. Wynn. "William

Edward Burghardt Du Bois: The Tennessee Connections to 'The Souls of Black Folk.'" *Tennessee Historical Quarterly* 63.1 (Spring 2004): 18–33.

39. Charles Hersch. "Poisoning Their Coffee: Louis Armstrong and Civil Rights." *Polity* 34.3 (Spring 2002): 371–392.

40. Robert Bookbinder. *The Films of Bing Crosby*. Secaucus, NJ: Citadel Press, 1977; Ted Crosby. *The Story of Bing Crosby*. Cleveland; New York: World Pub. Co., 1946; Todd Decker. "On the Scenic Route to Irving Berlin's *Holiday Inn* (1942)." *The Journal of Musicology* 28.4 (Fall 2011): 464–497; Gary Giddins. *Bing Crosby: A Pocketful of Dreams: The Early Years, 1903–1940*. Boston; London: Little Brown & Co., 2001; Richard Grudens. *Bing Crosby: Crooner of the Century*. Stony Brook, NY: Celebrity Profiles Pub., 2003; Randall G. Mielke. *Road to Box Office: The Seven Film Comedies of Bing Crosby, Bob Hope, and Dorothy Lamour, 1940–1962*. Jefferson, NC: McFarland & Co., 1997; Ruth Prigozy and Walter Raubicheck. *Going My Way: Bing Crosby and American Culture*. Rochester, NY: University of Rochester Press, 2007.

41. G. Anderson. "Blues for You Johnny: Johnny Dodds and His 'Wild Man Blues' Recordings of 1927 and 1928." *Annual Review of Jazz Studies*, 8 (1996): 39–62.

42. Louis Armstrong and Thomas David Brothers, ed. *Louis Armstrong, In His Own Words: Selected Writings*. Oxford; New York: Oxford University Press, 1999.

43. Louis Armstrong, Rudy Vallée, Dan Morgenstern, Horace Gerlach, and Benny Goodman. *Swing That Music*. New York: Da Capo Press, 1993.

44. Billie Holiday and William Dufty. *Lady Sings the Blues*. New York: Lancer Books, 1972.

45. Lawrence Gushee. "New Orleans: Area Musicians on the West Coast, 1908–1925." *Black Music Research Journal* 22, Supplement: Best of BMRJ (2002): 5–21; _____. *Pioneers of Jazz: The Story of the Creole Band*. New York: Oxford University Press, USA, 2010; Lawrence Gushee and Harry Carr. "How the Creole Band Came to Be." *Black Music Research Journal* 8.1 (1988): 83–100.

46. Davarian L. Baldwin. *Chicago's New Negroes: Modernity, the Great Migration, and Black Urban Life*. Chapel Hill: The University of North Carolina Press, 2009; James R. Grossman. *Land of Hope: Chicago, Black Southerners, and the Great Migration*. Chicago: The University of Chicago Press, 2011.

47. Robin Faith Bachin. *Building the South Side: Urban Space and Civic Culture in Chicago, 1890–1919*. Chicago: University of Chicago Press, 2004; Madrue Chavers-Wright. *The Guarantee: P.W. Chavers, Banker, Entrepreneur, Philanthropist in Chicago's Black Belt of the Twenties*. New York: Wright-Armstead Associates, 1985; Lionel Kimble, Jr. *A New Deal for Bronzeville: Housing, Employment, & Civil Rights in Black Chicago, 1935–1955*. Carbondale: Southern Illinois University Press, 2015; Christopher Robert Reed. *Knock at the Door of Opportunity: Black Migration to Chicago, 1900–1919*. Carbondale: Southern Illinois University Press, 2014; Elizabeth Schroeder Schlabach. *Along the Streets of Bronzeville: Black Chicago's Literary Landscape*. Urbana: University of Illinois Press, 2013; Rashad Shabazz. *Spatializing Blackness: Architectures of Confinement and Black Masculinity in Chicago*. Urbana: University of Illinois Press, 2015; Maren Stange and International Center of Photography. *Bronzeville: Black Chicago in Pictures, 1941–1943*. New York: New Press: Distributed by Norton, 2003; Jacqueline Najuma Stewart. *Migrating to the Movies: Cinema and Black Urban Modernity*. Berkeley: University of California Press, 2005; Steven C. Tracy. *Writers of the Black Chicago Renaissance*. Urbana: University of Illinois Press, 2011; Sylvia Hood Washington. *Packing Them In: An Archaeology of Environmental Racism in Chicago, 1865–1954*. Lanham, MD: Lexington Books, 2005.

48. Bruce Crowther. *Gene Krupa, His Life and Times*. Tunbridge Wells, Kent: Spellmount Ltd.; New York: Universe Books, 1987; George I. Hall and Stephen A. Kramer. *Gene Krupa and His Orchestra*. Laurel, MD: Jazz Discographies Unlimited, 1975; Bruce H. Klauber. *World of Gene Krupa: That Legendary Drummin' Man*. Ventura, CA: Pathfinder Pub., 1990.

49. James Lincoln Collier. *Benny Goodman and the Swing Era*. New York: Oxford University Press, 1989; D. Russell Connor. *Benny Goodman: Listen to His Legacy*. Metuchen, NJ: Scarecrow Press and the Institute of Jazz Studies, 1988; _____. *Benny Goodman: Wrappin' It Up*. Lanham, MD: Scarecrow Press, 1996.

50. Sandor Demlinger and John Steiner. *Destination Chicago Jazz*. Charleston, SC: Arcadia Publishing, 2003.

51. William Howland Kenney. *Chicago Jazz: A Cultural History, 1904–1930*. New York: Oxford University Press, 1993.

52. Gerald Majer. *The Velvet Lounge: On Late Chicago Jazz*. New York: Columbia University Press, 2005.

53. Jason Borge. "La Civilizada Selva: Jazz and Latin American Avant-Garde Intellectuals." *Chasqui* 37.1 (May 2008): 105–119; Ajay Heble and Rob Wallace. *People Get Ready: The Future of Jazz is Now!* Durham, NC: Duke University Press, 2013; Robin D. G. Kelley. "New Monastery: Monk and the Jazz Avant-Garde." *Black Music Research Journal* 19.2, New Perspectives on Thelonious Monk (Autumn 1999): 135–168; Howard Mandel. *Future Jazz*. Oxford; New York: Oxford University Press, 1999; Robert K. McMichael. "'We Insist-Freedom Now!': Black Moral Authority, Jazz, and the Changeable Shape of Whiteness." *American Music* 16.4 (Winter 1998): 375–416; Aldon Lynn Nielsen. *Black Chant: Languages of African-American Postmodernism*. Cambridge; New York: Cambridge University Press, 1997; Berndt Ostendorf. "The Afro-American Musical Avant-Garde: Bebop Jazz." *Angol Filológiai Tanulmányok / Hungarian Studies in English* 21 (1990): 45–57; Lloyd Peterson. *Music and the Creative Spirit: Innovators in Jazz, Improvisation, and the Avant Garde*. Lanham, MD: Scarecrow Press, 2006; Maeve Quigley. "Block Rockin' Beats." *Fortnight* 386 (June 2000): 22–23; David Glen Such. *Avant-Garde Jazz Musicians: Performing "Out There."* Iowa City, IA: University of Iowa Press, 1993.

54. Nicholas De Genova. *Working the Boundaries: Race, Space, and "Illegality" in Mexican Chicago*. Durham, NC: Duke University Press, 2005; Thomas A. Guglielmo. *White on Arrival: Italians, Race, Color, and Power in Chicago, 1890–1945*. New York: Oxford University Press, 2004; Arnold R. Hirsch. *Making the Second Ghetto: Race and Housing in Chicago, 1940–1960*. Cambridge; New York: Cambridge University Press, 1983; Huping Ling. *Chinese Chicago: Race, Transnational Migration, and Community Since 1870*. Stanford: Stanford University Press, 2012; Adam McKeown. *Chinese Migrant Networks and Cultural Change: Peru, Chicago, Hawaii, 1900–1936*. Chicago: University of Chicago Press, 2001; Eileen M. McMahon. *What Parish Are You From?: A Chicago Irish Community and Race Relations*. Lexington: University Press of Kentucky, 1995; Leonard G. Ramírez and Yenelli Flores. *Chicanas of 18th Street: Narratives of a Movement from Latino Chicago*. Urbana: University of Illinois Press, 2011.

55. Patrick Lawrence Burke. *Come in and Hear the Truth: Jazz and Race On 52nd Street*. Chicago: University of Chicago Press, 2008; Arnold Shaw. *The Street That Never Slept: New York's Fabled 52nd St*. New York: Coward, McCann & Geoghegan, 1971; Arnold Shaw and Abel Green. *52nd Street: The Street of Jazz*. New York: Da Capo Press, 1971; Travis A. Jackson. *Blowin' the Blues Away: Performance and Meaning on the New York Jazz Scene*. Berkeley: Chicago: University of California Press, 2012.

56. Jed Distler. *Art Tatum: Transcriptions of 6 Important Solo Piano Pieces as Played by the Legendary Art Tatum*. London: Jazzwise; New York London: Amsco, 1986; David Horn. "The Sound World of Art Tatum." *Black Music Research Journal* 20.2, European Perspectives on Black Music (Autumn 2000): 237–257; Arnold Laubich and Ray Spencer. *Art Tatum, A Guide to His Recorded Music*. [Newark, NJ]: Institute of Jazz Studies, Rutgers University; Metuchen, NJ: Scarecrow Press, 1982; James Lester. *Too Marvelous for Words: The Life and Genius of Art Tatum*. New York: Oxford University Press, 1994; Martin Williams. "Art Tatum: Not for the Left Hand Alone." *American Music* 1.1 (Spring 1983): 36–40.

57. Tom Nolan. *Three Chords for Beauty's Sake: The Life of Artie Shaw*. New York: W. W. Norton, 2010; _____. *Artie Shaw, King of the Clarinet: His Life and Times*. New York: W. W. Norton & Co., 2011; Artie Shaw. *Artie Shaw And His Orchestra*. Santa Monica, CA: Flashback Records, 1998; Vladimir Simosko. *Artie Shaw: A Musical Biography and Discography*. Lanham, MD: Scarecrow Press, 2000; John R. Tumpak. *When Swing Was the Thing: Personality Profiles of the Big Band Era*. Milwaukee, WI: Marquette University Press, 2008; John White. *Artie Shaw: His Life and Music*. New York: Continuum, 2004.

58. Andy Birtwistle. "Marking Time and Sounding Difference: Brubeck, Temporality and Modernity." *Popular Music* 29.3 (October 2010): 351–371; Dave Brubeck, Howard Brubeck,

and David C. Olsen. *The Genius of Dave Brubeck. Book 1: Piano Solos.* Hialeah, FL: Columbia Pictures, 1984; Stephen A. Crist. "Jazz as Democracy? Dave Brubeck and Cold War Politics." *The Journal of Musicology* 26.2 (Spring 2009): 133–174; Fred Hall. *It's About Time: The Dave Brubeck Story.* Fayetteville: University of Arkansas Press, 1996; Deborah Mawer. *French Music and Jazz in Conversation: From Debussy to Brubeck.* Cambridge; New York: Cambridge University Press, 2014; Jack Reilly. *The Harmony of Dave Brubeck.* New York: Music Sales America, 2013; Kevin Starr. *Golden Dreams: California in an Age of Abundance, 1950–1963.* Oxford; New York: Oxford University Press, 2009; Ilse Storb and Klaus-Gotthard Fischer. *Dave Brubeck, Improvisations and Compositions: The Idea of Cultural Exchange: With Discography.* New York: P. Lang, 1994.

59. Mary E. Davis and Warren Zanes. *Waiting for a Train: Jimmie Rodgers's America.* Burlington, MA: Rounder Books, 2009; Barry Mazor. *Meeting Jimmie Rodgers: How America's Original Roots Music Hero Changed the Pop Sounds of a Century.* Oxford; New York: Oxford University Press, 2009; Jocelyn R. Neal. *The Songs of Jimmie Rodgers: A Legacy in Country Music.* Bloomington: Indiana University Press, 2009; Ted Olson and Charles K. Wolfe. *The Bristol Sessions: Writings about the Big Bang of Country Music.* Jefferson, NC: McFarland, 2005; Mike Paris and Chris Comber. *Jimmie the Kid: The Life of Jimmie Rodgers.* New York: Da Capo Press, 1977; Nolan Porterfield. *Jimmie Rodgers: The Life and Times of America's Blue Yodeler.* Jackson: University Press of Mississippi, 2007; Carrie Rodgers. *My Husband, Jimmie Rodgers.* Nashville, TN: Country Music Foundation Press, 1995; Ben Wynne. *In Tune: Charley Patton, Jimmie Rodgers, and the Roots of American Music.* Baton Rouge: Louisiana State University Press, 2014.

60. Max Jones and John Chilton. *Louis: The Louis Armstrong Story, 1900–1971.* Boston: Little, Brown, 1971.

61. Brent Hayes Edwards. "Louis Armstrong and the Syntax of Scat." *Critical Inquiry* 28.3 (Spring 2002): 618–649; William Eric Perkins. *Droppin' Science: Critical Essays on Rap Music and Hip Hop Culture.* Philadelphia: Temple University Press, 1996.

62. Cab Calloway. *The New Cab Calloway's Hepsters Dictionary: Language of Jive.* New York: Cab Calloway, Inc., 1944; Cab Calloway and Bryant Rollins. *Of Minnie the Moocher & Me.* New York: Crowell, 1976; Alyn Shipton. *Hi-de-ho: The Life of Cab Calloway.* Oxford; New York: Oxford University Press, 2010.

63. Jürgen Wölfer. *Anita O'Day: An Exploratory Discography.* Zephyrhills, FL: Joyce Record Club Publication, 1990.

64. Abby Ellis. "Clark Terry: Ambassador of Music." *Music Educators Journal* 85.5 (March 1999): 36–38; Clark Terry and Gwen Terry. *Clark: The Autobiography of Clark Terry.* Berkeley: University of California Press, 2011.

65. Peter Ind. *Jazz Visions: Lennie Tristano and His Legacy.* London: Equinox, 2007; Jari Perkiömäki and Sibelius-Akatemia (Helsinki, Finland). *Lennie and Ornette: Searching for Freedom in Improvisation: Observations on the Music of Lennie Tristano and Ornette Coleman.* Helsinki: Sibelius Academy Jazz Department, 2009; Eunmi Shim. *Lennie Tristano: His Life in Music.* Ann Arbor: University of Michigan Press, 2007.

66. Jamey Aebersold. *Nothin' But Blues: Jazz and Rock.* New Albany, IN (1211 Aebersold Dr., New Albany, 47150): Jamey Aebersold, 1976; Harris M. Berger. *Metal, Rock, and Jazz: Perception and the Phenomenology of Musical Experience.* Hanover, NH: University Press of New England, 1999; Joachim-Ernst Berendt. *The Story of Jazz: From New Orleans to Rock Jazz.* Englewood Cliffs, NJ: Prentice-Hall, 1978; Ruth V. Brittin. "The Effect of Overtly Categorizing Music on Preference for Popular Music Styles." *Journal of Research in Music Education* 39.2 (Summer 1991): 143–151; Dick Grove. *Modern Harmonic Relationships: An Organization of Tonal Relationships in Jazz, Rock and Popular Musical Idioms.* Studio City, CA: Dick Grove Publications, 1977; Jonathan Kamin. "Parallels in the Social Reactions to Jazz and Rock." *The Black Perspective in Music* 3.3 (Autumn 1975): 278–298; Elizabeth West Marvin and Richard Hermann. *Concert Music, Rock, and Jazz since 1945: Essays and Analytical Studies.* Rochester, NY: University of Rochester Press, 1995; Gene Santoro. *Dancing in Your Head: Jazz, Blues, Rock, and Beyond.* New York: Oxford University Press, 1995.

67. Stephen Hartnett. "Cultural Postmodernism and Bobby McFerrin: A Case Study of Musical Production as the Composition of Spectacle." *Cultural Critique* 16 (Autumn 1990): 61–85.

68. Steven Block. "Pitch-Class Transformation in Free Jazz." *Music Theory Spectrum* 12.2 (Autumn 1990): 181–202; _____. "'Bemsha Swing': The Transformation of a Bebop Classic to Free Jazz." *Music Theory Spectrum* 19.2 (Autumn 1997): 206–231; Keren Omry. "Literary Free Jazz? "Mumbo Jumbo" and "Paradise": Language and Meaning." *African American Review* 41.1 (Spring 2007): 127–141.

69. Marc H. Miller, Donald Bogle, and Queens Museum of Art, eds. *Louis Armstrong: A Cultural Legacy*. Seattle: Queens Museum of Art, New York in association with University of Washington Press, 1994.

70. Gene Anderson. "The Origin of Armstrong's Hot Fives and Hot Sevens." *College Music Symposium* 43 (2003): 13–24; Gene Henry Anderson and Michael J. Budds. *The Original Hot Five Recordings of Louis Armstrong*. Hillsdale, NY: Pendragon Press, 2007; Brian Harker. *Louis Armstrong's Hot Five and Hot Seven Recordings*. New York: Oxford University Press, 2011.

71. Chet Falzerano, Judith Falzerano, Brooks Tegler, and Paul Testa. *Spinnin' the Webb: Chick Webb, The Little Giant*. Anaheim Hills, CA: Centerstream Publishing LLC, [Milwaukee, Wisconsin]: Exclusively distributed by Hal Leonard, 2014; Ron Fritts and Ken Vail. *Ella Fitzgerald: The Chick Webb Years & Beyond*. Lanham, MD: Scarecrow Press, 2003.

72. Scott Allen Nollen. *Louis Armstrong: The Life, Music, and Screen Career*. Jefferson, NC: McFarland, 2010; Klaus Stratemann. *Louis Armstrong on the Screen*. Copenhagen, Denmark: JazzMedia, 1996; Hans Westerberg. *Boy from New Orleans: Louis "Satchmo" Armstrong: On Records, Films, Radio, and Television*. Copenhagen: Jazzmedia, 1981.

73. Thomas Cripps. *Slow Fade to Black: The Negro in American Film, 1900–1942*. New York: Oxford University Press, 1977; Norman K. Denzin. *Reading Race: Hollywood and the Cinema of Racial Violence*. London; Thousand Oaks, CA: SAGE, 2002; Jaap van Ginneken. *Screening Difference: How Hollywood's Blockbuster Films Imagine Race, Ethnicity, and Culture*. Lanham, MD: Rowman & Littlefield, 2007; Herman Gray. *Cultural Moves: African Americans and the Politics of Representation*. Berkeley: University of California Press, 2005; Ed Guerrero. *Framing Blackness: The African American Image in Film*. Philadelphia: Temple University Press, 1993; Keith M. Harris. *Boys, Boyz, Bois: An Ethics of Black Masculinity in Film and Popular Media*. New York: Routledge, 2006; bell hooks. *Reel to Real: Race, Sex, and Class at the Movies*. New York: Routledge, 1996; Arthur Knight. *Disintegrating the Musical: Black Performance and American Musical Film*. Durham, NC: Duke University Press, 2002; André Seewood. *Slave Cinema: The Crisis of the African-American in Film*. Philadelphia: Xlibris Corp., 2008; Valerie Smith, ed. *Representing Blackness: Issues in Film and Video*. New Brunswick, NJ: Rutgers University Press, 1997; Lola Young. *Fear of the Dark: "Race," Gender, and Sexuality in the Cinema*. London; New York: Routledge, 1996.

74. Jeannette Eileen Jones. *In Search of Brightest Africa: Reimagining the Dark Continent in American Culture, 1884–1936*. Athens: University of Georgia Press, 2010; Christophe Konkobo. "Dark Continent, Dark Stage: Body Performance in Colonial Theatre and Cinema." *Journal of Black Studies* 40.6 (July 2010): 1094–1106.

75. Glenn T. Eskew. *Johnny Mercer: Southern Songwriter for the World*. Athens: The University of Georgia Press, 2013; Philip Furia. *Skylark: The Life and Times of Johnny Mercer*. New York: St. Martin's Press, 2003; Gene Lees. *Portrait of Johnny: The Life of John Herndon Mercer*. New York: Pantheon Books, 2004; Johnny Mercer. *Too Marvelous For Words: The Magic of Johnny Mercer*. Miami, FL: Warner Bros., 1985; Johnny Mercer, Bob Bach, and Ginger Mercer. *Johnny Mercer: The Life, Times, and Song Lyrics of Our Huckleberry Friend*. Atlanta, GA: Cherokee Pub., 2009.

76. Ben Dickenson. *Hollywood's New Radicalism: War, Globalisation and the Movies from Reagan to George W. Bush*. London; New York: I. B. Tauris, 2006; Gregory Frame. *The American President in Film and Television: Myth, Politics and Representation*. Oxford; New York: Peter Lang, 2014; Susan Jeffords. *Hard Bodies: Hollywood Masculinity in the Reagan Era*. New Brunswick, NJ: Rutgers University Press, 1994; Kenneth MacKinnon. *The Politics of Popular Representation: Reagan, Thatcher, AIDS, and the Movies*. Rutherford: London; Cran-

bury, NJ: Fairleigh Dickinson University Press, 1992; John W. Matviko. *The American President in Popular Culture.* Westport, CT: Greenwood Press, 2005; Alan Nadel. *Flatlining on the Field of Dreams: Cultural Narratives in the Films of President Reagan's America.* New Brunswick, NJ: Rutgers University Press, 1997; Stephen Prince and American Council of Learned Societies. *American Cinema of the 1980s: Themes and Variations.* New Brunswick, NJ: Rutgers University Press, 2007; Michael Paul Rogin. *Ronald Reagan, the Movie and Other Episodes in Political Demonology.* Berkeley: University of California Press, 1987.

77. James Gavin. *Stormy Weather: The Life of Lena Horne.* New York: Atria Books, 2009; James Haskins and Kathleen Benson. *Lena: A Personal and Professional Biography of Lena Horne.* New York: Stein and Day, 1984; Lena Horne, Helen Arstein, and Carlton Moss. *In Person, Lena Horne: As Told to Helen Arstein and Carlton Moss.* New York: Greenberg, 1950; Lena Horne and Richard Schickel. *Lena.* Garden City, NY: Doubleday, 1965; Megan E. Williams. "The 'Crisis' Cover Girl: Lena Horne, the NAACP, and Representations of African American Femininity, 1941–1945." *American Periodicals* 16.2 (2006): 200–218; _____. "'Meet the Real Lena Horne': Representations of Lena Horne in 'Ebony' Magazine, 1945–1949." *Journal of American Studies* 43.1 (2009): 117–130.

78. James Naremore. *"Uptown Folk: Blackness and Entertainment in Cabin in the Sky." An Invention Without a Future: Essays on Cinema.* Berkeley: University of California Press, 2014.

79. Stephane Dunn. *"Baad Bitches" and Sassy Supermamas: Black Power Action Films.* Urbana: University of Illinois Press, 2008; Mikel J. Koven. *Blaxploitation Films.* Harpenden [Hertfordshire]: Kamera, 2010; Novotny Lawrence. *Blaxploitation Films of the 1970s: Blackness and Genre.* New York: Routledge, 2008; Rikke Schubart. *Super Bitches and Action Babes: The Female Hero in Popular Cinema, 1970–2006.* Jefferson, NC: McFarland & Co., 2007; Christopher Sieving. *Soul Searching: Black-Themed Cinema From the March on Washington to the Rise of Blaxploitation.* Middletown, CT: Wesleyan University Press, 2011; Yvonne D. Sims. *Women of Blaxploitation: How the Black Action Film Heroine Changed American Popular Culture.* Jefferson, NC: McFarland, 2006.

80. Milly S. Barranger. *Unfriendly Witnesses: Gender, Theater, and Film in the McCarthy Era.* Carbondale: Southern Illinois University Press, 2008; Joanne J. Meyerowitz. *Not June Cleaver: Women and Gender in Postwar America, 1945–1960.* Philadelphia: Temple University Press, 1994; Greg Mitchell. *Tricky Dick and the Pink Lady: Richard Nixon vs. Helen Gahagan Douglas—Sexual Politics and the Red Scare, 1950.* New York: Random House, 1998.

81. Ossie Davis and Ruby Dee. *With Ossie and Ruby: In This Life Together.* New York: W. Morrow, 1998.

82. Scotty Barnhart. *The World of Jazz Trumpet: A Comprehensive History & Practical Philosophy.* Milwaukee, WI: Hal Leonard, 2005; Rudi Blesh. *Shining Trumpets, A History of Jazz.* New York: Knopf, 1958; John McNeil. *The Art of Jazz Trumpet.* Brooklyn, NY: Gerard & Sarzin, 1999; Krin Gabbard. "Signifyin(g) the Phallus: 'Mo' Better Blues' and Representations of the Jazz Trumpet." *Cinema Journal* 32.1 (Autumn 1992): 43–62; _____. *Hotter Than That: The Trumpet, Jazz, and American Culture.* New York: Faber and Faber, 2008; Michel Laplace. *Roger Guerin, or The Jazz Trumpet: 1946–1988.* Menden: Jazzfreund, 1993; Peter J. Levinson. *Trumpet Blues: The Life of Harry James.* New York: Oxford University Press, 1999; Albert J. McCarthy. *The Trumpet in Jazz.* London: Citizen Press, 1945; John Wallace and Alexander McGrattan. *The Trumpet.* New Haven: Yale University Press, 2011; Howard T. Weiner, Rutgers University. Institute of Jazz Studies., and Historic Brass Society. *Early Twentieth-Century Brass Idioms: Art, Jazz, and Other Popular Traditions: Proceedings of the International Conference Presented by the Institute of Jazz Studies of Rutgers University and the Historic Brass Society, November 4–5, 2005.* Lanham, MD: Scarecrow Press, 2009; Scott Yanow. *The Trumpet Kings: The Players Who Shaped the Sound of Jazz Trumpet.* San Francisco: Backbeat Books, 2001.

83. Aram Goudsouzian. *Sidney Poitier: Man, Actor, Icon.* Chapel Hill: University of North Carolina Press, 2004; Sharon Willis. *The Poitier Effect: Racial Melodrama and Fantasies of Reconciliation.* Minneapolis: University of Minnesota Press, 2015.

84. William H. Henney, III. "Le Hot: The Assimilation of American Jazz in France, 1917–1940." *American Studies* 25.1 (Spring 1984): 5–24.

85. Julian Bourg. *From Revolution to Ethics: May 1968 and Contemporary French Thought*. Montréal: McGill-Queen's University Press, 2014; Andrew Feenberg and Jim Freedman. *When Poetry Ruled the Streets: The French May Events of 1968*. Albany: State University of New York Press, 2001; Vladimir Claude Fišera. *Writing on the Wall, May 1968: A Documentary Anthology*. New York: St. Martin's Press, 1979; Marc Rohan. *Paris '68: Graffiti, Posters, Newspapers and Poems of the May 1968 Events*. London: Impact, 1988.

86. Tony Chafer and Emmanuel Godin. *The End of the French Exception?: Decline and Revival of the "French Model."* New York: Palgrave Macmillan, 2010; Lyombe Eko. *American Exceptionalism, The French Exception, and Digital Media Law*. Lanham, MD: Lexington Books, 2013; Emmanuel Godin and Tony Chafer. *The French Exception*. New York: Berghahn Books, 2005; Claude Imbert. "The End of French Exceptionalism." *Foreign Affairs* 68.4 (Fall 1989): 48–60; Hayward Kidd and Jack Ernest Shalom. *Fragmented France: Two Centuries of Disputed Identity*. Oxford; New York: Oxford University Press, 2007; William Kidd and Sian Reynolds. *Contemporary French Cultural Studies*. Hoboken: Taylor and Francis, 2014; Ahmet T. Kuru. "Secularism, State Policies, and Muslims in Europe: Analyzing French Exceptionalism." *Comparative Politics* 41.1 (October 2008): 1–19; Philippe Roger. "Global Anti-Americanism and the Lessons of the 'French Exception.'" *The Journal of American History* 93.2 (September 2006): 448–451.

87. Roger Célestin and Eliane Françoise DalMolin. *France from 1851 to the Present: Universalism in Crisis*. New York: Palgrave Macmillan, 2007; Enda McCaffrey. *The Gay Republic: Sexuality, Citizenship and Subversion in France*. Aldershot, England; Burlington, VT: Ashgate, 2005; Joan Wallach Scott. *Parité!: Sexual Equality and the Crisis of French Universalism*. Chicago: University of Chicago Press, 2005.

88. Hugh Dauncey and Steve Cannon, eds. *Popular Music in France From Chanson to Techno: Culture, Identity, and Society*. Burlington, VT: Ashgate, 2003.

89. Edward Brunner. "'Shuh! Ain't Nothin' To It': The Dynamics of Success in Jackie Ormes's 'Torchy Brown.' *Melus* 32.3, Coloring America: Multi-Ethnic Engagements with Graphic Narrative (Fall 2007): 23–49; James Haskins. *The Cotton Club*. New York: Random House, 1977; Howard Eugene Johnson and Wendy Johnson. *A Dancer in the Revolution: Stretch Johnson, Harlem Communist at the Cotton Club*. New York: Empire State Editions, 2014; Shane Vogel. "Performing 'Stormy Weather': Ethel Waters, Lena Horne, and Katherine Dunham." *South Central Review* 25.1, Staging Modernism (Spring 2008): 93–113.

90. Mita Banerjee. "Black Bottoms, Yellow Skin: From Ma Rainey to Maxine Hong Kingston's 'Tripmaster Monkey.'" *Amerikastudien / American Studies* 45.3 (2000): 405–423; Angela Y. Davis. *Blues Legacies and Black Feminism: Gertrude "Ma" Rainey, Bessie Smith, and Billie Holiday*. New York: Pantheon Books, 1998; David Evans. "Bessie Smith's 'Back-Water Blues': The Story Behind the Song." *Popular Music* 26.1, Special Issue on the Blues in Honour of Paul Oliver (January 2007): 97–116; Nicole L. B. Furlonge. "An Instrument Blues-Tinged: Listening, Language and the Everyday in Sterling Brown's 'Ma Rainey.'" *Callaloo* 21.4, Sterling A. Brown: A Special Issue (Autumn 1998): 968–984; Hao Huang. "Enter the Blues: Jazz Poems by Langston Hughes and Sterling Brown." *Hungarian Journal of English and American Studies* (HJEAS) 17.1 (Spring 2011): 9–44; Sandra R. Lieb. *Mother of the Blues: A Study of Ma Rainey*. Amherst: University of Massachusetts Press, 1981.

91. Andy Fry. *Paris Blues: African American Music and French Popular Culture, 1920–1960*. Chicago: The University of Chicago Press, 2014.

92. William Rubin. *"Primitivism" in 20th Century Art: Affinity of the Tribal and the Modern*. New York: Museum of Modern Art, 1994; Carole Sweeney. *From Fetish to Subject: Race, Modernism, and Primitivism, 1919–1935*. Westport, CT: Praeger Publishers, 2004.

93. Stan Hawkins and Sarah Niblock. *Prince: The Making of a Pop Music Phenomenon*. Farnham, Surrey, England; Burlington, VT: Ashgate, 2011; Per Nilsen. *Dance Music Sex Romance: Prince: The First Decade*. London: Firefly, 1999; James E. Perone. *The Words and Music of Prince*. Westport, CT: Praeger Publishers, 2008; Ronin Ro. *Prince: Inside the Music and the Masks*. New York: St. Martin's Press, 2011; Matt Thorne. *Prince: The Man and His Music*. Chicago: Bolden, 2016; Griffin Woodworth. "Prince, Miles, and Maceo: Horns, Masculinity, and the Anxiety of Influence." *Black Music Research Journal* 33.2 (Fall 2013): 117–150.

94. Thomas Bossius, Andreas Häger, and Keith Kahn-Harris. *Religion and Popular Music in Europe: New Expressions of Sacred and Secular Identity*. London; New York: I. B. Taurus, 2011; Alain-Philippe Durand. *Black, Blanc, Beur: Rap Music and Hip-Hop Culture in the Francophone World*. Lanham, MD: Scarecrow Press, 2002; Martin James. *French Connections: From Discothèque to Discovery*. London: Sanctuary, 2003; Felicia M. McCarren. *French Moves: The Cultural Politics of Le Hip Hop*. New York: Oxford University Press, 2012; André J. M. Prévos. "The Evolution of French Rap Music and Hip Hop Culture in the 1980s and 1990s." *The French Review* 69.5 (April 1996): 713–725; Francesca Canadé Sautman. "Hip-Hop/Scotch: 'Sounding Francophone' in French and United States Cultures." *Yale French Studies* 100, France/USA: The Cultural Wars (2001): 119–144; Seth Whidden. "French Rap Music Going Global: IAM, They Were, We Are." *The French Review* 80.5 (April 2007): 1008–1023.

95. Jeffrey H. Jackson. *Making Jazz French: Music and Modern Life in Interwar Paris*. Durham, NC: Duke University Press, 2003.

96. Matthew Jordan. *Le Jazz: Jazz and French Cultural Identity*. Urbana: University of Illinois Press, 2010.

97. Thabiti Asukile. "J. A. Rogers' 'Jazz at Home': Afro-American Jazz in Paris During the Jazz Age." *The Black Scholar* 40.3, Black Issues: 2010 (Fall 2010): 22–35; Bricktop and James Haskins. *Bricktop*. New York: Welcome Rain Publishers, 2000; Rachel Gillett. "Jazz and the Evolution of Black American Cosmopolitanism in Interwar Paris." *Journal of World History* 21.3, Cosmopolitanism in World History (September 2010): 471–495; Barbara Brewster Lewis. "Women Crossing Boundaries: A Field Report on the Paris Conference 'African Americans and Europe.'" *African American Review* 26.3, Fiction Issue (Autumn 1992): 515–519; T. Denean Sharpley-Whiting. *Bricktop's Paris: African American Women in Paris Between the Two World Wars*. Albany: State University of New York Press, 2015; Bruce Tucker. "Living Metaphors: Recent Black Music Biography." *Black Music Research Journal* 3 (1983): 58–69.

98. Rashida K. Braggs. *Jazz Diasporas: Race, Music, and Migration in Post-World War II Paris*. Oakland, CA: University of California Press, 2016; Ursula Broschke-Davis. *Paris Without Regret: James Baldwin, Kenny Clarke, Chester Himes, and Donald Byrd*. Iowa City: University of Iowa Press, 1986; Anthony Brown. "Modern Jazz Drumset Artistry." *The Black Perspective in Music* 18.1/2 (1990): 39–58; Leslie Gourse. *Timekeepers: The Great Jazz Drummers*. New York: F Watts, 1999; Michael Haggerty and Kenneth ("Kenny") Spearman Clarke. "Under Paris Skies." *The Black Perspective in Music* 13.2 (Autumn 1985): 195–221; Mike Hennessey. *Klook: The Story of Kenny Clarke*. Pittsburgh: University of Pittsburgh Press, 1994.

99. Richard N. Albert. "The Jazz-Blues Motif in James Baldwin's 'Sonny's Blues.'" *College Literature* 11.2 (Spring 1984): 178–185; James Campbell. "James Baldwin and the FBI." *The Threepenny Review* 77 (Spring 1999): 11; Dwight A. McBride. *James Baldwin Now*. New York: New York University Press, 1999; Therman B. O'Daniel. *James Baldwin, A Critical Evaluation*. Washington: Howard University Press, 1977; Sedat Pakay. *James Baldwin in Turkey: Bearing Witness from Another Place*. Seattle: Northwest African American Museum: Distributed by the University of Washington Press, 2012; Joel Alden Schlosser. "Socrates in a Different Key: James Baldwin and Race in America." *Political Research Quarterly* 66.3 (September 2013): 487–499; Magdalena Zaborowska. *James Baldwin's Turkish Decade: Erotics of Exile*. Durham: Duke University Press, 2009.

100. Germaine Brée. *Camus; A Collection of Critical Essays*. Englewood Cliffs, NJ: Prentice-Hall, 1962; Simone de Beauvoir. *The Second Sex*. New York: Knopf, 1952; James S. Williams. *Jean Cocteau*. Manchester: Manchester University Press, 2006.

101. Julius Adekunle and Hettie V. Williams. *Converging Identities: Blackness in the Modern African Diaspora*. Durham, NC: Carolina Academic Press, 2013; Susan L. Keller. "The Riviera's Golden Boy: Fitzgerald, Cosmopolitan Tanning, and Racial Commodities in 'Tender Is the Night.'" *The F. Scott Fitzgerald Review* 8 (2010): 130–159; Monica L. Miller. *Slaves to Fashion: Black Dandyism and the Styling of Black Diasporic Identity*. Durham, NC: Duke University Press, 2009; Malin Pereira. *Rita Dove's Cosmopolitanism*. Urbana: University of Illinois, 2003; Samantha Pinto. *Difficult Diasporas: The Transnational Feminist Aesthetic of the Black Atlantic*. New York: New York University Press, 2013; Sirpa Salenius. *An Abolition-*

ist Abroad: Sarah Parker Remond in Cosmopolitan Europe. Amherst: University of Massachusetts Press, 2016; L. Ayu. Saraswati. "Cosmopolitan Whiteness: The Effects and Affects of Skin-Whitening Advertisements in a Transnational Women's Magazine in Indonesia." *Meridians* 10.2 (2010): 15–41; Linda F. Selzer. "Barack Obama, the 2008 Presidential Election, and the New Cosmopolitanism: Figuring the Black Body." *Melus* 35.4, The Bodies of Black Folk (Winter 2010): 15–37; Tommie Shelby and Paul Gilroy. "Cosmopolitanism, Blackness, and Utopia." *Transition* 98 (2008): 116–135.

102. William Shack. *Harlem in Montmartre: A Paris Jazz Story Between the Great Wars*. Berkeley: University of California Press, 2001.

103. David Ake. "Re-Masculating Jazz: Ornette Coleman, 'Lonely Woman,' and the New York Jazz Scene in the Late 1950s." *American Music* 16.1 (Spring 1998): 25–44; Steve Day. *Ornette Coleman: Music Always*. Chelmsford, Essex: Soundworld, 2000; Brian Harker. "In Defense of Context in Jazz History: A Response to Mark Gridley." *College Music Symposium* 48 (2008): 157–159; David Lee. *The Battle of the Five Spot: Ornette Coleman and the New York Jazz Field*. Toronto, ON: Mercury Press, 2006; John Litweiler. *Ornette Coleman: A Critical Biography*. London: Quartet, 1990; _____. *Ornette Coleman: A Harmolodic Life*. New York: W. Morrow, 1992; A. B. Spellman. *Four Jazz Lives*. Ann Arbor, MI: University of Michigan Press, 2004; Peter Niklas Wilson. *Ornette Coleman: His Life and Music*. Berkeley, CA: Berkeley Hills Books, 1999.

104. Donald R. Browne. *The Voice of America: Policies and Problems*. [Lexington, KY]: Association for Education in Journalism, 1976; Alan L. Heil. *Voice of America: A History*. New York: Columbia University Press, 2003; David F. Krugler. *The Voice of America and the Domestic Propaganda Battles, 1945–1953*. Columbia: University of Missouri Press, 2000; Paul W. Massing. "Communist References to the Voice of America." *The Public Opinion Quarterly* 16.4, Special Issue on International Communications Research (Winter 1952–1953): 618–622; Arch Puddington. *Broadcasting Freedom: The Cold War Triumph of Radio Free Europe and Radio Liberty*. Lexington: University Press of Kentucky, 2000.

105. Elisabeth Armstrong. "Before Bandung: The Anti-Imperialist Women's Movement in Asia and the Women's International Democratic Federation." *Signs* 41.2 (Winter 2016): 305–331; Christopher J. Lee. *Making a World After Empire: The Bandung Moment and Its Political Afterlives*. Athens: Ohio University Press, 2010.

106. Louis Armstrong and Thomas David Brothers. *Louis Armstrong, In His Own Words: Selected Writings*. Oxford; New York: Oxford University Press, 1999.

107. Steven Brower. *Satchmo: The Wonderful World and Art of Louis Armstrong*. New York: Abrams, 2009.

Chapter Two

Duke Ellington

Elegant US Jazz Exceptionalist Symbol and Regal Transnational Hetero-Sexual

More than a world-famous composer and musician, Duke Ellington was a black-transnational symbol and countercultural artist, seeming to float atop twentieth-century US and transnational hierarchies with grace and sophistication. Ellington's personal style and suave demeanor projected a kind of royalty, earning him the nickname "Duke." An elegant man, Ellington maintained a regal disposition as he led his band and charmed transnational audiences. Considered the US and jazz's greatest composer and leader of its most significant band,[1] Ellington was a preeminent popular-cultural symbol of non-threatening black-transnational masculinity, refusing to be reduced to, even as he was marked by, his race, gender, sexuality, and body. A youngster who "practiced at being famous" and mourned at his funeral by more than 10,000 people, Ellington's charisma and sense of his own uniqueness was rooted in his childhood.[2]

The formation of Ellington's band includes some of jazz's greatest names, such as clarinetist and tenor saxophonist Barney Bigard (1906–1980), Johnny Hodges (1906–1970), saxophonist who was a featured soloist in Ellington's orchestra, renowned for the beauty of his tone, mastery of ballads, and one of jazz's most influential saxophonists,[3] Cootie Williams (1908?–1985), trumpeter whose mastery of mutes and expressive effects made him one of the most distinctive jazz musicians, Lawrence Brown (1907–1988), an acclaimed trombonist who achieved recognition with Ellington's orchestra, and Paul Gonsalves (1920–1974), tenor saxophonist best known for his association with Ellington. At the 1956 Newport Jazz Festival, Gonsalves played a twenty-seven-chorus solo in the middle of Ellington's

"Diminuendo and Crescendo in Blue" (1937), a performance credited with revitalizing Ellington's career.

As his experimentations with timbre and other approaches to tonal color were a result of his interest in such Impressionist composers as Claude Debussy, Ellington's panoptic, racialized, gendered, sexualized, and transnational twentieth-century histories include his "jungle music" performances at the legendary Cotton Club in 1920s Harlem and involvement with his white manager Irving Mills, music publisher, musician, and lyricist manipulating and cheating Ellington, putting his name on some of Ellington's compositions, and making him transnationally famous. Some attribute Ellington's 1930s success to Mills's marketing, appealing to multi-racial audiences and branding Ellington as a smooth, graceful genius.

Ellington's complicated personal and professional histories include his bond with his family, especially his troubled relationship with his son Mercer, and his marriage and many affairs, including liaisons with some of his musicians' women. As opposed to categorizing Ellington exclusively as a "composer" in the narrow sense of the word, broader definitions include Ellington's role as an improvising jazz musician whose instrument was his band. Ellington's dignity, willingness to take risks, and sense of organization enabled him to assemble and maintain one of the longest-lasting jazz bands.

Ellington's twentieth-century black-transnational biography and musical, rebel, and conventional global sojourns reveal his late introduction to music as a career possibility and lack of formal education. One of US music's most influential figures, Ellington was an accomplished and significant jazz pianist, composer, bandleader, and cultural diplomat. Jazz's twentieth-century evolution coincided with Ellington's long life, from ragtime and the 1930s big band era to post–World War II experimentations. Few US artists in any medium enjoyed Ellington's lasting transnational impact. From jazz standards, such as "Mood Indigo" (1930), to his orchestral suites to his leadership of the stellar big band he toured and performed with for decades after most big bands ceased to exist, Ellington represented a singular force in US popular culture for half a century, reaching the heights of international acclaim as he constantly evolved his approach to composition and performance and roles in the music business and US and transnational popular culture.

WASHINGTON, D.C., AND BEYOND

Born into a middle-class Washington, D.C., family at the turn of the twentieth century, Ellington acquired a strong sense of racial pride from Washington's African-American middle-class racial mores and his high school principal, a noted African-American historian.[4] A pampered and adored only son, Ellington's family encouraged his interests in the fine arts as he began studying piano at age seven. Ellington became engrossed in studying art during his high school years and was awarded, but did not accept, a scholarship to the Pratt Institute in Brooklyn, New York.

Echoing Forest Whitaker's performance of Cecil Gaines in *The Butler* (2013), serving eight presidents during the Civil Rights Movement, Vietnam War, and other major twentieth-century events,[5] Ellington's father was employed as a White House butler, noting the significance of this symbolic seat of the US government's executive branch to broader black-transnational histories.[6] As his father intended for him to become an artist, Ellington began to study piano and was influenced by ragtime pianists.

Ellington began to professionally perform at seventeen and first performed in 1923 in New York City. Later that year he moved there and, in Broadway nightclubs, led a sextet that grew into a ten-piece ensemble, featuring singular, blues-based melodies, harsh, vocalized sounds of trumpeter Bubber Miley, using a plunger ["wa-wa"] mute, and trombonist Joe ("Tricky Sam") Nanton, playing muted "growl" sounds. This influenced Ellington's early "jungle style," heard in such masterpieces as "East St. Louis Toodle-oo" (1926). Extended residencies in Cotton Club (1927–1932, 1937–1938) motivated Ellington to enlarge his band to fourteen musicians and expand his compositions' scope. During his engagement at the Cotton Club, Ellington began to share with Armstrong the leading position in the jazz world.

Ellington's first visit to New York, in early 1923, ended in financial failure, but on pianist Fats Waller's advice he moved there later that year with Elmer Snowden's Washington, D.C., band, the Washingtonians, featuring Snowden on banjo, Sonny Greer on drums, Otto Hardwick on saxophone, and Artie Whetsol on trumpet. Between 1923 and 1927, this small group, playing in Broadway's Hollywood and Kentucky clubs, was enlarged to a ten-piece orchestra with the addition of Bubber Miley on trumpet, "Tricky Sam" Nanton on trombone, Harry Carney on baritone saxophone, Rudy Jackson on clarinet and tenor saxophone, and Wellman Braud on double bass. As the band's early recordings emphasized an increasingly individualized sound, Ellington's orchestra grew to twelve musicians, including Barney Bigard on clarinet, Johnny Hodges on saxophone, and Cootie Williams on trumpet. The group went to Hollywood to perform in the film *Check and Double Check* (1930), featuring Amos 'n' Andy (blackface minstrel figures appearing in US radio and television).[7]

Once in New York, Ellington recorded approximately 200 compositions, many in the "jungle style" that was one of Ellington's most individual creations, an exotic label stemming from Ellington's hot music, and echoing jazz and its players' racialized and civilizational difference. Ellington selected his musicians for their expressive individuality. Several members of his ensemble were important jazz artists, including trumpeter Cootie Williams, cornetist Rex Stewart, trombonist Lawrence Brown, baritone saxophonist Harry

Carney, alto saxophonist Johnny Hodges, and clarinetist Barney Bigard. The most popular of these was Hodges, playing ballads with a full, creamy tone and long *portamentos* (a passing or gliding from one pitch or tone to another with a smooth progression). Performing with these exceptional musicians throughout the 1930s, Ellington appeared in films, on the radio, and in 1933 and 1939 Europe. His ensemble's expertise allowed Ellington to depart from band-section scoring conventions. Instead, Ellington used new harmonies to blend his musicians' individual sounds and emphasized compatible sections and a supple ensemble, featuring Carney's bass-clef sound.

Ellington illuminated subtle moods with instrumental combinations. Among the most well-known example is "Mood Indigo" (1930) for muted trumpet, unmuted trombone, and low-register clarinet, bringing Ellington transnational fame. By 1931, Ellington created extended works, including "Creole Rhapsody" (1931), "Reminiscing in Tempo" (1935), and "Diminuendo and Crescendo in Blue" (1937). Ellington composed works to highlight his soloists' talents. Williams performed his resourcefulness in Ellington's noted miniature concertos "Echoes of Harlem" (1936) and "Concerto for Cootie" (1940). Sidemen wrote some of Ellington's compositions, such as trombonist Juan Tizol's "Perdido" (1941).

The decade between 1932 and 1942 was Ellington's most creative, with Ellington reaching his greatest heights as a composer with such works as "Harlem Air Shaft" (1940) and "Main Stem" (1942).[8] Ellington's band, now made up of six brass instruments, four reeds, and a four-man rhythm section, performed in Europe and the United States. In 1939–1940, there were more band additions, including Jimmy Blanton on double bass and Ben Webster on tenor saxophone. Ellington created several outstanding short works, in particular "Concerto for Cootie," "Ko-Ko," and "Cotton Tail" (all 1940).

By the mid-1940s, Ellington's orchestra again expanded, so that by 1946 it included eighteen players. Previous personnel stability declined and Ellington's composing, based on his players' individualized styles, suffered from the constant changes. Some excellent soloists were added, such as Ray Nance on trumpet and violin, Shorty Baker on trumpet, and Jimmy Hamilton on clarinet. As the long-playing record allowed Ellington to create multiple-movement suites, from 1950, Ellington continued to expand his compositions and band-leading activities' scope. His transnational tours became more frequent and stimulated him to write large-scale suites.

Ellington recorded with younger jazz musicians, such as saxophonist, bandleader, and composer John Coltrane (1926–1967) and Max Roach (1924–2007), drummer, composer, and one of the most influential and widely recorded modern percussionists.[9] Among Ellington's many awards and honors were honorary doctorates from Howard University (1963) and Yale University (1967) and the Presidential Medal of Honor (1969). In 1970, Ellington was made a member of the National Institute of Arts and Letters and in 1971 he became the first jazz musician to be named a member of the Swedish Royal Academy of Music. Ellington directed his band until his death in 1974, when it was taken over by his son Mercer. Like Armstrong and Ella Fitzgerald, with whom he recorded, Ellington was an accepted, non-threatening racialized member of US and transnational cultural establishments.

SWING-ERA PREEMINENCE

A complex personality transversing multiple genres, eras, and transnational locales while negotiating subtle and explicit racial, gender, sexual, ethnic, class, and international hierarchies, Ellington's distinguished place in the 1930s and 1940s swing subgenre represents his musical gifts and preeminence. Between 1928 and 1932, such African-American arrangers and bandleaders as Ellington, Fletcher Henderson, and pianist Bennie Moten (1894–1935), one of the earliest known organizers of Midwest bands in jazz's emerging years,[10] experimented with different combinations of swing's timbral and rhythmic possibilities. 1920s bands led by Henderson disseminated various ideas, picked up by white orchestras performing swing. Orchestras of Jean Goldkette, Ben Pollack, Red Nichols, and Luis Russell, featuring soloists Benny Goodman, Jack Teagarden, and Jimmy Dorsey, were capable of reaching Henderson's mark. By the end of the 1920s, some of these bands, especially Ellington's, overshadowed Henderson's.

Part of swing's popularity and the rise of the big bands, Ellington's music featured a range of harmonies and sound colors. Ellington used the highly individualistic trombone trio of Joe "Tricky Sam" Nanton, Juan Tizol, and Lawrence Brown to enrich his elegant compositions. By 1926, Ellington's orchestra was making its first characteristic recordings. Ellington's group was the most celebrated swing band, yet it had only one foot in the swing camp, as his band was in it but not truly of it. Characteristic of his iconoclastic status as part of the jazz genre while transversing beyond it, Ellington developed his music along personal lines for a decade when the swing wave broke and did not completely base his music on sections' interplay, sometimes writing across the sections, combining three or four reeds and brass. More likely to write melodic lines than simple riffs, Ellington still employed standard swing band practices and his orchestra was perceived as a swing band.

The term "swing," used to describe the rhythmic "lilt" central to jazz, was current by the early 1930s and was applied to the big bands producing this rhythmic effect. Swing's early study was characterized by the analysis of style and genres of biography and autobiography, music appreciation, and criticism. Swing can be characterized as a quality attributed to jazz performance. Central to jazz's perception and identities, swing was a rhythmic phenomenon, resulting from the conflict between a fixed pulse and variety of accent and *rubato* (the disregarding of strict tempo to allow for an expressive quickening and slackening) a performer plays against it. Other properties are involved, of which one is the forward propulsion conveyed to each note through manipulations of timbre, *vibrato*, attack (the extent to which a note is performed), and intonation (the manner of producing tones and relation in pitch of tones to their key or harmony). This combines with the rhythmic placement of each note to produce swing. A way of performing music resulting in a feeling of forward motion and momentum, accompanied by a tendency to embody the music in some form of rhythmic movement, when music swings, it is the result of a combination of characteristics related to pulse (consisting of beats in a repeating series of identical yet distinct periodic short-duration stimuli) and how that pulse is divided, phrasing (a phrase is a unit of musical meter), and articulation (the direction or performative technique affecting the transition or continuity on a single note or between multiple notes or sounds).

A popular form of social dance[11] music, swing is characterized by four-to-the-bar rhythms, guitar, *pizzicato* (plucking an instrument's strings), double bass in the rhythm section, riff-based arrangements, and forceful drumming. Swing began to take shape around 1928 and became established by 1932. The main catalyst for this change was the emergence of the lindy hop,[12] a dance that, more than earlier social dances, emphasized four-to-the-bar rhythms and a high degree of physical vigor. Musicians responded to these changes by providing four-to-the-bar rhythms, driving riff-based arrangements, and more exciting drumming, spurring social dancers to new levels of physicality. Dancers and musicians' mutual responses continued to inform changes in swing music and dance into the 1930s. Radio broadcasting aided swing music and dance's dissemination and allowed access to previous performance practices.

Larger than earlier jazz ensembles, swing bands started with ten or eleven players during the late 1920s, and enlarged to seventeen by the early 1940s. Ensembles were divided into groups of like instruments, called sections. The brass section consisted of trumpets and trombones. The reeds section comprised musicians doubling on clarinets and saxophones in the late 1920s and early 1930s but came to be dominated by saxophones by the late 1930s. The rhythm section was made up of double bass, guitar, piano, and drums. Arrangers wrote "made-to-measure" scores for particular bands, standardized scores, and stock arrangements, meant for commercial publishers, and a combination of both. They used ideas taken from orally constructed "head" arrangements and composed sections, backgrounds, call-and-response sections, and riff-based choruses, adding interest to the music while providing momentum for the dancers. In addition to Ellington, swing arrangers include

Don Redman, Jimmy Mundy, Sy Oliver, and Benny Carter (1907–2003), influential alto saxophonist, composer, bandleader, trumpeter, and clarinetist.[13] Swing arrangers left space for improvisation, part of the performance of top players, such as trumpeter Roy "Little Jazz" Eldridge (1911–1989), one of the 1930s' great creative musicians.[14]

Swing rhythm sections played a four-beat rhythm, in contrast to the brass-bass and banjo two-beat rhythms typical of pre-swing jazz. Drummers became more energetic, reinforcing rhythmic figures played by the wind instruments, setting up different parts of the arrangements, and using the cymbals' noisier sounds to articulate the pulse. Although swing as a historical style coincided with swing as a musical practice, the music remained the norm for jazz performance after swing ceased to be popular. Swing was made possible by media transformations, as electronic recording provided the instrumental and performative conditions leading to swing. While guitar, *pizzicato* double bass, and assertive drumming were difficult to record with pre-1926 acoustic recording technology, post-1926 electronic recording made it possible to accurately capture these instruments' sounds.

By 1932, swing was gaining in popularity. By 1935, it became a national fad when Benny Goodman's band brought a particular brand of swing to white teenagers, combining African-American bands' practices with pop-song arrangements. Due to swing's popularity, the number of bands increased, divided into two major categories. "Sweet" bands played conventional dance music, while "hot" bands, such as those of Ellington, Goodman, Jimmie Lunceford, Cab Calloway, and Count Basie (1904–1984), noted for his spare, economical piano style and leadership of influential and widely heralded big bands,[15] featured hard-driving swing.

Swing music was part of a broader 1930s and 1940s subculture. This included fans and social dancers, or "jitterbugs," a segment of US popular culture critiqued by German philosopher and music critic Theodor Adorno (1903–1969) for representing the worst of the US culture industry, its homogenization and standardization, and loss of human beings' individuality and humanity.[16] The swing subculture also consisted of entrepreneurs, such as John Hammond[17] (1910–1987), US record producer, promoter, talent scout, music critic, advocate for racial integration in the music business, regarded as the most important non-musician in jazz histories, and "discoverer" and promoter of major popular music figures, from Count Basie and Billie Holiday in the 1930s to Bob Dylan and Bruce Springsteen during the rock era.

As radio stations and publications arose to nurture swing culture, critics, record collectors, the United Hot Clubs of America, booking agencies, the jukebox, live, commercially sponsored radio broadcasts, and mass-market magazines, such as *DownBeat*, established in 1939 as "the bible of jazz, blues, and beyond,"[18] were part of the swing era, whose popularity was also met with controversy. To some, swing was a commercial debasement of "authentic" New Orleans jazz. By the late 1940s, swing's popularity diminished, due to rising costs associated with traveling with a large band, the pop-song industry's development, and late swing's predictability. Rhythm and blues' emergence, appealing to social dancers, and bebop's appearance, taking jazz into the realm of art and distancing jazz from swing's assimilationist sounds and style, filled the vacuum.

A factor in big band jazz's development was the saxophone's popularity.[19] Although the instrument was invented in 1840, it did not play a significant role in US music until after the turn of the twentieth century, when it appeared as a novelty in vaudeville shows and various groups. By the early 1920s, the saxophone was an essential part of the dance band. The big band's creation was the result of a number of trends. When popular music emerged from the 1929 economic collapse,[20] which had far-reaching effects on entertainment and all areas of US culture, it was clear that the big band would be the shape of 1930s jazz. Its loud, harmonious sounds played well to audiences yearning for diversions from the economic situation and appealed to US cultural desires for optimistic, rose-colored, and innocent cultural products.

By 1930, the New Orleans ensemble was no longer popular and jazz was performed by the hot dance bands. Ellington's orchestra played a central role in this phenomenon and gained intellectuals and musicians' attention. By the early 1930s, Ellington was seen as jazz's pre-eminent figure. His group, at first a standard dance band, was drawn toward New Orleans jazz by Sidney Bechet, a 1920s member, and Bubber Miley, King Oliver's disciple. From 1927 to 1931, Ellington's band performed in the Cotton Club, the country's most famous cabaret, from which it regularly broadcast, and where Ellington's sophistication, regality, and racial emancipation contrasted with the Club's racialized primitivism, "jungle music," and segregation, as African Americans were hired to entertain, serve, and prepare food and drink but were not accepted as customers.

Though he had little formal musical training, Ellington's musical intelligence and judgment allowed him to create scores of popular hits and hundreds of small and large compositions. Ellington was aided in achieving this by his talent for surrounding himself with and drawing the best out of excellent musicians, such as saxophonists Johnny Hodges and Ben Webster,[21] trumpeters Cootie Williams and Clark Terry, drummer Sonny Greer, vocalist Alice Babs, organist Wild Bill Davis, tenor saxophonist Paul Gonsalves, and baritone saxophonist Harry Carney.

The 1930s and early to mid-1940s big band era was characterized by well-known leaders whose public and private lives were chronicled in the gossip columns, such as Goodman, Tommy and Jimmy Dorsey, and Glenn Miller, the most famous swing-era bandleader.[22] Their bands' repertory was not exclusively jazz. Disparaged by jazz fans as "mickey mouse" bands, they played "sweet music," with little jazz feel, and characterized by music that was fully arranged with little improvisation. Bands performed an instrumentation similar to 1930s jazz bands of reeds, brass, and a rhythm section supplemented by strings. These bands had to play ordinary popular music, though generally their sounds were rooted in jazz.

The big dance bands used rhythm sections to set a ground beat, employing a jazz feel in the section work, and making room for jazz solos. They produced excellent jazz, such as hard-swinging ensemble riffs interspersed with solos over driving rhythms. The best white orchestras were led by Goodman, Charlie Barnet, Woody Herman, and Bob Crosby, while the best African-American orchestras were those of Ellington, Jimmie Lunceford, Chick Webb, and Count Basie, whose orchestra exemplified a special strain in the big band movement. Though he was from New Jersey, as a young musician Basie spent his time in Kansas City. Crime-ridden, Kansas City had many rough cabarets where jazz was played, and these provided the setting for the development of the Kansas City jazz style,[23] heavily relying on the blues and simple riffs and invented on club bandstands in jam sessions.

Bands playing in this style depended more on head arrangements (a roughly outlined arrangement that is played from memory and often learned by ear), worked out by the musicians, and strong solo work than on the type of complex arrangements favored by Ellington, Henderson, and other East-Coast bandleaders. Besides Basie's band, those of Andy Kirk and Jay McShann were from Kansas City, and by the late 1930s they became influential. Central to Basie's place in jazz were soloists Dicky Wells, Buck Clayton, and especially Lester Young (1909–1959), tenor saxophonist who emerged in the mid-1930s Kansas City jazz world with the Count Basie band and introduced an approach to improvisation that provided much of the basis for modern jazz solo conception.[24]

Though Young was not widely known, he was highly regarded by many musicians, seeing him as tenor saxophone soloist Coleman Hawkins's chief rival. Whereas Hawkins's style was harmonically thick, busy, and powerful, Young employed a light tone and constructed simple, spare, yet highly imaginative statements. A group of followers, such as tenor saxophonist Stan Getz,[25] one of the best-known musicians of jazz's "cool school" and noted for his mellow, lush tone, Wardell Gray, tenor saxophonist straddling the swing and bebop periods, and Zoot Sims, tenor saxophonist known for his exuberance, mellow tone, and sense of swing, adopted Young's technique and style.

As swing became the first jazz idiom proving commercially successful, the swing era was an exercise in public relations. To nationally succeed, a band, especially its leader, had to be commercially exploitable, therefore he and his members had to be white. Though the African-American orchestras of Ellington, Count Basie, Chick Webb, and Jimmie Lunceford[26] became famous during this period, the swing era was mostly a white affair. While Benny Goodman was billed as the "King of Swing," Ellington's group was considered the best band.

Concurrent with the big band craze was a blossoming of the solo art of small-group musicians, such as pianists Fats Waller and Art Tatum, and big-band players with after-hours careers. Great virtuosos of this second category include saxophonists Lester Young, Johnny Hodges, Benny Carter, Coleman Hawkins, and Ben Webster, trumpeters Buck Clayton, Henry ("Red") Allen, and Cootie Williams, guitarist Charlie Christian, bassists Walter Page and Jimmy Blanton, trombonists Jack Teagarden and Dicky Wells, singer Billie Holiday, and pianists Earl Hines and Teddy Wilson.[27]

In addition to exceptional yet little-known Midwest "territory bands,"[28] Western swing bands dominated the airwaves and dance halls in 1930s Southwestern towns and rural settings. Though by the 1940s they spread their influence to California, these bands did not garner national fame but were local sensations to Southwesterners hungry for diversions and good dancing during the Great Depression and World War II. Wearing cowboy hats and boots and singing about "faded love," Western swing musicians performed on traditional country instruments, with all of jazz's required elements and outstanding solo improvisations.

A vibrant subgenre of mainstream jazz, Western swing pioneers included Cliff Bruner and Eldon Shamblin. Musicians made connections between the big band swing they heard on the radio and Western swing they created and played across the Southwest. Western swing culture included dance halls, recording studios, memorable personalities, stylistic growth, musical rivalries, touring, and live radio shows. Though performers came from the same rural roots nurturing country music, they considered themselves neither "hillbillies" nor "country pickers" but jazz musicians whose performance approach and repertory were not different from mainstream jazz.[29]

Western swing echoes in "King of Country" George Strait's recording of "Right or Wrong" (1983) (initially a 1936 hit by Milton Brown [1903–1936], "Father of Western Swing," band leader, and vocalist whose band was the first to fuse hillbilly hokum, jazz, and pop) and the band Asleep at the Wheel.[30] A period in country music histories during the 1930s and early 1940s, hundreds of thousands of "Okies," "Arkies," and other rural people from in and around the Southwest resettled in California in search of employment.[31] A country music scene quickly developed there, with performers playing Western swing, cowboy, and honky tonk country. After World War II, these styles influenced country music, leading to innovations of 1960s performers, such as Buck Owens and Merle Haggard, in creating the so-called "Bakersfield Sound." The Southwestern elements of the genre were distinct, especially before the 1950s, from more traditional Southeastern and

Midwestern styles. A powerful engine of music and poetry and link to rock and roll and rhythm and blues, Western swing has been an often-overlooked style of US popular music.[32] A subgenre of country music originating in the late 1920s in the West and South among the region's Western string bands, Western swing was popularized by artists Spade Cooley, The Light Crust Doughboys, Bob Wills and The Texas Playboys, and Milton Brown. Western swing legends also include Eldon Shamblin, Jimmy Wyble, Leon Rhodes, and Junior Benard (often called the first rockabilly).[33]

Though derided as mindless commercial entertainment for the masses, the era between 1935 and 1948, when big bands dominated US culture, has been described in glowing terms, echoing the Revolutionary War–era break from Europe as a golden age when US music shed the constrictions of European influence. Making its greatest impact during the Great Depression and World War II, swing, a collaboration between African Americans and immigrants' children, changed US culture. As young fans shaped swing's progression, their influence predated the impact young people continue to have on US popular culture. A lively music changing the United States's perception of itself, the swing era spurred transformations predating the 1960s counterculture and its emphasis on youth culture and generational divisions.[34]

Bandleaders Ellington, Count Basie, Benny Goodman, and Artie Shaw were crucial in confronting racial stereotypes and heralding integration. A cross section of the US population responded to swing, and fans' enthusiasm helped build the youth culture still active in the United States. Swing bands combined jazz and popular music to create fantasies for the Great Depression generation, capturing the imagination of US youth, music critics, and the music business. Swing was part of an era when the Great Depression was central to US citizens' lives. Jazz, literature, films, songs, and stories gave the population something to hope for by depicting a world of luxury. Innovations in technology and travel hinted at a utopian society, group sports and activities gave unemployed masses ways to spend their days, and a powerful demographic of the US teenager was courted by advertisers and entertainers. Racial mixing and musical swinging shook the United States in the big band era during its 1930s "golden years."

The early swing era (1930–1941) represented an extension of developments of the "Roaring Twenties" and an introduction of tendencies influencing subsequent periods in jazz histories. Major big bands and individual artists established styles bringing swing widespread popularity, while small groups created innovative approaches determining directions jazz would take. An era marked by colorful bandleaders, flashy instrumental soloists, showy orchestras, and such singers as Billie Holiday and her horn-like instrumental approach to singing, leading swing musicians from the World War II and post–World War II years include swing master Woody Herman, legendary big band leaders Les Brown, Dizzy Gillespie, Stan Kenton, Buddy

Rich,[35] and Vaughan Monroe, and small groups of Louis Jordan, Art Tatum, and Charlie Ventura. As World War II and postwar cultural changes affected performers, especially women and African Americans,[36] musicians from Basin Street in New Orleans to Harlem and Chicago's Southside[37] contributed to a period in US musical history from 1933 to 1945 when jazz was synonymous with US popular music, its social dances, and musical entertainment.[38]

John Nesbitt's groundbreaking compositions and arrangements helped shape swing-era styles through their influence on banjoist, guitarist, and arranger Gene Gifford and the famous Casa Loma Orchestra. In the big band era, when swing was giving a new shape and sound to US culture, bands were playing, audiences were dancing, and the music business was booming. In its music and broader subculture, swing revealed tensions over race, gender, sexuality, ethnicity, class, and nation mirroring those in the larger culture. Reinforcing and challenging racial attitudes and stereotypes, swing reflected US cultural impulses. Although its musical roots date to the 1920s, swing seemed to come out of nowhere in 1935, inspiring conflicting descriptions and explanations. Ellington, Goodman, and others' music caught many unaware and inspired contrasting interpretations.

As it linked to the evolving 1930s culture industry, at its commercial apex in the early 1940s, swing was adapted to suit the needs of World War II–era US culture, functioning as a symbol of national unity, even as this undermined the utopian values swing expressed. Syncretizing New Deal (US president Franklin D. Roosevelt's 1933–1939 domestic program, aimed to bring about immediate economic relief and reforms in industry, agriculture, finance, waterpower, labor, and housing, vastly increasing the scope of the federal government's activities to meet the ravages of the Great Depression, and embracing the concept of a government-regulated economy aimed at achieving a balance between conflicting economic interests) progressivism and utopian radicalism, though it failed to keep its New Deal coalition[39] together, swing became a quintessential expression of the New Deal ethos, emphasizing individualism within a cooperative national collective. Swing also reflected New Deal contradictions over race, gender, sexuality, ethnicity, class, and nation, fostering integration yet providing few opportunities for women and African Americans, who pioneered the form.

Emphasizing changes in US cultural codes and conventions, swing became the product of new technologies, allowing it to pervade US culture. A phenomenon forcing the United States to confront its indebtedness to African-American culture, swing exposed the role of white, wealthy, and progressive critics in crafting an ideology surrounding the music. Produced and consumed during a period of corporate consolidation in radio broadcasting and the recording industry and as the rising power of booking agencies combined to affect ways swing was disseminated, swing played a role in the

US war effort as the arts, activities, common items, and popular opinions impacted US culture.

In addition to Ellington, major swing-era figures include Fred Astaire, dancer of stage and film and regarded as the greatest popular music dancer, Ginger Rogers, stage and film dancer and actress primarily noted as Astaire's partner, Amelia Earhart, one of the world's most celebrated aviators who was the first woman to fly alone over the Atlantic Ocean, the Marx Brothers, a comedy team that was popular on stage, screen, and radio for thirty years, celebrated for their attacks on a socially respectable and ordered society, Margaret Mitchell, author of the sentimental, nostalgic Southern novel *Gone With the Wind* (1936) that was the source of the classic 1939 film of the same name, composer and lyricist Cole Porter, "Sultan of Swat" Babe Ruth, professional baseball player and one of the United States's most celebrated athletes, Shirley Temple, actress and diplomat who was an internationally popular 1930s child star, architect Frank Lloyd Wright, and Joe Louis, African-American world heavyweight champion boxer.[40]

Coinciding with dance bands' greatest popularity, the swing era was jazz's last great development before the late 1940s bebop explosion and this dissonant genre's harmonic experimentations, more conducive to cerebral listening than energetic dancing. While the homegrown US art form of swing produced some of jazz's most memorable figures, the pre-war and World War II–era marked the transition in jazz from the big band period to modern bebop. As swing achieved an art of improvisation, when harmonic conventions counterbalanced with its creators' stylistic individuality, the late swing era's harmonic innovations, evident in Woody Herman and bandleader and saxophonist Charlie Barnet's early 1940s bands, portended bebop and its chromaticism and defiance of swing's assimilationist style and substance.

Swing atrophied due to repetition, formularization, improvisational reduction, a loss of spontaneity, stylistic stultification, top-heavy sound, exuberant vulgarity, postwar changes, inflated musicians' salaries, fragmenting audiences, and television's rise. When singers who began as swing stylists, such as Frank Sinatra, Peggy Lee, Sarah Vaughan, and Nat "King" Cole became more popular than the swing bands they sang with, the swing era came to an end.[41]

FROM PROFANE TO SACRED

Proclaiming himself to be "God's messenger boy," Ellington's music was presented in the world's great cathedrals.[42] In his last decade, Ellington wrote mostly liturgical music. "In the Beginning God" (1965), for a standard jazz orchestra, narrator, chorus, two soloists, and dancer, was performed in Grace Cathedral, San Francisco, in 1965 and was followed by other "sacred services." To express the sadness of dancer Fredi Washington's[43] death in the short film *Black and Tan* (1929), Ellington uses gospel music,[44] predating his focus on sacred works toward the end of his career.

Ellington's sacred pieces echo the "sacred works" of Mary Lou Williams (1910–1981),[45] African-American jazz pianist and composer. Professionally playing from a very early age, in 1929, Williams served as deputy pianist and arranger for Andy Kirk's band until 1931, when she became a regular member. The 1930s fame of Kirk's band was largely due to the arrangements, compositions, and solo piano performances of Williams, also providing swing band scores for Benny Goodman, Earl Hines, and Tommy Dorsey. After leaving Kirk in 1942, Williams formed a small group in New York City and served as Ellington's staff arranger, composing the well-known "Trumpets No End" in 1946.

Williams became an important New York bebop figure, contributing scores to Dizzy Gillespie's big band and advancing younger musicians' careers. Williams lived in Europe from 1952 to 1954, when she retired from music to pursue religious and charitable interests. She restarted her career in 1957 and remained active in the 1960s and 1970s, leading groups in New York clubs and composing sacred works for jazz orchestra and voices. Long regarded as jazz's sole significant female musician, as an instrumentalist and composer, Williams was an important swing pianist, with a lightly rocking, *legato* (a smooth, flowing manner, without breaks between notes) manner based on stride and boogie-woogie bass patterns. As she explored her style, Williams retained the status of a modernist, adapting to the 1940s bebop idiom and in the 1960s attaining a level of complexity and dissonance rivalling avant-garde jazz pianists, all the while retaining a blues feeling.

Williams's work as a composer and arranger spans her expert swing band scores for Kirk, such as "Walkin' and Swingin'" (1936) and "Mary's Idea" (1938), to her 1960s and 1970s sacred works. These include the cantata "Black Christ of the Andes" (1963) and three masses, of which the third, *Mary Lou's Mass* (1970), was commissioned by the Vatican and became well known in a version choreographed by Alvin Ailey, Jr. (1931–1989), African-American dancer, choreographer, and director of the Alvin Ailey American Dance Theater.[46]

Williams's spiritual quest peaked in the mid-1950s. Returning from Europe in December 1954, she was financially unable to leave music. Her sporadic recorded output (six recording sessions between 1957 and 1962) suggests the strains involved as she attempted to negotiate her religious calling with her music. In 1955, Williams turned to the Abyssinian Baptist Church and preached in Harlem's streets. She found a lasting spiritual home in the Roman Catholic Church at Our Lady of Lourdes on 142nd Street in Harlem. Dizzy Gillespie introduced her to the Rev. John Crowley, a jazz-loving priest the trumpeter met in South America in 1956. Crowley urged

Williams to offer her playing as a prayer for others rather than leaving music. Fr. Anthony Woods became Williams's first spiritual mentor in the church. Williams was baptized on May 7, 1957, by Fr. Woods and confirmed a month later. In 1958, Williams founded the Bel Canto Foundation, assisting troubled musicians by establishing thrift stores in Harlem to raise money and help musicians return to their art, while she contributed 10 percent of her earnings.

Ellington's power in bringing people together and bringing out their best was credited to his spiritual side, an element strongly present, often overlooked, and reflected in Ellington's work, performances, and words. Ellington's spiritual objective was to share the wealth of his experiences, loves, and gifts and recognize the source of the African American tradition from which he drew. Ellington's centrality in jazz's shift from the brothel to the concert hall and profane to sacred did not allay critics, condemning jazz and labeling it "the Devil's music,"[47] threatening the fabric of US culture and Western civilization. By the 1920s, when jazz became the dominant influence on US popular music, some railed against it. Whites were shocked by its raw emotion and sexuality. Conservative African Americans castigated it for casting a negative light on their racial group. Others discovered meanings in jazz more significant than those in any other music or art form. For them, jazz provided ecstatic experiences that could not be found in any concert hall or church. These experiences, along with the charismatic personalities of such greats as Armstrong, Ellington, Charlie Parker, and John Coltrane, also merging jazz's profane and spiritual sides, generated strong communal feelings and sect-like groupings, generating rituals and myths to maintain jazz's mystique.

Part of broader relationships between music and religion, listeners regarded jazz as sacred and magical and fashioned mythologies to sustain this belief. During an era when conventional religions fell into a state of flux, jazz afforded a locus for spiritual impulses, tempered by contemporary anxieties and alienations. In the confluence of popular music and religious behavior in a secular time, jazz musicians and audiences participated in activities following patterns of religious behaviors. Such terms as "ritual," "convert," "prophet," and "sect" describe the reaction of jazz to the "church" of traditional nineteenth-century music in juxtapositions of religion and popular music.[48]

ON SCREEN

Following Armstrong and other early to mid-twentieth-century African-American film actors contending with mainstream cinema's dominant racial codes and conventions, Ellington expanded his professional marketability by performing in films, continuing the proliferation of racial musical stereotypes and the confluence of jazz and the moving image, all the while maintaining his regal disposition and performative demeanor. Film producers, knowing there was a market for films depicting popular African-American musicians, allowed performers, such as Ellington, to appear on screen when no one would risk putting a feature film's budget behind them, less cutting them off from markets that, while they may have had African-American customers, still had white theater owners and Jim Crow restrictions. As the first black film stars, such as Armstrong, light-skinned, "tragic mulatto" actresses Lena Horne and Dorothy Dandridge, singer, actor, and activist Paul Robeson,[49] and singer, actor, producer, and activist Harry Belafonte[50] emerged, films made much of the "authentic" connection between African Americans and musicality in the musical film genre, while films were shown to segregated audiences. Horne's film roles in particular were restricted to specialty performances, so her section of the film could be removed for Southern theaters.[51]

Ellington composed his first full-length film score for Otto Preminger's *Anatomy of a Murder* (1959) and first incidental music (music performed as part of the performance of a spoken drama) for Alain René Le Sage's *Turcaret* (1960). Ellington and his orchestra's cinematic performances include *Belle of the Nineties* (1934), *The Hit Parade* (1937), *Birth of the Blues* (1941), *Reveille with Beverly* (1943), *Symphony in Swing* (1949), and *The United States Steel Hour* (1957).

In *Black and Tan* (1929), Ellington performs in a jazz musical short with a tragic plotline. Ellington plays "hot jazz" in a story finding him down on his luck as he tries in vain to dissuade his friend, dancer Fredi Washington, from working with heart trouble even though it means work for his band. Although warned to give up dancing, Washington assures Ellington she is healthy enough to perform. However, she dances to her collapse to Ellington's "Cotton Club Stomp" (1929) and later dies as the orchestra and a vocal chorus perform Ellington's "Black and Tan Fantasy" (1927). Notable orchestra members include Arthur Whetsol, trumpeter and primary Ellington band member, Barney Bigard, tenor saxophonist and clarinetist, bassist Wellman Braud, and trombonist Joe "Tricky Sam" Nanton.

Black and Tan was written and directed by Dudley Murphy, one of the film industry's first independents and a guiding intelligence behind some of the key films of early twentieth-century cinema.[52] Murphy became involved in film starting in the early 1920s. He collaborated with African-American musicians to best express his films' concepts and became well known for his short films featuring popular music, such as *St. Louis Blues* (1929), starring Bessie Smith.[53] Murphy also wrote and directed *The Emperor Jones* (1933),[54] a film based on Eugene O'Neill's play and starring Paul Robeson as the unscrupulously ambitious Brutus Jones, who, after escaping from jail, finds himself emperor of a mysterious and exotic Caribbean island.

Along with being the first film to feature Ellington and his orchestra performing as a jazz band, *Black and Tan* was the film debut of actress Fredi

Washington. Representing African-American artists' emergence during the Harlem Renaissance, *Black and Tan* was selected in 2015 by the US Library of Congress for preservation in the National Film Registry due to its historical, cultural, and aesthetic significance. *Black and Tan* emphasizes the music and symbolism of African-American influences on jazz, 1920s Harlem struggles, and white supremacist realities.

In *A Bundle of Blues* (1933), Ellington and his orchestra perform two jazz compositions, plus "Stormy Weather," the song Lena Horne made famous in the film *Stormy Weather* (1943), sung as a "tragic mulatto"[55] against a backdrop of rain and the blues. *A Bundle of Blues* gives Ellington and his orchestra a few numbers to perform. As the Ellington band's 1930s female vocalist Ivie Anderson sings "Stormy Weather," she, like Horne, watches the rain pour over her "tragic" life. *A Bundle of Blues*'s final number depicts black dancers performing acrobatic feats, reminiscent of the famous African-Americandance duo The Nicholas Brothers. In *Belle of the Nineties* (1934), Ellington performs with Mae West (1893–1980), US stage and film actress and sex symbol whose bluntness, sensuality, leisurely postures, and blasé wisecracking became her trademarks as she portrayed women accepting their lives of dubious virtue with flippant humor.[56] In *Symphony in Swing* (1949), Ellington and his orchestra perform "Suddenly It Jumped," serving as an accompaniment to the spectacle of the Edwards Sisters tap dance team. Other numbers are "Turquoise Cloud," "Knock Me a Kiss," and "Frankie and Johnny."

BLACK-TRANSNATIONAL MUSICAL POLITICS

One of the most prominent African-American public figures in US history, helping to lower racial barriers on his Southern tours, Ellington demonstrated leadership on civil rights issues. Centering broader questions of racial justice in the United States and around the world, Ellington's life and career paralleled twentieth-century African-American history, including the Harlem Renaissance, Great Migration and move to urban areas, and the post–World War II Civil Rights Movement, while illuminating conflicting possibilities and limitations African Americans experienced in their economic, civic, and daily lives. Ellington's contributions to the cause of performative racial justice include being partly responsible for ending the routines of Stepin Fetchit, a physical comedian achieving 1930s superstar status, while characterized as a lazy, slow-witted, jive-talking "coon" racial stereotype.[57]

As he remarked during his successful 1933 tour of England, Ellington never denied his racial roots and was proud to compose and perform African-American folk music. Ellington's racially themed compositions include "Black Beauty" (1928), "Jubilee Stomp" (1928), "Harlem Flat Blues"

(1928), and "Saturday Night Function" (1929). The album *My People* (1964), released at the height of the Civil Rights Movement, chronicles African-American culture and Ellington's seminal work *Black, Brown, and Beige* (1943) represents African Americans' complex realities. A programmatic suite, jazz symphony, and "tone parallel" conceived in five sections, *Black, Brown and Beige* depicts African-American histories through African-American music.[58]

In January 1943, Ellington inaugurated a series of annual concerts at Carnegie Hall with his monumental work *Black, Brown and Beige*, showing a preoccupation with form in advance of his contemporaries. *Black, Brown and Beige* uses symphonic devices (the fragmentation and development of motifs, thematic recall, and mottoes) and symphonic proportions in its sections. Part of a legacy of implicit and explicitly political African-American performers, parallels are made between the music, thought, and cultural motivations of pioneering twentieth-century jazz musicians Ellington, Anthony Braxton (1945–), orchestrator, composer, woodwind improviser, and one of free jazz's most prolific artists, and Sun Ra, initial name Herman Blount, byname Sonny (1914–1993), experimentalist, composer, and keyboard player who led a free jazz big band known for its innovative instrumentation and theatrical performances.[59]

Ellington, Braxton, and Sun Ra were influenced by a common musical and spiritual heritage and participated in self-conscious efforts to create a utopian vision while using music to articulate black-transnational histories. While Braxton was a composer whose work created elaborate mythologies, Sun Ra was a bandleader who focused on cosmology, creating a self-mythology to accompany his innovative music and assert black people's cultural eminence and happy destiny, grounding his music and its presentation in myths and incorporating ancient Egyptian and science fictional[60] elements. Less hindered by overt racism, Braxton placed his compositions within an overarching dramatic structure as an allegory of his confrontations with attempts to delimit his music and people.[61]

Ellington, Braxton, and Sun Ra's influential work notes the confluence of twentieth-century African-American music, creativity, and histories while critiquing US music and culture. As each artist reacted to criticism and sought to break free of categorical constraints, Ellington, Braxton, and Sun Ra negotiated with misconceptions and misunderstandings regarding jazz and attempts to gain respect for the music. Noting jazz's democratic qualities and broader individual/communal tensions, Ellington, Braxton, and Sun Ra illuminate ways jazz, with its balance between individual invention and group coordination, acts as a democratic medium, metaphor, and model. The notion that jazz has been a democratic musical culture derives from players adjusting to each other to create an ideally safe space for individual self-expression amid a collective whole.

In their emphases on jazz's black-transnational routes, Ellington, Braxton, and Sun Ra challenge previous racial stereotyping of jazz and ways the majority of writing on black music and musicians incorporates racial stereotypes. Like other jazz artists, Braxton and Sun Ra were marginalized by critics and market forces. Black-transnational artists very much aware of their people's histories, Ellington, Braxton, and Sun Ra fought racism and the negative consequences of being part of a people forcibly torn from their homes, culture, and histories.

In his song "Sir Duke" (1976), Stevie Wonder, singer, songwriter, multi-instrumentalist, and child prodigy who became one of the most creative late twentieth-century musical figures, [62] centers Ellington in a black-transnational musical legacy. Ellington would also be hailed, especially in Europe, as a "high-art" practitioner equal to Igor Stravinsky (1882–1971), [63] Russian-born composer whose work had a revolutionary impact on musical thought and sensibility just before and after World War I, and whose compositions were a touchstone of modernism for much of his long working life, and Maurice Ravel (1875–1937), French composer of Swiss-Basque descent, noted for his craftsmanship in terms of form and style. [64]

WITH STRAYHORN

Ellington's stylistic qualities were shared by longtime friend, co-composer, arranger, and pianist Billy Strayhorn [65] (1915–1967). Between 1939 and 1967, Strayhorn collaborated so closely with Ellington it remains difficult to determine the extent that Strayhorn influenced and composed works attributed to Ellington. By the early 1940s, Strayhorn, composer of what would become the Ellington band's theme song, "Take the 'A' Train" (1939), was Ellington's composing-arranging partner and second pianist. One of the United States's greatest composers, Strayhorn was overshadowed by Ellington, with whom he worked for three decades as the Ellington Orchestra's top songwriter and arranger.

A giant of jazz, the "lush life" Strayhorn and other jazz musicians led in Harlem and Paris echoes jazz's transnational routes and multiple international manifestations. Composing some of the most memorable twentieth-century US music, Strayhorn labored under a complex agreement whereby Ellington took the credit for his work. A similarly "tragic" jazz musician, following Billie Holiday, Charlie Parker, and others, Strayhorn's life was cut short by cancer and alcohol abuse. Small and shy, Strayhorn carried himself with style and grace as one of the few jazzmen to be openly homosexual. The composer of many popular Ellington Orchestra tunes and worshipped by jazz aficionados as the creative power behind the Ellington throne, Strayhorn preferred to quietly live as he contributed to Ellington's "magic."

An attractive personality, perceived as Ellington's alter ego, Strayhorn collaborated with Ellington yet remained in his shadow, as his talents were recognized by other musicians and members of an elite circle of black performers, artists, and writers. With his male companions, Strayhorn lived lavishly, traveling in exclusive artistic and social spheres. Without the need to pursue a career of his own and part of jazz's broader queer black-transnational histories,[66] Strayhorn could be open about his homosexuality at a time when most queer men kept their sexual orientation secret. Strayhorn's powerful music and difficult life highlight hidden histories of New York's queer black artists.

Much of the music associated with Ellington's orchestra was Strayhorn's. Strayhorn composed "Chelsea Bridge" (1941) and "Lush Life" (1948) and collaborated on Ellington's suites and music for stage and film (including *Jump for Joy* (1941), a musical based on themes of African-American identity, the album *Such Sweet Thunder* (1957), and *Anatomy of a Murder* (1959). In return, Ellington provided Strayhorn a virtually all-expenses-paid life. An underappreciated voice in US popular music and little-studied figure central to jazz histories, "Strays" (also known as "Swee' Pea") grew up in working-class Pittsburgh and had high-society aspirations.

Strayhorn wrote a Gershwin-like musical revue a year out of high school, with advanced harmony and a sophisticated recitative (musical declamation of the kind usual in the narrative and dialogue parts of opera and oratorio, sung in the rhythm of ordinary speech with many words on the same note). Desiring a concert music career, Strayhorn was marked as a queer black man unwilling to hide his homosexuality. Strayhorn's break came in 1938, when he met Ellington. Possessing a steadfast business sense, Ellington knew Strayhorn was gifted and worked out the arrangement that Ellington give Strayhorn free rein to let his Ellington-influenced compositional sense run wild, while Strayhorn would have no by-line and publishing royalties. At first, Strayhorn submitted to Ellington's benevolent dictatorship. Eventually, his compositions moved beyond Ellington's influence. Depressed by his obscurity, Strayhorn left behind the ghostwriting arrangement to achieve his dark style and a small measure of fame. Both Ellington and Strayhorn's music was extraordinary, however Strayhorn's was perhaps fuller of the structures of feeling lacking from the oftentimes distant, detached, and regal Ellington.

STYLE AND MUSICAL INNOVATIONS

Despite his personal defects, few shared the stage as graciously as Ellington,[67] one of jazz's most romantic, flamboyant, and charismatic figures. As he extemporized solos and provided multiple variations in performance, Ellington's music became an integral part of US culture for most of the twenti-eth century.[68] An icon of US music, Ellington achieved a high level of sophistication while establishing foundations for US popular music. A jazz master, Ellington's compositions, such as "Mood Indigo" (1930) and "So-phisticated Lady" (1933), remain beloved standards. The music of Ellington and his sidemen include studio recordings, soundtracks, concerts, radio broadcasts, and private recordings.[69]

Ellington taught himself harmony at the piano and acquired the funda-mentals of orchestration by experimenting with his band. His orchestra was a workshop in which he consulted his players and tried alternative solutions. During his formative Cotton Club period, Ellington was required to perform in a variety of musical styles, including numbers for dancing, "jungle-style" and production numbers, popular songs, "blue" or "mood" pieces, and "pure" jazz instrumental compositions. During this period, Ellington developed a symbiotic relationship with his orchestra. More than the piano, it was his "instrument," enabling Ellington to experiment with the timbral colorings, tonal effects, and unusual voicings that became his style's trademark.

The "Ellington effect" was unique in that it depended on each player's timbre and style. While no two players in Ellington's orchestra sounded alike, they produced blends and ensembles of sonority. An early example of the "Ellington effect" can be heard on "Mood Indigo," in which the tradition-al roles of the three front-line instruments in New Orleans collective improv-isation—clarinet performing in the high register, trumpet playing the melody or theme, and trombone as bass or tenor counter-themes—are inverted so that the muted trumpet plays on top, plunger-muted trombone functions as a high-register second voice, and clarinet sounds more than an octave below.

In the early to mid-1920s, orchestral jazz arrangements were basic, serv-ing dance music's simplest functions. With arrangers Don Redman, Fletcher Henderson, and John Nesbitt, Ellington developed an elaborate, diversified arranging concept, incorporating the contemporary "hot" style of solo im-provisation. In this, he was influenced by the expressive and technical capa-bilities of his principal brass players, experts of the "growl and plunger" style. These powerful sounds, when juxtaposed with the saxophone's smoother sonority, provided Ellington with a colorful orchestral palette.

Faced with the problem posed by jazz arrangement of how best to inte-grate solo improvisations, Ellington learned to exploit the contrast produced by the soloist's entry, so as to project him into the music's movement and entrust him with its development. This explains why even Ellington's finest soloists seemed lackluster after leaving his orchestra. Few of Ellington's soloists, despite their importance to jazz histories, played as effectively in other contexts, finding it difficult to match Ellington's inspiration. Some of Ellington's musicians stayed with him for decades. While baritone saxo-phonist Harry Carney was a band member for forty-seven years, later replacements fit into roles created by their distinguished predecessors. After 1950, the Ben Webster–influenced Paul Gonsalves filled the band's solo tenor saxophone role originated by Webster. There were some exceptions to this generalization, such as trumpeter-violinist Ray Nance and high-note trumpet specialist Cat Anderson.

Ellington had a gift for formulating orchestral accompaniments for improvisation. Few arrangers, with the exception of Gil Evans and Sy Oliver, trumpeter, composer, and bandleader who was one of the 1930s and 1940s leading arrangers, imagined instrumental combinations as astonishing as those of "Mystery Song" (1931), "Saddest Tale" (1934), "Delta Serenade" (1934), "Azure" (1937), "Subtle Lament" (1939), "Dusk" (1940), "Ko-Ko" (1940), and "Moon Mist" (1942). Rarely featuring himself as a soloist and contributing to the broader "Ellington effect," Ellington viewed himself as a catalyst, accompanist, and contributor of ideas and rhythmic energy to his band and its soloists. In this inconspicuous role, playing only when necessary, Ellington was known for remaining silent throughout entire choruses and pieces.

Known as the "prince of the piano," Ellington's style as a pianist originated in ragtime and the stride piano idiom of James P. Johnson and Willie "The Lion" Smith (1897–1973), jazz pianist and one of the masters of the stride style, usually grouped with Johnson and Fats Waller as the three greatest practitioners of the genre in its golden age, from about 1920 to 1943. Ellington adapted his style for orchestral purposes, accompanying with vivid harmonic colors and, particularly in later years, offering swinging solos with angular melodies.

Ellington's talents as a pianist are generally neglected and underrated. However, his rich piano tone had the ability to energize his orchestra. Though as a soloist he could be erratic in his early years while relying on pianistic clichés, such as downward-fluttering arpeggios (the notes of a chord played in ascending or descending succession), Ellington could equal the best players. Examples of his work as a pianist-composer are *Piano Method for Blues* (1943), a short book by Ellington, and "Clothed Woman" (1947), noted for its atonality (music that lacks a key or tonal center). The piano was central to Ellington's achievements as a musician.[70] He composed at the keyboard, improvised there, led his musicians from the keyboard, and delivered, as the leading member of his rhythm section, his creations' energies on the keyboard. Practices in Ellington's piano work include an early foundational stride style, typical of his swing maturity, and an atypical, post-bop (a term stylistically and chronologically used to describe continuations and amalgamations of bop, modal jazz, and free jazz, encompassing swing and earlier styles, fusion, and "Third-World" styles, and emerging as an attempt to circumscribe the eclecticism characterizing jazz from the 1980s onward)[71]/modern style, all existing side by side from the 1940s to his career's end.

A copious writer and consummate performer, Ellington was the composer of such standards as "It Don't Mean a Thing (If It Ain't Got That Swing" (1931), "Solitude" (1934), and "Prelude to a Kiss" (1938). Ellington combined a flair for orchestration with gifts as a bandleader. While other jazz composers had comparable talent, they lacked the organizational abilities necessary to create and maintain a permanent orchestral vehicle. In "Concerto for Cootie" (1940), ten-bar phrases are combined into a complex, three-part form abandoning the chorus structure common to most jazz. In "Cotton Tail" (1940), Ellington uses a call-and-response technique to heighten the last climactic chorus's drama. Ellington worked best in the miniature forms dictated by the three-minute ten-inch disc. As his creativity somewhat declined after the 1940s, many of the late period extended compositions and multi-movement suites generally suffered from a diminished, less consistent originality and hasty work, occasioned by incessant touring.

A high point in Ellington's career came in the early 1940s, when he composed the masterworks "Concerto for Cootie," his fast-tempo showpieces "Cotton Tail" and "Ko-Ko," and the uniquely structured, compressed panoramas "Main Stem" and "Harlem Air Shaft," with soloists accompanied by diverse ensemble colors. These works, composed for three-minute, seventy-eight-rpm records, are inventive, as are their unique forms, ranging from flowing expositions to juxtapositions of line and mood. Major jazz artists, such as tenor saxophonist Ben Webster and bassist Jimmy Blanton, were with this classic Ellington band. Not restricting himself to jazz compositions, Ellington wrote such popular songs as "Rocks in My Bed" (1941) and "Satin Doll" (1953). In "I Let a Song Go Out of My Heart" (1938) and "Don't Get Around Much Any More" (1940), Ellington made wide interval leaps one of his trademarks.

Although his compositional interests and ambitions changed over the decades, Ellington's melodic, harmonic, and rhythmic features were mostly fixed by the late 1930s, when he was a swing-era star. Ellington recorded with musicians who were not band members, other swing-era luminaries, such as Armstrong, Ella Fitzgerald, and Coleman Hawkins, and, though bebop's melodies and polyrhythms did not have a major impact on him and the musical culture's anti-assimilation contrasted with his more integrationist stance, later bebop musicians John Coltrane and Charles Mingus. After World War II, the Ellington band often toured Europe and played in Asia (1963–1964, 1970), West Africa (1966), South America (1968), Australia (1970), and frequently toured North America.

Ellington continued to lead his band until shortly before his 1974 death. As his sense of musical drama and players' special talents were rare, Ellington's melodic gifts and mastery of sonic textures, rhythms, and composition-

al forms converted subtle, complex perceptions into a body of music un-
equaled in jazz histories. Charles Ives (1874–1954), US composer known for
innovations anticipating most of the twentieth century's later musical developments,[72] is one of Ellington's few rivals, along with such composers as
Aaron Copland (1900–1990), who achieved a distinctive musical character-
ization of US themes in an expressive modern style, and Philip Glass
(1937–), composer of innovative instrumental, vocal, and operatic music, for
the title of the United States's greatest composer.

A US JAZZ EXCEPTIONALIST AMBASSADOR

Though he lived his life as a globe-trotting world citizen, taking jazz back to
its transnational routes and demystifying the musical culture as exclusively
American, Ellington has been pigeonholed by those wishing to reduce jazz to
a US-centered definition. A State Department jazz ambassador and preeminent jazz cultural diplomat, the US jazz exceptionalism projected onto Ellington links to broader jingoistic exceptionalist discourses, permeating multiple US historical eras. One of the most powerful forces shaping US nation-
hood and featuring claims that the United States remains the world's indis-
pensable nation, US exceptionalism maintains that the US nation was a magical place God chose from all the peoples of the world, destined to lead and
provide an example to the myriad non-white and "uncivilized" populations
needing US guidance and deliverance. Part of the United States's highly
destructive, hyper-violent legacy, US exceptionalism encompasses Native
American removal,[73] slavery, and Manifest Destiny, or the supposed inevita-
bility, with religious backing, of the United States's continued territorial
expansion westward to the Pacific and beyond.[74]

US exceptionalism, or the notion that Americans have a distinct and
special destiny, distinct from other nations, can be understood through the
words of its champions and challengers, appearing in the speeches and writings of Rev. Dr. Martin Luther King, Jr.,[75] President Ronald Reagan, and
John Winthrop, first governor of the Massachusetts Bay Colony and chief
figure among the New England Puritan founders.[76] In 1630, Winthrop told
his fellow colonists that they were on the verge of establishing a "city on a
hill." The Massachusetts Bay colonists believed God intervened to create the
United States as a "redeemer nation."[77]

Revisions of the US exceptionalist myth are read in the novels of Larry
McMurtry, Thomas Pynchon, and Toni Morrison[78] and the writings of Mary
Rowlandson, William Bradford, and John Cotton. Works by Nathaniel Hawthorne and Herman Melville[79] articulate the nineteenth-century vision of
expansion, as anti-slavery writers wielded exceptionalist rhetoric against "the
peculiar institution." Engrossed with newness in politics and culture, US

exceptionalism's influence can be read in US political texts, such as the *Declaration of Independence* (1776), *The Federalist Papers* (1787–1788), Alexis de Tocqueville's *Democracy in America* (1835–1840), Henry David Thoreau's *Walden* (1854), and W. E. B. Du Bois's *The Souls of Black Folk* (1903).[80]

With a government transformed by an imperial presidency,[81] the culture of exceptionalism permeated US penchant for empire, sense of entitlement, and illusion of indestructibility. This was perpetuated despite the United States's failed wars, its recent performance in everything from fighting poverty to health care to political corruption, stacking up poorly against other nations, differing views of Native Americans, Chicanos, and non-Americans, and ways the United States has been an enemy to colonized people within and beyond its borders. Negative consequences ensued when US exceptionalism was embraced by elites in the Bush administration and when such events as the US invasions of Afghanistan and Iraq,[82] prisoner abuse at Abu Ghraib, and exposure of US governmental incompetence after Hurricane Katrina opened fissures in the exceptionalist myth. This was also fostered by an Obama administration conflicted between rhetoric and deeds, challenging the homeland security paradigm with an alternative, "post-racial"[83] state fantasy privileging fairness, inclusion, and justice,[84] as the long era of US transnational economic dominance entered a period of diminished expectations, and while the hold of white supremacy on US culture continued in an era of police brutality, gun violence, and rise in incarceration rates in a "new Jim Crow," targeting black men through the War on Drugs and decimating communities of color, as the US criminal justice system functioned as an updated system of racial control relegating millions to a permanent second-class status while adhering to a principle of "colorblindness."[85]

In national myths that have been part of the Washington establishment's delusions of omnipotence and crippling, consistently violent US foreign policy,[86] the United States considered itself an exceptional country of citizens unified by an allegiance to a common set of ideals of individualism, antistatism, populism, and egalitarianism. These ideologies define the limits of US political debate and shape its dominant culture. In US foreign policy's moralistic, crusading tendencies,[87] US exceptionalism has been celebrated, panned, emphasized, and denied for most of the country's histories by its population, visitors, and observers. US exceptionalist myths are revealed in the Vietnam War[88] and Hollywood films, especially the culture of Westerns and its celebration of the lone white hetero-normative male vigilante restoring violence to an untamed, virgin frontier and its "primitive" indigenous inhabitants. As exceptionalism provided the framework for US foreign policy discourses, each post–Vietnam War US presidential administration rhetorically revived the popular belief in exceptionalism and pursued foreign policies grounded in traditional US "values," as the "lessons" of Vietnam lingered in a "Vietnam Syndrome,"[89] or an aversion to further overseas military entanglements, and the exorcism of this syndrome through the Persian Gulf War (1990–1991) victory.[90]

For the first century after the Constitution went into effect, European observers and Americans understood the United States as exceptional, with political and civic cultures that had no counterparts. US geography, ideology, politics, and daily life set it apart from Europe,[91] and US exceptionalism was reformulated and redeployed through cultural works, political spectacles, and the construction of Islamic extremism as an official state enemy. As US exceptionalism came in exemplary and missionary versions, being exceptional offered an either/or choice postulating that the United States should either withdraw from the world like an isolated but inspiring "city on a hill" or that it was called on to lead the world to a better future.

Nineteenth-century US exceptionalism was illuminated through Americans' reactions to the 1848 European revolutions.[92] Since the recent US military victory over Mexico in the Mexican-American War (1846–1848), Americans celebrated news of European democratic revolutions as a further sign of divine providence. Others repudiated the 1848 revolutions and the thought of trans-Atlantic unity, interpreting European revolutionary radicalism, violence, socialism, and atheism as hostile to US "values." When the 1848 revolutions failed to create stable European democratic governments, Americans declared that their own revolutionary tradition was superior.[93]

Since its founding, the United States defined itself as the supreme global protector of freedom, pointing to its Constitution as the model of law to ensure democracy at home and internationally protect human rights.[94] Though the United States emphasized the importance of the international legal system, it distanced itself from international legal principles and institutions implementing them. The United States attempted to unilaterally reshape some international legal doctrines while ignoring others, such as the prohibition on torture and Geneva Conventions, a series of international treaties concluded in Geneva between 1864 and 1977 to ameliorate war's effects on soldiers and civilians.[95] To critics, the United States's selective self-exemption undermined legal institutions and led to the international rule of law's decreased effectiveness.

CONCLUSION

Making sense of Duke Ellington's legend and legacy requires an analysis of the composer from the standpoint of his musical gifts, place in transnational jazz histories, and relationships to broader hierarchies of race, gender, sexuality, ethnicity, class, and nation, the United States's understanding of itself and its relation to the rest of the world, and jazz's role in the US struggle for global supremacy and use as proof of US political and cultural exceptionalism. Ellington's standards and more ambitious suites reflect his refusal to accept limits on his creativity. Protective of his privacy, the calmest of men, while full of personal complications and contradictions, Ellington sought inspiration in a string of transient lovers, concealing his inner self behind a smiling mask of flowery language and ironic charm.

Ellington's public and private lives expose layers of evasion and deception, while reviews, essays, appreciations, profiles, ephemera, and texts by music critics, Ralph Ellison, Swiss writer Blaise Cendrars, Simone de Beauvoir, more than a dozen biographies, and memoirs by Ellington, his son Mercer, and band members highlight the notoriously elusive and not always admirable Ellington, whose traits included procrastination and manipulation. Composing a complex, ambitious art, onstage, Ellington was an effusive, electrifying personality. Offstage, he could be something of a cipher, leading a longtime associate to speculate that only some people "knew" Ellington, an enigma none of his orchestra members claim any profound intimacy with and an impenetrable personality whom no one, not even his closest friends, claimed to understand.

With five decades of hits and masterpieces and constantly breaking new ground, Ellington's art expressed varying black-transnational experiences, as Ellington drew on African-American traditions of ragtime and the blues. As he captured the sounds of trains, planes, babies, and animals with his orchestra, Ellington's career took him on a seemingly endless tour through North America, Europe, and the Near East. Most of the enormous number of works (over 1,500 compositions) Ellington recorded are his own. Ellington's compositions include hundreds of three-minute instrumental pieces (for seventy-eight-rpm recordings), popular songs (many consisting of instrumental pieces to which lyrics by Irving Mills were added), large-scale suites, several musical comedies, work for the stage,[96] many film scores, and *Boola*, an incomplete and unperformed opera.

One of the Jazz Age's defining composers, stages of Ellington's career extend from the 1920s Harlem Renaissance and early successes in the Harlem nightclub scene,[97] reign at the glamorous, gangster-owned Cotton Club (1927–1932), 1930s European tours, the swing era and challenging Great Depression years, pioneering explosion of form and genre in the 1940s, post–World War II critical acceptance, and acclaim during the next four decades. A major African-American musician and "King of Jazz," Ellington's histories define a half-century of jazz and US popular music. As much at home in the 1920s and 1930s Cotton Club as he was at a 1960s White House birthday celebration in his honor, Ellington was central to the expanding US school of music and its political and aesthetic mixtures.

Highlighting broad musical ideas of rhythm, melody, and harmony, Ellington was one of several iconic twentieth-century composers and performers across genres sharing the common pursuit of representing the rapidly changing conditions of contemporary existence. As vital to musical modernism as Igor Stravinsky and Arnold Schoenberg (1874–1951), Austrian American composer who created new methods of composition involving atonality,[98] comparisons are made between Ellington's techniques and Mozart and Béla Bartók (1881–1945), Hungarian composer, pianist, ethnomusicologist, and teacher, noted for the Hungarian flavor of his music, including orchestral works, string quartets, piano solos, stage pieces, a cantata, and folk songs for voice and piano.[99] With a lasting impact on jazz and popular music reaching from Gershwin to R&B, Ellington has been recognized as one of twentieth-century music's towering figures and one of jazz's preeminent musicians.

Among the transnational superstars Ellington influenced are "Godfather of Soul" James Brown (1933–2006),[100] Prince (1958–2016), singer, guitarist, songwriter, producer, dancer, and performer on keyboards, drums, and bass who was among the most talented musicians of his generation, Sly Stone (1943–), musician, songwriter, and record producer, most famous for his role as frontman for Sly and the Family Stone, a band playing a critical role in the development of soul, funk, rock, and psychedelia in the 1960s and 1970s,[101] Frank Zappa (1940–1993), composer, guitarist, satirist, cultural gadfly upsetting US suburban complacency and puncturing the hypocrisy and pretensions of the US political establishment and the counterculture that opposed it, rock band Steely Dan, a studio-based duo drawing from the gamut of US musical styles to create some of the 1970s' most intelligent and complex popular music, Ravi Shankar (1920–2012), Indian sitar player, composer, founder of the National Orchestra of India, and influential in stimulating Western appreciation of Indian music, and funk star George Clinton (1941–),[102] singer, songwriter, bandleader, record producer, principal architect of "P-Funk," the repertoire and performers associated with Clinton and the Parliament-Funkadelic collective and the distinctive style of funk music they performed, mastermind of the bands Parliament and Funkadelic during the 1970s and early 1980s, and cited as one of the foremost innovators of funk music, along with James Brown and Sly Stone. In the ultimate tribute, Miles Davis had himself interred next to Ellington in New York's Woodlawn Cemetery and said, "All the musicians should get together one certain day and get down on their knees and thank Duke."[103]

NOTES

1. Gunther Schuller. "Jazz and Composition: The Many Sides of Duke Ellington, the Music's Greatest Composer." *Bulletin of the American Academy of Arts and Sciences* 46.1 (October 1992): 36–51.

2. James Lincoln Collier. *Duke Ellington.* New York: Oxford University Press, 1987.

3. Benjamin Givan. "Swing Improvisation: A Schenkerian Perspective." *Theory and Practice* 35 (2010): 25–56; Herb Snitzer and Lewis Porter. "'Such Sweet Thunder': A Visual Journey." *The Georgia Review* 46.4 (Winter 1992): 663–680.

4. Anna Harwell Celenza. "Legislating Jazz." *Washington History* 26, Jazz in Washington (Spring 2014): 88–97; Michael Fitzgerald. "Researching Washington Jazz History." *Washington History* 26, Jazz in Washington (Spring 2014): 98–107; Rusty Hassan. "Jazz Radio in Washington: A Personal Retrospective." *Washington History* 26, Jazz in Washington (Spring 2014): 74–87; John Edward Hasse. "Washington's Duke Ellington." *Washington History* 26, Jazz in Washington (Spring 2014): 36–59.

5. David Garrett Izzo. *Movies in the Age of Obama: The Era of Post Racial and Neo-Racist Cinema.* Lanham, MD: Rowman & Littlefield, 2015; Ian G. Strachan and Mia Mask. *Poitier Revisited: Reconsidering a Black Icon in the Obama Age.* New York: Bloomsbury Academic, 2014.

6. "Blacks and the White House: From Slave Builders to the Master of the House." *The Journal of Blacks in Higher Education* 62 (Winter 2008/2009): 26–27; Michael Coard. "The 'Black' Eye on George Washington's 'White' House." *The Pennsylvania Magazine of History and Biography* 129.4 (October 2005): 461–471; Clarence Lusane. *The Black History of the White House.* San Francisco: City Lights Books, 2011.

7. "Brudder Bones: The New Acceptability of Ridiculing Black People." *The Journal of Blacks in Higher Education* 17 (Autumn 1997): 91–93; Thomas Cripps. "The Films of Spencer Williams." *Black American Literature Forum* 12.4 (Winter 1978): 128–134; Thomas Patrick Doherty. *Cold War, Cool Medium: Television, McCarthyism, and American Culture.* New York: Columbia University Press, 2003.

8. Stuart Nicholson. *Reminiscing in Tempo: A Portrait of Duke Ellington.* Boston: Northeastern University Press, 1999.

9. Amiri Baraka. *The Great Max Roach.* New York: Thunder's Mouth Press, 1991; Larry McShane. "In Memoriam: Max Roach (1924–2007): Jazz Master Max Roach Dies at Eighty-Three." *The Black Scholar* 37.3, Black Social Agenda (Fall 2007): 50–51; Ingrid T. Monson. *Freedom Sounds: Civil Rights Call Out to Jazz and Africa.* Oxford; New York: Oxford University Press, 2007; Njoroge Njoroge. "Dedicated to the Struggle: Black Music, Transculturation, and the Aural Making and Unmaking of the Third World." *Black Music Research Journal* 28.2 (Fall 2008): 85–104; Scott Saul. *Freedom Is, Freedom Ain't: Jazz and the Making of the Sixties.* Cambridge, MA: Harvard University Press, 2005.

10. Marc Rice. "Break o' Day Blues: The 1923 Recordings of the Bennie Moten Orchestra." *The Musical Quarterly* 86.2 (Summer 2002): 282–306; _____. "Prelude to Swing: The 1920s Recordings of the Bennie Moten Orchestra." *American Music* 25.3 (Fall 2007): 259–281.

11. Ralph G. Giordano. *Social Dancing in America: A History and Reference.* Westport, CT: Greenwood Press, 2007; _____. *Satan in the Dance Hall: Rev. John Roach Straton, Social Dancing, and Morality in 1920s New York City.* Lanham, MD: Scarecrow Press, 2008; Laam Hae. *The Gentrification of Nightlife and the Right to the City: Regulating Spaces of Social Dancing in New York.* New York: Routledge, 2012; Linda J. Tomko. *Dancing Class: Gender, Ethnicity, and Social Divides in American Dance, 1890–1920.* Bloomington: Indiana University Press, 1999.

12. Barbara Cohen-Stratyner. "Social Dance: Contexts and Definitions." *Dance Research Journal* 33.2, Social and Popular Dance (Winter 2001): 121–124; Lynne Fauley Emery. *Black Dance in the United States from 1619 to 1970.* Palo Alto, CA: National Press Books, 1972; Barbara Engelbrecht. "Swinging at the Savoy." *Dance Research Journal* 15.2, Popular Dance in Black America (Spring 1983): 3–10; Black Hawk Hancock. "Put a Little Color on That!" *Sociological Perspectives* 51.4 (Winter 2008): 783–802; _____. *American Allegory: Lindy Hop and the Racial Imagination.* Chicago: The University of Chicago Press, 2013; Jonathan

David Jackson. "Improvisation in African-American Vernacular Dancing." *Dance Research Journal* 33.2, Social and Popular Dance (Winter 2001): 40–53; Frankie Manning and Cynthia R. Millman. *Frankie Manning: Ambassador of Lindy Hop*. Philadelphia: Temple University Press, 2007; Howard Spring. "Swing and the Lindy Hop: Dance, Venue, Media, and Tradition." *American Music* 15.2 (Summer 1997): 183–207.

13. Morroe Berger, Edward Berger, and James Patrick. *Benny Carter, A Life in American Music*. Metuchen, NJ: Scarecrow Press, 1982; Jan Evensmo, Per Borthen, and Ib Skovsted Thomsen. *The Alto Saxophone, Trumpet and Clarinet of Benny Carter, 1927–1946: With a Critical Assessment of All His Known Records and Broadcasts*. Hosle: Jan Evensmo, 1982; Vincent Pelote. "The Institute of Jazz Studies." *Fontes Artis Musicae* 36.3 (July–September 1989): 177–181.

14. Pino Candini. "Musica Jazz: The Italian Jazz Magazine Which Is Also a Record." *Fontes Artis Musicae* 36.3 (July–September 1989): 219–220; John Chilton. *Roy Eldridge, Little Jazz Giant*. London; New York: Continuum, 2002; Jan Evensmo. *The Trumpet of Roy Eldridge, 1929–1944: With a Critical Assessment of All His Known Records and Broadcasts*. Hosle, Norway: [Jan Evensmo], 1979; Josephine R. B. Wright and John Birks 'Dizzy' Gillespie. "Conversation with John Birks 'Dizzy' Gillespie, Pioneer of Jazz." *The Black Perspective in Music* 4.1 (Spring 1976): 82–89.

15. Count Basie, Albert Murray, and Dan Morgenstern. *Good Morning Blues: The Autobiography of Count Basie*. Minneapolis: University of Minnesota Press, 2016; Stanley Dance. *The World of Count Basie*. New York: Da Capo Press, 1985; Raymond Horricks. *Count Basie and His Orchestra, Its Music and Its Musicians*. Westport, CT: Negro Universities Press, 1975; Chris Sheridan. *Count Basie: A Bio-Discography*. London: Greenwood/Eurospan, 1986; Mark Tucker. "Count Basie and the Piano That Swings the Band." *Popular Music* 5, Continuity and Change (1985): 45–79; Ken Vail. *Count Basie: Swingin' the Blues, 1936–1950*. Lanham, MD: Scarecrow Press, 2003.

16. Theodor W. Adorno. "On Popular Music." *Studies in Philosophy and Social Science* 9.1 (1941): 17–48.

17. John Hammond and Irving Townsend. *John Hammond on Record: An Autobiography*. New York: Ridge Press, 1977; Dunstan Prial. *The Producer: John Hammond and the Soul of American Music*. New York: Farrar, Straus and Giroux, 2006; Wendy Smith. "Recording: The Man Who Got His Way: John Hammond, Scion of White Privilege, Helped Integrate Popular Music." *The American Scholar* 75.3 (Summer 2006): 110–114.

18. Ron Welburn. "Jazz Magazines of the 1930s: An Overview of Their Provocative Journalism." *American Music* 5.3 (Autumn 1987): 255–270.

19. Tony Bacon and Dave Gelly. *Masters of Jazz Saxophone: The Story of the Players and Their Music*. London: Balafon Books, 2000; Johs Bergh, Jan Evensmo, and Norsk Jazzarkiv. *Jazz Tenor Saxophone in Norway: 1917–1959*. Oslo: Norwegian Jazz Archives, 1996; Stephen Cottrell. *The Saxophone*. New Haven: Yale University Press, 2013; William F. Lee. *Jazz Saxophone Players: A Biographical Handbook*. Silverspring, MD: Beckham Publications Group, 2010; Doug Miller. "The Moan within the Tone: African Retentions in Rhythm and Blues Saxophone Style in Afro-American Popular Music." *Popular Music* 14.2 (May 1995): 155–174; John O'Neill. *The Jazz Method for Saxophone*. London: Schott Educational, 1992; Michael Segell. *The Devil's Horn: The Story of the Saxophone, From Noisy Novelty to the King of Cool*. New York: Farrar, Straus and Giroux, 2005; Dennis Taylor. *Jazz Saxophone: An In-Depth Look at the Styles of the Tenor Masters*. Milwaukee, WI: Hal Leonard Corp., 2004; Ollie Weston. *Exploring Jazz Saxophone: An Introduction to Jazz Harmony, Technique and Improvisation*. London: Schott, 2009.

20. Robert W. D. Boyce. *The Great Interwar Crisis and the Collapse of Globalization*. Basingstoke: Palgrave Macmillan, 2009; John Kenneth Galbraith. *The Great Crash, 1929*. Boston, Houghton Mifflin, 1955; Paul N. Hehn. *A Low Dishonest Decade: The Great Powers, Eastern Europe, and the Economic Origins of World War II, 1930–1941*. New York: Continuum, 2002; Maury Klein. *Rainbow's End: The Crash of 1929*. Oxford; New York: Oxford University Press, 2001; Sidney Pollard. *Wealth & Poverty: An Economic History of the Twentieth Century*. Oxford; New York: Oxford University Press, 1990; Frank G. Steindl. *Understanding Economic Recovery in the 1930s: Endogenous Propagation in the Great Depression*. Ann

Arbor: University of Michigan Press, 2004; Jürgen von Kruedener. *Economic Crisis and Political Collapse: The Weimar Republic 1924–1933.* New York: Berg, 1990.

21. Frank Büchmann-Møller. *Someone to Watch Over Me: The Life and Music of Ben Webster.* Ann Arbor: University of Michigan Press, 2006; Hayden Carruth. "Ben Webster." *The American Poetry Review* 21.4 (July/August 1992): 17–19; _____. *Sitting In: Selected Writings on Jazz, Blues, and Related Topics.* Iowa City, IA: University of Iowa Press, 1993; Jeroen de Valk. *Ben Webster: His Life and Music.* Berkeley, CA: Berkeley Hills Books, [United States]: Distributed by Publishers Group West, 2001; Bill Dobbins. "Jazz and Academia: Street Music in the Ivory Tower." *Bulletin of the Council for Research in Music Education* 96, Research in Jazz Education II (Spring 1988): 30–41; Jan Evensmo. *The Tenor Saxophone of Ben Webster, 1931–1943.* Hosle, Norway: Jan Evensmo, 1978; Coleman Hawkins, Lester Young, and Ben Webster. *The Big Three Coleman Hawkins, Lester Young, Ben Webster.* New York: Doctor Jazz Records 1987; Nat Hentoff. "Jazz and the Intellectuals: Somebody Goofed." *Chicago Review* 9.3, Changing American Culture (Fall 1955): 110–121; Peter Hollerbach. "(Re)voicing Tradition: Improvising Aesthetics and Identity on Local Jazz Scenes." *Popular Music* 23.2 (May 2004): 155–171; Barry Ulanov. "Jazz: Issues of Identity." *The Musical Quarterly* 65.2 (April 1979): 245–256.

22. James J. Cooke. *American Girls, Beer, and Glenn Miller: GI Morale in World War II.* Columbia: University of Missouri Press, 2012; John Flower. *Moonlight Serenade; A Bio-discography of the Glenn Miller Civilian Band.* New Rochelle, NY: Arlington House, 1972; Edward F. Polic. *The Glenn Miller Army Air Force Band: Sustineo Alas = I Sustain the Wings.* Metuchen, NJ: Scarecrow Press; [New Brunswick, NJ]: Institute of Jazz Studies, Rutgers University, 1989; George Thomas Simon. *Glenn Miller and His Orchestra.* New York: Da Capo Press, 1980.

23. Leonard Brown and The Kansas City Jazz Museum. *Kansas City . . . And All That Jazz.* Riverside, NJ: Andrews McMeel Publishing, 1999; Frank Driggs and Chuck Haddix. *Kansas City Jazz: From Ragtime to Bebop—A History.* Oxford: Oxford University Press, 2005; Jacqueline Herschberg. "Kansas City: The Jazz Scene." *ALA Bulletin* 62.5 (May 1968): 517–518; Nathan W. Pearson. *Goin' to Kansas City.* Urbana: University of Illinois Press, 1987; _____. "Political and Musical Forces That Influenced the Development of Kansas City Jazz." *Black Music Research Journal* 9.2, Papers of the 1989 National Conference on Black Music Research (Autumn 1989): 181–192; Ross Russell. *Jazz Style in Kansas City and the Southwest.* Berkeley: University of California Press, 1971; Martin Williams. "Jazz: What Happened in Kansas City?" *American Music* 3.2 (Summer 1985): 171–179.

24. Frank Büchmann-Møller. *You Just Fight for Your Life: The Story of Lester Young.* New York: Praeger, 1990; Douglas Henry Daniels. "Lester Young: Master of Jive." *American Music* 3.3 (Autumn 1985): 313–328; _____. *Lester Leaps In: The Life and Times of Lester "Pres" Young.* Boston: Beacon Press, 2002; _____. "North Side Jazz: Lester 'Pres' Young in Minneapolis: The Formative Years." *Minnesota History* 59.3 (Fall 2004): 96–109; Luc Delannoy. *Pres: The Story of Lester Young.* Fayetteville: University of Arkansas Press, 1993; Dave Gelly. *Being Prez: The Life and Music of Lester Young.* New York: Oxford University Press, 2007; Lewis Porter. "Lester Leaps in: The Early Style of Lester Young." *The Black Perspective in Music* 9.1 (Spring 1981): 3–24; _____. *A Lester Young Reader.* Washington; London: Smithsonian Institution Press, United States of America, 1991.

25. Nicholas Churchill. *Stan Getz: An Annotated Bibliography and Filmography, with Song and Session Information for Albums.* Jefferson: McFarland & Company, Inc., Publishers, 2004; Dave Gelly. *Stan Getz: Nobody Else but Me.* San Francisco: Backbeat Books, 2002; Donald L. Maggin. *Stan Getz: A Life in Jazz.* New York: W. Morrow & Co., 1996; Richard Palmer. *Stan Getz.* London: Apollo, 1988.

26. Eddy Determeyer. *Rhythm Is Our Business: Jimmie Lunceford and the Harlem Express.* Ann Arbor: University of Michigan Press, 2006; Gene Lees. *Cats of Any Color: Jazz Black and White.* New York: Oxford University Press, 1994; Dempsey J. Travis. "Chicago's Jazz Trail, 1893–1950." *Black Music Research Journal* 10.1 (Spring 1990): 82–85; Christopher Wilkinson. "Hot and Sweet: Big Band Music in Black West Virginia before the Swing Era." *American Music* 21.2 (Summer 2003): 159–179.

27. Geoffrey L. Collier and James Lincoln Collier. "An Exploration of the Use of Tempo in Jazz." *Music Perception: An Interdisciplinary Journal* 11.3 (Spring 1994): 219–242; Leonard Lyons. *The Great Jazz Pianists: Speaking of Their Lives and Music*. New York: W. Morrow, 1983; Teddy Wilson, Arie Ligthart, and Humphrey Van Loo. *Teddy Wilson Talks Jazz*. New York: Continuum, 2001.

28. David W. Stowe. "Jazz in the West: Cultural Frontier and Region during the Swing Era." *The Western Historical Quarterly* 23.1 (February 1992): 53–73; Alex van der Tuuk. *Out of Anonymity: The Paramount and Broadway Territory Bands*. Glenwood Springs, CO: Rustbooks Publishing, 2014; Patrice Madura Ward-Steinman. "Musical Training and Compensation in the Big Band Era: A Case Study of Madura's Danceland from 1930–1950." *Journal of Historical Research in Music Education* 24.2 (April 2003): 164–177; Christopher Wilkinson. "A National Band from the Southwest: The Don Albert Orchestra." *American Music* 14.3 (Autumn 1996): 313–351; _____. *Jazz on the Road: Don Albert's Musical Life*. Berkeley: University of California Press; [Chicago]: Center for Black Music Research Columbia College, Chicago, 2001; John Wriggle. "Chappie Willet, Frank Fairfax, and Phil Edwards' Collegians: From West Virginia to Philadelphia." *Black Music Research Journal* 27.1 (Spring 2007): 1–22.

29. Jean Ann Boyd. *The Jazz of the Southwest: An Oral History of Western Swing*. Austin: University of Texas Press, 1998; _____. *Dance All Night: Those Other Southwestern Swing Bands, Past and Present*. Lubbock: Texas Tech University Press, 2012.

30. Cary Ginell and Roy Lee Brown. *Milton Brown and the Founding of Western Swing*. Urbana: University of Illinois Press, 1994.

31. Emily K. Abel. *Tuberculosis and the Politics of Exclusion: A History of Public Health and Migration to Los Angeles*. New Brunswick, NJ: Rutgers University Press, 2007; Martin Butler. *Voices of the Down and Out: The Dust Bowl Migration and the Great Depression in the Songs of Woody Guthrie*. Heidelberg: Winter, 2007; Joan M. Crouse. *The Homeless Transient in the Great Depression: New York State, 1929–1941*. Albany NY: State University of New York Press, 1986; James N. Gregory. *American Exodus: The Dust Bowl Migration and Okie Culture in California*. New York: Oxford University Press, 1989; Dan Morgan. *Rising in the West: The True Story of an "Okie" Family from the Great Depression through the Reagan Years*. New York: Knopf: Distributed by Random House, 1992; Charles J. Shindo. *Dust Bowl Migrants in the American Imagination*. Lawrence: University Press of Kansas, 1997; Walter J. Stein. *California and the Dust Bowl Migration*. Westport, CT: Greenwood Press, 1973; Sarah D. Wald. *The Nature of California: Race, Citizenship, and Farming since the Dust Bowl*. Seattle: University of Washington Press, 2016.

32. Richard Kienzle. *Southwest Shuffle: Pioneers of Honky Tonk, Western Swing, and Country Jazz*. New York: Routledge, 2003.

33. Travis T. J. Walker. *Western Swing Music: A Complete Reference Guide*. [Charleston, SC]: [CreateSpace Independent Publishing Platform], 2016.

34. Mathew J. Bartkowiak and Yuya Kiuchi. *The Music of Counterculture Cinema: A Critical Study of 1960s and 1970s Soundtracks* . Jefferson, NC: McFarland & Company, Inc., 2015; David W. Bernstein. *The San Francisco Tape Music Center: 1960s Counterculture and the Avant-Garde*. Berkeley: University of California Press, 2008; Peter Braunstein and Michael William Doyle. *Imagine Nation: The American Counterculture of the 1960s and '70s*. New York: Routledge, 2002; David Mark Chalmers. *And the Crooked Places Made Straight: The Struggle for Social Change in the 1960s*. Baltimore: Johns Hopkins University Press, 1991; Robert C. Cottrell. *Sex, Drugs, and Rock 'n' Roll: The Rise of America's 1960s Counterculture*. Lanham, MD: Rowman & Littlefield, 2015; Christoph Grunenberg, Jonathan Harris, and Tate Gallery Liverpool. *Summer of Love: Psychedelic Art, Social Crisis and Counterculture in the 1960s*. Liverpool: Liverpool University Press, 2005; Jeff Kisseloff. *Generation on Fire: Voices of Protest from the 1960s: An Oral History*. Lexington, KY: University Press of Kentucky, 2007; Rebecca E. Klatch. *A Generation Divided: The New Left, The New Right, and the 1960s*. Berkeley: University of California Press, 1999.

35. Burt Korall. *Drummin' Men: The Heartbeat of Jazz, The Swing Years*. New York: Schirmer Books; Toronto: Collier Macmillan Canada; New York: Maxwell Macmillan International, 1990; _____. *Drummin' Men: The Heartbeat of Jazz: The Bebop Years*. Oxford; New

York: Oxford University Press, 2002; Mel Tormé. *Traps, The Drum Wonder: The Life of Buddy Rich*. New York: Oxford University Press, 1991.

36. Lawrence McClellan. *The Later Swing Era, 1942 to 1955*. Westport, CT: Greenwood, 2004.

37. Maureen Reilly. *Swing Style: Fashions of the 1930s–1950s*. Atglen, PA: Schiffer, 1999.

38. Lewis Erenberg. *Swingin' the Dream: Big Band Jazz and the Rebirth of American Culture*. Chicago: University of Chicago Press, 1999; Ira Gitler. *Swing to Bop: An Oral History of the Transition in Jazz in the 1940s*. New York: Oxford University Press, USA, 1987; Dave Oliphant. *The Early Swing Era, 1930 to 1941*. Westport, CT: Greenwood Press, 2002; Gunther Schuller. *The Swing Era: The Development of Jazz, 1930–1945*. New York: Oxford University Press, USA, 1991.

39. Kenneth S. Davis. *FDR, The New Deal Years, 1933–1937: A History*. New York: Random House, 1986; Michael A. Hiltzik. *The New Deal: A Modern History*. New York: Free Press, 2011; William E. Leuchtenburg. *Franklin D. Roosevelt and the New Deal, 1932–1940*. New York: Harper & Row, 1963; _____. *The New Deal: A Documentary History*. Columbia: University of South Carolina Press, 1968; Robert S. McElvaine. *The Depression and New Deal: A History in Documents*. New York: Oxford University Press, 2000; Broadus Mitchell. *Depression Decade; From New Era through New Deal, 1929–1941*. New York, Rinehart, 1947.

40. Richard Bak. *Joe Louis: The Great Black Hope*. New York: Da Capo Press, 1998; Art Evans. "Joe Louis as a Key Functionary: White Reactions Toward a Black Champion." *Journal of Black Studies* 16.1 (September 1985): 95–111; Anthony Foy. "Joe Louis's Talking Fists: The Auto/Biopolitics of 'My Life Story.'" *American Literary History* 23.2 (Summer 2011): 311–336; Lew Freedman. *Joe Louis: The Life of a Heavyweight*. Jefferson, NC: McFarland & Company, Inc., Publishers, 2013; Thomas R. Hietala. *The Fight of the Century: Jack Johnson, Joe Louis, and the Struggle for Racial Equality*. Armonk, NY: M. E. Sharpe, 2004; Joe Louis, Edna Rust, and Art Rust. *Joe Louis: My Life*. Hopewell, NJ: Ecco Press, 1997; David Margolick. *Beyond Glory: Joe Louis vs. Max Schmeling and a World on the Brink*. New York: Vintage Books, 2006; Donald McRae. *In Black & White: The Untold Story of Joe Louis and Jesse Owens*. London: Simon & Schuster, 2014; Patrick Myler. *Ring of Hate: The Brown Bomber and Hitler's Hero, Joe Louis v. Max Schmeling and the Bitter Propaganda War*. Edinburgh: Mainstream, 2006; Randy Roberts. *Joe Louis: Hard Times Man*. New Haven: Yale University Press, 2010; Lauren Rebecca Sklaroff. "Constructing G.I. Joe Louis: Cultural Solutions to the 'Negro Problem' during World War II." *The Journal of American History* 89.3 (December 2002): 958–983.

41. Leslie Gourse. *Unforgettable: The Life and Mystique of Nat King Cole*. New York: St. Martin's Press, 1991; Karen McNally. "'Where's the Spinning Wheel?' Frank Sinatra and Working-Class Alienation in 'Young at Heart.'" *Journal of American Studies* 41.1 (April 2007): 115–133; _____. *When Frankie Went to Hollywood: Frank Sinatra and American Male Identity*. Urbana: University of Illinois Press, 2008; Gerald Meyer. "Frank Sinatra: The Popular Front and an American Icon." *Science & Society* 66.3 (Fall 2002): 311–335; Steven Petkov and Leonard Mustazza. *The Frank Sinatra Reader*. New York: Oxford University Press, 1995; Gene Ringgold and Clifford McCarty. *The Films of Frank Sinatra*. New York: Citadel Press, 1971; Chris Rojek. *Frank Sinatra*. Cambridge; Malden, MA: Polity, 2004; David Stowe. *Swing Changes: Big-Band Jazz in New Deal America*. Cambridge, MA: Harvard University Press, 1996; Brian Ward. "Civil Rights and Rock and Roll: Revisiting the Nat King Cole Attack of 1956." *OAH Magazine of History* 24.2 (April 2010): 21–24.

42. Janna Tull Steed. *Duke Ellington: A Spiritual Biography*. New York: Crossroad Pub. Co., 1999.

43. Matthew H. Bernstein and Dana F. White. "'Imitation of Life' in a Segregated Atlanta: Its Promotion, Distribution and Reception." *Film History* 19.2, Film and Copyright (2007): 152–178; Karen M. Bowdre. "Passing Films and the Illusion of Racial Equality." *Black Camera* 5.2 (Spring 2014): 21–43; Jonathan Dewberry. "Black Actors Unite: The Negro Actors' Guild." *The Black Scholar* 21.2, Black Cinema (March–April–May 1990): 2–11; Miriam J. Petty. *Stealing the Show: African American Performers and Audiences in 1930s Hollywood*. Oakland, CA: University of California Press, 2016; Charlene B. Regester. *African American*

Actresses: The Struggle for Visibility, 1900–1960. Bloomington: Indiana University Press, 2010; Ellen Scott. "More than a 'Passing' Sophistication: Dress, Film Regulation, and the Color Line in 1930s American Films." *Women's Studies Quarterly* 41.1/2, Fashion (Spring/ Summer 2012): 60–86.

44. Ezra Chitando and Nordiska Afrikainstitutet. *Singing Culture: A Study of Gospel Music in Zimbabwe*. Uppsala: Nordiska Afrikainstitutet; Somerset, NJ: Transaction Publishers (distributor), 2002; Don Cusic. *The Sound of Light: A History of Gospel Music*. Bowling Green, OH: Bowling Green State University Popular Press, 1990; Douglas Harrison. *Then Sings My Soul: The Culture of Southern Gospel Music*. Urbana: University of Illinois Press, 2012; Mark W. Lewis. *The Diffusion of Black Gospel Music in Postmodern Denmark: How Mission and Music Are Combining to Affect Christian Renewal*. Lexington, KY: Emeth Press, 2010; Robert M. Marovich. *A City Called Heaven: Chicago and the Birth of Gospel Music*. Urbana: University of Illinois Press, 2015; William Lynwood Montell. *Singing the Glory Down: Amateur Gospel Music in South Central Kentucky, 1900–1990*. Lexington: University Press of Kentucky, 1991; Timothy Rommen. *"Mek Some Noise": Gospel Music and the Ethics of Style in Trinidad*. Berkeley: University of California Press; Chicago: Center for Black Music Research, Columbia College, 2007.

45. Linda Dahl. *Morning Glory: A Biography of Mary Lou Williams*. New York: Pantheon Books, 2000; D. Antoinette Handy and Mary Lou Williams. "First Lady of the Jazz Keyboard." *The Black Perspective in Music* 8.2 (Autumn 1980): 194–214; Tammy Lynn Kernodle. "This Is My Story, This Is My Song: The Historiography of Vatican II, Black Catholic Identity, Jazz, and the Religious Compositions of Mary Lou Williams." *U.S. Catholic Historian* 19.2, African American Spirituality and Liturgical Renewal (Spring 2001): 83–94; _____. *Soul on Soul: The Life and Music of Mary Lou Williams*. Boston: Northeastern University Press, 2004; Gayle Murchison. "Mary Lou Williams's Hymn 'Black Christ of the Andes (St. Martin de Porres)': Vatican II, Civil Rights, and Jazz as Sacred Music." *The Musical Quarterly* 86.4 (Winter 2002): 591–629; Kimberly Hannon Teal. "Posthumously Live: Canon Formation at Jazz at Lincoln Center through the Case of Mary Lou Williams." *American Music* 32.4 (Winter 2014): 400–422.

46. Alvin Ailey and A. Peter Bailey. *Revelations: The Autobiography of Alvin Ailey*. Secaucus, NJ: Carol Pub. Group, 1995; Thomas DeFrantz. *Dancing Many Drums: Excavations in African American Dance*. Madison, WI: University of Wisconsin Press, 2002; _____. *Dancing Revelations: Alvin Ailey's Embodiment of African American Culture*. New York: Oxford University Press, 2004; _____. "Composite Bodies of Dance: The Repertory of the Alvin Ailey American Dance Theater." *Theatre Journal* 57.4, Black Performance (December 2005): 659–678; Brenda Dixon. "Black Dance and Dancers and the White Public: A Prolegomenon to Problems of Definition." *Black American Literature Forum* 24.1 (Spring 1990): 117–123; Jennifer Dunning. *Alvin Ailey: A Life in Dance*. Reading, MA: Addison-Wesley, 1996; Julia L. Foulkes. *Modern Bodies: Dance and American Modernism from Martha Graham to Alvin Ailey*. Chapel Hill: University of North Carolina Press, 2002.

47. Giles Oakley. *The Devil's Music: A History of the Blues*. London: British Broadcasting Corp., 1983.

48. Neil Leonard. *Jazz: Myth and Religion*. New York: Oxford University Press, 1987.

49. Scott Allen Nollen. *Paul Robeson: Film Pioneer*. Jefferson, NC: McFarland, 2010; Tony Perucci. *Paul Robeson and the Cold War Performance Complex: Race, Madness, Activism*. Ann Arbor: University of Michigan Press, 2012; Paul Robeson. *The Negro People and the Soviet Union*. New York: New Century Publishers, 1950.

50. Ben Kamin. "Harry Belafonte, Janet Levison, and a Totally Different 'Kennedy.'" *Dangerous Friendship: Stanley Levison, Martin Luther King Jr., and the Kennedy Brothers*. East Lansing: Michigan State University Press, 2014, 67–82; Michelle Stephens. "The First Negro Matinee Idol: Harry Belafonte and American Culture in the 1950s." In *Left of the Color Line: Race, Radicalism, and Twentieth-Century Literature of the United States*, edited by Bill Mullen and James Edward Smethurst. Chapel Hill: University of North Carolina Press, 2003, 223–238.

51. Elizabeth Abel. *Signs of the Times: The Visual Politics of Jim Crow*. Berkeley, CA: University of California Press, 2010; Garna L. Christian. *Black Soldiers in Jim Crow Texas, 1899–1917*. College Station: Texas A & M University Press, 1995; Douglas Flamming. *Bound*

for Freedom: Black Los Angeles in Jim Crow America. Berkeley: University of California Press, 2005; Alan Howard Levy. *Tackling Jim Crow: Racial Segregation in Professional Football*. Jefferson, NC: McFarland & Co, 2003; Catherine M. Lewis and J. Richard Lewis. *Jim Crow America: A Documentary History*. Fayetteville: University of Arkansas Press, 2009; Francesca Morgan. *Women and Patriotism in Jim Crow America*. Chapel Hill: University of North Carolina Press, 2005; Brian Norman and Piper Kendrix Williams. *Representing Segregation: Toward an Aesthetics of Living Jim Crow, and Other Forms of Racial Division*. Albany: State University of New York Press, 2010; Mark R. Schneider. *Boston Confronts Jim Crow, 1890–1920*. Boston: Northeastern University Press, 1997; Stephanie J. Shaw. *What a Woman Ought To Be and To Do: Black Professional Women Workers During the Jim Crow Era*. Chicago: University of Chicago Press, 1996; Katherine S. Van Wormer, David W. Jackson, and Charletta Sudduth. *The Maid Narratives: Black Domestic and White Families in the Jim Crow South*. Baton Rouge: Louisiana State University Press, 2012.

52. Susan Delson. *Dudley Murphy, Hollywood Wild Card*. Minneapolis: University of Minnesota Press, 2006.

53. Peter Stanfield. "An Excursion into the Lower Depths: Hollywood, Urban Primitivism, and 'St. Louis Blues,' 1929–1937." *Cinema Journal* 41.2 (Winter 2002): 84–108.

54. Ruby Cohn. "Black Power on Stage: Emperor Jones and King Christophe." *Yale French Studies* 46, From Stage to Street (1971): 41–47; Garrett Eisler. "Backstory as Black Story: The Cinematic Reinvention of O'Neill's 'The Emperor Jones.'" *The Eugene O'Neill Review* 32 (2010): 148–162; Rebecca B. Gauss. "O'Neill, Gruenberg and 'The Emperor Jones.'" *The Eugene O'Neill Review* 18.1/2 (Spring/Fall 1994): 38–44; Carme Manuel. "A Ghost in the Expressionist Jungle of O'Neill's 'The Emperor Jones.'" *African American Review* 39.1/2 (Spring–Summer 2005): 67–85; Brenda Murphy. "McTeague's Dream and 'The Emperor Jones': O'Neill's Move from Naturalism to Modernism." *The Eugene O'Neill Review* 17.1/2 (Spring/Fall 1993): 21–29; Eugene O'Neill. *The Emperor Jones, The Straw, and Diff'rent: Three Plays*. London: J. Cape, 1922; Alexander Pettit, James Baird, and Jacqueline Vanhoutte. "Bob Dylan and The Emperor Jones Revisited." *The Eugene O'Neill Review* 33.2 (2012): 273–274; Peter R. Saiz. "The Colonial Story in 'The Emperor Jones.'" *The Eugene O'Neill Review* 17.1/2 (Spring/Fall 1993): 30–38; Jennie Saxena, Ken Weissman, and James Cozart. "Preserving African-American Cinema: The Case of 'The Emperor Jones' (1933)." *The Moving Image: The Journal of the Association of Moving Image Archivists* 3.1 (Spring 2003): 42–58; Shannon Steen. "Melancholy Bodies: Racial Subjectivity and Whiteness in O'Neill's "The Emperor Jones." *Theatre Journal* 52.3 (October 2000): 339–359.

55. Suzanne Bost. *Mulattas and Mestizas: Representing Mixed Identities in the Americas, 1850–2000*. Athens: The University of Georgia Press, 2003; Kimberly Snyder Manganelli and American Literatures Initiative. *Transatlantic Spectacles of Race: The Tragic Mulatta and the Tragic Muse*. New Brunswick, NJ: Rutgers University Press, 2012; Joel Williamson. *New People: Miscegenation and Mulattoes in the United States*. New York: Free Press, 1980.

56. Pamela Robertson. *Guilty Pleasures: Feminist Camp from Mae West to Madonna*. Durham: Duke University Press, 1996.

57. Champ Clark. *Shuffling to Ignominy: The Tragedy of Stepin Fetchit*. New York: iUniverse, 2005; Kimberly Fain. *Black Hollywood: From Butlers to Superheroes, The Changing Role of African American Men in the Movies*. Santa Barbara, CA: Praeger, an imprint of ABC-Clio, 2015; Paul Loukides and Linda K. Fuller. *Beyond the Stars: Stock Characters in American Popular Film*. Bowling Green, OH: Bowling Green University Popular Press, 1990; Yuval Taylor and Jake Austen. *Darkest America: Black Minstrelsy From Slavery to Hip-Hop*. New York: W. W. Norton, 2012; Mel Watkins. *Stepin Fetchit: The Life and Times of Lincoln Perry*. New York: Pantheon Books, 2005. Llc, 2015.

58. Harvey G. Cohen. "Duke Ellington and 'Black, Brown and Beige': The Composer as Historian at Carnegie Hall." *American Quarterly* 56.4 (December 2004): 1003–1034; Scott DeVeaux. "'Black, Brown and Beige' and the Critics." *Black Music Research Journal* 13.2 (Autumn 1993): 125–146; Kurt Dietrich. "The Role of Trombones in 'Black, Brown and Beige.'" *Black Music Research Journal* 13.2 (Autumn 1993): 111–124; Sjef Hoefsmit and Andrew Homzy. "Chronology of Ellington's Recordings and Performances of 'Black, Brown and Beige,' 1943–1973." *Black Music Research Journal* 13.2 (Autumn 1993): 161–173; An-

drew Homzy. "'Black, Brown and Beige' in Duke Ellington's Repertoire, 1943–1973." *Black Music Research Journal* 13.2 (Autumn 1993): 87–110; Wolfram Knauer. "'Simulated Improvisation' in Duke Ellington's 'Black, Brown and Beige.'" *The Black Perspective in Music* 18.1/2 (1990): 20–38; Maurice Peress. "My Life with 'Black, Brown and Beige.'" *Black Music Research Journal* 13.2 (Autumn 1993): 147–160; Mark Tucker. "The Genesis of 'Black, Brown and Beige.'" *Black Music Research Journal* 22 Supplement: Best of BMRJ (2002): 131–150.

59. Ayé Aton and John Corbett. *Sun Ra + Ayé Aton: Space, Interiors and Exteriors, 1972.* Brooklyn, NY: PictureBox, 2013; John Corbett, Anthony Elms, Terri Kapsalis, Hyde Park Art Center (Chicago, Ill.). *Pathways to Unknown Worlds: Sun-Ra, El Saturn and Chicago's Afro-Futurist Underground 1954–68.* Chicago: WhiteWalls, 2006; Tam Fiofori and Leni Sinclair. *Sun Ra: Myth, Music & Media.* London: Karnak House, 2014; Daniel Kreiss. "Performing the Past to Claim the Future: Sun Ra and the Afro-Future Underground, 1954–1968." *African American Review* 45.1/2 (Spring/Summer 2012): 197–203; Sun Ra. *The Immeasurable Equation: The Collected Poetry and Prose.* Wartaweil: Waitawhile, 2005; Sun Ra and John Corbett. *The Wisdom of Sun-Ra: Sun Ra's Polemical Broadsheets and Streetcorner Leaflets.* Chicago: WhiteWalls, 2006; J. Griffith Rollefson. "The 'Robot Voodoo Power' Thesis: Afrofuturism and Anti-Anti-Essentialism from Sun Ra to Kool Keith." *Black Music Research Journal* 28.1, Becoming: Blackness and the Musical Imagination (Spring 2008): 83–109; John F. Szwed. *Space is the Place: The Lives and Times of Sun Ra.* New York: Pantheon Books, 1997; Paul Youngquist. *A Pure Solar World: Sun Ra and the Birth of Afrofuturism.* Austin: University of Texas Press, 2016.

60. André M. Carrington. *Speculative Blackness: The Future of Race in Science Fiction.* Minneapolis: University of Minnesota Press, 2016; Sharon DeGraw. *The Subject of Race in American Science Fiction.* New York: Routledge, 2007; Samuel R. Delany. *Silent Interviews: On Language, Race, Sex, Science Fiction, and Some Comics: A Collection of Written Interviews.* Hanover, NH: Wesleyan University Press, 1994; Jason Haslam. *Gender, Race, and American Science Fiction: Reflections on Fantastic Identities.* Hoboken: Taylor and Francis, 2015; Isiah Lavender, III. *Race in American Science Fiction.* Bloomington: Indiana University Press, 2011; _____. *Black and Brown Planets: The Politics of Race in Science Fiction.* Jackson: University Press of Mississippi, 2014; Adilifu Nama. *Black Space: Imagining Race in Science Fiction Film.* Austin: University of Texas Press, 2008.

61. Graham Lock. *Blutopia: Visions of the Future and Revisions of the Past in the Work of Sun Ra, Duke Ellington, and Anthony Braxton.* Durham: Duke University Press, 1999.

62. James E. Perone. *The Sound of Stevie Wonder: His Words and Music.* Westport, CT: Praeger, 2006; Mark Ribowsky. *Signed, Sealed, and Delivered: The Soulful Journey of Stevie Wonder.* Hoboken, NJ: John Wiley & Sons, 2010; Terry Rowden. *The Songs of Blind Folk: African American Musicians and the Cultures of Blindness.* Ann Arbor: University of Michigan Press, 2009; Craig Hansen Werner. *Higher Ground: Stevie Wonder, Aretha Franklin, Curtis Mayfield, and the Rise and Fall of American Soul.* New York: Crown Publishers, 2004.

63. Roger Nichols. *Stravinsky.* Milton Keynes: Open University Press, 1978; Igor Stravinsky. *Igor Stravinsky, An Autobiography.* New York: W. W. Norton & Company, Inc., 1962; Igor Stravinsky and Robert Craft. *Conversations with Igor Stravinsky.* Garden City, NY: Doubleday, 1959; Vera Stravinsky, Robert Craft, and Otto Klemperer Archive (Library of Congress). *Stravinsky in Pictures and Documents.* New York: Simon & Schuster, 1978; Roman Vlad, Frederick Fuller, and Ann Fuller. *Stravinsky.* London; New York: Oxford University Press, 1967.

64. Steven Baur. "Ravel's 'Russian' Period: Octatonicism in His Early Works, 1893–1908." *Journal of the American Musicological Society* 52.3 (Autumn 1999): 531–592; Roger Delage and Frayda Lindemann. "Ravel and Chabrier." *The Musical Quarterly* 61.4 (October 1975): 546–552; Jessie Fillerup. "Ravel, 'La Valse,' and the Purloined Plot." *College Music Symposium* 49/50 (2009/2010): 345–355; _____. "Ravel and Robert-Houdin, Magicians." *19th-Century Music* 37.2 (Fall 2013): 130–158; Edward Burlingame Hill. *Maurice Ravel. The Musical Quarterly* 13.1 (January 1927): 130–146; Emily Kilpatrick. "Into the Woods: Retelling the Wartime Fairytales of Maurice Ravel." *The Musical Times* 149.1902 (Spring 2008): 57–66; Arbie Orenstein. "Maurice Ravel's Creative Process." *The Musical Quarterly* 53.4 (October 1967): 467–481; _____. *Ravel: Man and Musician.* New York: Columbia University Press,

1975; Maurice Ravel and Arbie Orenstein. *A Ravel Reader: Correspondence, Articles, Interviews*. New York: Columbia University Press, 1990; Maurice Ravel, Vlado Perlemuter, Hélène Jourdan-Morhange, and Harold Taylor. *Ravel According to Ravel*. London: Kahn & Averill, 1988.

65. David Hajdu. *Lush Life: A Biography of Billy Strayhorn*. New York: North Point Press, 1996; Walter van de Leur. *Something To Live For: The Music of Billy Strayhorn*. New York: Oxford University Press, 2002.

66. Lisa Barg. "Queer Encounters in the Music of Billy Strayhorn." *Journal of the American Musicological Society* 66.3 (Fall 2013): 771–824; Patrick Burke. "Oasis of Swing: The Onyx Club, Jazz, and White Masculinity in the Early 1930s." *American Music* 24.3 (Autumn 2006): 320–346; Benjamin Piekut. "New Thing? Gender and Sexuality in the Jazz Composers Guild." *American Quarterly* 62.1 (March 2010): 25–48.

67. A. H. Lawrence. *Duke Ellington and His World: A Biography*. New York: Routledge, 2001.

68. Ken Rattenbury. *Duke Ellington, Jazz Composer*. London; New Haven: Yale University Press, 1990.

69. W. E. Timner. *Ellingtonia: The Recorded Music of Duke Ellington and his Sidemen*. Metuchen, NJ: Institute of Jazz Studies: Scarecrow Press, 1988.

70. Matthew J. Cooper and Michael J. Budds. *Duke Ellington as Pianist: A Study of Styles*. Missoula, MT: The College Music Society, 2013; Duke Ellington. *Duke Ellington Piano Method for Blues*. New York: Robbins Music Corp., 1943; Luvenia A. George. "Duke Ellington the Man and His Music." *Music Educators Journal* 85.6 (May 1999): 15–21; Gene Rizzo. *The Fifty Greatest Jazz Piano Players of all Time: Ranking, Analysis & Photos*. Milwaukee, WI: Hal Leonard Corporation, 2005.

71. Fritz Gysin. "Double-Jointed Time in Nathaniel Mackey's Jazz Fiction." *Amerikastudien/American Studies* 45.4, Time and the African-American Experience (2000): 513–518; George Kerr. "Belfast, Home of Amazing Jazz." *Fortnight* 410 (January 2003): 19; John R. Sansevere and Erica Farber. *Post-Bop Hip-Hop: A Tribe Called Quest*. [Racine, WI]: Western Pub. Co., 1993; Jeremy Yudkin. *Miles Davis, Miles Smiles, and the Invention of Post Bop*. Bloomington: Indiana University Press, 2008.

72. Geoffrey Holden Block and J. Peter Burkholder. *Charles Ives and the Classical Tradition*. New Haven: Yale University Press, 1996; J. Peter Burkholder. *Charles Ives, The Ideas Behind The Music*. New Haven: Yale University Press, 1985; _____. *All Made of Tunes: Charles Ives and the Uses of Musical Borrowing*. New Haven: Yale University Press, 1995; _____. *Charles Ives and His World*. Princeton, NJ: Princeton University Press, 1996; Henry Cowell and Sidney Robertson Cowell. *Charles Ives and His Music*. New York: Oxford University Press, 1955; Henry Cowell, Sidney Robertson Cowell, and Paul Avrich Collection (Library of Congress). *Charles Ives and His Music*. London; New York: Oxford University Press, 1969; Stuart Feder. *The Life of Charles Ives*. Cambridge; New York: Cambridge University Press, 1999; Charles Ives and Thomas Clarke Owens. *Selected Correspondence of Charles Ives*. Berkeley: University of California Press, 2007; Philip Lambert. *The Music of Charles Ives*. New Haven: Yale University Press, 1997; Gayle Sherwood Magee. *Charles Ives Reconsidered*. Urbana: University of Illinois Press, 2008; David C. Paul. *Charles Ives in the Mirror: American Histories of an Iconic Composer*. Urbana; Chicago; Springfield: University of Illinois Press, 2013; Vivian Perlis. *Charles Ives Remembered: An Oral History*. New Haven: Yale University Press, 1974; Rosalie Sandra Perry. *Charles Ives and the American Mind*. Kent, OH: Kent State University Press, 1974; Joseph W. Reed. *Three American Originals: John Ford, William Faulkner & Charles Ives*. Middletown, CT: Wesleyan University Press; Scranton, PA: Distributed by Harper & Row, 1984; Larry Starr. *A Union of Diversities: Style in the Music of Charles Ives*. New York: Schirmer Books; Toronto: Maxwell Macmillan Canada; New York: Maxwell Macmillan International, 1992; Jan Swafford. *Charles Ives: A Life With Music*. New York: W. W. Norton, 1996.

73. Wilbur R. Jacobs. *Dispossessing the American Indian: Indians and Whites on the Colonial Frontier*. New York: Scribner, 1972; Janet A. McDonnell. *The Dispossession of the American Indian, 1887–1934*. Bloomington: Indiana University Press, 1991; Peter Nabokov. *Native American Testimony: A Chronicle of Indian-White Relations from Prophecy to the*

Present, 1492–1992. New York: Viking, 1991; George D. Pappas. *The Literary and Legal Genealogy of Native American Dispossession: The Marshall Trilogy Cases.* Abingdon, Oxon; New York: Routledge, Taylor & Francis Group, 2017.

74. Donald V. Gawronski. *Transcendentlism: An Ideological Basis for Manifest Destiny.* Thesis/dissertation: Ann Arbor, MI, University Microfilms, 1969; Laura E. Gómez. *Manifest Destinies: The Making of the Mexican American Race.* New York: New York University, 2007; David W. Haines and Carol A. Mortland. *Manifest Destinies: Americanizing Immigrants and Internationalizing Americans.* Westport, CT: Praeger, 2001; Reginald Horsman. *Race and Manifest Destiny: The Origins of American Racial Anglo-Saxonism.* Cambridge, MA: Harvard University Press, 1981; Frederick Merk and Lois Bannister Merk. *Manifest Destiny and Mission in American History: A Reinterpretation.* Cambridge, MA: Harvard University Press, 1995.

75. "Colleges and Universities That Don't Observe the Martin Luther King Jr. Holiday." *The Journal of Blacks in Higher Education* 19 (Spring 1998): 26–27; Renée Ater. "Communities in Conflict: Memorializing Martin Luther King Jr. in Rocky Mount, North Carolina." *Indiana Magazine of History* 110.1, Special Issue—Art, Race, Space (March 2014): 32–39; Clayborne Carson, Peter Holloran, Ralph E. Luker, and Penny Russell. "Martin Luther King, Jr., as Scholar: A Reexamination of His Theological Writings." *The Journal of American History* 78.1 (June 1991): 93–105; Michael Eric Dyson. *I May Not Get There With You: The True Martin Luther King, Jr.* New York: Free Press, 2000; _____. *April 4, 1968: Martin Luther King, Jr.'s Death and How It Changed America.* New York: Basic Civitas Books, 2008; Robert Kelly and Erin Cook. "Martin Luther King, Jr., and Malcolm X: A Common Solution." *OAH Magazine of History* 19.1, Martin Luther King, Jr. (January 2005): 37–40; Martin Luther King, Jr. and Clayborne Carson. *The Autobiography of Martin Luther King, Jr.* New York: Intellectual Properties Management in association with Warner Books, 1998; Martin Luther King, Jr., Clayborne Carson, Peter Holloran, Ralph E. Luker, and Penny A. Russell. *The Papers of Martin Luther King, Jr.* Berkeley: University of California Press, 1992; Martin Luther King, Jr. and Coretta Scott King. *The Words of Martin Luther King, Jr.* New York: Newmarket Press, 1983; Martin Luther King, Jr. and Cornel West. *The Radical King.* Boston: Beacon Press, 2014; Levering Lewis, David. "Failing to Know Martin Luther King, Jr." *The Journal of American History* 78.1 (June 1991): 81–85; Keith D. Miller. "Composing Martin Luther King, Jr." *PMLA* 105.1, Special Topic: African and African American Literature (January 1990): 70–82; Douglas Sturm. "Martin Luther King, Jr., as Democratic Socialist." *The Journal of Religious Ethics* 18.2 (Fall 1990): 79–105.

76. Francis J. Bremer. *John Winthrop: America's Forgotten Founding Father.* New York: Oxford University Press, 2003; _____. *John Winthrop: Biography as History.* New York: Continuum, 2009; Edmund S. Morgan and Oscar Handlin. *The Puritan Dilemma: The Story of John Winthrop.* Boston: Little, Brown, and Company, 1958; John Winthrop, Richard S. Dunn, James Savage, and Laetitia Yeandle. *The Journal of John Winthrop, 1630–1649.* Cambridge, MA: Harvard University Press, 1996; John Winthrop and James K. Hosmer. *Winthrop's Journal, "History of New England," 1630–1649.* New York: C. Scribner's Sons, 1908; Robert C. Winthrop. *Life and Letters of John Winthrop: Governor of the Massachusetts-Bay Company at Their Emigration to New England, 1630.* Boston: Little, Brown, 1869; Walter William Woodward and Omohundro Institute of Early American History & Culture. *Prospero's America: John Winthrop, Jr., Alchemy, and the Creation of New England Culture, 1606–1676.* Chapel Hill: Published for the Omohundro Institute of Early American History and Culture by the University of North Carolina Press, 2010.

77. Barbara Reeves-Ellington, Kathryn Kish Sklar, and Connie Anne Shemo. *Competing Kingdoms: Women, Mission, Nation, and the American Protestant Empire, 1812–1960.* Durham [NC]: Duke University Press, 2010; Orrin Schwab. *Redeemer Nation: America and the World in the Technocratic Age, 1914 to the Present.* Salt Lake City, UT: American University & Colleges Press, 2004; William V. Spanos. *Redeemer Nation in the Interregnum: An Untimely Meditation on the American Vocation.* New York: Fordham University Press, 2015; Ernest Lee Tuveson. *Redeemer Nation: The Idea of America's Millennial Role.* Chicago: University of Chicago Press, 1968.

78. Jill L. Matus. *Toni Morrison*. Manchester; New York: Manchester University Press, 1998; Toni Morrison. *Playing in the Dark: Whiteness and the Literary Imagination*. Cambridge, MA: Harvard University Press, 1992; Toni Morrison and Danille Kathleen Taylor-Guthrie. *Conversations with Toni Morrison*. Jackson: University Press of Mississippi, 1994.

79. Julian Hawthorne. *Nathaniel Hawthorne and His Wife; A Biography*. Hamden, CT: Archon Books, 1968; Nathaniel Hawthorne. *The Complete Works of Nathaniel Hawthorne*. Boston: Houghton, Mifflin, 1882–1899; Leon Howard. *Herman Melville*. Minneapolis: University of Minnesota Press, 1961; James R. Mellow. *Nathaniel Hawthorne in His Times*. Boston: Houghton Mifflin, 1980; Herman Melville. *The Letters of Herman Melville*. New Haven: Yale University Press, 1960; Herman Melville & Douglas Robillard. *The Poems of Herman Melville*. Kent, OH: Kent State University Press, 2000.

80. Philip Abbott. *Exceptional America: Newness and National Identity*. New York: P. Lang, 1999.

81. Ryan C. Hendrickson. *Obama at War: Congress and the Imperial Presidency*. Lexington: The University Press of Kentucky, 2015; Mark J. Rozell and Gleaves Whitney. *Testing the Limits: George W. Bush and the Imperial Presidency*. Lanham, MD: Rowman & Littlefield, 2009; Andrew Rudalevige. *The New Imperial Presidency: Renewing Presidential Power After Watergate*. Ann Arbor: University of Michigan Press, 2006; Arthur M. Schlesinger, Jr., *The Imperial Presidency*. Boston: Houghton Mifflin, 1973.

82. Dan Berger. *Struggle Within: Prisons, Political Prisoners, and Mass Movements in the United States*. Oakland, CA: PM Press; Montreal, QC: Kersplebedeb, 2014; Philip Sheldon Foner and Richard C. Winchester. *The Anti-Imperialist Reader: A Documentary History of Anti-Imperialism in the United States*. New York: Holmes & Meier, 1984; E. Berkeley Tompkins. *Anti-Imperialism in the United States: The Great Debate, 1890–1920*. Philadelphia: University of Pennsylvania Press, 1970.

83. Dorinda Carter Andrews and Frank Tuitt. *Contesting the Myth of a "Post Racial Era": The Continued Significance of Race in U.S. Education*. New York: Peter Lang, 2013; David Ikard and Martell L. Teasley. *Nation of Cowards: Black Activism in Barack Obama's Post-Racial America*. Bloomington: Indiana University Press, 2012; Sarah E. Turner and Sarah Nilsen. *The Colorblind Screen: Television in Post-Racial America*. New York: NYU Press, 2014; Tim J. Wise. *Colorblind: The Rise of Post-Racial Politics and the Retreat from Racial Equity*. San Francisco, CA: City Lights Books, 2010.

84. Donald E. Pease. *The New American Exceptionalism*. Minneapolis: University of Minnesota Press, 2009.

85. Michelle Alexander. *The New Jim Crow: Mass Incarceration in the Age of Colorblindness*. New York: The New Press, 2010; _____. "The War on Drugs and the New Jim Crow." *Race, Poverty & the Environment* 17.1, 20th Anniversary Issue (Spring 2010): 75–77; V. P. Franklin. "Commentary: Predatory Capitalists, The New Jim Crow, and Restitutive Justice." *The Journal of African American History* 96.2 (Spring 2011): 147–150; Andy Kroll. "The African American Jobs Crisis and the New Jim Crow." *Race, Poverty & the Environment* 18.2, Autumn Awakening: From Civil Rights to Economic Justice (2011): 49–52.

86. Andrew J. Bacevich. *The Limits of Power: The End of American Exceptionalism*. New York: Metropolitan Books, 2008.

87. Seymour Martin Lipset. *American Exceptionalism: A Double-Edged Sword*. New York: W. W. Norton, 1996.

88. Trevor B. McCrisken. *American Exceptionalism and the Legacy of Vietnam: US Foreign Policy Since 1974*. Basingstoke, Hampshire; New York: Palgrave Macmillan, 2003; Siobhán McEvoy-Levy. *American Exceptionalism and US Foreign Policy: Public Diplomacy at the End of the Cold War*. Houndmills, Basingstoke, Hampshire; New York: Palgrave, 2001.

89. Arnold R. Isaacs and Rogers D. Spotswood Collection. *Vietnam Shadows: The War, Its Ghosts, and Its Legacy*. Baltimore: Johns Hopkins University Press, 1997; Michael T. Klare. *Beyond the "Vietnam Syndrome": U.S. Interventionism in the 1980s*. Washington, D.C.: Institute for Policy Studies, 1981; G. L. Simons. *Vietnam Syndrome: Impact on US Foreign Policy*. New York: St. Martin's Press, 1998.

90. Stephen A. Bourque and John W. Burdan. *The Road to Safwan: The 1st Squadron, 4th Cavalry in the 1991 Persian Gulf War*. Denton, TX: University of North Texas Press, 2007;

Lawrence Freedman and Efraim Karsh. *The Gulf Conflict, 1990–1991: Diplomacy and War in the New World Order*. Princeton, NJ: Princeton University Press, 1993; Susan Jeffords and Lauren Rabinovitz. *Seeing Through the Media: The Persian Gulf War*. New Brunswick, NJ: Rutgers University Press, 1994; Peter Liberman. "Punitiveness and U.S. Elite Support for the 1991 Persian Gulf War." *The Journal of Conflict Resolution* 51.1 (Feburary 2007): 3–32.

91. Charles A. Murray. *American Exceptionalism: An Experiment in History*. Washington, D.C.: AEI Press, 2013.

92. John A. Davis. *Naples and Napoleon: Southern Italy and the European Revolutions (1780–1860)*. Oxford; New York: Oxford University Press, 2006; Josef V. Polišenský. *Aristocrats and the Crowd in the Revolutionary Year 1848: A Contribution to the History of Revolution and Counter-Revolution in Austria*. Albany: State University of New York Press, 1980; Priscilla Smith Robertson. *Revolutions of 1848, A Social History*. Princeton: Princeton University Press, 1952; Jonathan Sperber. *The European Revolutions, 1848–1851*. Cambridge [England]; New York: Cambridge University Press, 1994; Guy P. C. Thomson. *The European Revolutions of 1848 and the Americas*. London: Institute of Latin American Studies, 2002.

93. Timothy Mason Roberts. *Distant Revolutions: 1848 and the Challenge to American Exceptionalism*. Charlottesville: University of Virginia Press, 2009.

94. Natsu Taylor Saito. *Meeting the Enemy: American Exceptionalism and International Law*. New York: New York University Press, 2010.

95. "International Committee of the Red Cross: Letter on Application of Geneva Conventions in Viet-Nam, and Replies of the United States and Republic of Viet-Nam." *International Legal Materials* 4.6 (November 1965): 1171–1174; Francois Bugnion. "The Geneva Conventions of 12 August 1949: From the 1949 Diplomatic Conference to the Dawn of the New Millennium." *International Affairs* (Royal Institute of International Affairs 1944–) 76.1 (January 2000): 41–50; Andrew Clapham, Paola Gaeta, Marco Sassòli, Iris van der Heijden, and Académie de droit International Humanitaire et de droits Humains à Genève. *The 1949 Geneva Conventions: A Commentary*. Oxford: Oxford University Press, 2015; Renée de Nevers. "The Geneva Conventions and New Wars." *Political Science Quarterly* 121.3 (Fall 2006): 369–395; Theodor Meron. "The Geneva Conventions as Customary Law." *The American Journal of International Law* 81.2 (April 1987): 348–370; Sarah Perrigo and Jim Whitman. *The Geneva Conventions Under Assault*. London; New York: Pluto Press, 2010.

96. John Charles Franceschina. *Duke Ellington's Music for the Theatre*. Jefferson, NC: McFarland, 2001.

97. Maria Balshaw. "'Black Was White': Urbanity, Passing and the Spectacle of Harlem." *Journal of American Studies* 33.2 (August 1999): 307–322; Lewis A. Erenberg. "From New York to Middletown: Repeal and the Legitimization of Nightlife in the Great Depression." *American Quarterly* 38.5 (Winter 1986): 761–778; Anne Rasmussen. "'An Evening in the Orient'": The Middle Eastern Nightclub in America." *Asian Music* 23.2 (Spring–Summer 1992): 63–88; Debra B. Silverman. "Nella Larsen's Quicksand: Untangling the Webs of Exoticism." *African American Review* 27.4 (Winter 1993): 599–614; Cheryl A. Wall. "Passing for What? Aspects of Identity in Nella Larsen's Novels." *Black American Literature Forum* 20.1/2 (Spring–Summer 1986): 97–111; Shane Vogel. "Closing Time: Langston Hughes and the Queer Poetics of Harlem Nightlife." *Criticism* 48.3 (Summer 2006): 397–425; _____. *The Scene of Harlem Cabaret: Race, Sexuality, Performance*. Chicago: The University of Chicago Press, 2009.

98. Joseph Henry Auner and Arnold Schoenberg. *A Schoenberg Reader: Documents of a Life*. New Haven: Yale University Press, 2003; George Perle. *Serial Composition and Atonality; An Introduction to the Music of Schoenberg, Berg, and Webern*. Berkeley: University of California Press, 1962; Arnold Schoenberg and Egbert M. Ennulat. *Arnold Schoenberg Correspondence: A Collection of Translated and Annotated Letters Exchanged with Guido Adler, Pablo Casals, Emanuel Feuermann, and Olin Downes*. Metuchen, NJ: Scarecrow Press, 1991; Arnold Schoenberg, Erwin Stein, Eithne Wilkins, and Ernst Kaiser. *Arnold Schoenberg Letters*. New York: St. Martin's Press, 1964; Arnold Schoenberg and Leonard Stein. *Style and Idea: Selected Writings of Arnold Schoenberg*. New York: St. Martin's Press, 1975.

99. Michael Fjeldsøe. "Different Images: A Case Study on Bartók Reception in Denmark." *Studia Musicologica Academiae Scientiarum Hungaricae* 47.3/4, Bartók's Orbit. The Context

and Sphere of Influence of His Work. Proceedings of the International Conference Held by the Bartók Archives, Budapest (22–24 March 2006). Part I. (September 2006): 453–465; Emőke Tari Solymosi. "'Bartók Always Called Me Latin': The Influence of Béla Bartók on László Lajtha's Life and Art." *Studia Musicologica* 48.1/2 (March 2007): 215–223; Lujza Tari. "Bartók's Collection of Hungarian Instrumental Folk Music and Its System." *Studia Musicologica Academiae Scientiarum Hungaricae* 47.2 (June 2006): 141–166; Richard Taruskin. "Why You Cannot Leave Bartók Out." *Studia Musicologica Academiae Scientiarum Hungaricae* 47.3/4, Bartók's Orbit. The Context and Sphere of Influence of His Work. Proceedings of the International Conference Held by the Bartók Archives, Budapest (22–24 March 2006). Part I. (September 2006): 265–277.

100. David Brackett. "James Brown's 'Superbad' and the Double-Voiced Utterance." *Popular Music* 11.3 (October 1992): 309–324; James Brown and Bruce Tucker. *James Brown, The Godfather of Soul.* New York: Thunder's Mouth Press, 2002; Yamma Brown and Robin Gaby Fisher. *Cold Sweat: My Father James Brown and Me.* Chicago: Chicago Review Press, 2014; Anne Danielsen. *Presence and Pleasure: The Funk Grooves of James Brown and Parliament.* Middletown, CT: Wesleyan University Press, 2006; Alice Echols. "The Land of Somewhere Else: Refiguring James Brown in Seventies Disco." *Criticism* 50.1, Special Issue: Disco (Winter 2008): 19–41; Charlie Ford. "The Very Best of James Brown?" *Popular Music* 21.1 (January 2002): 127–131; Michael Hanson. "Suppose James Brown Read Fanon: The Black Arts Movement, Cultural Nationalism and the Failure of Popular Musical Praxis." *Popular Music* 27.3 (October 2008): 341–365; James McBride. *Kill 'Em and Leave: Searching for James Brown and the American Soul.* New York: Spiegel & Grau, 2016; Cynthia Rose. *Living in America: The Soul Saga of James Brown.* London: Serpent's Tail, 1990; R. J. Smith. *The One: The Life and Music of James Brown.* New York: Gotham Books, 2012; Alexander Stewart. "Make It Funky: Fela Kuti, James Brown and the Invention of Afrobeat." *American Studies* 52.4, The Funk Issue (2013): 99–118.

101. Michael Collins. "'I'm Interested as a Writer in Less Exalted Persons': An Interview with Jessica Hagedorn." *Callaloo* 31.4, Cutting Down "The Wrath-Bearing Tree": The Politics Issue (Fall, 2008): 1217–1228; Kandia Crazy Horse. *Rip It Up: The Black Experience in Rock 'n' Roll.* New York: Palgrave Macmillan, 2004; Manthia Diawara. "The Song of the Griot." *Transition*, No. 74 (1997): 16–30; Patricia Spears Jones. "Sly and the Family Stone under the Big Tit, Atlanta, 1973." *The Kenyon Review, New Series* 15.4 (Autumn 1993): 66–68; Jeff Kaliss. *I Want to Take You Higher: The Life and Times of Sly & the Family Stone.* New York: Backbeat Books, 2008; Cheryl L. Keyes. "'She Was Too Black for Rock and Too Hard for Soul': (Re)discovering the Musical Career of Betty Mabry Davis." *American Studies* 52.4, The Funk Issue (2013): 35–55; Joel Selvin and Dave Marsh. *Sly and the Family Stone: An Oral History.* New York: Avon Books, 1998; Chris Stone. "'My Beliefs Are in My Song': Engaging Black Politics through Popular Music." *OAH Magazine of History* 20.5, Social Movements in the 1960s (October 2006): 28–32.

102. George Clinton and Ben Greenman. *Brothers Be "Yo Like George, Ain't That Funkin' Kinda Hard On You?": A Memoir.* New York: Atria Books, 2014; Horace J. Maxile, Jr. "Extensions on a Black Musical Tropology: From Trains to the Mothership (and Beyond)." *Journal of Black Studies* 42.4 (May 2011): 593–608; David Mills and Dave Marsh. *George Clinton and P-Funk: An Oral History.* New York: Avon Books, 1998; Kris Needs. *George Clinton & The Cosmic Odyssey of the P-Funk Empire.* London: Omnibus Press, 2014.

103. Terry Teachout. *Duke: A Life of Duke Ellington.* New York: Gotham Books, 2013.

Chapter Three

Miles Davis

Popular Musical and Transnational Border Crosser

With Louis Armstrong and Duke Ellington, Miles Davis, the great jazz trumpeter, bandleader, and composer, has been one of the most influential musicians in jazz and the musical culture's most eclectic practitioner, transversing a variety of genres and transnational styles. A lyrical, creative soloist and demanding group leader, since the late 1940s, Davis was jazz's most consistently innovatory musician. A jazz fusion[1] innovator, Davis was the epitome of the aloof, suave jazzman, offering the world his musical gifts while abusive to himself and others.

In small group formats, Davis pioneered the delicate, dry, and understated styles of cool[2] and modal jazz, developed in the late 1950s, in which modal scales dictate the melodic and harmonic content, sounds are free of frequent harmonic interruption, creating an unhurried and meditative feeling, and featuring the absence of frequent chord changes. Davis was also a forerunner of hard bop,[3] a bebop substyle dating from the mid-1950s. Hard bop took a countercultural stance and assumed a kind of "direct action," with an emancipatory musical-politics challenging white supremacy. Emphasizing bebop's black-transnational routes, as hard bop reaffirmed straightforward musical and emotional qualities, evolving from and incorporating gospel and rhythm and blues, its musicians reacted against cool and West Coast jazz's aloofness and refined intimacy. While Horace Silver (1928–2014) was the most prominent pianist, composer, and bandleader of this period,[4] alto saxophonist Cannonball Adderley (1928–1975), one of the most prominent and popular jazz musicians of the 1950s and 1960s, whose exuberant music was firmly in the bop school while employing the melodic sense of traditional jazz as a multi-instrumentalist best-known for his work on alto saxophone and recordings with Miles Davis and with his own small groups, and Art Blakey, also called Abdullah Ibn Buhaina (1919–1990), drummer and bandleader noted for his extraordinary drum solos, helping define the offshoot of bebop known as "hard bop," giving the drums a significant solo status, and whose style was characterized by thunderous press rolls, cross beats, and drum rolls that began as quiet tremblings that grew into frenzied explosions,[5] led other hard bop combos.

Though he was the product of an upper-middle-class family, Davis cultivated the demeanor of a surly street hustler. In later years, Davis spoke of his comfortable upbringing, sometimes to rebuke critics assuming that a background of poverty and suffering was common to all great jazz artists. Davis was raised in East St. Louis, a town in southwestern Illinois along the Mississippi River. There, his father was a prosperous dental surgeon and one of the worst incidents of US racial violence occurred in 1917.[6] The East Saint Louis Race Riot was a bloody outbreak of violence, stemming from the employment of black workers in a factory holding government contracts. Whites turned on blacks, indiscriminately stabbing, clubbing, and hanging them and driving 6,000 from their homes; forty blacks and eight whites were killed. At thirteen, Davis took up the trumpet and was professionally playing two years later. In light of his later stylistic development, Davis's first teacher advised him to play without vibrato. Davis played with St. Louis–area jazz bands, part of the St. Louis music scene of riverboats, dance halls, and territory bands.[7] Davis moved to New York City in September 1944, apparently to enter the Institute of Musical Art (now Juilliard) but actually to locate his idol Charlie Parker.

In New York, Davis skipped many classes and was schooled through jam sessions with jazz masters, such as Parker and Dizzy Gillespie. As he and Parker recorded together between 1945–1948, Davis's early playing was sometimes tentative and not always fully in tune. However, his unique, intimate tone and prolific musical imagination outweighed his technical deficiencies. By the early 1950s, Davis turned his limitations into assets. Rather than emulate the busy, wailing style of such bebop pioneers as Gillespie, Davis explored the trumpet's middle register, experimenting with harmonies and rhythms and varying his improvisational phrasing. With the exception of multi-note flurries, Davis's melodic style was direct and unornamented, based on quarter notes and rich with inflections. His improvisations' deliberation, pacing, and lyricism are remarkable.

Joining Parker in live appearances and recording sessions, Davis played in other groups and toured in big bands led by composer, arranger, bandleader, alto saxophonist, trumpeter, and clarinetist Benny Carter and Billy Eckstine (1914–1993), singer and bandleader who achieved great personal success while fostering younger jazz musicians' careers.[8] In 1948, Davis began to lead bebop groups. Davis composed several bebop themes, such as "Donna Lee" (1956) and "Half Nelson" (1959) (recorded with Parker) and "Bo-plicity" (1957) (with the nonet). Participating in an experimental workshop centered on the arranger Gil Evans, Davis and Evans's collaborations with Gerry Mulligan,[9] baritone saxophonist, arranger, and composer noted for his role in popularizing cool jazz, John Lewis, pianist and composer-arranger who was an influential member of the Modern Jazz Quartet, and trumpeter and composer Johnny Carisi culminated in a series of nonet (a group of nine musicians/a musical composition for nine voices or instruments) recordings for Capitol under Davis's name and later collected and reissued as *Birth of the Cool* (1957).

In 1949, Davis performed with Art Blakey, Sonny Rollins (1930–), tenor saxophonist who was among the finest improvisers on the instrument to appear since the mid-1950s,[10] and Tadd Dameron (1917–1965), pianist, ar-ranger, composer, and bandleader especially noted during the bop era for the melodic beauty and warmth of the songs he composed, until heroin addiction intermittently interrupted his career from mid-1949 to 1953. Although con-tinuing to record with famous bebop musicians, such as Parker, Rollins, Blakey, Horace Silver, J. J. Johnson (1924–2001), trombonist, composer, and arranger, and members of the Modern Jazz Quartet, Davis infrequently worked in clubs and with accompanists until 1954. In 1955, Davis informally appeared at the Newport Jazz Festival, where his improvisations brought him widespread publicity and enough engagements to establish a quintet (1955–1957) with Red Garland on piano, Paul Chambers on double bass, Philly Joe Jones on drums, and John Coltrane, who joined in 1956 and was later replaced by Rollins. As a leader, Davis followed the widespread prac-tice of appropriating music. Pieces popularized by and credited to Davis include "Four" (1954), "Solar" (1954), "Tune Up" (1957), and "Blue in Green" (1959). Several pieces from the 1950s, such as "Milestones" (1958), "So What" (1959), "All Blues" (1959), and "Freddie Freeloader" (1959), are Davis's own.

In May 1957, Davis made the first of several solo recordings on trumpet and flugelhorn with Gil Evans's unusual jazz orchestrations. That fall, Davis organized a short-lived quintet, joined by Cannonball Adderley. Also in 1957, Davis composed and recorded music in Paris for the film *Ascenseur Pour L'Echafaud* (*Elevator to the Gallows*) (1958) by Louis Malle (1932–1995), French director whose eclectic films were noted for their emo-tional realism and stylistic simplicity.

On his US return, Davis reformed his 1955 quintet with Adderley as a sixth member. For the next five years, Davis drew the rhythm sections of his various sextets and quintets from a small pool of players, including the pianists Garland, Bill Evans, and Wynton Kelly, drummers Jones and Jimmy Cobb, and bass player Chambers. Personnel changes increased in early 1963, and Davis engaged a new rhythm section as the nucleus of another quintet with pianist Herbie Hancock (1963–1968),[11] percussionist Tony Williams (1963–1969), and double bassist and cellist Ron Carter (1963–1968).[12] To replace Coltrane, who left in 1960, Davis experimented with a string of saxophonists, including Sonny Stitt,[13] Jimmy Heath, Hank Mobley (1961), George Coleman (1963–1964), Sam Rivers, and ultimately settling on Wayne Shorter[14] (1964–1970), also a composer, jazz-rock fusion pioneer, and among the most influential hard bop and modal musicians.

Because of Davis's prickly temperament and need for frequent periods of inactivity, these sidemen were not exclusively committed to him. Still, the 1955–1968 groups were steadier than Davis's later ones of 1969–1975. Often, the instrumentation and style of Davis's changing recording ensembles (up to fourteen players) diverged from his working groups (generally sextets and septets). In the late 1960s and early 1970s, influential musicians joined Davis, such as Chick Corea,[15] classically trained pianist, composer, and bandleader, Joe Zawinul, soulful Austrian keyboardist and composer who was a leading practitioner in jazz-rock fusion, most famously in the combo Weather Report, jazz and classical pianist Keith Jarrett,[16] English guitarist, bandleader, and composer John McLaughlin, whose energetic, eclectic soloing made him one of the most popular and influential jazz-rock musicians,[17] Dave Holland, double bassist, composer, and bandleader, Jack DeJohnette, drummer, pianist, composer, and jazz-fusion figure, Billy Cobham, Jr., Panamanian-American drummer, composer, and bandleader who came to prominence in the late 1960s and early 1970s with Davis and then with the Mahavishnu Orchestra, a transnational jazz-rock fusion band, and generally acclaimed as fusion's greatest drummer, and Airto Moreira, a Brazilian jazz[18] drummer and percussionist. Similar to his previous colleagues, these sidemen's outstanding playing were testament to Davis's stature among jazz musicians.

Davis's rejection of the 1940s standards for jazz trumpeters set by Dizzy Gillespie's bebop improvisations was partly due to his limited technique (some of his early recordings were tarnished by errors), but mostly because his interests were elsewhere. Composing relaxed, tuneful melodies in the middle register, and not hesitant to repeat ideas, Davis drew from a small collection of melodic formula, so that many solos seem as much composed as improvised. Davis was harmonically conservative and performed in close accord with his accompanists. Underneath his apparent simplicity was a subtle sense of rhythmic placement and expressive nuance. These characteristics were central to Davis's performances throughout his career. They can be heard on the nonet sessions, especially "Move"/"Budo," "Jeru"/"Godchild," and "Boplicity"/"Israel" (all 1949), inspiring the cool jazz movement. Davis's preference for moderation fused with his arranger's concern for smooth instrumental textures, restrained dynamics and rhythms, and a balance between ensemble and solo passages.

In the 1950s, as cool jazz became popular, Davis ignored this style, instead surrounding himself with passionate bebop players. Davis's unproductive early 1950s period came to an end with his celebrated blues improvisation album *Walkin'* (1954). In a session with Sonny Rollins in the same year, he introduced the stemless Harmon Mute to jazz. Its sound led to subtle and gentle recordings by his first quintet, for example, "Bye Bye Blackbird" and "'Round Midnight" on *'Round about Midnight* (1957). Many jazz trumpeters turned to flugelhorn after Davis showcased its potential in his Gil Evans collaborations (notably "Summertime" on *Porgy and Bess* [1958]. These recordings offer examples of lush orchestral settings with sustained emotional substance, presenting an ideal foil for Davis's improvisations' relaxed tunefulness, melodic and harmonic simplicity, and subtle swing.

Until 1965, Davis's groups performed a small selection of bebop, blues, popular songs, and compositions featuring ostinato (a constantly recurring melodic fragment). In this period, Davis's technical and emotional performances expanded, heard on the sophisticated *My Funny Valentine*[19] sophistication and the live album *Four and More* (both 1964). Wayne Shorter's addition to the ensemble led to a change in repertory, beginning with the album *E.S.P.* (1965). Discarding standard tunes, Davis's groups recorded improvisations in a chordless, tonally unclear bebop style and ostinato pieces on which the Hancock-Carter-Williams rhythm section discovered malleable ways of expressing 4/4 rhythms.

In 1968–1969, Davis turned to jazz-rock. The albums *In a Silent Way* and *Bitches Brew* (both 1969) merge acoustic and electronic instruments and melodic jazz improvisations with rock accompaniment. From this point on, Davis regularly edited his recordings from lengthy live and studio taped performances. Teo Macero, with whom he had a turbulent yet creative relationship, was Davis's recording engineer and producer from 1959 to 1983, becoming an important "member" of his ensembles.

In 1980, Davis made new recordings, and in the summer of 1981, he began touring with new quintets and sextets. During Davis's 1980s efforts to resume his career, the results were a juxtaposition of disparate sounds rather than fusion. The album *Decoy* (1984) offers examples of Davis's style. As Davis played trumpet and synthesizer, his performance on both can be heard on the title track of the album *Star People* (1983).

Though debilitated by a stroke in February 1982, Davis resumed his career in the spring of that year. Only the drummer Al Foster remained with Davis, serving as a sideman in 1975 and again from 1980 to 1985. New young members of Davis's groups included saxophonist, composer, and bandleader Branford Marsalis,[20] guitarist and composer John Scofield, and saxophonist Kenny Garrett. In his final decade, Davis was described as a "living legend," a title he loathed because it went against his inclination to be associated with new popular music and energetic, youthful activities, but one that was accurate as it reflected Davis's position as Parker and Coltrane's former partner. In 1986, Davis received an honorary Doctorate of Music from the New England Conservatory in honor of his achievements.

COOL JAZZ

In the summer of 1948, Davis formed a nonet, including such renowned performers as baritone saxophonist Gerry Mulligan, trombonist, composer, and arranger J. J. Johnson, Kenny Clarke (1914–1985), drummer who was a major exponent of the 1940s modern jazz movement, Lee Konitz (1927–), leading cool jazz figure and one of the most distinctive alto saxophonists,[21] and players on French horn and tuba, instruments rarely heard in jazz. Mulligan, Gil Evans, and pianist John Lewis did most of the band's arrangements, contrasting bebop's flexible, improvisatory nature with a thickly textured, orchestral sound. During its brief histories, the group recorded a dozen tracks, first released as singles (1949–1950). Altering the course of modern jazz and paving the way for 1950s West Coast styles, these tracks were immortalized in the *Birth of the Cool* (1957) album.

While Davis was a pioneer of cool jazz, such musicians as tenor saxophonist Lester Young exerted vast influence, contrasting with the "hot" modern style of saxophonist Charlie Parker and trumpeter Dizzy Gillespie. Cool jazz emerged in the late 1940s as a reaction against bebop, even as it was a natural outgrowth of its predecessor. The term "cool" derives from what journalists perceived as an understated and subdued feeling in the music of Davis, The Modern Jazz Quartet, saxophonist Gerry Mulligan, and pianist Lennie Tristano. Tone colors tended toward pastels, vibratos were slow or non-existent, and drummers played softer and less interactively than in bebop, hard bop, and other modern styles.

There was a renewed interest in contrapuntal collective improvisation among melody instruments, with variety in emotional range, level of intricacy, and instrumentation. While cool jazz derived from bebop, it promoted a moderation of the musical, emotional, and ritualistic qualities associated with its parent style. Most cool jazz musicians pursued a soft level of dynamics, favoring drum brushes rather than sticks, while avoiding a distinct use of vibrato. This moderation included the restrained lyricism of Stan Getz's solo on "Early Autumn" (1949) with Woody Herman's "Second Herd" band, elimination of cutting sharply differentiated articulation, heard in the highly chromatic and unmelodic unison themes and improvised lines of Lennie Tristano's group (1949), an emphasis on mid-range register and subdued timbres, and a balance between improvisation[22] and composition, practiced by Davis's *Birth of the Cool* nonet (1949–1950). Powerful, transparent, and contrapuntal dialogues were improvised by Gerry Mulligan in Mulligan's quartet (also from 1952) and Chet Baker (1929–1988), trumpeter and vocalist noted for the wistful, fragile tone of his playing and singing. Baker was a cult figure whose well-publicized struggles with drug addiction shortened his career.[23]

WEST COAST JAZZ

As cool jazz led to West Coast jazz, another bebop substyle, the term "cool" also referred to the tuneful and light-hearted sounds of Los Angeles–based saxophonist Dave Pell. The West Coast jazz label was applied despite the fact that most of its performers were not born there and some only briefly remained there. While white saxophonists Gerry Mulligan and Art Pepper were making names for themselves in Los Angeles in the West Coast style, leading African-American saxophonists Wardell Gray and Dexter Gordon[24] (each influenced by Parker) were playing in the same city, with neither called "West Coast" players. Simultaneously, in Boston,[25] white saxophonist John LaPorta and trumpeter Herb Pomeroy were playing in the cool style that was considered West Coast. In the early twentieth century, leading creole string player Bill Johnson established himself on the West Coast, and he soon brought New Orleans musicians to form his Creole Orchestra. Jelly Roll Morton went to California and in 1917 brought cornetist Buddie Petit (ca. 1890?–1931) and a group to play there. Kid Ory went to 1919 Los Angeles and formed a band with musicians he brought from New Orleans.

By 1919, drummer Art Hickman's orchestra, consisting of trumpet, trombone, two saxophones, and a rhythm section, became well known on the West Coast and began to develop a national reputation, unique for a dance band at that time. King Oliver's group performed in 1921–1922 Los Angeles and San Francisco, and the first jazz recordings to be released by a New Orleans African-American band, Ory's "Sunshine" sides, were made in Los Angeles late in 1921 and early in 1922. Much recording activity and publicity surrounded a white jazz subculture, including saxophonist Gerry Mulligan, trumpeter and flugelhornist Milton "Shorty" Rogers (one of West Coast jazz's principal creators), and others based in early to mid-1950s California.

Experimental musicians, such as Chet Baker and Stan Kenton (1912–1979), bandleader, pianist, and composer who commissioned and promoted the works of many modern composer-arrangers and thrust formal education and big band jazz together into what became the 1960s and 1970s stage (or concert) band movement, involving thousands of high school and college musicians, stood at the forefront of West Coast jazz and the Los Angeles scene. The laidback, cool style of pianist Dave Brubeck, bringing elements of classical music into jazz, epitomized West Coast jazz.[26]

Foreshadowing late twentieth-century debates surrounding East Coast versus West Coast hip hop, schisms emerged over West Coast cool versus East Coast bebop, with some critics arguing that West Coast jazz lacked intensity. Though jazz historiography neglected West Coast players, West Coast jazz performers include cool jazz trumpeter Chet Baker, muscular-sounding Dexter Gordon, trumpeters Andy Blakeney, George Orendorff, and McLure "Red Mack" Morris, pianists Betty Hall Jones, Chester Lane, and Gideon Honore, saxophonists Chuck Thomas, Jack McVea, and Caughey Roberts, Jr., drummers Jesse Sailes, Red Minor Robinson, and Nathaniel "Monk" McFay, Clifford Brown (1930–1956), trumpeter noted for his lyricism, clarity of sound, and grace of technique and principal figure in the hard bop subgenre,[27] Eric Dolphy (1928–1964), virtuoso improviser on woodwinds and a major influence on free jazz,[28] Wardell Gray (1921–1955), tenor saxophonist who straddled the swing and bebop periods, Art Pepper (1925–1982), noted for the beauty of his sound and improvisations on alto saxophone and a major figure in 1950s West Coast jazz, and Milton "Shorty" Rogers (1924–1994), one of the principal creators of West Coast jazz who was in demand for his skills as an arranger.

The political-culture surrounding West Coast jazz includes California's multi-racial and ethnic diversity, Southern Californian urban sprawl, the Los Angeles jazz scene's excitement and multi-faceted nature, supportive jazz clubs, critics, and such record companies as Fantasy, Contemporary, Capitol, and Pacific Jazz. Musicians performed on Los Angeles's Central Avenue,[29] occupying a central place in twentieth-century African-American cultural history. By day, Central Avenue was the economic, political, and cultural center of African-American Angelenos. By night, it was a magnet for African-American and white Southern Californians desiring the latest in jazz. Music on Central Avenue thrived in a context of Hollywood's effects on local culture, the precedent-setting merger of African-American and white musicians' unions, and repercussions from Los Angeles Police Department racism.[30] As West Coast jazz's influence became as significant in the jazz world as Harlem, New Orleans, and Chicago, artistic production and communal life coexisted in public spaces as the "Avenue" and West Coast artists' creativity nurtured and sustained a golden age. In the West Coast's equivalent of the Harlem Renaissance, Central Avenue became a center of political-cultural ferment and showplace for artistic achievement, part of Los Angeles's rich African-American cultural history.[31]

From the late 1910s to the early 1950s, segregationist policies toward Los Angeles's rapidly expanding African-American subculture inadvertently led to one of the most culturally rich avenues in the United States. From Downtown Los Angeles to the largely undeveloped city of Watts to the south, which would experience a massive uprising in 1965,[32] Central Avenue became West Coast jazz's center, nurturing homegrown talents like Charles

Mingus, bebop tenor, saxophonist Dexter Gordon (1923–1990), and flutist, saxophonist, and clarinetist Buddy Collette (1921–2010), while hosting touring jazz legends, such as Armstrong and Ellington.

As sounds of live jazz came out of nightclubs, restaurants, hotel lobbies, and music schools, jazz combos performed for nearly fifty years, helping to define and advance the musical culture.[33] The development of jazz and swing in Los Angeles's African-American area before World War II received an enhancement from the arrival of a significant number of musicians from Chicago and Southwestern states. The Central Avenue scene produced an energy leading to West Coast jazz becoming among the most vibrant of US jazz subcultures. Arriving in Los Angeles when African Americans faced restrictions on where they could live and work, non-white jazz artists found themselves limited to the Central Avenue area. This scene, supplemented by road travel, constituted their daily wages.

Pre-bebop jazz in California was a world of luxurious white nightclubs with African-American bands, ghetto clubs, and after-hours joints resulting from African-American musicians' West Coast migration.[34] Histories include postwar efforts to end discrimination in the film industry and recording studios, the development of community-based arts organizations, creation of intense films critiquing conditions in the African-American working-class neighborhoods of a city touting its diversity, and the political-cultural significance of African-American arts in Los Angeles between World War II and the 1992 uprising associated with the video-taped beating of African-American motorist Rodney King.[35]

During decades of neglect of Los Angeles's African-American and other non-white areas, amid the lives and work of African-American writers, visual artists, musicians, and filmmakers, black cultural politics changed as altered political realities generated new forms of artistic and cultural expressions. Those invested in the politics of black art and culture in post–World War II Los Angeles included African-American artists, black nationalists, affluent white liberals, elected officials, and federal bureaucrats.

As the "Watts Renaissance" revised pictures of Los Angeles's art and literary scenes, the turbulent 1960s and 1970s Los Angeles Black Arts Movement illuminated the dynamic cultural politics fueling it.[36] The rise of regional, Southern Californian black arts was part of a larger national and transnational Black Arts Movement, a period of artistic and literary development among African Americans in the 1960s and early 1970s. Based on black nationalism's cultural politics, developed into a set of theories referred to as the "Black Aesthetic," the Black Arts Movement sought to create a populist art form to promote the idea of black separatism. Advocates and practitioners viewed the artist as an activist, responsible for the establishment of racially separate publishing houses, theater troupes, and study groups. The movement's literature, written in black vernacular and reflecting the era's separatism and struggles for autonomy, addressed such issues as inter-racial tensions, political-cultural awareness, and the relevance of African histories, politics, and culture to African Americans.[37]

Deriving in wartime cultural activists' efforts, the Southern California Black Arts Movement was rooted in the African-American working class and characterized by struggles for artistic autonomy and improved living and working conditions for African-American artists. As new ideas concerning art, racial politics, and African-American artists' institutional position emerged, dozens of collectives appeared, from the Watts Writers Workshop to the Inner City Cultural Center to the New Art Jazz Ensemble. Spread across generations of artists, the Southern California Black Arts Movement was more than the artistic affiliate of local civil rights and Black Power efforts. Connections proliferated between Los Angeles expressive culture and politics, across musical, theater, cinematic, literary, economic, intellectual, and urban histories. These provide revisions of black Los Angeles, beyond its most sensational and destructive moments, such as the 1992 Los Angeles uprising, a major outbreak of violence, looting, and arson that began on April 29, 1992, in response to the acquittal of four white Los Angeles policemen on all but one charge (on which the jury was deadlocked), connected with the severe beating of Rodney King in March 1991. During several days of violence, more than fifty people were killed, more than 2,300 were injured, and thousands were arrested. More than 1,000 buildings were damaged and total property damage was about $1 billion.[38]

In a dynamic and affirmative network of political-cultural activities, dating to African Americans' World War II–era arrival in the region, a particular aesthetic emerged due to the deliberate efforts of African-American artists in Los Angeles. Emphasizing relationships between race and class[39] in Los Angeles, artists, cultural movements, and community organizations illuminate national and transnational struggles around cultural production and black radicalism's relationships to African-American expressive culture.[40] Creating one of the most significant periods of African-American cultural production, texts across a range of genres note the confluence of politics and culture, such as Jayne Cortez and Harry Dolan's poetry, Bobby Bradford's music, John Outterbridge and Betye Saar's visual art, and Charles Burnett and Billy Woodberry's films.

While in his twenties, jazz pianist and composer Horace Tapscott gave up a successful career in Lionel Hampton's band and returned home to Los Angeles. There, Tapscott formed the Pan Afrikan Peoples Arkestra (also known as P.A.P.A., or The Ark) in 1961 and led the ensemble through the 1990s. The P.A.P.A. was a community arts group providing affordable, community-oriented jazz and jazz training. For close to forty years, the Arkestra, with the related Union of God's Musicians and Artists Ascension (UGMAA) Foundation, were at the vanguard of the vital community-based arts movements in African-American Los Angeles. More than 300 musicians, vocalists, poets, playwrights, painters, sculptors, and graphic artists passed through these organizations, many remaining in Southern California and others achieving transnational fame.

Part of the overlooked community arts movement of African-American Los Angeles, as some worked to make the arts integral to everyday life, Tapscott stayed in Los Angeles to develop a musical and arts legacy. The P.A.P.A. can be understood in a broader context of African culture, the use of art among African nations to impose order, and similar use of the P.A.P.A. in Los Angeles as an enormous community and artistic resource. Artistic goals, political aspirations, internal conflicts, and socio-economic terrain shaped the P.A.P.A. as West Coast black arts figures in the Arkestra and jazz musicians worked within and gained sustenance from working-class African-American people, while observers deemed their music irrelevant.[41]

KIND OF BLUE

In the early 1950s, Davis struggled with a drug addiction that affected his playing, yet he recorded albums ranking among his best, including several with such notable performers as tenor saxophonist Sonny Rollins, Thelonious Monk, and Milt Jackson, the first and most influential vibraphone improviser of the post–World War II, modern jazz era. In 1954, after overcoming his addiction, Davis embarked on a two-decade period during which he was considered jazz's most innovative musician. Davis formed classic 1950s small groups featuring saxophone legends John Coltrane and Cannonball Adderley, pianists Red Garland and Bill Evans, bassist Paul Chambers, and drummers "Philly" Joe Jones and Jimmy Cobb. The albums Davis recorded during this era, such as *'Round About Midnight* (1956), *Workin'* (1956), *Steamin'* (1956), *Relaxin'* (1956), and *Milestones* (1958), influenced many artists.

Davis topped off this period with *Kind of Blue* (1959), jazz history's most celebrated album and its best-selling piece of music.[42] An automatic inclusion in critics' list of the great jazz albums, *Kind of Blue* has been the one record people who own no other jazz records possess, selling 250,000 copies a year in the United States and over three million copies to date. Mellow and relaxed, *Kind of Blue* includes some of the finest recorded examples of modal jazz,[43] a style developed in the late 1950s in which improvisations are based on sparse chords and non-standard scales rather than on complex, frequently changing chords, with modal scales dictating the melodic and harmonic content.[44] The modal style lent itself to solos focused on a piece's melody, giving it an accessible quality.

Since its release, *Kind of Blue* was hailed as a jazz classic, embraced by fans of multiple music genres. A watershed moment in jazz history, *Kind of Blue* helped usher in the first great jazz revolution since bebop. Recorded with pianist Bill Evans, tenor saxophonist John Coltrane, and pianist, composer, and music theorist George Russell,[45] *Kind of Blue* was an unexpected fusion of jazz giants when they were at the top of their game. The result was a recording that would change the face of jazz.

Released during the Civil Rights Movement and last years of the Eisenhower administration, Davis was nearing the end of his bebop period when he began to work on *Kind of Blue*. Signaling the rise of space-giving modal jazz, a new approach to the genre, contributing to the legend of pianist Bill Evans and his controversial playing style, and highlighting the often-overlooked alto saxophonist Cannonball Adderley, *Kind of Blue* was a milestone in contemporary jazz's development. The album provided a bridge over which jazz's young stars left the structured world of bebop and popularized modal jazz's freer, more spontaneous, and emotive style. It led Davis to greater fame in his rapidly developing career, paved the way for his sidemen, such as Coltrane, Evans, and Adderley, to launch their careers, and made lifelong jazz fans out of millions of listeners.

Featuring familiar Davis collaborators, such as producer Teo Macero, involved in the artistic process,[46] *Kind of Blue* revolutionized twentieth-century popular music. Paradoxically offering the most singular of sounds, a sound of isolation, while selling itself to millions, *Kind of Blue* ranks among the twentieth century's most haunting works and affected its musicians' subsequent performances. *Kind of Blue* influenced such diverse artists as James Brown, classical Minimalist composers,[47] rock experimentalist John Cale, English producer, composer, keyboardist, and singer Brian Eno, helping to define and reinvent the sound of some of the most popular 1980s and 1990s bands while creating the ambient music genre,[48] 1960s US band the Velvet Underground, whose primal guitar sound and urban-*noir* lyrics, influenced by avant-garde art and modern literature, inspired the 1970s and 1980s punk and alternative rock movements, English guitarist, composer, and record producer Robert Fripp, and Duane Allman, guitarist, session musician, and co-founder and leader of the Allman Brothers Band.

As Davis and his sextet walked into a church basement in midtown Manhattan that had been converted into a music studio, they recorded *Kind of Blue* in nine hours. Like Coltrane, Davis introduced Western listeners to a music immersed in a kind of jazz exoticism with roots in Eastern philosophies. While critics did not know what to make of *Kind of Blue*, others recognized its power as an album that pervaded other cultural forms and ushered in changes in various parts of US culture. *Kind of Blue*'s antecedents include Davis's just-previous album *Milestones* (1958). The title track of *Milestones*, based in modes rather than chord progressions, thereby fostering a slower-seeming overall pace and soloists' freer improvisations, anticipated all of *Kind of Blue*'s tracks. *Kind of Blue*'s predecessors also include Davis's impressionist-influenced *Birth of the Cool* (1948) and the significance of blue in literature and early modernist painting, such as Pablo Picasso (1881–1973), Spanish ex-patriate painter, sculptor, printmaker, ceramicist, and stage designer, one of the twentieth century's greatest and most influential artists, and creator (with Georges Braque) of Cubism, and his blue period between 1901 and mid-1904, when blue was the predominant color in Picasso's paintings.[49]

Miles Davis was part of a continuum of twentieth-century jazz innovators, stretching the musical culture beyond its mainstream limits and US exceptionalist definitions by performing music, such as bebop, that challenged the dominant culture's politics and aesthetics and incorporating musical styles that would reintroduce jazz to its transnational routes. This includes pianist, composer, bandleader, and educator Ahmad Jamal.[50] Though Jamal has been overlooked by jazz critics and historians, he has been credited with having a great influence on Davis, impressed by Jamal's rhythmic sense and concept of space, lightness of touch, and understatement. Jamal and Davis became friends in the 1950s and Davis continued to support Jamal, performing versions of Jamal's songs, such as "New Rhumba" (1955) and "Ahmad's Blues" (1959).

Davis's experimentations can be understood in a larger context of avant-garde groups, such as the experimental Revolutionary Ensemble, a free jazz trio consisting of violinist Leroy Jenkins, a member of the Chicago-based Association for the Advancement of Creative Musicians (AACM),[51] a cooperative organization of musicians, including several major figures of free jazz, bassist Sirone, and percussionist/pianist Jerome Cooper. This trio, active from 1971 to 1977, has been described as one of the most crucial groups to form in the decade and reunited in 2004.

Davis can also be heard in relation to the free jazz of Ornette Coleman and John Coltrane, while creating jazz rock with a broader commercial appeal. The "Lost Quintet" consisted of Davis, saxophonist Wayne Shorter, Chick Corea on keyboards, bassist Dave Holland, and drummer Jack DeJohnette. Later, Keith Jarrett joined as a second keyboardist and percussionist Airto Moreira was also added. Shorter was replaced by Steve Grossman who, in turn, was replaced by Gary Bartz, and Michael Henderson stepped in for Holland, all in 1970. The "quintet" toured during the *Bitches Brew* period and recorded in the studio, though years later, live recordings and bootlegs surfaced. A "musical economy" separated The Lost Quintet from groups on the commercial margins, such as Circle and The Revolutionary Ensemble. The Lost Quintet was a band in its own right, not just a transition to better known ensembles.[52]

Belonging to networks animating 1970s experimental music making, relationships among highly innovative musicians shaped the music of the time, including the cultural, political, and philosophical elements of late 1960s and early 1970s cutting-edge groups. Davis's relationships with avant-garde bands include the mid-1970s New York City loft jazz scene,[53] occurring at venues such as Environ, Ali's Alley, and Studio Rivbea, in former industrial loft spaces in the SoHo district. Loft jazz was a continuation of the free jazz and avant-garde jazz traditions inaugurated by saxophonist, composer, and bandleader John Coltrane, saxophonist, composer, and bandleader Ornette Coleman, Albert Ayler (1936–1970), tenor saxophonist whose innovations in style and technique were a major influence on free jazz, saxophonist Pharoah Sanders (1940–),[54] and composer and keyboard player Sun Ra. Not following one specific jazz style or idiom, few loft jazz musicians continuously played atonal or arhythmic music in the style of Coltrane's legendary albums *Ascension* (1966) and *Om* (1968). They combined conventional melodic elements with free jazz, used instruments less familiar to jazz, such as the bass saxophone, oboe, and cello, and combined instruments in non-traditional formats, like the World Saxophone Quartet, whose changing members used a variety of saxophones and flutes, usually without any rhythm section.

In addition to Davis, Ornette Coleman and Cecil Taylor (1929–), composer and among the leading free jazz pianists,[55] revolutionized music from the end of the twentieth century through the twenty-first, expanding jazz traditions with distinct concepts of composition, improvisation, instrumentation, and performance. Davis, Coleman, and Taylor remain controversial figures due to their musical, political, and transnational border crossing. Icons of the African-American avant-garde,[56] lionized by some critics and reviled by others, Davis, Coleman, and Taylor influenced musicians across divides of race, gender, sexuality, ethnicity, class, nation, and genre.[57]

With keyboardists Chick Corea and Joe Zawinul and guitarist John McLaughlin, Davis recorded *In a Silent Way* (1969), regarded as the seminal album of the jazz-fusion movement and considered by purists to be Davis's last true jazz album. Davis won new fans and alienated old ones with the release of *Bitches Brew* (1969), an album utilizing rock rhythms, electronic instrumentation, and studio effects. A combination of layered sounds, rhythms, and textures, *Bitches Brew*'s influence was heard in such 1970s fusion groups as Weather Report and Corea's *Return to Forever* (1972). Davis continued in this style for several years, with the album *Live-Evil* (1970) and film soundtrack *A Tribute to Jack Johnson* (1970).

THREATENING AND NON-THREATENING BLACK-TRANSNATIONAL MASCULINITIES

Davis's connection to Jack Johnson (1878–1946), the first black boxer to win the world heavyweight championship and considered one of the greatest heavyweights of all time,[58] notes his centrality to the creation of the mythology of black masculinity,[59] the various incarnations of its threatening and non-threatening representations in visual culture, and similarities in the personas of black-transational boxers and jazz musicians. Obsessed with sports, Davis, who had sickle-cell anemia, major hip operations, and suffering from a stomach ulcer and gallstones, combated the effects of his disease by hand exercises. Training as a boxer, in 1975 Davis's joints' deterioration forced him into retirement.

In 1970, Davis was asked to record music for a documentary on Jack Johnson's life. Johnson resonated with Davis, an African-American male celebrity similarly negotiating US culture's interwoven hierarchies of race, gender, sexuality, class, and nation while part of a hyper-mediated gaze surveilling males of color as part of the visual-culture industry and criminal justice system. Echoing his own style, Davis wrote in his album's liner notes of Johnson's mastery as a boxer, affinity for jazz, fast cars, clothes, and beautiful women. Johnson's "unapologetic blackness" and threatening image to white men was similar to Davis's image of a black man unafraid to explore his creative inclinations, turning his back on his audience, and defying racial norms, heard in his dissonant bebop and other experimental, transnational, and countercultural music, and seen in his refusal to "mug" in ways Armstrong and others did.

Jack Johnson professionally fought from 1897 to 1928 and engaged in exhibition matches as late as 1945. He won the title by knocking out champion Tommy Burns in Sydney, Australia, on December 26, 1908, and lost it on a knockout by Jess Willard in twenty-six rounds in Havana, Cuba, on April 5, 1915. Until his fight with Burns, racism limited Johnson's opportunities and purses. When he became champion, a cry for a "Great White Hope" produced numerous opponents. At his career's height, the mainstream press attacked the outspoken Johnson for his flashy lifestyle and for having twice married white women. Johnson continued to transgress the transnational color line in 1910 by knocking out former champion James J. Jeffries, induced to come out of retirement as a "Great White Hope." Billed as the "Fight of the Century," the Johnson-Jeffries bout led to nationwide celebrations by African Americans and was met with white violence, resulting in more than twenty deaths across the United States.

In 1912, Johnson was convicted of violating the Mann Act due to transporting his wife-to-be across state lines before their marriage. A landmark of Progressive-era legislation, the Mann Act, also known as the "White Slave

Traffic Act," made it a crime to transport women across state lines for the purpose of prostitution, debauchery, or for any other "immoral" purpose. Designed to combat forced prostitution, the law was so broadly worded that courts held it to criminalize many forms of consensual sexual activities, and it was soon being used as a tool for blackmail and political persecution of Johnson and others. Sentenced to a year in prison, Johnson was released on bond, pending appeal.

Disguised as a member of a black baseball team, Johnson fled to Canada, made his way to Europe, and was a fugitive for seven years. Johnson defended his championship three times in Paris before agreeing to fight Jess Willard in Havana. Some thought Johnson, mistakenly believing that the charge against him would be dropped if he forfeited his championship to a white man, intentionally lost to Willard. From 1897 to 1928, Johnson had 114 bouts, winning 80, 45 by knockouts. In 1920, Johnson surrendered to US marshals, served his sentence, and fought in bouts in the Leavenworth, Kansas, federal prison. After his release, Johnson occasionally fought and entered US cultural, racialized "freak show"[60] traditions by performing in vaudeville and carnival acts, appearing at one point with a trained flea. Johnson wrote two memoirs, *Mes Combats* (in French, 1914) and *Jack Johnson in the Ring and Out* (1927; reprinted 1975). Johnson died in a car accident and was a member of the inaugural class of inductees into the International Boxing Hall of Fame in 1990.

In the years after his death, Johnson's reputation was gradually rehabilitated. His criminal record came to be regarded as more a result of racial bigotry than a reflection of any wrongdoing, and members of the US Congress attempted to obtain a posthumous presidential pardon for Johnson several times. Represented in the hit play *The Great White Hope* (1967; filmed 1970), Johnson was the subject of Ken Burns's documentary *Unforgivable Blackness* (2004), a title playing on the type of black-transnational masculinity Johnson and Davis lived and performed.

Transversing hegemonies of race, gender, sexuality, class, nation, colonization, sports, and popular culture, Johnson's transnational career highlights intersecting US, English, and French colonial histories. Johnson's impact on race relations during his exile was at least as great in countries outside the United States as it was stateside. When he fought outside the United States, Johnson became a model of freedom for colonial populations seeking liberation and an object of exotic fascination and detestation for whites trying to maintain their power in a changing world. Inspiring colonial people from Fiji to Jamaica to India, as Western imperialists grew alarmed at his popularity and success, Johnson's transnationalism exposed ways itinerant black workers who left the United States contributed to resistive politics in Europe, Latin America, Australia, Asia, and Africa.

As heavyweight champion, Johnson was the most prominent example of the confluence of defiance to global white supremacy in sports and entertainment. Born in Texas and the son of former slaves, Johnson was the most famous black man on the planet. As the first African-American World Heavyweight Champion (1908–1915), he publicly challenged white supremacy at home and abroad, enjoying an audacious lifestyle of conspicuous consumption, masculine bravado, and interracial romance as he struggled against the transnational color line from London to Cape Town, Paris, and Mexico City.

Injured in a 1972 car accident, Davis curtailed his activities, then retired from 1975 through 1980. When he returned to public attention with *The Man with the Horn* (1981), critics felt Davis's erratic playing showed the effects of his five-year layoff. Regaining his powers during the next few years, Davis dabbled in a variety of musical styles in the 1980s, concentrating mostly on jazz-rock dance music. Experiments in other styles included Davis's return to his blues roots in the album *Star People* (1983). Davis won several Grammy Awards during this period for the albums *We Want Miles* (1982), *Tutu* (1986), and *Aura* (1989). Though critics dismissed much of the music Davis released after *Bitches Brew*, his experimentations kept jazz popular with mainstream audiences.

ANTI-ASSIMILATIONIST BEBOP

Davis's excursions into bebop, a modern jazz subgenre that split jazz into two camps in the last half of the 1940s, signified his ability to buck mid-twentieth-century US racial codes by performing a music that shed the constraints of swing's integrationism and happy endings as just one of several musical, racial, gender, sexual, ethnic, and transnational border crossings and experimentations Davis would enact throughout his career. When bebop, an onomatopoeic rendering of a staccato two-tone phrase distinctive in this type of music, emerged, it was considered unacceptable to the general public and many musicians.

Bebop took old jazz harmonies and superimposed on them "substituted" chords, broke up the metronomic regularity of the drummer's rhythmic pulse, and produced solos played in double time, with several bars packed with sixteenth notes, leading to complex improvisational results. Offering a unique sound, raw emotionality, and sophisticated technique, bebop was a modernist movement that had a major impact on jazz histories. Musicians superimposed on the harmonic structure of standard songs' melodic themes closer to the spirit of jazz improvisations, creating a new repertory. Improvisations became more searching and the speed of harmonic, rhythmic, and melodic motion led to dense, compact performances. Instrumental sounds (without vibrato) became more tense and mobile. The rhythm section was thinned out, guitars were omitted, and pianists irregularly spaced accompanying chords. Drummers explored tensions between a permanent beat on the cymbal (supported by a walking bass) and syncopated strokes divided among the snare, tom-tom, and bass drums, closely interacting with the solo line's implied polyrhythms. The range of tempos became wider, with a tendency to the extremely fast.

Initiating in early 1940s, World War II–era Harlem, heard in the playing of trumpeter Dizzy Gillespie, guitarist Charlie Christian, pianist Thelonious Monk, drummer Kenny Clarke, Billy Eckstine, and especially alto saxophonist Charlie Parker, bebop was a central chapter in jazz history and provided a shift from dominant US culture, offering an alternative music, style, and way of being and knowing that challenged staid, bourgeois norms in the decades before the Civil Rights Movement.

As Davis participated in bebop's evolution, his musical experimentations from that point on can be understood as part of a larger trajectory the birth of bebop initiated, as contemporary ideas of jazz flow from that pivotal moment. Departing from the swing era's (racial and musical) harmonies, African-American musicians' position altered due to bebop, as their performances linked to broader developments in US culture, such as World War II–era turmoil and pervasive mid-twentieth-century racism. At once an artistic movement, ideological statement, and commercial phenomenon, the self-effacing, clownish term of bebop does not do justice to its aesthetic and political complexities and consequences.

Synonymous with a new musical sensibility, bebop burst onto the cultural scene as additional musical and literary forms challenged cultural conservatism. In its modernism, bebop connected to the music of Arnold Schoenberg and writing of Irish novelist James Joyce (1882–1941), noted for his experimental use of language and exploration of new literary methods in such large works of fiction as *Ulysses* (1922) and *Finnegans Wake* (1939).[61] Featuring elements defying meaningful representation in musical notation and created by a small cadre of primarily New York–based jazzmen, bebop was a melodically and harmonically complicated chamber music with unusual rhythms demanding serious listening. Bebop impacted US culture in economic, political, and cultural terms in its rich and alternative sounds. Political-cultural forces fostering bebop include the post–World War II economic slump, ongoing racism, the Civil Rights Movement's beginnings, and rise of small venues for performance, leading to the shift from an interest in big bands toward more specialized music, including small combo jazz.

As jazz aficionados began to desire virtuosos, such as Charlie Parker and Dizzy Gillespie, they deserted big bands for small combo bebop improvisations. A revolutionary break simultaneously representing an evolutionary stage in jazz histories, bebop represented an epochal shift in jazz, provided the pivot on which jazz histories turn, and represented the juncture at which the lived experience of music became transformed into cultural memory.

As its creators negotiated a position on the shifting terrain of World War II–era US culture, bebop was the result of musical decisions, the nexus of economics, jazz, and race, its time's musical aesthetics and cultural spirit, perspectives of Harlem Renaissance–era figures, such as W. E. B. Du Bois and Marcus Garvey (1887–1940), charismatic black leader who organized a black nationalist movement (1919–1926) based in Harlem,[62] and ways Islam played a role in the music's development.

In addition to Davis and his unique individual and musical persona that was part of bebop's renegade identity, a variety of iconoclastic jazz players contributed to mid-twentieth-century modern jazz. In its initial stages, many jazz musicians and most of the jazz audience heard bebop as radical, chaotic, and bewildering. For a nation swinging to big bands' smoothly orchestrated sounds, bebop seemed destined for a short span on the musical fringe. However, due to Davis, Parker, Gillespie, and others, bebop became jazz's *lingua franca*, serving as jazz musicians' principal musical language.

One of jazz's greatest and most "mysterious" stars and an enigmatic giant of black modernism, Bud Powell was a great bebop pianist.[63] A dynamic and adventurous musical mind, Powell's expansive musicianship, riveting performances, and inventive compositions expanded bebop and pushed jazz musicians to higher performance levels. Powell remains one of US music's most misunderstood figures. His talents overshadowed by his alcohol abuse, mental instability, and brutalization at the hands of white authorities, Powell expanded his artistic horizons and moved his chosen idiom into new realms.

WITH COLTRANE

When Davis chose members of his quintet in 1955, he passed over well-known, respected saxophonists, such as Sonny Rollins, to pick out the young, still inexperienced John Coltrane. Acclaimed African-American jazz tenor and soprano saxophonist, bandleader, composer, and iconic twentieth-century figure, Coltrane, a seminal force in jazz, changed the face of the musical culture. What might have seemed like an insignificant decision at the time would impact Davis and Coltrane's careers and jazz histories more broadly. During Davis and Coltrane's collaboration, each influenced the other and in doing so made a tremendous impact on US and transnational popular culture. In the drama of their collaboration, from their initial partnership to their breakup, Davis and Coltrane made progress toward each other's artistic goals.

In their public personas, private lives, and racial, gender, sexual, national, transnational, and popular musical border crossing, Davis and Coltrane paralleled changing standards of African-American culture, part and parcel of a respectability politics, a key component of African Americans' attempts to counter stereotypes demeaning their racial, gender, sexual, class, and national positions.[64] In their personal and musical styles, Davis and Coltrane radically contrasted, with Davis typifying the tough, closemouthed 1950s cool while Coltrane transitioned from an unfocused junkie to religious pilgrim, inspiring others to pursue spiritual enlightenment.

On *Kind of Blue*, Davis and Coltrane's musical gifts can be heard. Each establishes his style in "So What's" warm, confident tones. As neither Davis nor Coltrane elaborated on their work in words, in a symbiotic relationship of two mavericks, rewriting jazz's rules, Davis was a prodigy, possessing a great talent and desire to expand his sound's limits, while Coltrane was a late bloomer with a resolute focus on his music. While Davis's bold trumpet and Coltrane's searching saxophone mixed in harmony, their off-stage relationship was not as amicable, though their time-honored performances brought enduring legacies to "The Chief" and "Trane."[65]

After Charlie Parker, Coltrane was the most revolutionary and widely imitated jazz saxophonist. Growing up in High Point, North Carolina, Coltrane learned to play Eb alto horn, clarinet, and, at about fifteen, alto saxophone. He performed alto saxophone in bands led by Joe Webb and King Kolax, then changed to the tenor to work with Eddie "Cleanhead" Vinson (1947–mid-1948). Coltrane performed on either instrument while in groups led by Jimmy Heath, Gillespie (with whom he recorded in 1949), Earl Bostic, and other rhythm-and-blues musicians. After Gillespie broke up his big band in May 1950, Coltrane joined his sextet for engagements in New York's Birdland and in Detroit during the first months of 1951.

When he joined Johnny Hodges's septet in 1954, Coltrane was committed to the tenor saxophone. Early in October 1955, Coltrane received an offer to replace tenor saxophonist Sonny Rollins in Miles Davis's quintet with Red Garland (1923–1984), a modern jazz pianist known for his work as a bandleader and during the 1950s with Davis and helping to popularize the block chord style of piano playing, Paul Chambers, Jr. (1935–1969), double bassist, a fixture of 1950s and 1960s rhythm sections, whose importance in the development of jazz bass can be measured by the length and breadth of his work in this short period and his impeccable timing, intonation, and virtuosic improvisations, known for his bowed solos, recording some dozen albums as a leader or co-leader, and prolifically as a sideman, especially as the anchor of Davis's "first great quintet" (1955–1963), with pianist Wynton Kelly (1963–1968), and Philly Joe Jones (1923–1985), among the most recorded percussionists of the bop era (1955–1957).

In 1955, Coltrane came to prominence when he joined Davis's quintet. His drug and alcohol abuse led to unreliability and in early 1957 Davis fired him. Davis replaced Coltrane, although Coltrane is heard on the quintet's famous albums. Coltrane played in Thelonious Monk's legendary quartet (July–December 1957), rejoined Davis, and worked in quintets and sextets with alto saxophonist Adderley, drummers Jones and Jimmy Cobb, double bassist Chambers, pianists Garland and Bill Evans, and Wynton Kelly (1931–1971), Jamaican American jazz pianist and composer known for his lively, blues-based playing and as one of the finest accompanists in jazz (1958–July 1959 and late August 1959–mid-April 1960).

With Davis, Coltrane discovered the soprano saxophone and purchased his own instrument in February 1960. Leading studio sessions, Coltrane established a reputation as a composer and emerged as the leading jazz tenor saxophonist. Ready to form his own group, upon returning with Davis from a European tour, Coltrane made his début as a leader at New York's Jazz Gallery in early May 1960. In November 1961, Coltrane put together a quartet that would remain together for several years and gain legendary status.

As Coltrane turned to alternative styles in the mid-1960s, his controversial experiments attracted large audiences, and by 1965 Coltrane became wealthy. From the fall of 1965, Coltrane's quest for new sounds resulted in frequent changes of personnel in his group. New members included saxophonist Pharoah Sanders, bass clarinet, ney (an end-blown flute prominent in Middle Eastern music), shakuhachi (a Japanese end-blown bamboo flute derived from the Chinese xiao [flute] in the eighth century), and double bass player Donald Garrett, Alice Coltrane (his second wife, also a jazz musician and composer, and playing piano during the last years of Coltrane's life), drummer Rashied Ali (with Frank Butler, Beaver Harris, and Jack DeJohnette as seconds to Ali), and African-influenced percussionists. In his final years and after his death, Coltrane gained a saintly reputation among listeners and musicians for his support of young avant-garde performers, religious beliefs, peaceful disposition, and striving for a musical ideal.

As his 1950s performances' success were dependent on their tempo, Coltrane played ballad themes with little or no embellishments, as in his performances of "Naima" in 1959. In other ballads, such as his version of Thelonious Monk's "Round Midnight" (September–October 1956), Coltrane alternated paraphrases of the theme with elaborations and brief thematic references. Coltrane's priority was beautiful sounds and he was a skilled, romantic interpreter of ballads. One of Coltrane's goals was to elaborate bebop chord progressions. At moderate speeds, Coltrane could do this without ignoring rhythmic and expressive nuances, for example in his varying improvisations on "All of You" (1956), "Blues by Five" (1956), and "Blue Train" (1957). The faster the piece, the more focused was his exploration of harmony.

Like Parker, Coltrane improvised rapid bop melodies from formula. Unlike Parker, Coltrane drew on a small collection of formula, failed to juxtapose these in new combinations, and placed them in predictable relationships to the beat. Early solos on "Salt Peanuts" and "Tune-up" (both 1956) exemplify this practice, also heard in his intense performance in "Giant Steps" (1959). This solo was due to Coltrane's driving tone, technical facility, and complex harmonic ideas. By seeking to escape harmonic clichés in such pieces as "Giant Steps," Coltrane inadvertently created a confining, one-dimensional improvisatory style. Whereas Coltrane was more important as an improviser than a composer, he did write several pieces that became jazz standards (including "Moment's Notice" [1958], "Naima" [1959], "Equinox" [1960], and "Impressions" [1962]. From May 1959 to his death in 1967, the majority of Coltrane's recordings as a leader were of his own compositions.

In the late 1950s, Coltrane pursued two directions. First, his expanding technique enabled him to play "sheets of sound," part of his fascination with chords and harmony,[66] exemplified in his very fast sixteenth-note runs during a live performance of "Ah-leu-cha," recorded at Newport in 1958. Such flurries replaced the clarity of his approach in "Giant Steps" and hid his excessive replication of formula. Coltrane claimed he would start in the middle of a sentence and move both directions at once. The cascade of notes during his powerful solos showed his infatuation with chord progressions, culminating in his virtuoso performance of "Giant Steps."

When Davis discarded bebop chord progressions in favor of relaxed ostinatos, Coltrane abandoned formula in favor of motivic development. Davis's "So What" on the *Kind of Blue* (1959) album was the first recording on which Coltrane varied motifs throughout a solo. This became prominent in his most famous recordings, such as Richard Rodgers and Oscar Hammerstein's[67] "My Favorite Things" and "Equinox" (1960), "Teo" and "Impressions" (1961), "Crescent" (1964), and the album *A Love Supreme* (1964). Initially, Coltrane developed motifs only in performances when neither tempo nor harmonic rhythm was fast, as he could avoid repetitive responses at high speeds. Coltrane's famous early 1960s recordings are often referred to as being "modal" or exemplifying "modal improvisation" or "modal playing." This had less to do with Coltrane, whose chromatic lines defied modal analysis, than with pianist McCoy Tyner's accompaniments, some of which suggest modal scales.

While consolidating his manner of organizing melody, Coltrane embarked on a quest for new sonorities. Coltrane used "false" fingerings to protract the tone-color and upper range of his instrument. This followed tenor saxophonist Lester Young and tenor saxophonist and bandleader Illinois Jacquet (1922–2004), playing solos full of riffs, honking tones, and screaming, high-register notes. Jacquet's soulful blues playing and crowd-pleasing "freak" sounds were a major influence on rhythm-and-blues saxophonists. He was most noted for his big tone and aggressive, extroverted antics, a sweetly melodic way of playing ballads, and care for solo form that made him a lasting influence on jazz saxophonists. Jacquet joined the troupe of Jazz at the Philharmonic, the title of a series of concerts, tours, and recordings produced by Norman Granz (1918–2001), US concert and record producer, for annual tours of the United States and, eventually, around the world.[68]

Coltrane performed on the soprano saxophone, rivaling the tenor as his main instrument. On both he learned to leap between extreme registers at high speeds and convey the impression of an overlapping dialogue between two voices, as in the latter part of "My Favorite Things." Radical timbres, akin to human cries, dominate Coltrane's late improvisations as his concern with tonality and pitch diminished. Coltrane's expansion of individual sonority linked with an expansion of group texture.

In the quartet, pianist McCoy Tyner kept time and established tonal centers with chordal fluctuations, thus freeing Philly Joe Jones to create masses of drum and cymbal accents. Jones (later Rashied Ali) and Coltrane engaged in extended coloristic duets. The addition of double bass, bass clarinetist, alto saxophonist, and flutist Eric Dolphy's bird- and speech-like sounds on wind instruments and Pharoah Sanders's powerful tenor saxophone intensified the group's textures.

Coltrane moved to experimental jazz's[69] forefront with the album *Ascension* (1966), presenting a density of dissonant sounds unheard of in jazz. Two alto and three tenor saxophonists, two trumpeters, a pianist, two double bass players, and drummer played through a scarcely tonal, loosely structured scheme. Their collective improvisation and "solos" stressed timbral and registral extremes rather than conventional melodies. Coltrane's ensembles concentrated on maintaining high levels of intensity by filling a spectrum of frequencies, tone-colors, and, when he utilized extra percussionists, accents. The albums *Meditations* (1966) and *Om* (1968), late versions of "My Favorite Things" and "Naima" (1966), and other recordings demonstrate this final stage of Coltrane's evolution. Coltrane had a great impact on his contemporaries. Though they could not match his technical mastery, performers imitated Coltrane's sound on tenor saxophone. Coltrane was responsible for demonstrating the potential of the soprano saxophone as a modern jazz instrument. By the 1970s, most alto and tenor saxophonists doubled on this once archaic instrument. Selling hundreds of thousands of albums in his final years, Coltrane achieved the atypical accomplishment of temporarily establishing avant-garde jazz as popular music.

Coltrane, whose first musical influence was his father, a tailor and part-time musician, studied clarinet and alto saxophone as a youth and moved to Philadelphia in 1943 to continue his studies. Drafted into the navy in 1945, Coltrane played alto saxophone with a navy band until 1946 and switched to tenor saxophone in 1947. During the late 1940s and early 1950s, Coltrane played in nightclubs and on recordings with such musicians as Gillespie,

Eddie Vinson (1917–1988), jump blues, bebop, and R&B alto saxophonist and blues shouter nicknamed "Cleanhead" after an incident in which his hair was accidentally destroyed by lye contained in a hair straightening product, and Earl Bostic (1913–1965), alto saxophonist performing with a characteristic growl on the horn, pioneer of the post–World War II rhythm-and-blues style, and one of Coltrane's major influences.

With his first recorded solo appearing on Gillespie's "We Love to Boogie" (1951), Coltrane embarked on a six-month stint with Thelonious Monk and recorded under his own name. Each undertaking demonstrated a new level of technical discipline and increased harmonic and rhythmic sophistication. Coltrane performed a huge and dark tone on the tenor saxophone, with clear definition and full body, even in the highest and lowest registers. His vigorous, intense style was original, but traces of his idols, saxophonists Johnny Hodges and Lester Young, can be heard in his *legato* phrasing and *portamento*. From Monk, Coltrane learned the technique of multiphonics, when a reed player simultaneously produces multiple tones by using a relaxed embouchure (position of the lips, tongue, and teeth), varied pressure, and special fingerings. In the late 1950s, Coltrane used multiphonics for simple harmony effects (as on "Harmonique" [1959]. In the 1960s, Coltrane more frequently employed this technique in passionate, screeching passages.

Coltrane returned to Davis's group in 1958, contributing to the "modal phase" albums *Milestones* (1958) and *Kind of Blue* (1959), each considered quintessential 1950s modern jazz examples. During this period, Davis was experimenting with modes, or scale patterns other than major and minor. Coltrane's work on these recordings was proficient and brilliant, though relatively cautious and subdued. After ending his association with Davis in 1960, Coltrane formed his acclaimed quartet, featuring pianist Tyner, bassist Jimmy Garrison, and drummer Elvin Jones. Throughout the early 1960s, Coltrane focused on mode-based improvisation, in which solos were played atop one- or two-note accompanying figures, repeated for extended periods, and typified in his recordings of "My Favorite Things."

Coltrane's various influences, together with a unique interplay with the drums and steady vamping of the piano and bass, made the Coltrane quartet one of the 1960s' most noteworthy jazz groups. Between 1965 and his 1967 death, Coltrane's work expanded into a free, collective (simultaneous) improvisation based on prearranged scales. This was the most radical period of Coltrane's career and his avant-garde experiments divided critics and audiences. Coltrane's best-known work spanned the period between 1955 and 1967. His tentative, relatively melodic early style can be heard on the Davis-led albums recorded for the Prestige and Columbia labels during 1955 and 1956.

Thelonious Monk With John Coltrane (1957) demonstrates Coltrane's growth in terms of technique and harmonic sense, an evolution further chronicled on *Milestones* and *Kind of Blue*. Most of Coltrane's early solo albums are of a high quality, particularly *Blue Train* (1957), one of the best-recorded examples of his early hard bop style. Recordings from the end of the 1950s, such as "Giant Steps" (1959) and "My Favorite Things" (1960), offer evidence of Coltrane's developing virtuosity. Almost all of the many early 1960s albums Coltrane recorded are considered classics. Coltrane's last examples of avant-garde and free jazz are heard in the albums *Ascension* (1966) and *Meditations* (1966) and several albums posthumously released.

Coltrane's jazz innovations were part of the 1960s political-cultural upheavals of the Civil Rights Movement, anti–Vietnam War activism, and broader counterculture.[70] Though creating his new sound was difficult and risky, Coltrane's recordings stand among the greatest of all jazz achievements. Coltrane's life, thoughts, and words have been inspiring. Gracious and conscientious as an interviewee, Coltrane's responses were thoughtful and measured. Self-critical, Coltrane rarely said anything negative about others and gave credit to those influencing him. A quiet man whose music was volcanic, interviewers noted how different Coltrane was from his music.[71]

Tracing the development of Coltrane's playing style and critical reception to it notes shifts in Coltrane's histories and mythologies, from his early days as a semi-anonymous sideman to his final, increasingly experimental recordings to the growth of his legacy after his death. Coltrane's constantly changing sound, noting jazz's collaborative nature, influenced various musical forms. A soloist dominating jazz as Armstrong and Parker had, Coltrane's sounds highlight his individualized style, from his initial fame in Davis and Thelonious Monk's bands and as a leader on 1950s recordings.

In his last seven years, Coltrane led the most successful 1960s quartet and engaged in more experimental ventures after disbanding it. The first period was one of greater complexity in Coltrane's solos, the second of increasing tonal variety and extra-musical and spiritual motivation but decreasing structural underpinnings, as Coltrane exploited modal scales over sparse or no Western chord changes. Performing jazz with an expansive imagination in transnational, political, cultural, and religious terms, Coltrane distinguished himself from other musicians.

Not staying with any style for long, Coltrane grew so involved in his music that he confused many listeners. A cultural, musical, and political force and one of the most influential and widely imitated jazz musicians, Coltrane wished to reach and inspire, not alienate. As he traveled an immense spiritual and aesthetic distance in the last decade of his short life, Coltrane left his listeners behind in his quest for music reflecting other worlds. In his early, middle, and late periods, Coltrane transversed from a "journeyman bopper" addicted to alcohol and heroin to a spiritual warrior seeking knowledge of God through music.

Coltrane's career can be followed from his earliest recordings with Dizzy Gillespie and work as a member of Davis's legendary late 1950s quintet through his classic ensembles and later free jazz experimentations. In his relationships with fellow musicians, such as the egotistical Davis, far-out Sun Ra, and Pharaoh Sanders, Coltrane's close associate during his final, most radical years, Coltrane revealed his personal and musical excesses, demonstrating courage in following his muse. Exhibiting an enormous amount of self-sacrifice and continual growth, Coltrane's inspiration came from complex rhythmic bases of non-Western, modal music as he influenced numerous musicians, from psychedelic rock stars to fans of world music. [72]

Even before his death in 1967 at the age of forty, more verbose prose has been written about Coltrane than any other musician. By experimenting with new concepts of time, integrating Eastern philosophies into Western music, and exploring multiphonics and other new sounds on his saxophone, Coltrane opened multiple avenues of expression. As Coltrane the musician and Coltrane the religious person were interrelated, both aspects were bound up with Coltrane's identification as an African American. Accepting the traditional African belief in sounds' magical powers, Coltrane connected his music to its African roots via a devout religiosity. Coltrane's influences extended from tribal tone languages to speeches by Martin Luther King, Jr., adapting King's rhythmic inflections into a saxophone solo.

Coltrane developed a type of meditative, slow, *rubato* (subtle rhythmic manipulation and nuance) melody based on African-American gospel preaching. [73] In "Alabama" (1963), Coltrane interpreted a speech by King and in "Psalm" from *A Love Supreme* (1964), he instrumentally "narrates" his own prayer. This technique also appears in several late recordings, such as "Reverend King" (1966) and the album *Expression* (1967). Immersed in trance-inducing African and Indian musical traditions, Coltrane was influenced by additional, "exotic" ancient legacies, such as Kabbalah, an esoteric Jewish mysticism appearing in the twelfth and following centuries. [74] Coltrane's study of Indian and African music affected his approach to the soprano saxophone. His sense of mission played a central role in transforming US artistic and cultural consciousness. In his music, life, and thought, Coltrane became a key jazz figure and intensely emotional force.

Coltrane's *A Love Supreme* (1965), one of the twentieth century's most moving and spiritual albums, was deeply personal as it reflected Coltrane's religious commitment and spirituality. [75] After he was fired for a second time, in April 1957, Coltrane overcame his problems and later in his career, *A Love Supreme* celebrated his victory and the religious experience associated with it. Few albums in the popular music canon have had *A Love Supreme*'s influence, resonance, and endurance, proving jazz was a fitting medium for spiritual exploration and the expression of the sublime. With Davis's seminal album *Kind of Blue*, *A Love Supreme* became one of the most influential

recordings in jazz histories and one of the greatest and top-selling jazz albums of all time. Recorded with pianist McCoy Tyner, bassist Jimmy Garrison, and drummer Elvin Jones over the course of one evening in 1964, *A
Love Supreme* caught Coltrane at a pivotal point in his creative trajectory,
including the crystallizing of his four years with his renowned quartet and
before the turn toward his career's final, most debated phase.

Reaching a broad audience, *A Love Supreme* was a spiritual manifesto
highlighting many issues, such as mid-1960s cultural movements, expression
of spiritual values, and technical musical challenges. As he fulfilled his desire to record in one finite session without regard to commercial pressures,
Coltrane was able to pull together much of his previous work and focus it in
one piece. *A Love Supreme* is considered Coltrane's magnum opus. Its musical complexities and seminal importance to jazz histories note Coltrane's
transition from his earlier recordings' bebop and hard bop to the free jazz of
the rest of his career. *A Love Supreme* exemplifies the deep spirituality characterizing Coltrane's final years. The titles of the four-part suite "Acknowl-
edgment," "Resolution," "Pursuance," and "Psalm," with the poem Coltrane
composed for inclusion in the liner notes, which he instrumentally "recites"
in "Psalm," reflect *A Love Supreme*'s religious aspects, contributing to its
mystique and symbolic importance.

Challenging traditional, unreflective assumptions permeating jazz culture,
binary oppositions between improvisation and composition, black and white
music, and live performance and studio recording, mythical narratives surround how *A Love Supreme* was conceived and recorded and what it signifies
in terms of the trajectory of Coltrane's personal and professional lives. Despite criticism of late Coltrane, there are ways of listening to *A Love Supreme*
departing from conventional ideologies of mainstream jazz, while opening a
wide range of responses to the album, whose afterlife and contested meanings center cultural politics of race, gender, sexuality, ethnicity, class, and
nation in US and transnational popular-cultural histories. [76]

EXTRA-MUSICAL GIFTS

In his celebrated and revealing autobiography *Miles* (1989), Davis frankly
wrote of his hedonistic past and music industrial racism. Davis discusses the
women in his life and talks about music and musicians, including the legends
he played with over the years, such as Coltrane, Charlie Parker, Dizzy Gillespie, Charles Mingus, Thelonious Monk, Gil Evans, and John McLaughlin.
Davis expresses opinions on topics ranging from friendship, sex, drugs,
women, and cars. [77] Complex and contradictory, secretive at times and revealing at others, Davis was compelling, exasperating, and entertaining in

interviews, varying from polite to outrageous, from straight-ahead to contrarian.

Conducted by leading journalists, such as Leonard Feather, Stephen Davis, Ben Sidran, Mike Zwerin, and Nat Hentoff,[78] Davis could be contemplative, defiant, elegant, uncompromising, and humorous. In his classic 1962 *Playboy* interview by Alex Haley, Davis shows a typically truculent attitude and reticent demeanor. From Davis's first *DownBeat* interview in 1950 to his death in 1991, this iconic jazz magazine captured each phase of Davis's career through cover stories, features, news items, and reviews.[79] Characterized as moody and dangerous, Davis experienced tempestuous relationships with film stars, police busts, and later fusion ventures infuriating jazz and rock purists. Davis's turbulent last decade included the musical lows of his final "freaky deaky" years, tender family moments and the family turmoil erupting over his last will and testament, his Jekyll and Hyde behavior, swings between sobriety and prodigious drug use, destructive selfishness, search for marital stability, obsession with younger women, exalted musical talent, ever-present personal demons, role as younger musicians' mentor, and struggles with age and ill health.

Davis negotiated demands of art and fame with a desire to return jazz to African-American youth culture's center.[80] His emblematic green shirt, echoing Charlie Parker's overindulgence and extravagant behavior, Thelonious Monk's beatnik weirdness, and Charlie Mingus's rebel soul, appeared on the cover of *Milestones* (1958), one of a few late 1950s albums turning Davis from a talented bebop performer into a mythical figure. Davis's green shirt, a symbol of taste and elegance, was the mark of a cool outsider seeking jazz and popular-cultural preeminence.[81]

In addition to his musical talents, around 1980, Davis turned to sketching and painting. Davis's hobby became a serious passion and Davis approached it with the same creativity he applied to his music. The resulting archive of distinctive and evocative visual work showcased Davis's artistic skills. In the 1980s, Davis regularly studied with Jo Gelbard, a New York painter with a unique graphic style, whose collaborative work was transnationally exhibited. Featuring bright colors and geometric shapes, Davis's art recalls and responds to Pablo Picasso, Russian-born artist Wassily Kandinsky, US artist Jean-Michel Basquiat, and African tribal art.[82] Though few of Davis's pieces were exhibited during his lifetime, not many people were aware of the extent of Davis's commitment to sketching and painting.

Davis's estate worked with gallery owners and private parties to compile a comprehensive collection of his artwork. Such celebrities as Quincy Jones,[83] performer, producer, arranger, and composer whose work encompasses virtually all forms of popular music, have been among Davis's most adamant collectors. Possessing multiple creative talents, Davis's visual art also appeared on album covers. Beginning in 1980 until his 1991 death,

Davis made art as much a part of his life as music, bringing to it the same quest for fresh expression. Davis's subjects include highly stylized and powerful female figures, funky characters he called his "robots," and totem pole faces. A bold and skilled colorist, Davis conveyed a sense of movement in his vibrant, dynamic, and lushly textured compositions. Part of his multifaceted creativity, Davis's drawings and paintings became an additional creative outlets.[84]

From 1975 to 1981, Davis temporarily retired. Almost completely reclusive, very few people knew what was happening to him. A combination of contempt and desire for recognition drove controversy in Davis's public and private lives, resulting in his lengthy self-imposed isolation.[85] Davis lived a controversial life, from his early days in New York City with Charlie Parker to the *Birth of the Cool* (1957) to his early 1950s drug addiction and years of achievements (1954–1960), during which he signed with Columbia and collaborated with Coltrane, pianist Bill Evans, pianist and composer Wynton Kelly, and saxophonist Cannonball Adderley. Davis's dark, reclusive period (1975–1980), descent into addiction, and dramatic return to music encompassed highs and lows of a performer whose inner creativity and expressions spilled over into his personal life and public persona.

Throughout his career, Davis seemed enigmatic, brusque, rude, yet capable of a warm lyricism in his art. Davis exposed a harsh temperament, inscrutability, unpredictability, refusal to be pinned down, and sudden juxtapositions of gentleness and violence. Similar attributes can be heard in Davis's art, as he moved from the pioneering bebop days and his apprenticeship with the music's founder, Charlie Parker, to his series of innovations, the "cool" and orchestral recordings with arranger Gil Evans, modal-based postbop with his 1950s and 1960s small groups, work with electric bands, 1980s "post-modernist" works syncretizing styles, and late funk, pop, and hip hop recordings.[86]

Davis's music evolved according to the perspectives of the musicians with whom he performed. Some of Davis's closest associates and friends include singer, songwriter, actress, activist, and "Queen of Funk" Chaka Khan,[87] Paul Buckmaster, Grammy Award–winning English artist, arranger, conductor, and composer best known for his 1970s orchestral collaborations with Elton John and The Rolling Stones, and George Duke, US musician and record producer transversing jazz and popular music borders during his more than forty-year career of playing soulful music on keyboard instruments (especially the synthesizer), composing, producing hit recordings, helping pioneer jazz fusion and funk, dabbling in Brazilian jazz, and arranging music for Davis.

Davis's landmark albums *Birth of the Cool* (1957), *Miles Ahead* (1957), *Kind of Blue* (1959), *In a Silent Way* (1969), and *Bitches Brew* (1970) were central to his development as an instrumentalist, group leader, and composer.

While the "last Miles" bands have been overlooked, Davis's recorded work and live tours in his last decade were in keeping with the experimentations stretching over his career. Some dismissed this aspect of Davis's body of work, claiming that in the 1980s Davis was only good for performing live, and condemning Davis's pop phase.[88]

TRANSNATIONAL ROUTES

Claimed by keepers of US jazz history as somehow quintessentially American, part of US jazz exceptionalist claims, Davis, like Armstrong, Ellington, and other supposedly exclusive US jazz musicians had a distinct interest in jazz's transnational possibilities and expressed those interests in multiple albums. Creating music consumed across continents, one of the most memorable events of Davis's later years occurred at the 1991 Montreux, Switzerland, Jazz Festival, where Davis joined with an orchestra conducted by Quincy Jones to perform some of the classic late 1950s Gil Evans arrangements.

From 1969 to 1975, Davis's groups made use of electronically altered trumpet, Indian sitār and tablā, African and Brazilian percussion,[89] and African-American dance rhythms, heard on the albums *On the Corner* (1972) and *Big Fun* (1974). Evans-influenced orchestral numbers are heard on *Music from Siesta* (1987). Davis's albums, with pieces arranged and conducted by Evans, such as *Miles Ahead* (1957), *Porgy and Bess* (1958), and *Sketches of Spain* (1960), were monuments of the genre. The Davis-Evans collaborations were marked by complex arrangements, a near-equal emphasis on orchestra and soloist, and some of Davis's most soulful and emotionally powerful playing. Davis and Evans occasionally collaborated in later years, but never again so memorably as on these three albums.

With *'Round About Midnight* (1957), *Kind of Blue* (1959), and *In a Silent Way* (1969), *Sketches of Spain* is one of Davis's most enduring and inventive achievements. Recorded between November 1959 and March 1960, after Coltrane and Cannonball Adderley left his group, Davis teamed with Gil Evans for the third time. Davis brought Evans the album's signature piece, "Concierto de Aranjuez," after hearing a classical version of it at bassist Joe Mondragon's house. Evans was as equally taken with it as Davis, and ventured to create an entire album of material around it, with the resulting product considered a masterpiece of modern art.

On the "Concierto," Evans's arrangement provided an orchestra and jazz band of Paul Chambers, Jimmy Cobb, and Elvin Jones the opportunity to record a classical work. The piece, with its striking colors and sophisticated *adagio* (a movement or composition marked to be played in slow tempo), performed by Davis on a flugelhorn with a Harmon Mute, is one of twentieth-century popular music's most memorable works. Davis was noted for his control over his instrument and Evans for his flawless conducting. Also noteworthy are "Saeta," with one of the most remarkable technical solos of Davis's career, and the album's closer "Solea," a narrative piece based on an Andalusian folk song about a woman encountering the procession taking Christ to Calvary. She sings of his passion and the procession with full brass accompaniment.

Cobb and Jones perform with flamenco-flavored percussion and allow the orchestra to indulge in the lushly impassioned arrangement Evans provided to accompany Davis, at his most challenged, even as he delivers with grace and verve. The lavish and romantic *Sketches of Spain* features timbres, tonalities, and harmonic structures rarely heard in jazz and stands as an exemplary recording of "Third Stream," a fusion of jazz, European classical, and world music.[90]

Davis sought to broaden his audience by fusing qualities of other musical cultures, such as flamenco, classical, rock, and funk. "Flamenco Sketches" (1959) characterizes Davis's common approach to composition, in which Davis would develop an idea from a sideman (Evans) according to his approach at the time. During his jazz-fusion decades, this collaborative approach characterized Davis's music making. A form of song, dance, and instrumental (mostly guitar) music associated with the Andalusian Roma (Gypsies) of southern Spain, flamenco's roots, though somewhat mysterious, lie in the Roma migration from Rajasthan (in northwest India) to Spain between the ninth and fourteenth centuries. These migrants brought with them tambourines, bells, and wooden castanets and an extensive repertoire of songs and dances. In Spain, they encountered Sephardic Jews and Moors's rich cultures. Their centuries-long cultural intermingling produced the flamenco art form.[91]

The use of modes in Davis's 1958–1959 recordings, such as "Milestones" on *Milestones* (1958) and "So What" and "Flamenco Sketches" on *Kind of Blue* (1959), had less impact than the slowing of harmonic rhythm. In place of fast-moving, functional chord progressions, Davis used half-tone oscillation, common in flamenco music, diatonic ostinatos (vamps), drones, and tone-dominant alternation in the bass line. The French theme of The Davis Quintet's *Filles de Kilimanjaro* (1968) adds to Davis's transnational output. The studio recordings released by The Davis Quintet contributed to improvisational strategies, jazz composition, and mediation between mainstream and avant-garde jazz, yet most critical attention focused on live performances and the political-cultural contexts of the work.[92]

The "Second Quintet," Davis's mid-1960s group, was one of the most innovative and influential in jazz histories. Among its influential recordings are *Live at the Plugged Nickel* (1965), *E.S.P.* (1965), *Miles Smiles* (1967), *Sorcerer* (1967), and *Nefertiti* (1968), also the name of a West Coast rapper with Nation of Islam roots and gang experiences, borrowing her stage name from an ancient Egyptian queen, and corresponding to Queen Latifah's Muslim International[93] and Afro-centric renaming (*latifah* has been translated as "delicate" and "sensitive" in Arabic), part of a broader hip hop trend to reassert a type of black nationalism and pride in the face of hyper-commodification and an excessive focus on sexuality and violence.

Though the early 1960s were transitional, less innovative years for Davis, his music and playing remained top-caliber. Davis began forming another soon-to-be-classic small group in late 1962 with bassist Ron Carter, pianist Herbie Hancock, and teenage drummer Tony Williams, with tenor saxophonist Wayne Shorter joining the lineup in 1964. This quintet was characterized by a light, free sound and repertoire extending from the blues to avant-garde and free jazz. Compared with innovations of other 1960s modern jazz groups, the Davis quintet's experimentations in polyrhythm and polytonality were subtler but just as audacious. Around the time of *Filles de Kilimanjaro* (1968), Davis began performing with electronic instruments. *Miles Smiles* (1966), an album overlooked as "classic Davis," use schematics and sheet music changes. One of Davis's lesser known albums, *Miles Smiles* constituted a new direction for Davis and the mark of Davis's creation of post-bop, as The Second Quintet's mid-1960s formation was central to the invention of this additional jazz subgenre.

GOING ELECTRIC

When Davis experimented with African and rock music in the late 1960s, he alienated many of his fans. However, his electric explorations persisted and their impact on popular music continues. Davis's music produced between 1967 and 1991 has been neglected and misunderstood, with accolades from jazz critics and fans usually ending with his late 1960s work. Around that time, Davis abandoned conventional jazz practices to experiment with avant-garde improvisation, rock music, and electric instruments, using elaborate, electronic post-production techniques to sharpen his studio recordings. These explorations became known as "fusion." A misunderstood and critically dismissed period, critics and listeners denigrated Davis's electric recordings. Some argued Davis succumbed to rock influences to the detriment of his jazz stylings.

Davis's experimentations culminated in the masterful *Bitches Brew* (1970), one of jazz and rock's most influential albums.[94] *Bitches Brew* attracted criticism and listeners welcoming the music of 1969–1975 and the work following Davis's 1981 return from retirement. The album strongly impacted Davis's career and the musicians involved, including Wayne Shorter, Chick Corea, John McLaughlin, Joe Zawinul, and Bennie Maupin, multi-reedist performing on bass clarinet, flute, and various saxophones.

One of the most iconic albums in US music, *Bitches Brew* was the preeminent landmark of jazz-fusion. Abdul Mati Klarwein, a painter best known for his works used on the covers of music albums, designed the artwork for *Bitches Brew*'s cover. The complexity of the *Bitches Brew* cover captures the multi-layered and interwoven understandings of jazz fusion, as *Bitches Brew*'s sounds and images were linked to the political-cultural times of its release, especially early 1970s racial upheavals. The cover of *Bitches Brew*'s Afro-centric[95] and psychedelic connotations resonated in the Black Power Movement[96] and early 1970s progressive counterculture. Critics believed *Bitches Brew* represented jazz's death. They thought Davis left behind racially identifiable music for the commercial success of white rock and the countercultural lifestyle that became mainstream after Woodstock in 1969.[97] Others saw *Bitches Brew* as a decisive moment in jazz and a remarkable and daring album ahead of its time.

Following the grooves and ambiance of *In a Silent Way* (1969) and a tour with a quintet called "The Lost Band" with Wayne Shorter, Chick Corea, Dave Holland, and Jack DeJohnette, Davis went into the studio with guitarist John McLaughlin and keyboardist Joe Zawinul. Working with his essential producer, Teo Macero, Davis set a variety of ideas loose, producing a different direction for jazz and rock. Fusing the two, *Bitches Brew* blends the most avant-garde aspects of Western music with rhythmic sounds while rejecting jazz and rock for an alternative way of how music can be made. Incorporating rock influences and an unprecedented use of jazz recording techniques, featuring extraordinary technical features on each of the six items of the double LP, a constellation of musical, political, and psychological forces came together to produce one of contemporary music's most radical works. *Bitches Brew* became the album transforming jazz with its electric sound and rock-influenced style.

During the first twenty years of Davis's prolific career, few critics could find anything negative to say about his music. But when Davis went electric in the late 1960s, traditionalists turned on him with charges of "selling out" to commercial interests and record company politics. "The greatest example of self-violation in the histories of art," wrote Stanley Crouch, quoting Nietzsche's evaluation of Wagner.[98] Though Davis's "electric period" continues to influence contemporary music, jazz purists detest this phase, encompassing his career's second half, from 1967 to his 1991 death. As electric music became more important to Davis's career and jazz more generally, connections were made between Davis, iconic and exoticized rock guitarist, singer, and songwriter Jimi Hendrix,[99] and Sly Stone, especially the ways each fed one another's creativity.[100]

As "electric Miles" plugged into the zeitgeist, trading his suits for hipster finery and opening up his music to distortion and groove-based repetition, repudiating jazz's acoustic roots, the longtime debate about Davis's electric music echoed Bob Dylan, also "going electric" and embracing jazz, with his improvising less a continuation of a folk tradition than of jazz and electric blues. Dylan's followers experienced shock when he traded his acoustic sound, a hallmark of the folk scene regarding him as its spokesman, for an electric guitar at the 1965 Newport Folk Festival. There, some in the audience tried to boo Dylan off stage, as he incurred the wrath of folkies by having the audacity to express himself through an electric guitar. On his album *Bringing It All Back Home* (1965), electric instruments were used in a violation of folk dogma. As Dylan's mainstream audience increased, his purist folk fans fell off. His mid-1960s recordings, backed by rock musicians, reached the top of the charts while attracting denunciation from those in the folk movement. By the late 1960s, Dylan was a leading rock performer, distancing himself from the early 1960s urban folk movement.

CONCLUSION

An innovator of cool, modal, and free jazz and acclaimed as one of the greatest influences on jazz, during his forty-six-year career, Miles Davis provided the impetus for major changes in jazz and popular music. A transnational popular-cultural icon and trend-setting "hipster,"[101] Davis's career extended from his recordings with Charlie Parker and the *Birth of the Cool* nonet through the Coltrane quintet, 1960s Gil Evans–arranged masterpieces, landmark *Kind of Blue* album, Shorter/Hancock/Carter/Williams group, and success of his 1970s fusion recordings.

Davis was one of the crucial influences on modern jazz's development. Regularly changing styles and incorporating multiple transnational influences, Davis left his inimitable impact on many jazz forms, whether he created them or developed others' work, from bebop to modal jazz, his seminal quintet and big band performances to later jazz-funk[102] experimentations. Davis knew and worked with everyone who was anyone in jazz, from Coltrane to Monk. He was a friend of French philosopher and author Jean-Paul Sartre,[103] lover of French actress and popular *chanson* singer Juliette Gréco, and collaborator with a multitude of musicians, including German composer Karlheinz Stockhausen.[104] One of the great and archetypal jazz artists and virtuosos, myth making about Davis's life by Davis himself and biographers tells the story of his childhood, depressions, heroin use, and more familiar public career.[105]

As jazz audiences followed Davis, from Ivy League suits to silks and velvets to his electronic bands' wild funk, they gazed at the middle-class son of an East St. Louis dentist who became a teenage bebop apprentice on 52nd Street and ended up a restless veteran who spent his final years collaborating with the likes of Prince and investigating hip hop's possibilities. An incomparably influential artist and one of the legendary musicians in jazz, Davis shifted from a polite young trumpeter making a name for himself to bombastic innovator to mythic legend.

Jazz's most enigmatic, elusive, and enduring star and an extraordinarily complex artist living a turbulent life and leaving behind a conflicted legacy, since he arrived in late 1940s New York to work with Charlie Parker and Dizzy Gillespie, Davis transformed the jazz idiom, initiating a series of jazz movements, beginning with the early 1950s cool jazz period and continuing with the release of *Kind of Blue*. One of the United States's greatest musical innovators, in a career continuing to fascinate, Davis's contemplative, defiant, and elegant personality meshed with his art to form one of the most compelling figures in transnational popular-music histories.

NOTES

1. Joachim-Ernst Berendt and Günther Huesmann. *The Jazz Book: From Ragtime to Fusion and Beyond*. Brooklyn, NY: Lawrence Hill Books, 1992; Gary Carner. "Introduction: [Literature of Jazz]." *Black American Literature Forum* 25.3, Literature of Jazz Issue (Autumn 1991): 441–448; Charles D. Carson. "'Bridging the Gap': Creed Taylor, Grover Washington Jr., and the Crossover Roots of Smooth Jazz." *Black Music Research Journal* 28.1, Becoming: Blackness and the Musical Imagination (Spring 2008): 1–15; Julie Coryell and Laura Friedman. *Jazz-Rock Fusion, The People, The Music*. Milwaukee, WI: Hal Leonard Corp., 2000; Kevin Fellezs. *Birds of Fire: Jazz, Rock, Funk, and the Creation of Fusion*. Durham [NC]: Duke University Press, 2011; Jens Jørgen Gjedsted. "Electric Jazz." *Fontes Artis Musicae* 30.3 (July–September 1983): 132–136; Yvetta Kajanová. "The Rock, Pop and Jazz in Contemporary Musicological Studies." *International Review of the Aesthetics and Sociology of Music* 44.2 (December 2013): 343–359; Andrew Kania. "All Play and No Work: An Ontology of Jazz." *The Journal of Aesthetics and Art Criticism* 69.4 (Fall 2011): 391–403; Stuart Nicholson. *Jazz Rock: A History*. New York: Schirmer Books, 1998.

2. John Gennari. *Blowin' Hot and Cool: Jazz and Its Critics*. Chicago: University of Chicago Press, 2006.

3. Paul R. Farnsworth. "The Effects of Role-Taking on Artistic Achievement." *The Journal of Aesthetics and Art Criticism* 18.3 (March 1960): 345–349; Mark C. Gridley. *Jazz Styles: History & Analysis*. Upper Saddle River, NJ: Prentice Hall, 2000; Kenny Mathieson. *Cookin': Hard Bop and Soul Jazz, 1954–65*. Edinburgh: Canongate, 2002; David H. Rosenthal. "Jazz in the Ghetto: 1950–70." *Popular Music* 7.1 (January 1988): 51–56; _____. "Hard Bop and Its Critics." *The Black Perspective in Music* 16.1 (Spring 1988): 21–29; _____. *Hard Bop: Jazz and Black Music, 1955–1965*. New York: Oxford University Press, 1992; Evan Sarzin and Charley Gerard. *Hard Bop Piano Jazz Compositions of the 50s and 60s*. New York: Gerard & Sarzin 1992.

4. Anush Apoyan. *The Preacher: A Tribute to Horace Silver*. Saarbrücken AV Akademikerverlag 2013; Horace Silver. *Horace Silver: The Art of Small Combo Jazz Playing, Composing and Arranging*. Milwaukee, WI: Hal Leonard Corp., 1995; Horace Silver and Philip Pastras. *Let's Get to the Nitty Gritty: The Autobiography of Horace Silver*. Berkeley, CA: University of California Press, 2006.

5. Wayne Enstice and Paul Rubin. *Jazz Spoken Here: Conversations with Twenty-Two Musicians*. Baton Rouge: Louisiana State University Press, 1992; Alan Goldsher. *Hard Bop*

Academy: The Sidemen of Art Blakey and the Jazz Messengers. Milwaukee, WI: Hal Leonard, 2002; Leslie Gourse. *Art Blakey, Jazz Messenger*. New York: Schirmer Trade Books, 2002; Sandy Warren. *Art Blakey Cookin' and Jammin': Recipes and Remembrances from a Jazz Life*. Donaldsonville, LA: Margaret Media, 2010.

6. Mike Acquaviva and Elliott M. Rudwick. *A Guide to The East St. Louis Race Riot of 1917*. Frederick, MD: University Publications of America, 1985; Harper Barnes. *Never Been a Time: The 1917 Race Riot that Sparked the Civil Rights Movement*. New York: Walker & Co.: Distributed to the trade by Macmillan, 2008; D. S. Bailey. *Up in Flames: [The Torching of East St. Louis 1917: Based on a True Story]*. St. Louis, MO: Voices Books & Pub., 2004; Joseph Boskin. *Urban Racial Violence in the Twentieth Century*. Beverly Hills, CA: Glencoe Press, 1976; Jennifer Hamer. *Abandoned in the Heartland: Work, Family, and Living in East St. Louis*. Berkeley: University of California Press, 2011; Charles L. Lumpkins. *American Pogrom: The East St. Louis Race Riot and Black Politics*. Athens, OH: Ohio University Press, 2008; Malcolm McLaughlin. *Power, Community, and Racial Killing in East St. Louis*. New York: Palgrave Macmillan, 2005; Elliott M. Rudwick. *Race Riot at East St. Louis, July 2, 1917*. Carbondale, IL: Southern Illinois University Press, 1964; Elliott M. Rudwick and Mike Acquaviva. *The East St. Louis Race Riot of 1917*. Frederick, MD: University Publications of America, 1985; State Council of Defense of Illinois. Labor Committee. *Report to the Illinois State Council of Defense on the Race Riots at East St. Louis*. Chicago: Illinois State Council of Defense, 1917; United States Congress House Special Committee to Investigate the East St. Louis Riots. *East St. Louis Riots: Report of the Special Committee Authorized by Congress to Investigate the East St. Louis Riots*. [Washington, D.C.]: [U.S. G.P.O.], 1918.

7. Lyn Driggs Cunningham and Jimmy Jones. *Sweet, Hot, and Blue: St. Louis' Musical Heritage*. Jefferson, NC: McFarland, 1989; Samuel A. Floyd, Jr. "A Black Composer in Nineteenth-Century St. Louis." *19th-Century Music* 4.2 (Autumn 1980): 121–133; William H. Kenney. "James Scott and the Culture of Classic Ragtime." *American Music* 9.2 (Summer 1991): 149–182; Benjamin Looker. *BAG: "Point from Which Creation Begins": The Black Artists' Group of St. Louis*. St. Louis: Missouri Historical Society Press, [Columbia, MO]: Distributed by University of Missouri Press, 2004; Harriet Ottenheimer. "The Blues Tradition in St. Louis." *Black Music Research Journal* 9.2, Papers of the 1989 National Conference on Black Music Research (Autumn 1989): 135–151; Dennis Owsley, Clark Terry, and Sheldon Art Galleries. *City of Gabriels: The History of Jazz in St. Louis, 1895–1973*. St. Louis, MO: Reedy Press, 2006.

8. Cary Ginell. *Mr. B.: The Life and Music of Billy Eckstine*. Montclair: Hal Leonard Books, 2013; Max Jones. *Jazz Talking: Profiles, Interviews, and other Riffs on Jazz Musicians*. Boulder, CO: Da Capo Press, 2000; Eileen Southern and William Clarence ("Billy") Eckstine. "'Mr. B' of Ballad and Bop." *The Black Perspective in Music* 8.1 (Spring 1980): 54–64; Dempsey J. Travis. *Billy Eckstine: The Ballad Singer of the Century*. Chicago: Urban Research Press, 1994.

9. Jerome Klinkowitz. *Listen, Gerry Mulligan: An Aural Narrative in Jazz*. New York: Schirmer Books, 1991.

10. David Baker. *The Jazz Style of Sonny Rollins: A Musical and Historical Perspective*. Lebanon, IN: Studio 224: Sole distributorship Studio P/R, 1980; Charles Blancq. *Sonny Rollins, The Journey of a Jazzman*. Boston, MA: Twayne, 1983; Bob Blumenthal and John Abbott. *Saxophone Colossus: A Portrait of Sonny Rollins*. New York: Abrams, 2010; Eric Nisenson. *Open Sky: Sonny Rollins and His World of Improvisation*. New York: St. Martin's Press, 2000; Richard Palmer. *Sonny Rollins: The Cutting Edge*. New York: Continuum, 2004; Gene Santoro. "Jazz: The Edgy Optimist: At 76, Saxist Sonny Rollins Is Still on Top of His Game." *The American Scholar* 76.1 (Winter 2007): 125–129; Peter Niklas Wilson. *Sonny Rollins: The Definitive Musical Guide*. Berkeley, CA: Berkeley Hills Books, 2001.

11. Bob Gluck. *You'll Know When You Get There: Herbie Hancock and the Mwandishi Band*. Chicago; London: The University of Chicago Press, 2012; Herbie Hancock and Lisa Dickey. *Herbie Hancock: Possibilities*. New York: Viking, 2014; Marco Meier. *All That Funk James Brown, Herbie Hancock, George Clinton*. Zürich: TA-Media AG, 1999; Keith Waters. "Modes, Scales, Functional Harmony, and Nonfunctional Harmony in the Compositions of Herbie Hancock." *Journal of Music Theory* 49.2 (Fall 2005): 333–357.

12. Ron Carter and Oliver Nelson. *Building a Jazz Bass Line*. Jamaica, NY: Noslen Music Co., 1966; Sherry Turner DeCarava, Roy DeCarava, and Ron Carter. "Inventory: A Conversation between Roy DeCarava and Ron Carter." *MoMA* 21 (Winter–Spring 1996): 2–7; Dan Ouellette and Nat Hentoff. *Ron Carter: Finding the Right Notes*. New York: Retrac Productions, 2014.

13. Gerald Early. "The Passing of Jazz's Old Guard: Remembering Charles Mingus, Thelonious Monk, and Sonny Stitt." *The Kenyon Review*, New Series 7.2 (Spring 1985): 21–36; Gary Giddins. *Rhythm-a-ning: Jazz Tradition and Innovation in the '80s*. New York: Oxford University Press, 1985.

14. Patricia Julien. "'Sakeena's Vision': The Trifocal Organization of Harmonic Relations in One of Wayne Shorter's Early Compositions." *Theory and Practice* 34 (2009): 107–140; Michelle Mercer. *Footprints: The Life and Work of Wayne Shorter*. New York: J. P. Tarcher/Penguin, 2004; Steven Strunk. "Notes on Harmony in Wayne Shorter's Compositions, 1964–67." *Journal of Music Theory* 49.2 (Fall 2005): 301–332.

15. Dale A. Craig. "Trans-Cultural Composition in the 20th Century." *Tempo, New Series* 156 (March 1986): 16–18; Steven Strunk. "Chick Corea's 1984 Performance of 'Night and Day.'" *Journal of Music Theory* 43.2 (Autumn 1999): 257–281; William "Billy" Taylor. "Jazz: America's Classical Music." *The Black Perspective in Music* 14.1, Special Issue: Black American Music Symposium 1985 (Winter 1986): 21–25.

16. Gernot Blume. "Blurred Affinities: Tracing the Influence of North Indian Classical Music in Keith Jarrett's Solo Piano Improvisations." *Popular Music* 22.2 (May 2003): 117–142; Ian Carr. *Keith Jarrett: The Man and His Music*. London: Paladin, 1991; Peter Elsdon. *Keith Jarrett's the Köln Concert*. New York: Oxford University Press, 2013; Anders Friberg and Andreas Sundström. "Swing Ratios and Ensemble Timing in Jazz Performance: Evidence for a Common Rhythmic Pattern." *Music Perception: An Interdisciplinary Journal* 19.3 (Spring 2002): 333–349; Leonard Lyons. *The Great Jazz Pianists: Speaking of Their Lives and Music*. New York: W. Morrow, 1983; Jairo Moreno. "Body 'n' Soul?: Voice and Movement in Keith Jarrett's Pianism." *The Musical Quarterly* 83.1 (Spring 1999): 75–92; Dariusz Terefenko. *Keith Jarrett's Transformation of Standard Tunes: Theory, Analysis, and Pedagogy*. Saarbrücken, Germany: VDM Verlag Dr. Müller, 2009; _____. "Keith Jarrett's Art of Solo Introduction: 'Stella by Starlight'—A Case Study." *Intégral* 24, Special Issue in Honor of Robert Wason (2010): 81–114.

17. Colin Harper. *Bathed in Lightning: John McLaughlin, the 60s, and the Emerald Beyond*. London: Jawbone Press: Distributed by Hal Leonard Corporation, 2014; Walter Kolosky. *Follow Your Heart: John McLaughlin Song by Song: A Listener's Guide*. Cary, NC: Abstract Logix Books, 2010; Alyn Shipton. *Jazz Makers: Vanguards of Sound*. Oxford; New York: Oxford University Press, 2002; Paul Stump. *Go Ahead John: The Music of John McLaughlin*. London: SAF Publishing Ltd, 1999; Ken Trethewey. *John McLaughlin: The Emerald Beyond*. Jazz-Fusion Books, 2013.

18. Derrick Bang. *Vince Guaraldi at the Piano*. Jefferson, NC: McFarland & Co., 2012; Luiz Costa-Lima Neto, Laura Coimbra, and Tom Moore. *The Experimental Music of Hermeto Pascoal and Group (1981–1993): Conception and Language*. Hillsdale, NY: Pendragon Press, 2015; Cary Ginell and Hubert Laws. *The Evolution of Mann: Herbie Mann & The Flute in Jazz*. Milwaukee, WI: Hal Leonard Books, 2014; Deborah Mawer. *Darius Milhaud: Modality & Structure in Music of the 1920s*. Aldershot, England: Scolar Press; Brookfield, VT: Ashgate Pub. Co., 1997; Charles A. Perrone and Christopher Dunn. *Brazilian Popular Music and Globalization*. Gainesville: University Presses of Florida, 2001.

19. Howard Brofsky. "Miles Davis and 'My Funny Valentine': The Evolution of a Solo." *Black Music Research Journal* 3 (1983): 23–45.

20. Trey Ellis. "The New Black Aesthetic." *Callaloo* 38 (Winter 1989): 233–243; Bruce Boyd Raeburn. "'They're Tryin' to Wash Us Away': New Orleans Musicians Surviving Katrina." *The Journal of American History* 94.3, Through the Eye of Katrina: The Past as Prologue? (December 2007): 812–819; Ben Ratliff. *The Jazz Ear: Conversations Over Music*. New York: Times Books, 2008; Ben Sidran. *Talking Jazz: An Oral History*. New York: Da Capo Press, 1995; Don Sweeney. *Backstage at The Tonight Show: From Johnny Carson to Jay Leno*. Lanham, MD: Taylor Trade Pub., 2006; Mark Small, Andrew Taylor, Jonathan Feist, and

Berklee College of Music. *Masters of Music: Conversations with Berklee Greats*. Boston, MA: Berklee Press; Milwaukee, WI: Distributed by H. Leonard, 1999.

21. Matthew W. Butterfield. "Why Do Jazz Musicians Swing Their Eighth Notes?" *Music Theory Spectrum* 33.1 (Spring 2011): 3–26; Andy Hamilton and Lee Konitz. *Lee Konitz: Conversations on the Improviser's Art*. Ann Arbor: University of Michigan Press, 2007.

22. Christopher Smith. "A Sense of the Possible: Miles Davis and the Semiotics of Improvised Performance." *TDR* (1988–) 39.3 (Autumn 1995): 41–55.

23. Chet Baker. *As Though I Had Wings: The Lost Memoir*. New York: St. Martin's Press, 1997; William Claxton. *Young Chet: The Young Chet Baker*. New York: Te Neues Pub. Co., 1998; Jeroen de Valk. *Chet Baker: His Life and Music*. Berkeley, CA: Berkeley Hills Books: Distributed to the trade by Publishers Group West, 2000; James Gavin. *Deep in a Dream: The Long Night of Chet Baker*. Chicago: Chicago Review Press, 2011; Hans Henrik Lerfeldt and Thorbjørn Sjøgren. *Chet: The Discography of Chesney Henry Baker*. Copenhagen, Denmark: Distribution, Tiderne Skifter Publishers, 1985; Jim Merod and Frank Strazzeri. "Paint Another Picture: An Interview with Frank Strazzeri." *Boundary 2* 22.2, Jazz as a Cultural Archive (Summer 1995): 191–206.

24. "Dexter Keith Gordon." *The Black Perspective in Music* 18.1/2 (1990): 218–219; Stan Britt. *Dexter Gordon: A Musical Biography*. New York: Da Capo Press, 1989; Michael Dempsey. "All the Colors: Bertrand Tavernier Talks about 'Round Midnight.'" *Film Quarterly* 40.3 (Spring 1987): 2–11; Jürgen E. Grandt. "Kinds of Blue: Toni Morrison, Hans Janowitz, and the Jazz Aesthetic Kinds of Blue: Toni Morrison, Hans Janowitz, and the Jazz Aesthetic." *African American Review* 38.2 (Summer 2004): 303–322; William Lawlor. *Beat Culture: Icons, Lifestyles, and Impact*. Santa Barbara, CA: ABC-CLIO, 2005; Thorbjørn Sjøgren. *Long Tall Dexter: The Discography of Dexter Gordon*. Copenhagen: Thorbjørn Sjøgren, 1986.

25. Richard Vacca. *The Boston Jazz Chronicles: Faces, Places, and Nightlife, 1937–1962*. Belmont, MA: Troy Street Publishing, 2012.

26. Walter Bruyninckx. *Jazz, Modern Jazz: Be-Bop, Hard Bop, West Coast*. Mechelen, Belgium, 60 Years of Recorded Jazz Team, 1986; William Claxton and Hitoshi Namekata. *Jazz West Coast: Artwork of Pacific Jazz Records*. Tokyo: Bijutsu Shuppan-Sha, 1992; Dwight Dickerson. "Jazz in Los Angeles: The Black Experience." *Black Music Research Journal* 31.1 (Spring 2011): 179–192; Jacqueline Cogdell DjeDje and Eddie S. Meadows. *California Soul: Music of African Americans in the West*. Berkeley: University of California Press, 1998; K. O. Eckland. *Jazz West, 1945–1985: The A-Z Guide to West Coast Jazz Music*. Carmel-by-the-Sea, CA: Cypress, 1986; Jo Brooks Fox and Jules L. Fox. *The Melody Lingers On: Scenes from the Golden Years of West Coast Jazz*. Santa Barbara, CA: Fithian Press, 1996; Ted Gioia. *West Coast Jazz: Modern Jazz in California, 1945–1960*. New York: Oxford University Press, 1992; Robert Gordon, M. A. *Jazz West Coast: The Los Angeles Jazz Scene of the 1950s*. London; New York: Quartet Books, 1986; Anthony Macías. "California's Composer Laureate: Gerald Wilson, Jazz Music, and Black-Mexican Connections." *Boom: A Journal of California* 3.2 (Summer 2013): 34–51; Elizabeth Pepin and Lewis Watts. *Harlem of the West: The San Francisco Fillmore Jazz Era*. San Francisco: Chronicle Books, 2006; Michael T. Spencer. "Jazz Education at the Westlake College of Music, 1945–61." *Journal of Historical Research in Music Education* 35.1 (October 2013): 50–65; Geoffrey Wheeler. *Dial Records: West Coast Jazz and the Be-Bop Era*. Ft. Wayne, IN: Hillbrook Press, 2009; Scott Yanow. *Jazz: A Regional Exploration*. Westport, CT: Greenwood Press, 2005.

27. David Baker. *The Jazz Style of Clifford Brown: A Musical and Historical Perspective*. Hialeah, FL: Studio P/R, 1982; Nick Catalano. *Clifford Brown: The Life and Art of the Legendary Jazz Trumpeter*. Oxford; New York: Oxford University Press, 2000; Eddie S. Meadows. "Clifford Brown in Los Angeles." *Black Music Research Journal* 31.1 (Spring 2011): 45–63.

28. Amiri Baraka. *Digging: The Afro-American Soul of American Classical Music*. Berkeley: University of California Press, 2009; Raymond Horricks. *The Importance of Being Eric Dolphy*. Tunbridge Wells: Costello, 1988; Fred Moten. *In the Break: The Aesthetics of the Black Radical Tradition*. Minneapolis: University of Minnesota Press, 2003; Vladimir Simosko and Barry Tepperman. *Eric Dolphy: A Musical Biography and Discography*. Washington: Smithsonian Institution Press; [distributed in the United States and Canada by G. Braziller, New York] 1971; Lorenzo Thomas and Aldon Lynn Nielsen. *Don't Deny My Name: Words*

and Music and the Black Intellectual Tradition. Ann Arbor: University of Michigan Press, 2008.

29. Bette Yarbrough Cox. *Central Avenue—Its Rise and Fall, 1890–c. 1955: Including the Musical Renaissance of Black Los Angeles.* Los Angeles: BEEM Publications, 1996; Los Angeles (CA). Grand Avenue Committee. *Reimagining Grand Avenue: Creating a Center for Los Angeles.* Los Angeles: Grand Avenue Committee, 2005; Lawrance Marable, Steven Louis Isoardi, and University of California, Los Angeles. Oral History Program. *Central Avenue Sounds Oral History Transcript, 1996: Lawrance Marable.* Los Angeles: Oral History Program, University of California, Los Angeles, 2001; Kenneth H. Marcus. "Living the Los Angeles Renaissance: A Tale of Two Black Composers." *The Journal of African American History* 91.1, The African American Experience in the Western States (Winter 2006): 55–72; Gary Marmorstein. "Central Avenue Jazz: Los Angeles Black Music of the Forties." *Southern California Quarterly* 70.4 (Winter 1988): 415–426; Johnny Otis. *Upside Your Head!: Rhythm and Blues on Central Avenue.* Hanover, NH: University Press of New England, 1993.

30. Joan C. Barker. *Danger, Duty, and Disillusion: The Worldview of LosAngeles Police Officers.* Prospect Heights, IL: Waveland Press, 1999; Lou Cannon. *Official Negligence: How Rodney King and the Riots Changed Los Angeles and the LAPD.* New York: Times Books, 1997; Edward J. Escobar. "The Dialectics of Repression: The Los Angeles Police Department and the Chicano Movement, 1968–1971." *The Journal of American History* 79.4 (March 1993): 1483–1514; _____. *Race, Police, and the Making of a Political Identity: Mexican Americans and the Los Angeles Police Department, 1900–1945.* Berkeley: University of California Press, 1999; Steve Herbert. "Morality in Law Enforcement: Chasing 'Bad Guys' with the Los Angeles Police Department." *Law & Society Review* 30.4 (1996): 799–818; _____. "The Normative Ordering of Police Territoriality: Making and Marking Space with the Los Angeles Police Department." *Annals of the Association of American Geographers* 86.3 (September 1996): 567–582; _____. *Policing Space: Territoriality and the Los Angeles Police Department.* Minneapolis: University of Minnesota Press, 1997; Marshall W. Meyer. "Police Shootings at Minorities: The Case of Los Angeles." *The Annals of the American Academy of Political and Social Science* 452, The Police and Violence (November 1980): 98–110.

31. Janet L. Abu-Lughod. *Race, Space, and Riots in Chicago, New York, and Los Angeles.* Oxford; New York: Oxford University Press, 2007; Eric Avila. *Popular Culture in the Age of White Flight: Fear and Fantasy in Suburban Los Angeles.* Berkeley: University of California Press, 2004; Lawrence Bobo. *Prismatic Metropolis: Inequality in Los Angeles.* New York: Russell Sage Foundation, 2000; Edward T. Chang and Jeannette Diaz-Veizades. *Ethnic Peace in the American City: Building Community in Los Angeles and Beyond.* New York: New York University Press, 1999; Jerry Cohen and William S. Murphy. *Burn, Baby, Burn! The Los Angeles Race Riot, August, 1965.* New York, Dutton, 1966; Darnell M. Hunt and Ana-Christina Ramón. *Black Los Angeles: American Dreams and Racial Realities.* New York: New York University Press, 2010; Josh Kun and Laura Pulido. *Black and Brown in Los Angeles: Beyond Conflict and Coalition.* Berkeley: University of California Press, 2013; Laura Pulido. *Black, Brown, Yellow, and Left: Radical Activism in Los Angeles.* Berkeley: University of California Press, 2006.

32. Paul Bullock. *Watts; the Aftermath; an Inside View of the Ghetto.* New York: Grove Press, 1969; Gerald Horne. *Fire This Time: The Watts Uprising and the 1960s.* Charlottesville: University Press of Virginia, 1995; Ronald N. Jacobs. *Race, Media and the Crisis of Civil Society: From the Watts Riots to Rodney King.* Cambridge: Cambridge University Press, 2000; David O. Sears and John B. McConahay. *The Politics of Violence; The New Urban Blacks and the Watts Riot.* Boston: Houghton Mifflin, 1973; Errol Wayne Stevens. *Radical L.A.: from Coxey's Army to the Watts Riots, 1894–1965.* Norman: University of Oklahoma Press, 2009.

33. Sean J. O'Connell. *Los Angeles's Central Avenue Jazz.* Charleston, SC: Arcadia Publishing, 2014.

34. Peter Vacher. *Swingin' on Central Avenue: African American Jazz in Los Angeles.* Lanham, MD: Rowman & Littlefield, 2015.

35. Ian Gerrie. "Knowledge on the Horizon: A Phenomenological Inquiry into the 'Framing' of Rodney King." *Human Studies* 29.3 (September 2006): 295–315; Ronald N. Jacobs. "Civil Society and Crisis: Culture, Discourse, and the Rodney King Beating." *American Jour-

nal of Sociology 101.5 (March 1996): 1238–1272; Phylis Johnson. *KJLH-FM and the Los Angeles Riots of 1992: Compton's Neighborhood Station in the Aftermath of the Rodney King Verdict*. Jefferson, NC: McFarland & Co., Publishers, 2009; Alfred H. Knight. *The Life of the Law: The People and Cases That Have Shaped Our Society, from King Alfred to Rodney King*. Oxford; New York: Oxford University Press, 1998; Los Angeles Times (Firm). *Understanding the Riots: Los Angeles before and after the Rodney King Case*. Los Angeles, CA: Los Angeles Times, 1992; William L. Solomon and William S. Solomon. "Images of Rebellion: News Coverage of Rodney King." *Race, Gender & Class* 11.1, Race, Gender, Class and the 1992 L.A. "Riots" (2004): 23–38.

36. Daniel Widener. *Black Arts West: Culture and Struggle in Postwar Los Angeles*. Durham, NC: Duke University Press, 2010.

37. Amiri Baraka and Larry Neal. *Black Fire; An Anthology of Afro-American Writing*. New York: Morrow, 1968; Cheryl Clarke. *"After Mecca": Women Poets and the Black Arts Movement*. New Brunswick, NJ: Rutgers University Press, 2005; Lisa Gail Collins and Margo Natalie Crawford. *New Thoughts on the Black Arts Movement*. New Brunswick, NJ: Rutgers University Press, 2006; Larry Neal, Amiri Baraka, and Michael Schwartz. *Visions of a Liberated Future: Black Arts Movement Writings*. New York: Thunder's Mouth Press; St. Paul, MN: Distributed by Consortium Book Sales and Distribution, 1989; Carmen L. Phelps. *Visionary Women Writers of Chicago's Black Arts Movement*. Jackson: University Press of Mississippi, 2013; Mike Sell. *Avant-Garde Performance & the Limits of Criticism: Approaching the Living Theatre, Happenings/Fluxus, and the Black Arts Movement*. Ann Arbor: University of Michigan Press, 2005; James Edward Smethurst. *The Black Arts Movement: Literary Nationalism in the 1960s and 1970s*. Chapel Hill: The University of North Carolina Press, 2005; James Edward Smethurst, Sonia Sanchez, and John H. Bracey. *SOS/Calling All Black People: A Black Arts Movement Reader*. Amherst: University of Massachusetts Press, 2014.

38. Kamran Afary. *Performance and Activism: Grassroots Discourse After the Los Angeles Rebellion of 1992*. Lanham, MD: Lexington Books, 2009; Louise I. Gerdes. *The 1992 Los Angeles Riots*. Detroit: Greenhaven Press, a part of Gale, Cengage Learning, 2014; Haki R. Madhubuti. *Why L.A. Happened: Implications of the '92 Los Angeles Rebellion*. Chicago: Third World Press, 1993; Manning Marable. *Black America: Multicultural Democracy in the Age of Clarence Thomas, David Duke and LA Uprisings*. Westfield, NJ: Open Media, 1992; Carina Spaulding and Josephine Metcalf. *African American Culture and Society after Rodney King: Provocations and Protests, Progression and "Post-Racialism."* Aldershot, Hampshire: Ashgate Publishing 2015; University of California, Los Angeles. Asian American Studies Center. *Los Angeles Since 1992: Commemorating the 20th Anniversary of the Uprisings*. Los Angeles: Asian American Studies Center, University of California, Los Angeles, 2012.

39. David Cole. *No Equal Justice: Race and Class in the American Criminal Justice System*. New York: New Press: Distributed by W. W. Norton, 1999; Gail Dines and Jean McMahon Humez. *Gender, Race, and Class in Media: A Text-Reader*. Thousand Oaks, CA: Sage, 1995; Chris Gaine and Rosalyn George. *Gender, "Race," and Class in Schooling: A New Introduction*. London; Philadelphia, PA: Falmer Press, 1999; John H. Hinshaw. *Steel and Steelworkers: Race and Class Struggle in Twentieth-Century Pittsburgh*. Albany: State University of New York Press, 2002; John L. Jackson, Jr. *Harlem World: Doing Race and Class in Contemporary Black America*. Chicago: University of Chicago Press, 2001; Mary E. Pattillo. *Black on the Block: The Politics of Race and Class in the City*. Chicago: University of Chicago Press, 2007; B. J. Widick. *Detroit: City of Race and Class Violence*. Detroit: Wayne State University Press, 1989.

40. Brian W. Alleyne. *Radicals Against Race: Black Activism and Cultural Politics*. Oxford; New York: Berg, 2002; Davarian L. Baldwin. "Black Cultural Production and the Promises and Pitfalls of American Pluralism." *American Studies* 45.2 (Summer 2004): 133–140; Robin D. G. Kelley. *Race Rebels: Culture, Politics, and the Black Working Class*. New York: Free Press; Toronto: Maxwell Macmillan Canada; New York: Maxwell Macmillan International, 1994; Bill Lyne. "God's Black Revolutionary Mouth: James Baldwin's Black Radicalism." *Science & Society* 74.1 (January 2010): 12–36; Melani McAlister. "One Black Allah: The Middle East in the Cultural Politics of African American Liberation, 1955–1970." *American Quarterly* 51.3 (September 1999): 622–656; Jeffrey Babcock Perry. *Hubert Harrison: The Voice of Harlem*

Radicalism, 1883–1918. New York: Columbia University Press, 2009; Daniel Walden. "Black Music and Cultural Nationalism: The Maturation of Archie Shepp." *Negro American Literature Forum* 5.4 (Winter 1971): 150–154; Pnina Werbner and Muhammad Anwar. *Black and Ethnic Leaderships in Britain: The Cultural Dimensions of Political Action*. London; New York: Routledge, 2003.

41. Steven Louis Isoardi. *The Dark Tree: Jazz and the Community Arts in Los Angeles*. Berkeley: University of California Press, 2006.

42. Ashley Kahn and Jimmy Cobb. *Kind of Blue: The Making of the Miles Davis Masterpiece*. Cambridge, MA: Da Capo Press, 2007.

43. Samuel Barrett. "'Kind of Blue' and the Economy of Modal Jazz." *Popular Music* 25.2 (May 2006): 185–200.

44. Yuri Broze and Daniel Shanahan. "Diachronic Changes in Jazz Harmony: A Cognitive Perspective." *Music Perception: An Interdisciplinary Journal* 31.1 (September 2013): 32–45; Scott Knowles DeVeaux and Gary Giddins. *Jazz: Essential Listening*. New York: W. W. Norton, 2011; Gary Iseminger. "Sonicism and Jazz Improvisation." *The Journal of Aesthetics and Art Criticism* 68.3 (Summer 2010): 297–299; John Litweiler. *The Freedom Principle: Jazz after 1958*. New York: W. Morrow, 1984; Bruno Nettl and Melinda Russell. *In the Course of Performance: Studies in the World of Musical Improvisation*. Chicago: University of Chicago Press, 1998; Keren Omry. *Cross-Rhythms: Jazz Aesthetics in African-American Literature*. London; New York: Continuum, 2008; Tom Piazza. *The Guide to Classic Recorded Jazz*. Iowa City, IA: University of Iowa Press, 1995.

45. Lee B. Brown. "'Feeling My Way': Jazz Improvisation and Its Vicissitudes—A Plea for Imperfection." *The Journal of Aesthetics and Art Criticism* 58.2, Improvisation in the Arts (Spring 2000): 113–123; Duncan Heining. *George Russell: The Story of an American Composer*. Lanham, MD: Scarecrow Press, 2010; George Russell. *George Russell's Lydian Chromatic Concept of Tonal Organization*. Brookline, MA: Concept Pub. Co., 2001; Julian Silverman. "What Theory Says and What Musicians Do: Some Thoughts on the George Russell Event." *Tempo* 57.226 (October 2003): 32–39; Peter Niklas Wilson. "Living Time: Ancient to the Future. Concepts and Fantasies of Micro- and Macro-Time in Contemporary Jazz." *Amerikastudien / American Studies* 45.4, Time and the African-American Experience (2000): 567–574; Robert Witmer and James Robbins. "A Historical and Critical Survey of Recent Pedagogical Materials for the Teaching and Learning of Jazz." *Bulletin of the Council for Research in Music Education* 96, Research in Jazz Education II (Spring 1988): 7–29.

46. Eric Nisenson. *The Making of Kind of Blue: Miles Davis and His Masterpiece*. New York: St. Martin's Press, 2000; Richard Williams. *The Blue Moment: Miles Davis' Kind of Blue and the Remaking of Modern Music*. London: Faber, 2009.

47. Keith Potter. *Four Musical Minimalists: La Monte Young, Terry Riley, Steve Reich, Philip Glass*. Cambridge; New York: Cambridge University Press, 2000; Steve Reich and Paul Hillier. *Writings on Music, 1965–2000*. Oxford; New York: Oxford University Press, 2002; Simon Shaw-Miller. *Visible Deeds of Music: Art and Music from Wagner to Cage*. New Haven: Yale University Press, 2002.

48. DJ Spooky That Subliminal Kid. *Sound Unbound: Sampling Digital Music and Culture*. Cambridge, MA: MIT Press, 2008; Christopher Scoates. *Brian Eno: Visual Music*. San Francisco: Chronicle Books, 2013; David Sheppard. *On Some Faraway Beach: The Life and Times of Brian Eno*. London: Orion, 2015.

49. Mary Mathews Gedo. "A Youthful Genius Confronts His Destiny: Picasso's 'Old Guitarist' in The Art Institute of Chicago." *Art Institute of Chicago Museum Studies* 12.2, The Helen Birch Bartlett Memorial Collection (1986): 152–165; Temma Kaplan. *Red City, Blue Period: Social Movements in Picasso's Barcelona*. Berkeley, CA: University of California Press, 1992; Pablo Picasso and Laszlo Glozer. *Picasso: Masterpieces of the Blue Period: 38 Paintings*. New York: W. W. Norton, 1988.

50. George Avakian. "Jazz-1962." *Transition* 6/7 (October 1962): 59–60; Charles Fair. "Poetry and Jazz." *Chicago Review* 29.1 (Summer 1977): 22–29; Bettye Gardner and Bettye Thomas. "The Cultural Impact of the Howard Theatre on the Black Community." *The Journal of Negro History* 55.4 (October 1970): 253–265; Vijay Iyer. "Embodied Mind, Situated Cognition, and Expressive Microtiming in African-American Music." *Music Perception: An Interdis-*

ciplinary Journal 19.3 (Spring 2002): 387–414; Warren R. Pinckney. "Toward a History of Jazz in Bermuda." *The Musical Quarterly* 84.3 (Autumn 2000): 333–371.

51. Craig Hansen Werner. *Playing the Changes: From Afro-modernism to the Jazz Impulse.* Urbana: University of Illinois Press, 1994; George Lewis. *A Power Stronger Than Itself: The AACM and American Experimental Music.* Chicago: University of Chicago Press, 2008.

52. Bob Gluck. *The Miles Davis Lost Quintet: And Other Revolutionary Ensembles.* Chicago; London: University of Chicago Press, 2016.

53. Michael C. Heller. *Loft Jazz: Improvising New York in the 1970s.* Oakland, CA: University of California Press, 2017.

54. John Coltrane and Pharoah Sanders. *John Coltrane Live in Seattle Featuring Pharoah Sanders.* New York: The Verve Music Group, 2011; L. L. Dickson. "'Keep It in the Head': Jazz Elements in Modern Black American Poetry." *Melus* 10.1, Ethnic Literature and Music (Spring 1983): 29–37; Christopher Funkhouser. "LeRoi Jones, Larry Neal, and 'The Cricket': Jazz and Poets' Black Fire." *African American Review* 37.2/3 Amri Baraka Issue (Summer–Autumn 2003): 237–244; John Gennari. "Baraka's Bohemian Blues." *African American Review* 37.2/3, Amri Baraka Issue (Summer–Autumn 2003): 253–260; Guy-Marc Hinant and Michael Novy. "Artist's Notebook: TOHU BOHU: Considerations on the Nature of Noise, in 78 Fragments." *Leonardo Music Journal* 13, Groove, Pit and Wave: Recording, Transmission and Music (2003): 43–46; Frank Kofsky. "The State of Jazz." *The Black Perspective in Music* 5.1 (Spring 1977): 44–66; _____. "Indecent Coverage." *The Threepenny Review* 1 (Winter–Spring 1980): 21–22; Terry S. Koger, Mark Martin, Gary Richardson, Hassan Sabree, Anthony Wade, and Dominique-René de Lerma. "Fifty Years of 'Down Beat' Solo Jazz Transcriptions: A Register." *Black Music Research Journal* 5 (1985): 43–79; Catrin Lorch. "Drawings of Removal." *Afterall: A Journal of Art, Context and Enquiry* 10 (Autumn/Winter 2004): 76–80; Nathaniel Mackey. "Some Thoughts on 'Fusion.'" *The Threepenny Review* 1 (Winter–Spring 1980): 23–24; Donald M. Morales. "The Pervasive Force of Music in African, Caribbean, and African American Drama." *Research in African Literatures* 34.2 (Summer 2003): 145–154; Arun Nevader. "John Coltrane: Music and Metaphysics." *The Threepenny Review* 10 (Summer 1982): 26–27; William L. Van Deburg. *New Day in Babylon: The Black Power Movement and American Culture, 1965–1975.* Chicago: University of Chicago Press, 1992.

55. Andrew W. Bartlett. "Cecil Taylor, Identity Energy, and the Avant-Garde African American Body." *Perspectives of New Music* 33.1/2 (Winter–Summer 1995): 274–293; Brent Hayes Edwards. "Middle Ear Recitation (A Transcription of Cecil Taylor's 'Erzulie Maketh Scent')." *Callaloo* 22.4 (Autumn 1999): 771–774; Aldon L. Nielsen. "Clark Coolidge and a Jazz Aesthetic." *Pacific Coast Philology* 28.1 (September 1993): 94–112; Lynette Westendorf. "Cecil Taylor: Indent—'Second Layer.'" *Perspectives of New Music* 33.1/2 (Winter–Summer 1995): 294–326.

56. Susan M. Asai. "Cultural Politics: The African American Connection in Asian American Jazz-Based Music." *Asian Music* 36.1 (Winter–Spring 2005): 87–108; Michael Bérubé. "Masks, Margins, and African American Modernism: Melvin Tolson's Harlem Gallery." *PMLA* 105.1, Special Topic: African and African American Literature (January 1990): 57–69; Robert Elliot Fox. "Ted Joans and the (B)reach of the African American Literary Canon." *Melus* 29.3/4, Pedagogy, Canon, Context: Toward a Redefinition of Ethnic American Literary Studies (Autumn–Winter 2004): 41–58; Allan M. Gordon. "The Art Ensemble of Chicago as Performance Art." *Lenox Avenue: A Journal of Interarts Inquiry* 3 (1997): 55–58; Rebecca Peabody. "African American Avant-Gardes, 1965–1990." *Getty Research Journal* 1 (2009): 211–217; James Smethurst. "'Pat Your Foot and Turn the Corner': Amiri Baraka, the Black Arts Movement, and the Poetics of a Popular Avant-Garde." *African American Review* 37.2/3, Amri Baraka Issue (Summer–Autumn 2003): 261–270; Daniel Won-gu Kim. "'In the Tradition': Amiri Baraka, Black Liberation, and Avant-Garde Praxis in the U.S." *African American Review* 37.2/3, Amri Baraka Issue (Summer–Autumn 2003): 345–363; Timothy Yu. *Race and the Avant-Garde: Experimental and Asian American Poetry since 1965.* Stanford, CA: Stanford University Press, 2009.

57. Howard Mandel. *Miles, Ornette, Cecil: Jazz Beyond Jazz: How Miles Davis, Ornette Coleman, and Cecil Taylor Revolutionized the World of Jazz.* London [u.a.]: Routledge, 2008.

58. Finis Farr. *Black Champion: The Life and Times of Jack Johnson*. London: Macmillan, 1964; Jack Johnson. *Jack Johnson in the Ring and Out*. Chicago: National Sports Pub. Co., 1927; _____. *Jack Johnson Is a Dandy: An Autobiography*. New York: Chelsea House, 1969; Randy Roberts. *Papa Jack: Jack Johnson and the Era of White Hopes*. New York: London: Free Press, 1983; Theresa Runstedtler. *Jack Johnson, Rebel Sojourner: Boxing in the Shadow of the Global Color Line*. Berkeley: University of California Press, 2012.

59. Zain Abdullah. "Narrating Muslim Masculinities: The Fruit of Islam and the Quest for Black Redemption." *Spectrum: A Journal on Black Men* 1.1 (Autumn 2012): 141–177; Stephanie Brown and Keith Clark. "Melodramas of Beset Black Manhood?: Meditations on African-American Masculinity as Scholarly Topos and Social Menace an Introduction." *Callaloo* 26.3 (Summer 2003): 732–737; Ronald Cummings. "Jamaican Female Masculinities: Nanny of the Maroons and the Genealogy of the Man-Royal." *Journal of West Indian Literature* 21.1/2, Caribbean Masculinities (November 2012/April 2013): 129–154; Michael K. Johnson. *Black Masculinity and the Frontier Myth in American Literature*. Norman, OK: University of Oklahoma Press, 2002; Arlene R. Keizer. *Black Subjects: Identity Formation in the Contemporary Narrative of Slavery*. Ithaca, NY: Cornell University Press, 2004; Amy Abugo Ongiri. "We Are Family: Black Nationalism, Black Masculinity, and the Black Gay Cultural Imagination." *College Literature* 24.1, Queer Utilities: Textual Studies, Theory, Pedagogy, Praxis (Feburary 1997): 280–294; Peter Kerry Powers. "Gods of Physical Violence, Stopping at Nothing: Masculinity, Religion, and Art in the Work of Zora Neale Hurston." *Religion and American Culture: A Journal of Interpretation* 12.2 (Summer 2002): 229–247.

60. Rachel Adams. *Sideshow U.S.A: Freaks and the American Cultural Imagination*. Chicago: The University of Chicago Press, 2001; Robert Bogdan. *Freak Show: Presenting Human Oddities for Amusement and Profit*. Chicago: University of Chicago Press, 1990; Robert M. Lewis. *From Traveling Show to Vaudeville: Theatrical Spectacle in America, 1830–1910*. Baltimore, MD: Johns Hopkins University Press, 2003.

61. James Joyce. *Selected Letters of James Joyce*. New York: Viking Press, 1975; James Joyce and Stuart Gilbert. *Letters of James Joyce*. New York: Viking Press, 1957; James Joyce, Michael Groden, Hans Walter Gabler, David Hayman, A. Walton Litz, and Danis Rose. *The James Joyce Archive*. New York: Garland, 1977–1979; James Joyce and Harry Levin. *The Essential James Joyce*. Harmondsworth, Middlesex: Penguin Books, 1948; James Joyce, Ellsworth Mason, and Richard Ellmann. *The Critical Writings of James Joyce*. New York: Viking Press, 1959.

62. John Henrik Clarke. *Marcus Garvey and the Vision of Africa*. New York, Vintage Books, 1974; Edmund David Cronon. *Black Moses: The Story of Marcus Garvey and the Universal Negro Improvement Association*. Madison: University of Wisconsin Press, 1969; Marcus Garvey and Robert Blaisdell. *Selected Writings and Speeches of Marcus Garvey*. Mineola, NY: Dover Publications, 2004; Marcus Garvey and Amy Jacques Garvey. *Philosophy and Opinions of Marcus Garvey*. New York: Arno Press, 1968–69; Marcus Garvey, Robert A. Hill, and Universal Negro Improvement Association. *The Marcus Garvey and Universal Negro Improvement Association Papers. Vol. 10, Africa for the Africans, 1923–1945*. Berkeley, CA; London: University of California Press, 2006; Marcus Garvey and Tony Martin. *The Poetical Works of Marcus Garvey*. Dover, MA: Majority Press, 1983; Wallace Thurman. *Marcus Garvey*. New Brunswick, NJ: Rutgers University Press, 2003.

63. Alan Groves. *Bud Powell*. New York: Universe Books, 1987; Peter Pullman. *Wail: The Life of Bud Powell*. New York: Peter Pullman LLC, 2012; Alan Groves and Alyn Shipton. *The Glass Enclosure: The Life of Bud Powell*. New York: Continuum, 2001; Francis Paudras. *Dance of the Infidels: A Portrait of Bud Powell*. New York: Da Capo Press, 1998; Guthrie P. Ramsey. *The Amazing Bud Powell: Black Genius, Jazz History, and the Challenge of Bebop*. Berkeley: Chicago: University of California Press, 2013; Carl Smith and Chick Corea. *Bouncing with Bud: All the Recordings of Bud Powell*. Brunswick, ME: Biddle Pub. Co., 1997.

64. Carla Freeman. *Entrepreneurial Selves: Neoliberal Respectability and the Making of a Caribbean Middle Class*. Durham: Duke University Press, 2014; Cheryl D. Hicks. *Talk With You Like a Woman: African American Women, Justice, and Reform in New York, 1890–1935*. Chapel Hill: University of North Carolina Press, 2010; E. Frances White. *Dark Continent of Our Bodies: Black Feminism and the Politics of Respectability*. Philadelphia: Temple Univer-

sity Press, 2001; Victoria W. Wolcott. *Remaking Respectability: African American Women in Interwar Detroit*. Chapel Hill: University of North Carolina Press, 2001.

65. Farah Jasmine Griffin and Salim Washington. *Clawing at the Limits of Cool: Miles Davis, John Coltrane and the Greatest Jazz Collaboration Ever*. New York: Thomas Dunne Books, 2008.

66. Ben Ratliff. *Coltrane: The Story of a Sound*. New York: Farrar, Straus and Giroux, 2007.

67. Geoffrey Holden Block. *The Richard Rodgers Reader*. Oxford: Oxford University Press, 2002; _____. *Richard Rodgers*. New Haven: Yale University Press, 2003; Stanley Green. *The Rodgers and Hammerstein Story*. New York: The John Day Company, 1963; Thomas S. Hischak. *The Rodgers and Hammerstein Encyclopedia*. Westport, CT: Greenwood Press, 2007; Frederick W. Nolan. *The Sound of Their Music: The Story of Rodgers and Hammerstein*. New York: Walker, 1978; Richard Rodgers and Oscar Hammerstein, II. *6 Plays by Rodgers and Hammerstein*. New York: Random House, 1955; Max Wilk. *Overture and Finale: Rodgers & Hammerstein and the Creation of Their Two Greatest Hits*. New York: Back Stage Books, 1999.

68. Colin Fleming. "Jazz: The Quiet Sideman: Tenor Saxist 'Chu' Berry Emerged from the Pack at the End of His Short Life." *The American Scholar* 77.1 (Winter 2008): 110–111; Benjamin Franklin. *Commentaries on Jazz Musicians and Jazz Songs: A History of Jazz in Retrospect*. Lewiston, NY: E. Mellen Press, 2011; Michael S. Harper. "Dear Old Stockholm." *The Georgia Review* 35.1 (Spring 1981): 140–141; Hank O'Neal. *The Ghosts of Harlem: Sessions with Jazz Legends*. Nashville, TN: Vanderbilt University Press, 2009; Michael Segell. *The Devil's Horn: The Story of the Saxophone, From Noisy Novelty to the King of Cool*. New York: Farrar, Straus and Giroux, 2005; Arnold Shaw. *Honkers and Shouters: The Golden Years of Rhythm and Blues*. New York: Macmillan, 1978.

69. Thom Holmes and Terence M. Pender. *Electronic and Experimental Music: Technology, Music, and Culture*. New York: Routledge, 2012; Michael Magee. *Emancipating Pragmatism: Emerson, Jazz, and Experimental Writing*. Tuscaloosa: University of Alabama Press, 2004; Mary S. Pollock and Susanne Vincenza. "Feminist Aesthetics in Jazz: An Interview with Susanne Vincenza of Alive!" *Frontiers: A Journal of Women Studies* 8.1 (1984): 60–63.

70. Frank Kofsky. *John Coltrane and the Jazz Revolution of the 1960s*. New York: Pathfinder Press, 1998.

71. Chris DeVito and John Coltrane. *Coltrane on Coltrane: The John Coltrane Interviews*. Chicago: Chicago Review Press, 2010.

72. Michael B. Bakan. *World Music: Traditions and Transformations*. Boston: McGraw-Hill, 2007; Philip V. Bohlman. *World Music: A Very Short Introduction*. Oxford: Oxford University Press, 2002; _____. *The Cambridge History of World Music*. New York: Cambridge University Press, 2013; Terry E. Miller and Andrew C. Shahriari. *World Music: A Global Journey*. New York: Routledge, 2009; Bruno Nettl. *The Western Impact on World Music: Change, Adaptation, and Survival*. New York: Schirmer Books; London: Collier Macmillan, 1985; _____. *Excursions in World Music*. Upper Saddle River, NJ: Prentice Hall, 1997; Bruno Nettl, Ruth M. Stone, James Porter, and Timothy Rice. *The Garland Encyclopedia of World Music*. New York: Garland Pub., 1998–2002; Richard Nidel. *World Music: The Basics*. New York: Routledge, 2005; Ian Peddie. *Popular Music and Human Rights. Vol. 2: World Music*. Farnham, Surrey, England; Burlington, VT: Ashgate, 2011; Andrew C. Shahriari. *Popular World Music*. Upper Saddle River, NJ: Prentice Hall/Pearson, 2011; Ted Solís. *Performing Ethnomusicology: Teaching and Representation in World Music Ensembles*. Berkeley: University of California Press, 2004; Timothy Dean Taylor. *Global Pop: World Music, World Markets*. New York: Routledge, 1997; Michael Tenzer. *Analytical Studies in World Music*. Oxford; New York: Oxford University Press, 2006; Elijah Wald. *Global Minstrels: Voices of World Music*. New York: Routledge, 2007.

73. Adam Bond. *The Imposing Preacher: Samuel DeWitt Proctor and Black Public Faith*. Minneapolis: Fortress Press, 2013; Katie G. Cannon. *Teaching Preaching: Isaac Rufus Clark and Black Sacred Rhetoric*. New York; London: Continuum, 2003; James H. Cone. *Black Theology and Black Power*. Maryknoll, NY: Orbis Books, 1997; Carl F. Ellis. *Beyond Liberation: The Gospel in the Black American Experience*. Downers Grove, IL: InterVarsity Press,

1983; Kenyatta R. Gilbert. *A Pursued Justice: Black Preaching from the Great Migration to Civil Rights*. Waco, TX: Baylor University Press, 2016; Martha J. Simmons and Frank A. Thomas. *Preaching with Sacred Fire: An Anthology of African American Sermons, 1750 to the Present*. New York: W. W. Norton, 2010; Gerald Lamont Thomas. *African American Preaching: The Contribution of Dr. Gardner C. Taylor*. New York: Peter Lang, 2004; Amos Yong and Estrelda Alexander. *Afro-Pentecostalism: Black Pentecostal and Charismatic Christianity in History and Culture*. New York: New York University Press, 2011.

74. Eric Nisenson. *Ascension: John Coltrane and His Quest*. New York: Da Capo Press, 1995.

75. William C. Banfield. *Cultural Codes: Makings of a Black Music Philosophy: An Interpretive History from Spirituals to Hip Hop*. Lanham, MD: Scarecrow Press, 2010; Franya J. Berkman. "Appropriating Universality: The Coltranes and 1960s Spirituality." *American Studies* 48.1 (Spring 2007): 41–62; _____. *Monument Eternal: The Music of Alice Coltrane*. Middletown, CT: Wesleyan University Press, 2010; Leonard L. Brown. *John Coltrane and Black America's Quest for Freedom: Spirituality and the Music*. New York City: Oxford University Press, 2010; Marcel Cobussen. *Thresholds: Rethinking Spirituality through Music*. Aldershot, Hampshire, England; Burlington, VT: Ashgate, 2008; Bill Cole. *John Coltrane*. New York: Schirmer Books, 1976; Harvey Cox. "Jazz and Pentecostalism." *Archives de sciences sociales des religions, 38e Année* 84, La religion aux États-Unis (October–December 1993): 181–188; Jay Keister. "Seeking Authentic Experience: Spirituality in the Western Appropriation of Asian Music." *The World of Music* 47.3, The Music of "Others" in the Western World (2005): 35–53; Michael Bruce McDonald. "Traning the Nineties, or the Present Relevance of John Coltrane's Music of Theophany and Negation." *African American Review* 29.2, Special Issues on The Music (Summer 1995): 275–282; Lewis Porter. *John Coltrane: His Life and Music*. Ann Arbor: University of Michigan Press, 1998; Vijay Prashad. *The Karma of Brown Folk*. Minneapolis: University of Minnesota Press, 2000; Allison Welch. "Meetings along the Edge: Svara and Tāla in American Minimal Music." *American Music* 17.2 (Summer 1999): 179–199; Ann Willey. "A Bridge over Troubled Waters: Jazz, Diaspora Discourse, and E. B. Dongala's 'Jazz and Palm Wine' as Response to Amiri Baraka's 'Answers in Progress.'" *Research in African Literatures* 44.3 (Fall 2013): 138–151.

76. Ashley Kahn. *A Love Supreme: The Story of John Coltrane's Signature Album*. New York: Viking, 2002; Tony Whyton. *Beyond A Love Supreme: John Coltrane and the Legacy of an Album*. New York: Oxford University Press, 2013.

77. Miles Davis and Quincy Troupe. *Miles: The Autobiography*. New York: Simon & Schuster, 1990.

78. Nat Hentoff. *Listen to the Stories: Nat Hentoff on Jazz and Country Music*. New York: HarperCollins, 1995; _____. *The Nat Hentoff Reader*. Cambridge, MA: Da Capo Press, 2001; _____. *At the Jazz Band Ball: Sixty Years on the Jazz Scene*. Berkeley: University of California Press, 2010; Nat Shapiro and Nat Hentoff. *Hear Me Talkin' To Ya: The Story of Jazz by the Men Who Made It*. New York: Rinehart, 1955.

79. Miles Davis, Paul Maher, and Michael K. Dorr. *Miles on Miles: Interviews and Encounters with Miles Davis*. Chicago: Lawrence Hill Books, 2009; Gerald Lyn Early. *Miles Davis and American Culture*. St. Louis: Missouri Historical Society Press, 2001.

80. Paul Tingen. *Miles Beyond: The Electric Explorations of Miles Davis, 1967–1991*. New York: Billboard Books, 2001.

81. Richard Williams. *Miles Davis: The Man in the Green Shirt*. New York: H. Holt, 1993.

82. William Russell Bascom. *African Art in Cultural Perspective; An Introduction*. New York: Norton, 1973; Daniel P. Biebuyck. *Tradition and Creativity in Tribal Art*. Berkeley: University of California Press, 1969; René A. Bravmann. *Islam and Tribal Art in West Africa*. London; New York: Cambridge University Press, 1974; Hart House. *African Tribal Art from the Collection of Sam and Ayala Zacks, Hart House Art Gallery, March 8 to 28, 1970*. Toronto: University of Toronto Press, 1970; Bettina von Lintig and Hughes Dubois. *African Impressions: Tribal Art and Currents of Life*. Milan, Italy: 5 Continents Editions, 2011.

83. Clarence Bernard Henry. *Quincy Jones: His Life in Music*. Jackson: University Press of Mississippi, 2013; _____. *Quincy Jones: A Research and Information Guide*. New York;

London: Routledge, Taylor and Francis Group, 2014; Quincy Jones. *Q: The Autobiography of Quincy Jones*. New York: Doubleday, 2001.

84. Miles Davis and Scott Gutterman. *Miles Davis: The Collected Artwork*. San Rafael, CA: Editions, 2013.

85. Jack Chambers. *Milestones: The Music and Times of Miles Davis*. Toronto: University of Toronto Press, 1990; Richard Cook. *It's About That Time: Miles Davis On and Off Record*. Oxford; New York: Oxford University Press, 2007; Gregory Davis and Les Sussman. *Dark Magus: The Jekyll and Hyde Life of Miles Davis*. San Francisco, CA: Backbeat Books; Berkeley, CA: Distributed to the book trade in the United States and Canada by Publishers Group West, 2006; Eric Nisenson. *'Round About Midnight: A Portrait of Miles Davis*. New York: Dial Press, 1982.

86. Ian Carr. *Miles Davis: The Definitive Biography*. New York: Thunder's Mouth Press, 1998.

87. Chaka Khan and Tonya Bolden. *Chaka!: Through the Fire*. Emmaus, PA: Rodale; [New York]: Distributed to the book trade by St. Martin's Press, 2003; Adam Krims. *Music and Urban Geography*. New York: Routledge, 2007; Treva B. Lindsey. "If You Look in My Life: Love, Hip-Hop Soul, and Contemporary African American Womanhood." *African American Review* 46.1, Special issue: Hip Hop and the Literary (Spring 2013): 87–99; William H. McClendon. "Black Music: Sound and Feeling for Black Liberation." *The Black Scholar* 7.5 Black Popular Culture (January–February 1976): 20–25; David Nathan. *The Soulful Divas: Personal Portraits of Over a Dozen Divine Divas, from Nina Simone, Aretha Franklin & Diana Ross to Patti LaBelle, Whitney Houston & Janet Jackson*. New York: Billboard Books, 1999; Sonja H. Stone. "An Ethno/Youth Perspective for Teaching Afro-American Culture." *The High School Journal* 60.2, Cultural Diversity (November 1976): 77–85; Allan Tannenbaum, Peter Occhiogrosso, and Debbie Harry. *Grit and Glamour: The Street Style, High Fashion, and Legendary Music of the 1970s*. San Rafael, CA: Insight Editions, 2016.

88. George Cole. *The Last Miles: The Music of Miles Davis, 1980–1991*. London: Equinox Pub., 2005.

89. Kenneth Bilby. "Distant Drums: The Unsung Contribution of African-Jamaican Percussion to Popular Music at Home and Abroad." *Caribbean Quarterly* 56.4; Pioneering Icons of Jamaican Popular Music, Part II (December 2010): 1–21; Serge Blanc and Percudanse Association. *African Percussion: The Djembe*. Paris, France: Percudanse Association, 1997; Kirk Brundage. *Afro-Brazilian Percussion Guide: Instruments and Rhythms from Salvador, Bahia, Brazil*. Los Angeles, CA: K. Brundage, 2011; Larry Crook. *Brazilian Music: Northeastern Traditions and the Heartbeat of a Modern Nation*. Santa Barbara, CA: ABC-CLIO, 2005; Gilson de Assis. *Brazilian Percussion*. [Rottenburg], Germany: Advance Music, 2003; Lynne Jessup and Isaac Hirt-Manheimer. *All Hands On!: An Introduction to West African Percussion Ensembles*. Danbury, CT: World Music Press, 1997; Frederick Moehn. "A Carioca Blade Runner, or How Percussionist Marcos Suzano Turned the Brazilian Tambourine into a Drum Kit, and Other Matters of (Politically) Correct Music Making." *Ethnomusicology* 53.2 (Spring/Summer 2009): 277–307; Alberto Netto. *Brazilian Rhythms for Drum Set and Percussion*. Boston, MA: Berklee Press, 2003; Art Rosenbaum and Johann S. Buis. *Shout Because You're Free: The African American Ring Shout Tradition in Coastal Georgia*. Athens: University of Georgia Press, 1998; Kenneth George Schweitzer. *The Artistry of Afro-Cuban Batá Drumming: Aesthetics, Transmission, Bonding, and Creativity*. Jackson: University Press of Mississippi, 2013; Patricia Tang. *Masters of the Sabar: Wolof Griot Percussionists of Senegal*. Philadelphia: Temple University Press, 2007; Ed Uribe. *The Essence of Brazilian Percussion and Drum Set: With Rhythm Section Parts: Rhythms, Songstyles, Techniques, Applications*. Van Nuys, CA: Alfred Publishing, 2006.

90. Don Banks. "Third-Stream Music." *Proceedings of the Royal Musical Association* 97 (1970–1971): 59–67; Edward Berger. *Softly, With Feeling: Joe Wilder and the Breaking of Barriers in American Music*. Philadelphia: Temple University Press, 2014; Ran Blake. "Teaching Third Stream." *Music Educators Journal* 63.4 (December 1976): 30–33; _____. "Third Stream and the Importance of the Ear: A Position Paper in Narrative Form." *College Music Symposium* 21.2 (Fall 1981): 139–146; Christopher Coady and Project Muse. *John Lewis and the Challenge of "Real" Black Music*. Ann Arbor: University of Michigan Press, 2016; David

Dennen. "The Third Stream: Oḍiśī Music, Regional Nationalism, and the Concept of 'Classical.'" *Asian Music* 41.2 (Summer/Fall 2010): 149–179.

91. Ninotchka Bennahum. *Antonia Mercé, "LaArgentina": Flamenco and the Spanish Avant Garde.* Middletown: Wesleyan University Press, 2014; Ken Haas and Gwynne Edwards. *Flamenco!* London: Thames and Hudson, 2000; Michelle Heffner Hayes. *Flamenco: Conflicting Histories of the Dance.* Jefferson, NC: McFarland & Co., 2009; Paul Hecht. *The Wind Cried; An American's Discovery of the World of Flamenco.* New York: Dial Press, 1968; Bernard Leblon and Centre de recherches tsiganes (Université René Descartes). *Gypsies and Flamenco: The Emergence of the Art of Flamenco in Andalusia.* Hatfield: University of Hertfordshire Press, 2003; D. E. Pohren. *Lives and Legends of Flamenco; A Biographical History.* Madrid: Society of Spanish Studies; [distribution: H. Howell, La Mesa, CA], 1964; Dixie Salazar. *Flamenco Hips and Red Mud Feet.* Tucson: University of Arizona Press, 2010; Claus Schreiner, Madeleine Claus, and Reinhard G. Pauly. *Flamenco: Gypsy Dance and Music from Andalusia.* Portland, OR: Amadeus Press, 1990; Robin Totton. *Song of the Outcasts: An Introduction to Flamenco.* Portland, OR: Amadeus Press, 2003; William Washabaugh. *Flamenco: Passion, Politics, and Popular Culture.* Oxford; Washington, D.C.: Berg, 1996; _____. *Flamenco Music and National Identity in Spain.* Farnham, Surrey; Burlington, VT: Ashgate, 2012; Jason Webster. *Duende: A Journey in Search of Flamenco.* London: Doubleday, 2003.

92. Keith Waters. *The Studio Recordings of the Miles Davis Quintet, 1965–68.* New York: Oxford University Press, 2011.

93. Hisham Aidi. *Rebel Music: Race, Empire, and the New Muslim Youth Culture.* New York: Pantheon Books, 2014; Sohail Daulatzai. *Black Star, Crescent Moon: The Muslim International and Black Freedom Beyond America.* Minneapolis: University of Minnesota Press 2012; Sylviane A. Diouf. *Servants of Allah: African Muslims Enslaved in the Americas.* New York: New York University Press, 1998; Carolyn Moxley Rouse. *Engaged Surrender: African American Women and Islam.* Berkeley: University of California Press, 2004.

94. George Grella, Jr. *Bitches Brew.* New York: Bloomsbury Academic, 2015; Victor Svorinich. *Listen to This: Miles Davis and Bitches Brew.* Jackson: University Press of Mississippi, 2015.

95. Algernon Austin. *Achieving Blackness: Race, Black Nationalism, and Afrocentrism in the Twentieth Century.* New York: New York University Press, 2006; Errol Anthony Henderson. *Afrocentrism and World Politics: Towards a New Paradigm.* Westport, CT: Praeger, 1995; Cheryl Jeanne Sanders. *Living the Intersection: Womanism and Afrocentrism in Theology.* Minneapolis: Fortress Press, 1995.

96. James L. Conyers. *Engines of the Black Power Movement: Essays on the Influence of Civil Rights Actions, Arts, and Islam.* Jefferson, NC: McFarland & Co., 2007; Devorah Heitner. *Black Power TV.* Durham; London: Duke University Press, 2013; J. L. Jeffries. *Black Power in the Belly of the Beast.* Urbana: University of Illinois, 2006; Peniel E. Joseph. *Waiting 'til the Midnight Hour: A Narrative History of Black Power in America.* New York: Henry Holt and Co., 2006; _____. *The Black Power Movement: Rethinking the Civil Rights-Black Power Era.* New York: Routledge, 2006; John T. McCartney. *Black Power Ideologies: An Essay in African-American Political Thought.* Philadelphia: Temple University Press, 1992; Danielle L. McGuire. *At the Dark End of the Street: Black Women, Rape, and Resistance—A New History of the Civil Rights Movement from Rosa Parks to the Rise of Black Power.* New York: Alfred A. Knopf, 2010; Göran Hugo Olsson and Goran Olsson. *The Black Power Mixtape: 1967–1975.* Chicago: Haymarket Books, 2013; Amy Abugo Ongiri. *Spectacular Blackness: The Cultural Politics of the Black Power Movement and the Search for a Black Aesthetic.* Charlottesville: University of Virginia Press, 2010; Hugh Pearson. *The Shadow of the Panther: Huey Newton and the Price of Black Power in America.* Reading, MA: Addison-Wesley Pub. Co., 1994; Kate Quinn. *Black Power in the Caribbean.* Gainesville: University Press of Florida, 2014; Fabio Rojas. *From Black Power to Black Studies: How a Radical Social Movement Became an Academic Discipline.* Baltimore: Johns Hopkins University Press, 2007; Nico Slate. *Black Power Beyond Borders: The Global Dimensions of the Black Power Movement.* New York: Palgrave Macmillan, 2012; Denise Sullivan. *Keep on Pushing: Black Power Music from Blues to Hip-Hop.* Chicago: Lawrence Hill Books, 2011.

97. Andy Bennett. *Remembering Woodstock*. Aldershot, Hampshire, England; Burlington, VT: Ashgate, 2004; Louise I. Gerdes. *Woodstock*. Detroit: Greenhaven Press, 2012; Ronald Helfrich. "'What Can a Hippie Contribute to our Community?' Culture Wars, Moral Panics, and The Woodstock Festival." *New York History* 91.3 (Summer 2010): 221–244; Ian Inglis. *Performance and Popular Music: History, Place and Time*. Aldershot, Hants, England; Burlington, VT: Ashgate, 2006; Elliott Landy. *Woodstock Vision: The Spirit of a Generation*. New York: Backbeat Books, 2009; Michael Lang and Holly George-Warren. *The Road to Woodstock*. New York: Ecco, 2009; James E. Perone. *Woodstock: An Encyclopedia of the Music and Art Fair*. Westport, CT: Greenwood Press, 2005; Bob Spitz. *Barefoot in Babylon: The Creation of the Woodstock Music Festival, 1969*. New York: Viking Press, 1979.

98. Dietrich Fischer-Dieskau. *Wagner and Nietzsche*. New York: Seabury Press, 1976; Andrea Gogröf-Voorhees. *Defining Modernism: Baudelaire and Nietzsche on Romanticism, Modernity, Decadence, and Wagner*. New York: P. Lang, 1999; Roger Hollinrake. *Nietzsche, Wagner, and the Philosophy of Pessimism*. London; Boston: Allen and Unwin, 1982; Joachim Köhler and Ronald Taylor. *Nietzsche and Wagner: A Lesson in Subjugation*. New Haven: Yale University Press, 1998; Friedrich Wilhelm Nietzsche. *The Case of Wagner: Nietzsche contra Wagner. The Twilight of the Idols. The Antichrist*. London: Fisher Unwin, 1899; _____. *The Birth of Tragedy, and the Case of Wagner*. New York: Vintage Books, 1967; Friedrich Wilhelm Nietzsche, Anthony M. Ludovici, and John McFarland Kennedy. *I. The Case of Wagner; II. Nietzsche Contra Wagner; III. Selected Aphorisms*. Edinburgh: T. N. Foulis, 1911; Friedrich Wilhelm Nietzsche, Richard Wagner, Elisabeth Förster-Nietzsche, Caroline V. Kerr, and H. L. Mencken. *The Nietzsche-Wagner Correspondence*. New York: Boni and Liveright, 1921; Brayton Polka. *Modernity Between Wagner and Nietzsche*. Lanham; Boulder; New York; London: Lexington Books, 2015; Martine Prange. *Nietzsche, Wagner, Europe*. Berlin; Boston: De Gruyter, 2013; T. K. Seung. *Goethe, Nietzsche, and Wagner: Their Spinozan Epics of Love and Power*. Lanham, MD: Lexington Books, 2006.

99. Geoffrey Becker. "Jimi Hendrix, Bluegrass Star." *Prairie Schooner* 78.1 (Spring 2004): 6–18; Lawrence Chenoweth. "The Rhetoric of Hope and Despair: A Study of the Jimi Hendrix Experience and the Jefferson Airplane." *American Quarterly* 23.1 (Spring 1971): 25–45; David Henderson. *Jimi Hendrix: Voodoo Child of the Aquarian Age*. Garden City, NY: Doubleday, 1978; _____. "Jimi Hendrix Deep Within the Blues and Alive Onstage at Woodstock—25 Years after Death." *African American Review* 29.2, Special Issues on The Music (Summer 1995): 213–216; Leon Hendrix and Adam D. Mitchell. *Jimi Hendrix: A Brother's Story*. New York: Thomas Dunne Books, 2012; Jimi Hendrix and Steven Roby. *Hendrix on Hendrix: Interviews and Encounters with Jimi Hendrix*. Chicago: Chicago Review Press, 2012; Monifa Love. "Listening to Jimi Hendrix Near Lafayette Park." *The Massachusetts Review* 43.4 (Winter 2002/2003): 616–617; Marie-Paule Macdonald. *Jimi Hendrix: Soundscapes*. London, UK: Reaktion Books, 2016; David V. Moskowitz. *The Words and Music of Jimi Hendrix*. Santa Barbara: Praeger, 2010; Charles Shaar Murray. *Crosstown Traffic: Jimi Hendrix and Post-War Pop*. London: Faber, 1989; Jeff Schwartz. "Writing Jimi: Rock Guitar Pedagogy as Postmodern Folkloric Practice." *Popular Music* 12.3 (October 1993): 281–288; Harry Shapiro and Caesar Glebbeek. *Jimi Hendrix, Electric Gypsy*. New York: St. Martin's Press, 1991, 1990; Greg Tate. *Midnight Lightning: Jimi Hendrix and the Black Experience*. Chicago: Lawrence Hill Books, 2003; Sheila Whiteley. "Progressive Rock and Psychedelic Coding in the Work of Jimi Hendrix." *Popular Music* 9.1 (January 1990): 37–60; Albin J. Zak III. "Bob Dylan and Jimi Hendrix: Juxtaposition and Transformation 'All along the Watchtower.'" *Journal of the American Musicological Society* 57.3 (Fall 2004): 599–644.

100. Phil Freeman. *Running the Voodoo Down: The Electric Music of Miles Davis*. San Francisco: Backbeat Books, 2005.

101. Roy Carr, Brian Case, and Fred Dellar. *The Hip: Hipsters, Jazz, and the Beat Generation*. London; Boston: Faber and Faber, 1986; George Cotkin. "The Photographer in the Beat-Hipster Idiom: Robert Frank's the Americans." *American Studies* 26.1 (Spring 1985): 19–33; Philip Ford. "Somewhere/Nowhere: Hipness as an Aesthetic." *The Musical Quarterly* 86.1 (Spring 2002): 49–81; Benjamin Lee. "Avant-Garde Poetry as Subcultural Practice: Mailer and Di Prima's Hipsters." *New Literary History* 41.4, What Is an Avant-Garde? (Autumn 2010): 775–794; Andrea Levine. "'The (Jewish) White Negro': Norman Mailer's Racial Bodies."

Melus 28.2, Haunted by History (Summer 2003): 59–81; Douglas Malcolm. "'Jazz America': Jazz and African American Culture in Jack Kerouac's 'On the Road.'" *Contemporary Literature* 40.1 (Spring 1999): 85–110; Paul McCann. *Race, Music, and National Identity: Images of Jazz in American Fiction, 1920–1960*. Madison [NJ]: Fairleigh Dickinson University Press, 2008; Peter Stanfield. "Crossover: Sam Katzman's 'Switchblade Calypso Bop Reefer Madness Swamp Girl' or 'Bad Jazz,' Calypso, Beatniks and Rock 'n' Roll in 1950s Teenpix." *Popular Music* 29.3 (October 2010): 437–455.

102. Matthew Davies, Guy Madison, Pedro Silva, and Fabien Gouyon. "The Effect of Microtiming Deviations on the Perception of Groove in Short Rhythms." *Music Perception: An Interdisciplinary Journal* 30.5 (June 2013): 497–510; Orlando Enrique Fiol. "Grooves and Waves: Cyclicity and Narrativity in Cuban 'Timba' Piano." *Latin American Music Review/ Revista de Música Latinoamericana* 33.1 (Spring/Summer 2012): 1–26 ; Sharony Andrews Green. *Grant Green: Rediscovering the Forgotten Genius of Jazz Guitar*. San Francisco: Miller Freeman Books, 1999; Kirk Marcy. "Vocal Jazz: 'What's in Your Folder?' Balanced Programming for Vocal Jazz Ensembles." *The Choral Journal* 51.10 (May 2011): 56–59; Steven F. Pond. "'Chameleon' Meets 'Soul Train': Herbie, James, Michael, Damita Jo, and Jazz-Funk." *American Studies* 52.4, The Funk Issue (2013): 125–140; Terry Silverlight, Felipe Orozco, and Adrian Hopkins. *Jazz, Funk & Fusion: Over 60 Classic Grooves in Standard Notation*. London: Wise, 2011; Mark Cotgrove. *From Jazz Funk & Fusion to Acid Jazz: The History of the UK Jazz Dance Scene*. London: Chaser Publications; Milton Keynes [England]: AuthorHouse, 2009.

103. Allen Belkind. *Jean-Paul Sartre: Sartre and Existentialism in English: A Bibliographical Guide*. Kent, OH: Kent State University Press, 1970; Francois Bondy. "Jean-Paul Sartre and Politics." *Journal of Contemporary History* 2.2, Literature and Society (April 1967): 25–48; Norman N. Greene. *Jean-Paul Sartre: The Existentialist Ethic*. Ann Arbor: University of Michigan Press, 1960; Jacques Hardré. "Jean-Paul Sartre: Literary Critic." *Studies in Philology* 55.1 (January 1958): 98–106; Jonathan Judaken. *Jean-Paul Sartre and the Jewish Question: Anti-Antisemitism and the Politics of the French Intellectual*. Lincoln: University of Nebraska Press, 2006; Edith Kern. *Sartre, A Collection of Critical Essays*. Englewood Cliffs, NJ: Prentice-Hall, 1962; Joseph H. McMahon. *Humans Being: The World of Jean-Paul Sartre*. Chicago: University of Chicago Press, 1971; Jean-Paul Sartre and Robert Denoon Cumming. *The Philosophy of Jean-Paul Sartre*. New York: Random House, 1965.

104. Barry Bergstein. "Miles Davis and Karlheinz Stockhausen: A Reciprocal Relationship." *The Musical Quarterly* 76.4 (Winter 1992): 502–525; Cornelius Cardew. *Stockhausen Serves Imperialism, and Other Articles: With Commentary and Notes*. London: Latimer New Dimensions, 1974; M. J. Grant and Imke Misch. *The Musical Legacy of Karlheinz Stockhausen: Looking Back and Forward*. Hofheim am Taunus: Wolke, 2016; Jonathan Harvey. *The Music of Stockhausen: An Introduction*. Berkeley: University of California Press, 1975; Martin Iddon. *New Music at Darmstadt: Nono, Stockhausen, Cage, and Boulez*. New York: Cambridge University Press, 2013; Robin Maconie. *The Works of Karlheinz Stockhausen*. London; New York: Oxford University Press, 1976; _____. *Other Planets: The Music of Karlheinz Stockhausen*. Lanham, MD: Scarecrow Press, 2005; Karlheinz Stockhausen. *Towards a Cosmic Music*. Longmead, Shaftesbury, Dorset: Element, 1989; Karlheinz Stockhausen and Robin Maconie. *Stockhausen on Music: Lectures and Interviews*. London; New York: M. Boyars; New York: Distributed in the United States by Kampmann, 1989; Karlheinz Stockhausen and Mya Tannenbaum. *Conversations with Stockhausen*. Oxford [Oxfordshire]: Clarendon Press; Oxford [Oxfordshire]; New York: Oxford University Press, 1987; Thomas Ulrich and Jayne Obst. *Stockhausen: A Theological Interpretation*. Kürten, Germany: Stockhausen-Stiftung für Musik, 2012; Gregg Wager. *Symbolism as a Compositional Method in the Works of Karlheinz Stockhausen*. College Park, MD: G. Wager, 1998; Karl H. Wörner and Bill Hopkins. *Stockhausen; Life and Work*. Berkeley: University of California Press, 1973.

105. John F. Szwed. *So What: The Life of Miles Davis*. New York: Simon & Schuster, 2002.

Conclusion

Louis Armstrong, Duke Ellington, and Miles Davis's twentieth-century transnational biographies highlight jazz's internationalization, debunking any notion of jazz as indicative of a particularly exceptional US character. Markers of an intense fascination and simultaneous disdain of surveilled black-transnational masculinity, part of Armstrong, Ellington, and Davis's enduring appeal remains due to their exotic racial, gender, and sexual difference. Their pre-political images still internationally circulating, prized members of US cultural boasting, and crossing national borders to transnational locales, structures of feeling, ontologies, epistemologies, and musical experimentations, Armstrong, Ellington, and Davis's use and abuse by the US culture industry emphasizes the precarious positions non-white performers negotiate in a culture fetishizing and commodifying them.

Even as each iconoclastic performer was a particular kind of jazz star, Armstrong, Ellington, and Davis's interwoven transnational histories and intersecting racial, gender, and sexual formations and struggles disrupt mythic, individualistic notions of innocent, pure, and US-centered jazz, while emphasizing ways jazz and Afro-Diasporic traditions unfold as one. Transversing the Black Atlantic and beyond, Armstrong, Ellington, and Davis highlight black-transnational musicians' economic, political, and cultural histories, related to currents in African-American thought, nationalism, and various racial formations, from accidental, incidental, intentional, to unforgiveable blackness.

Cutting across crucial moments in twentieth-century jazz and broader US and transnational popular-cultural histories, from turn-of-the-century New Orleans to the 1920s and 1930s formative years, bebop's 1940s emergence, and 1950s, 1960s, and 1970s experimental sounds, as Armstrong, Ellington, and Davis expressed themselves in print and through additional creative endeavors, they shaped and were shaped by the institutional structures through which jazz was created, distributed, and consumed. Aligning themselves with other artists and activists, and influenced by forces of race, gender, sexuality, ethnicity, class, and nation, Armstrong, Ellington, and Davis were three among numerous African-American jazz musicians struggling against US and global white supremacy and prescriptive definitions of black-transnational masculinity and authenticity propagated by jazz's white and black advocates.

Black-transnational jazz musicians making verbal and artistic sense of their accomplishments, demonstrating self-awareness as they engaged in discourses about their vocation, Armstrong, Ellington, and Davis demonstrate ways black-transnational jazz musicians positioned themselves as creators, thinkers, and politically conscious individuals, navigating their political-cultural contexts and constructing a critical, philosophical, and political framework for analyzing their craft. Focusing attention on jazz's formal qualities and providing historical interpretations and theoretical reflections, Armstrong, Ellington, and Davis were composer-performers whose critical, historical, and aesthetic contributions illuminate artists' concerns and how black-transnational jazz musicians sought to realize ambitious, concrete goals through direct action in sound, building alternative institutions emphasizing the importance of political-cultural involvement, and noting jazz's impact on additional artistic expressions and the musical culture's role in US and transnational visual cultures.

As Armstrong, Ellington, and Davis represent the heroic, hetero-normative image of black male jazz icons, they link to African-American performers making popular music the soundtrack of the twentieth-century US experience, while disentangling jazz from any patriotic definition and exceptional claims. Noting jazz's impact on US and transnational popular culture, ways jazz histories have been riven by upheaval, and highlighting jazz as a musical style and cultural form intimately influenced by and influential on US and transnational conceptions of race, gender, sexuality, ethnicity, class, and nation, Armstrong, Ellington, and Davis were jazz performers interpreting and evaluating performances based on contested political-aesthetic criteria, whose transnational dimensions emphasize jazz musicians' multiple cultural sources, contexts, rituals, meanings, and race, gender, sexuality, ethnicity, class, and nation's instability as concepts inflecting jazz performance and reception in the political, capitalistic, and visual-cultural transmissions of a global art.

If jazz's more melancholic practitioners include Davis, Billie Holiday, Charlie Parker, and Nina Simone, creating an emotional intensity by singing songs of love, protest, and black empowerment in a dramatic style with a rough-edged voice, Louis Armstrong, along with Fats Waller, Art Tatum, and Ella Fitzgerald, offered listeners an emotional lift, as Armstrong articulated an ecstatic explosion of sound. Though his "mugging" may have been interpreted as confirming racial stereotypes, Armstrong exploited a blues sensibility, making it consonant with US and transnational popular cultures as part of broader desires for racial harmony and fetishization. The greatest of the New Orleans jazz musicians, used to perpetuate the myth that music can magically transcend racial, cultural, and national differences, Armstrong remains frozen in caricatures stereotyping him as a "true American original" and one of the United States's greatest and most beloved musical icons, hiding the complexities of his image and representations.

Duke Ellington, the first jazz composer of transnational status, was one of the twentieth century's most significant cultural figures and one of the greatest US composers and orchestra leaders. A slave's grandson, Ellington dropped out of high school to become a showman of unsurpassed suavity who was as comfortable in Carnegie Hall as in the nightclubs where he honed his style. Jazz's most important and influential composer and greatest bandleader, Ellington was one of the first musicians to concern himself with composition and musical form in jazz, as distinct from improvisation, songwriting, and arranging. One of big band jazz's initiators, Ellington led his band for more than half a century, composed thousands of scores, and created one of music's most distinctive ensemble sounds.

Surviving the deaths of Armstrong, Ellington, Parker, and Coltrane, the creative momentum of the twentieth century's most vital musical language passed on to Miles Davis, described as a protean and mercurial musical genius. Davis was one of the most influential musicians in the world and one of the twentieth century's most significant musicians. Producing some of the century's most exciting music, for more than forty years Davis remained at post–World War II popular music's vanguard as the world's most acclaimed jazz trumpeter, composer, bandleader, and musical visionary. One of the most innovative and respected figures in jazz histories, at the forefront of bebop, cool jazz, hard bop, modal jazz, and jazz-rock fusion, Davis remains a favorite and best-selling jazz artist, beloved worldwide. Depicted as "the bad man of jazz trumpetry," "prince of cool," "prince of darkness," "jazz's evil genius," "American Knight," and "American Knave," myths continue to surround Davis, contributing to jazz's racially tinged "mysteries," also implicated in Billie Holiday and other mythical jazz figures, as one of the United States's rarest creative artists performing an uncompromising jazz.

Bibliography

Abdullah, Zain. "Narrating Muslim Masculinities: The Fruit of Islam and the Quest for Black Redemption." *Spectrum: A Journal on Black Men* 1.1 (Autumn 2012): 141–177.

Abel, Elizabeth. *Signs of the Times: The Visual Politics of Jim Crow.* Berkeley, CA: University of California Press, 2010.

Abel, Emily K. *Tuberculosis and the Politics of Exclusion: A History of Public Health and Migration to Los Angeles.* New Brunswick, NJ: Rutgers University Press, 2007.

Abu-Lughod, Janet L. *Race, Space, and Riots in Chicago, New York, and Los Angeles.* Oxford; New York: Oxford University Press, 2007.

Acquaviva, Mike, and Elliott M. Rudwick. *A Guide to The East St. Louis Race Riot of 1917.* Frederick, MD: University Publications of America, 1985.

Adams, Rachel. *Sideshow U.S.A: Freaks and the American Cultural Imagination.* Chicago: The University of Chicago Press, 2001.

Adams, Vincanne. *Markets of Sorrow, Labors of Faith: New Orleans in the Wake of Katrina.* Durham, NC: Duke University Press, 2013.

Adekunle, Julius, and Hettie V. Williams. *Converging Identities: Blackness in the Modern African Diaspora.* Durham, NC: Carolina Academic Press, 2013.

Adorno, Theodor W. "On Popular Music." *Studies in Philosophy and Social Science* 9.1 (1941) 17–48.

Aebersold, Jamey. *Nothin' But Blues: Jazz and Rock.* New Albany, IN (1211 Aebersold Dr., New Albany, 47150): Jamey Aebersold, 1976.

Afary, Kamran. *Performance and Activism: Grassroots Discourse After the Los Angeles Rebellion of 1992.* Lanham, MD: Lexington Books, 2009.

African Jazz Pioneers. *The African Jazz Pioneers: Live at the Montreux Jazz Festival.* South Africa: Gallo Music Productions, 1991.

Agawu, Kofi. *African Rhythm: A Northern Ewe Perspective.* Cambridge; New York: Cambridge University Press, 1995.

Agostinelli, Anthony J. *The Newport Jazz Festival, Rhode Island, 1954–1971: A Bibliography, Discography, and Filmography.* Providence, RI: Agostinelli, 1977.

Aidi, Hisham. *Rebel Music: Race, Empire, and the New Muslim Youth Culture.* New York: Pantheon Books, 2014.

Ailey, Alvin, and A. Peter Bailey. *Revelations: The Autobiography of Alvin Ailey.* Secaucus, NJ: Carol Pub. Group, 1995.

Ake, David. "Re-Masculating Jazz: Ornette Coleman, "Lonely Woman," and the New York Jazz Scene in the Late 1950s." *American Music* 16.1 (Spring 1998): 25–44.

Albert, Richard N. "The Jazz-Blues Motif in James Baldwin's 'Sonny's Blues.'" *College Literature* 11.2 (Spring 1984): 178–185.

Albertson, Chris. *Bessie*. New Haven, Connecticut: Yale University Press, 2003.

Albertson, Chris, George N. Terry, Clifford Richter, and Gunther Schuller. *Bessie Smith: Empress of Blues*. New York: Collier Macmillan, 1975.

Alexander, Michael. *Jazz Age Jews*. Princeton, NJ: Princeton University Press, 2001.

Alexander, Michelle. *The New Jim Crow: Mass Incarceration in the Age of Colorblindness*. New York: The New Press, 2010.

_____. "The War on Drugs and the New Jim Crow." *Race, Poverty & the Environment* 17.1, 20th Anniversary Issue (Spring 2010): 75–77.

Alleyne, Brian W. *Radicals Against Race: Black Activism and Cultural Politics*. Oxford; New York: Berg, 2002.

Anderson, Gene. "Blues for You Johnny: Johnny Dodds and His 'Wild Man Blues' Recordings of 1927 and 1928," *Annual Review of Jazz Studies*, viii (1996), 39–62.

_____. "The Origin of Armstrong's Hot Fives and Hot Sevens." *College Music Symposium* 43 (2003): 13–24.

Anderson, Gene Henry, and Michael J. Budds. *The Original Hot Five Recordings of Louis Armstrong*. Hillsdale, NY: Pendragon Press, 2007.

Anderson, Paul Allen. *Deep River: Music and Memory in Harlem Renaissance Thought*. Durham: Duke University Press, 2001.

Andrews, Dorinda Carter, and Frank Tuitt. *Contesting the Myth of a "Post Racial Era": The Continued Significance of Race in U.S. Education*. New York: Peter Lang, 2013.

Apoyan, Anush. *The Preacher: A Tribute to Horace Silver*. Saarbrücken AV Akademikerverlag 2013.

Arceneaux, Pamela D. "Guidebooks to Sin: The Blue Books of Storyville." *Louisiana History: The Journal of the Louisiana Historical Association* 28.4 (Autumn 1987): 397–405.

Armstrong, Elisabeth. "Before Bandung: The Anti-Imperialist Women's Movement in Asia and the Women's International Democratic Federation." *Signs* 41.2 (Winter 2016): 305–331.

Armstrong, Lil Hardin. "Satchmo and Me." *American Music* 25.1 (Spring 2007): 106-118.

Armstrong, Louis, and Thomas David Brothers, Ed. *Louis Armstrong, In His Own Words: Selected Writings*. Oxford; New York: Oxford University Press, 1999.

Armstrong, Louis, Rudy Vallée, Dan Morgenstern, Horace Gerlach, and Benny Goodman. *Swing That Music*. New York: Da Capo Press, 1993.

Asai, Susan M. "Cultural Politics: The African American Connection in Asian American Jazz-Based Music." *Asian Music* 36.1 (Winter–Spring 2005): 87–108.

Asukile, Thabiti. "J.A. Rogers' "Jazz at Home": Afro-American Jazz in Paris During the Jazz Age." *The Black Scholar* 40.3, Black Issues: 2010 (Fall 2010): 22–35.

Ater, Renée. "Communities in Conflict: Memorializing Martin Luther King Jr. in Rocky Mount, North Carolina." *Indiana Magazine of History* 110.1, Special Issue—Art, Race, Space (March 2014): 32–39.

Aton, Ayé, and John Corbett. *Sun Ra + Ayé Aton: Space, Interiors and Exteriors, 1972*. Brooklyn, New York: PictureBox, 2013.

Auner, Joseph Henry, and Arnold Schoenberg. *A Schoenberg Reader: Documents of a Life*. New Haven, CT: Yale University Press, 2003.

Austin, Algernon. *Achieving Blackness: Race, Black Nationalism, and Afrocentrism in the Twentieth Century*. New York: New York University Press, 2006.

Avakian, George. "Jazz-1962." *Transition* 6/7 (October 1962): 59–60.

Avila, Eric. *Popular Culture in the Age of White Flight: Fear and Fantasy in Suburban Los Angeles*. Berkeley: University of California Press, 2004.

Bacevich, Andrew J. *The Limits of Power: The End of American Exceptionalism*. New York: Metropolitan Books, 2008.

Bachin, Robin Faith. *Building the South Side: Urban Space and Civic Culture in Chicago, 1890–1919*. Chicago: University of Chicago Press, 2004.

Bacon, Tony, and Dave Gelly. *Masters of Jazz Saxophone: The Story of the Players and Their Music*. London: Balafon Books, 2000.

Badger, Reid. *A Life in Ragtime: A Biography of James Reese Europe*. New York: Oxford University Press, 1995.

Bailey, D. S. *Up in Flames: [The Torching of East St. Louis 1917: Based on a True Story]*. St. Louis, MO: Voices Books & Pub., 2004.

Bak, Richard. *Joe Louis: The Great Black Hope*. New York: Da Capo Press, 1998.

Bakan, Michael B. *World Music: Traditions and Transformations*. Boston: McGraw-Hill, 2007.

Baker, Bruce E, and Barbara Hahn. *The Cotton Kings: Capitalism and Corruption in Turn-of-the-Century New York and New Orleans*. Oxford; New York: Oxford University Press, 2016.

Baker, Chet. *As Though I Had Wings: The Lost Memoir*. New York: St. Martin's Press, 1997.

Baker, David. *The Jazz Style of Sonny Rollins: A Musical and Historical Perspective*. Lebanon, IN: Studio 224: Sole distributorship Studio P/R, 1980.

_____. *The Jazz Style of Clifford Brown: A Musical and Historical Perspective*. Hialeah, FL: Studio P/R, 1982.

Baldwin, Davarian L. "Black Cultural Production and the Promises and Pitfalls of American Pluralism." *American Studies* 45.2 (Summer 2004): 133–140.

_____. *Chicago's New Negroes: Modernity, the Great Migration, and Black Urban Life*. Chapel Hill: The University of North Carolina Press, 2009.

Balliett, Whitney. *Jelly Roll, Jabbo, and Fats: Nineteen Portraits in Jazz*. New York: Oxford University Press, 1983.

Balshaw, Maria. "'Black Was White': Urbanity, Passing and the Spectacle of Harlem." *Journal of American Studies* 33.2 (August 1999): 307–322.

Banerjee, Mita. "Black Bottoms, Yellow Skin: From Ma Rainey to Maxine Hong Kingston's 'Tripmaster Monkey.'" *Amerikastudien / American Studies* 45.3 (2000): 405–423.

Banfield, William C. *Cultural Codes: Makings of a Black Music Philosophy: An Interpretive History from Spirituals to Hip Hop*. Lanham, MD: Scarecrow Press, 2010.

Bang, Derrick. *Vince Guaraldi at the Piano*. Jefferson, NC: McFarland & Co., 2012.

Banks, Don. "Third-Stream Music." *Proceedings of the Royal Musical Association* 97 (1970–1971): 59–67.

Baraka, Amiri. *The Great Max Roach*. New York: Thunder's Mouth Press, 1991.

_____. *Digging: The Afro-American Soul of American Classical Music*. Berkeley: University of California Press, 2009.

Baraka, Amiri, and Larry Neal. *Black Fire; An Anthology of Afro-American Writing*. New York: Morrow, 1968.

Barg, Lisa. "Queer Encounters in the Music of Billy Strayhorn." *Journal of the American Musicological Society* 66.3 (Fall 2013): 771–824.

Barker, Danny and Alyn Shipton. *Buddy Bolden and the Last Days of Storyville*. London; New York: Continuum, 2001.

Barker, Joan C. *Danger, Duty, and Disillusion: The Worldview of Los Angeles Police Officers*. Prospect Heights, IL: Waveland Press, 1999.

Barnes, Catherine A. *Journey from Jim Crow: The Desegregation of Southern Transit*. New York: Columbia University Press, 1983.

Barnes, Harper. *Never Been a Time: The 1917 Race Riot that Sparked the Civil Rights Movement*. New York: Walker & Co.: Distributed to the trade by Macmillan, 2008.

Barnhart, Scotty. *The World of Jazz Trumpet: A Comprehensive History & Practical Philosophy*. Milwaukee, WI: Hal Leonard, 2005.

Barranger, Milly S. *Unfriendly Witnesses: Gender, Theater, and Film in the McCarthy Era*. Carbondale: Southern Illinois University Press, 2008.

Barrett, Samuel. "'Kind of Blue' and the Economy of Modal Jazz." *Popular Music* 25.2 (May 2006): 185–200.

Bartkowiak, Mathew J., and Yuya Kiuchi. *The Music of Counterculture Cinema: A Critical Study of 1960s and 1970s Soundtracks*. Jefferson, NC: McFarland & Company, Inc., 2015.

Bartlett, Andrew W. "Cecil Taylor, Identity Energy, and the Avant-Garde African American Body." *Perspectives of New Music* 33.1/2 (Winter–Summer 1995): 274–293.

Bascom, William Russell. *African Art in Cultural Perspective; An Introduction*. New York: Norton, 1973.

Basie, Count, Albert Murray, and Dan Morgenstern. *Good Morning Blues: The Autobiography of Count Basie.* Minneapolis: University of Minnesota Press, 2016.

Battle, Lois. *Storyville.* New York: Viking, 1993.

Baur, Steven. "Ravel's "Russian" Period: Octatonicism in His Early Works, 1893–1908." *Journal of the American Musicological Society* 52.3 (Autumn 1999): 531–592.

Bean, Annemarie, James V. Hatch, Brooks McNamara, and Mel Watkins. *Inside the Minstrel Mask: Readings in Nineteenth-Century Blackface Minstrelsy.* Middletown, CT: Wesleyan University Press 1996.

Bearden, Romare, Mary Schmidt Campbell, Sharon F. Patton, and Studio Museum in Harlem. *Memory and Metaphor: The Art of Romare Bearden, 1940-1987.* New York: Studio Museum in Harlem: Oxford University Press, 1991.

Bearden, Romare, Ruth Fine, Mary Lee Corlett, and National Gallery of Art (U.S.). *The Art of Romare Bearden.* Washington: National Gallery of Art, 2003.

Bearden, Romare, Carla M. Hanzal, Ruth Fine, and Mint Museum (Charlotte, NC). *Romare Bearden: Southern Recollections.* Charlotte, NC: Mint Museum, 2011.

Bearden, Romare, and M. Bunch Washington. *The Art of Romare Bearden: The Prevalence of Ritual.* New York: Abrams, 1973.

Becker, Geoffrey. "Jimi Hendrix, Bluegrass Star." *Prairie Schooner* 78.1 (Spring 2004): 6–18.

Behr, Edward. *Prohibition: Thirteen Years That Changed America.* New York: Arcade Pub.; [Boston]: Distributed by Little, Brown and Co., 1996.

Belkind, Allen. *Jean-Paul Sartre: Sartre and Existentialism in English: A Bibliographical Guide.* Kent, OH: Kent State University Press, 1970.

Bell, Monta. "Movies and Talkies." *The North American Review* 226.4 (October 1928): 429–435.

Bellocq, Ernest James, Lee Friedlander, and John Szarkowski. *Storyville Portraits: Photographs from the New Orleans Red-Light District, circa 1912.* New York: Museum of Modern Art, cop. 1970.

Bennahum, Ninotchka. *Antonia Mercé, "LaArgentina": Flamenco and the Spanish Avant Garde.* Middletown, CT: Wesleyan University Press, 2014.

Bennett, Andy. *Remembering Woodstock.* Aldershot, Hampshire, England; Burlington, VT: Ashgate, 2004.

Berendt, Joachim-Ernst. *The Story of Jazz: From New Orleans to Rock Jazz.* Englewood Cliffs, NJ: Prentice-Hall, 1978.

Berendt, Joachim-Ernst, and Günther Huesmann. *The Jazz Book: From Ragtime to Fusion and Beyond.* Brooklyn, NY: Lawrence Hill Books, 1992 .

Berg, Stefan. *Let That Bad Air Out: Buddy Bolden's Last Parade.* Erin, ON: Porcupine's Quill, 2007.

Berger, Dan. *Struggle Within: Prisons, Political Prisoners, and Mass Movements in the United States.* Oakland, CA: PM Press; Montreal, Quebec: Kersplebedeb, 2014.

Berger, Edward. *Softly, With Feeling: Joe Wilder and the Breaking of Barriers in American Music.* Philadelphia: Temple University Press, 2014.

Berger, Harris M. *Metal, Rock, and Jazz: Perception and the Phenomenology of Musical Experience.* Hanover, NH: University Press of New England, 1999.

Berger, Morroe, Edward Berger, and James Patrick. *Benny Carter, A Life in American Music.* Metuchen, NJ: Scarecrow Press, 1982.

Bergh, Johs, Jan Evensmo, and Norsk Jazzarkiv. *Jazz Tenor Saxophone in Norway: 1917–1959.* Oslo: Norwegian Jazz Archives, 1996.

Bergreen, Laurence. *As Thousands Cheer: The Life of Irving Berlin.* New York: Viking, 1990.

Bergstein, Barry. "Miles Davis and Karlheinz Stockhausen: A Reciprocal Relationship." *The Musical Quarterly* 76.4 (Winter 1992): 502–525.

Berish, Andrew S. *Lonesome Roads and Streets of Dreams: Place, Mobility, and Race in Jazz of the 1930s and '40s.* Chicago: London: The University of Chicago Press, 2012.

Berkman, Franya J. "Appropriating Universality: The Coltranes and 1960s Spirituality." *American Studies* 48.1 (Spring 2007): 41–62.

———. *Monument Eternal: The Music of Alice Coltrane.* Middletown, CT: Wesleyan University Press, 2010.

Bernstein, David W. *The San Francisco Tape Music Center: 1960s Counterculture and the Avant-Garde* . Berkeley: University of California Press, 2008 .

Bernstein, Leonard. *The Unanswered Question: Six Talks at Harvard*. Cambridge, MA: Harvard University Press, 1976.

Bernstein, Leonard, and Nigel Simeone. *The Leonard Bernstein Letters*. New Haven: Yale University Press, 2013.

Bernstein, Matthew H., and Dana F. White. "'Imitation of Life' in a Segregated Atlanta: Its Promotion, Distribution and Reception." *Film History* 19.2, Film and Copyright (2007): 152–178.

Berry, David Carson. "Dynamic Introductions: The Affective Role of Melodic Ascent and Other Linear Devices in Selected Song Verses of Irving Berlin." *Intégral* 13 (1999): 1–62.

_____. "Gambling with Chromaticism? Extra-Diatonic Melodic Expression in the Songs of Irving Berlin." *Theory and Practice* 26 (2001): 21–85.

Berton, Ralph. *Remembering Bix; A Memoir of the Jazz Age*. New York, Harper & Row, 1974.

Bérubé, Michael. "Masks, Margins, and African American Modernism: Melvin Tolson's Harlem Gallery." *PMLA* 105.1, Special Topic: African and African American Literature (January 1990): 57–69.

Bicknell, Jeanette. "Just a Song? Exploring the Aesthetics of Popular Song Performance." *The Journal of Aesthetics and Art Criticism* 63.3 (Summer 2005): 261–270.

Biebuyck, Daniel P. *Tradition and Creativity in Tribal Art*. Berkeley, University of California Press, 1969.

Bilby, Kenneth. "Distant Drums: The Unsung Contribution of African-Jamaican Percussion to Popular Music at Home and Abroad." *Caribbean Quarterly* 56.4; Pioneering Icons of Jamaican Popular Music, Part II (December 2010): 1–21.

Birkbeck, Matt. *Deconstructing Sammy: Music, Money, Madness, and the Mob*. New York: Amistad, 2008.

Birtwistle, Andy. "Marking Time and Sounding Difference: Brubeck, Temporality and Modernity." *Popular Music* 29.3 (October 2010): 351–371.

Bisso, Ray. *Buddy Bolden of New Orleans: A Jazz Poem*. Santa Barbara, CA: Fithian Press, 1998.

Blake, Ran. "Teaching Third Stream." *Music Educators Journal* 63.4 (December 1976): 30–33.

_____. "Third Stream and the Importance of the Ear: A Position Paper in Narrative Form." *College Music Symposium* 21.2 (Fall 1981): 139–146.

Blanc, Serge, and Percudanse Association. *African Percussion: The Djembe*. Paris, France: Percudanse Association, 1997.

Blancq, Charles. *Sonny Rollins, The Journey of a Jazzman*. Boston, MA: Twayne, 1983.

Blesh, Rudi. *Shining Trumpets, A History of Jazz*. New York, Knopf, 1958.

Bloch, Avital H., and Lauri Umansky. *Impossible to Hold: Women and Culture in the 1960's*. New York: New York University Press, 2005.

Block, Geoffrey Holden. *The Richard Rodgers Reader*. Oxford: Oxford University Press, 2002.

_____. *Richard Rodgers*. New Haven, CT: Yale University Press, 2003.

Block, Geoffrey Holden, and J. Peter Burkholder. *Charles Ives and the Classical Tradition*. New Haven, CT: Yale University Press, 1996.

Block, Steven. "Pitch-Class Transformation in Free Jazz." *Music Theory Spectrum* 12.2 (Autumn 1990): 181–202.

_____. "'Bemsha Swing': The Transformation of a Bebop Classic to Free Jazz." *Music Theory Spectrum* 19.2 (Autumn 1997): 206–231.

Bloom, Jack M. *Class, Race, and the Civil Rights Movement*. Bloomington: Indiana University Press, 1987.

Blum, Edward J., and Jason R. Young. *The Souls of W. E. B. Du Bois: New Essays and Reflections*. Macon, GA: Mercer University Press, 2009.

Blume, Gernot. "Blurred Affinities: Tracing the Influence of North Indian Classical Music in Keith Jarrett's Solo Piano Improvisations." *Popular Music* 22.2 (May 2003): 117–142.

Blumenthal, Bob, and John Abbott. *Saxophone Colossus: A Portrait of Sonny Rollins*. New York: Abrams, 2010.

Bobo, Lawrence. *Prismatic Metropolis: Inequality in Los Angeles.* New York: Russell Sage Foundation, 2000.

Bogdan, Robert. *Freak Show: Presenting Human Oddities for Amusement and Profit.* Chicago: University of Chicago Press, 1990.

Bohlman, Philip V. *World Music: A Very Short Introduction.* Oxford: Oxford University Press, 2002.

_____. *The Cambridge History of World Music.* New York: Cambridge University Press, 2013.

Boisvert, Patricia Anne, and Adrienne Lepore. *Jazz in Newport.* Providence, RI: New Press, 1977.

Bolden, Tony. *The Funk Era and Beyond: New Perspectives on Black Popular Culture.* New York: Palgrave Macmillan, 2008.

_____. "Groove Theory: A Vamp on the Epistemology of Funk." *American Studies* 52.4, The Funk Issue (2013): 9–34.

Bond, Adam. *The Imposing Preacher: Samuel DeWitt Proctor and Black Public Faith.* Minneapolis: Fortress Press, 2013.

Bondy, Francois. "Jean-Paul Sartre and Politics." *Journal of Contemporary History* 2.2, Literature and Society (April 1967): 25–48.

Bone, Robert. *Richard Wright.* Minneapolis: University of Minnesota Press, 1969.

Bookbinder, Robert. *The Films of Bing Crosby.* Secaucus, NJ: Citadel Press, 1977, Ted Crosby. *The Story of Bing Crosby.* Cleveland, New York: World Pub. Co., 1946.

Borge, Jason. "La Civilizada Selva: Jazz and Latin American Avant-Garde Intellectuals." *Chasqui* 37.1 (May 2008): 105–119.

Bornstein, George. "W. E. B. Du Bois and the Jews: Ethics, Editing, and The Souls of Black Folk." *Textual Cultures* 1.1 (Spring 2006): 64–74.

Boskin, Joseph. *Urban Racial Violence in the Twentieth Century.* Beverly Hills, CA: Glencoe Press, 1976.

Bossius, Thomas, Andreas Häger, and Keith Kahn-Harris. *Religion and Popular Music in Europe: New Expressions of Sacred and Secular Identity.* London; New York: I.B. Taurus, 2011.

Bost, Suzanne. *Mulattas and Mestizas: Representing Mixed Identities in the Americas, 1850–2000.* Athens: The University of Georgia Press, 2003.

Bourg, Julian. *From Revolution to Ethics: May 1968 and Contemporary French Thought.* Montréal: McGill-Queen's University Press, 2014.

Bourque, Stephen A., and John W. Burdan. *The Road to Safwan: The 1st Squadron, 4th Cavalry in the 1991 Persian Gulf War.* Denton, TX: University of North Texas Press, 2007.

Bowdre, Karen M. "Passing Films and the Illusion of Racial Equality." *Black Camera* 5.2 (Spring 2014): 21–43.

Boyce, Robert W. D. *The Great Interwar Crisis and the Collapse of Globalization.* Basingstoke: Palgrave Macmillan, 2009.

Boyd, Jean Ann. *The Jazz of the Southwest: An Oral History of Western Swing.* Austin: University of Texas Press, 1998.

_____. *Dance All Night: Those Other Southwestern Swing Bands, Past and Present.* Lubbock: Texas Tech University Press, 2012.

Boyden, Matthew. *Richard Strauss.* Boston: Northeastern University Press, 1999.

Brackett, David. "James Brown's "Superbad" and the Double-Voiced Utterance." *Popular Music* 11.3 (October 1992): 309–324.

Braggs, Rashida K. *Jazz Diasporas: Race, Music, and Migration in Post-World War II Paris.* Oakland: University of California Press, 2016.

Bratcher, Melanie E. *Words and Songs of Bessie Smith, Billie Holiday, and Nina Simone: Sound Motion, Blues Spirit, and African Memory.* New York: Routledge, 2007.

Braunstein, Peter, and Michael William Doyle. *Imagine Nation: The American Counterculture of the 1960s and '70s .* New York: Routledge, 2002 .

Bravmann, René A. *Islam and Tribal Art in West Africa.* London, New York: Cambridge University Press, 1974.

Brée, Germaine. *Camus; A Collection of Critical Essays*. Englewood Cliffs, NJ, Prentice-Hall, 1962.

Bremer, Francis J. *John Winthrop: America's Forgotten Founding Father*. New York: Oxford University Press, 2003.

_____. *John Winthrop: Biography as History*. New York: Continuum, 2009.

Bricktop and James Haskins. *Bricktop*. New York: Welcome Rain Publishers, 2000.

Briggs, John. *Leonard Bernstein: The Man, His Work, and His World*. Cleveland; New York: World Pub. Co.; Popular Library, 1961.

Britt, Stan. *Dexter Gordon: A Musical Biography*. New York: Da Capo Press, 1989.

Brittin, Ruth V. "The Effect of Overtly Categorizing Music on Preference for Popular Music Styles." *Journal of Research in Music Education* 39.2 (Summer 1991): 143–151.

Brodwin, Stanley. "The Veil Transcended: Form and Meaning in W. E. B. DuBois' 'The Souls of Black Folk.'" *Journal of Black Studies* 2.3 (March 1972): 303–321.

Brofsky, Howard. "Miles Davis and "My Funny Valentine": The Evolution of a Solo." *Black Music Research Journal* 3 (1983): 23–45.

Brooks, Edward. *The Bessie Smith Companion: A Critical and Detailed Appreciation of the Recordings*. Wheathampstead, Herts, UK: Cavendish Pub. Co.; New York: Da Capo Press, 1982.

Broschke-Davis, Ursula. *Paris Without Regret: James Baldwin, Kenny Clarke, Chester Himes, and Donald Byrd*. Iowa City: University of Iowa Press, 1986.

Brothers, Thomas David. *Louis Armstrong's New Orleans*. New York: W. W. Norton, 2006.

_____. *Louis Armstrong, Master of Modernism*. New York: W. W. Norton & Company, 2014.

Brower, Steven. *Satchmo: The Wonderful World and Art of Louis Armstrong*. New York: Abrams, 2009.

Brown, Anthony. "Modern Jazz Drumset Artistry." *The Black Perspective in Music* 18.1/2 (1990): 39–58.

Brown, James, and Bruce Tucker. *James Brown, The Godfather of Soul*. New York: Thunder's Mouth Press, 2002.

Brown, Lee B. "'Feeling My Way': Jazz Improvisation and Its Vicissitudes—A Plea for Imperfection." *The Journal of Aesthetics and Art Criticism* 58.2, Improvisation in the Arts (Spring 2000): 113–123.

Brown, Leonard L. *John Coltrane and Black America's Quest for Freedom: Spirituality and the Music*. New York City: Oxford University Press, 2010.

Brown, Leonard, and The Kansas City Jazz Museum. *Kansas City...And All That Jazz*. Riverside, NJ: Andrews McMeel Publishing, 1999.

Brown, Scot. "The Blues/Funk Futurism of Roger Troutman." *American Studies* 52.4, The Funk Issue (2013): 119–123.

Brown, Scott E., and Robert Hilbert. *James P. Johnson: A Case of Mistaken Identity*. Metuchen, NJ: Scarecrow Press and the Institute of Jazz Studies, Rutgers University, 1986.

Brown, Stacy, and Todd Barmann. *Jelly Roll Morton: New Orleans Style! Chicago Style! Kansas City Style! It's all Jelly Roll Style!* New York: Select; Lancaster: Gazelle [distributor], 2011.

Brown, Stephanie. "Bourgeois Blackness and Autobiographical Authenticity in Ellen Tarry's 'The Third Door.'" *African American Review* 41.3 (Fall 2007): 557–570 .

Brown, Stephanie, and Keith Clark. "Melodramas of Beset Black Manhood?: Meditations on African-American Masculinity as Scholarly Topos and Social Menace an Introduction." *Callaloo* 26.3 (Summer 2003): 732–737.

Brown, Yamma, and Robin Gaby Fisher. *Cold Sweat: My Father James Brown and Me*. Chicago: Chicago Review Press, 2014.

Browne, Donald R. *The Voice of America: Policies and Problems*. [Lexington, KY]: Association for Education in Journalism, 1976.

Browne, Ray B. "Shakespeare in American Vaudeville and Negro Minstrelsy." *American Quarterly* 12.3 (Autumn 1960): 374–391.

_____. "Wellerisms in Negro Minstrelsy and Vaudeville." *Western Folklore* 20.3 (July 1961): 201-202.

Broze, Yuri, and Daniel Shanahan. "Diachronic Changes in Jazz Harmony: A Cognitive Perspective." *Music Perception: An Interdisciplinary Journal* 31.1 (September 2013): 32–45.

Brubeck, Dave, Howard Brubeck, and David C. Olsen. *The Genius of Dave Brubeck. Book 1: Piano Solos.* Hialeah, FL: Columbia Pictures, 1984.

Brundage, Kirk. *Afro-Brazilian Percussion Guide: Instruments and Rhythms from Salvador, Bahia, Brazil.* Los Angeles, CA: K. Brundage, 2011.

Brunner, Edward. "'Shuh! Ain't Nothin' To It': The Dynamics of Success in Jackie Ormes's "Torchy Brown." *Melus* 32.3, Coloring America: Multi-Ethnic Engagements with Graphic Narrative (Fall 2007): 23–49.

Bruyninckx, Walter. *Jazz, Modern Jazz: Be-bop, Hard Bop, West Coast.* Mechelen, Belgium, 1986.

Büchmann-Møller, Frank. *You Just Fight for Your Life: The Story of Lester Young.* New York: Praeger, 1990.

————. *Someone to Watch Over Me: The Life and Music of Ben Webster.* Ann Arbor: Univ. of Michigan Press, 2006.

Bugnion, Francois. "The Geneva Conventions of 12 August 1949: From the 1949 Diplomatic Conference to the Dawn of the New Millennium." *International Affairs* (Royal Institute of International Affairs 1944-) 76.1 (January 2000): 41–50.

Bullock, Paul. *Watts; the Aftermath; an Inside View of the Ghetto.* New York: Grove Press, 1969.

Burke, Patrick. "Oasis of Swing: The Onyx Club, Jazz, and White Masculinity in the Early 1930s." *American Music* 24.3 (Autumn 2006): 320–346.

————. *Come in and Hear the Truth: Jazz and Race On 52nd Street.* Chicago: University of Chicago Press, 2008.

Burkholder, J. Peter. *Charles Ives, The Ideas Behind The Music.* New Haven, CT: Yale University Press, 1985.

————. *All Made of Tunes: Charles Ives and the Uses of Musical Borrowing.* New Haven, CT: Yale University Press, 1995.

————. *Charles Ives and His World.* Princeton, NJ: Princeton University Press, 1996.

Butler, Martin. *Voices of the Down and Out: The Dust Bowl Migration and the Great Depression in the Songs of Woody Guthrie.* Heidelberg: Winter 2007.

Butsch, Richard. *The Making of American Audiences: From Stage to Television, 1750–1990.* Cambridge; New York: Cambridge University Press, 2000.

Butterfield, Matthew W. "Why Do Jazz Musicians Swing Their Eighth Notes?" *Music Theory Spectrum* 33.1 (Spring 2011): 3–26.

Caldwell, Ryan Ashley. *Fallgirls: Gender and the Framing of Torture at Abu Ghraib.* Farnham, Surrey; Burlington, VT: Ashgate, 2012.

Calloway, Cab. *The New Cab Calloway's Hepsters Dictionary: Language of Jive.* New York: Cab Calloway, Inc., 1944.

Calloway, Cab, and Bryant Rollins. *Of Minnie the Moocher and Me.* New York: Crowell, 1976.

Campbell, James. "James Baldwin and the FBI." *The Threepenny Review* 77 (Spring 1999): 11.

Candini, Pino. "Musica Jazz: the Italian Jazz Magazine Which is Also a Record." *Fontes Artis Musicae* 36.3 (July–September 1989): 219–220.

Cannon, Katie G. *Teaching Preaching: Isaac Rufus Clark and Black Sacred Rhetoric.* New York; London: Continuum, 2003.

Cannon, Lou. *Official Negligence: How Rodney King and the Riots Changed Los Angeles and the LAPD.* New York: Times Books, 1997.

Cardew, Cornelius. *Stockhausen Serves Imperialism, and Other Articles: With Commentary and Notes.* London: Latimer New Dimensions, 1974.

Carmichael, Hoagy, and Stephen Longstreet. *Sometimes I Wonder: The Story of Hoagy Carmichael.* New York: Farrar, Straus and Giroux, 1965.

Carner, Gary. "Introduction: [Literature of Jazz]." *Black American Literature Forum* 25.3, Literature of Jazz Issue (Autumn 1991): 441–448.

Carr, Ian. *Keith Jarrett: The Man and His Music.* London: Paladin, 1991.

————. *Miles Davis: The Definitive Biography.* New York: Thunder's Mouth Press, 1998.

Carr, Roy, Brian Case, and Fred Dellar. *The Hip: Hipsters, Jazz, and the Beat Generation.* London; Boston: Faber and Faber, 1986.

Carringer, Robert L., Alfred A. Cohn, and Samson Raphaelson. *The Jazz Singer.* Madison: Published for the Wisconsin Center for Film and Theater Research by the University of Wisconsin Press, 1979.

Carrington, André M. *Speculative Blackness: The Future of Race in Science Fiction.* Minneapolis: University of Minnesota Press, 2016.

Carruth, Hayden. "Ben Webster." *The American Poetry Review* 21.4 (July/August 1992): 17–19.

_____. *Sitting In: Selected Writings on Jazz, Blues, and Related Topics.* Iowa City: University of Iowa Press, 1993.

Carson, Charles D. "'Bridging the Gap': Creed Taylor, Grover Washington Jr., and the Crossover Roots of Smooth Jazz." *Black Music Research Journal* 28.1, Becoming: Blackness and the Musical Imagination (Spring 2008): 1–15.

Carson, Clayborne, Peter Holloran, Ralph E. Luker, and Penny Russell. "Martin Luther King, Jr., as Scholar: A Reexamination of His Theological Writings." *The Journal of American History* 78.1 (June 1991): 93–105.

Carter, Marva Griffin. "Removing the "Minstrel Mask" in the Musicals of Will Marion Cook." *The Musical Quarterly* 84.2 (Summer 2000): 206–220.

_____. *Swing Along: The Musical Life of Will Marion Cook.* New York: Oxford University Press, 2008.

Carter, Ron, and Oliver Nelson. *Building a Jazz Bass Line.* Jamaica, NY: Noslen Music Co., 1966.

Cassidy, Donna. *Painting the Musical City: Jazz and Cultural Identity in American Art, 1910–1940.* Washington, D.C.: Smithsonian Institution Press, 1997.

Catalano, Nick. *Clifford Brown: The Life and Art of the Legendary Jazz Trumpeter.* Oxford; New York: Oxford University Press, 2000.

Cawthra, Benjamin. *Blue Notes in Black and White: Photography and Jazz.* Chicago; London: University of Chicago Press, 2011.

Celenza, Anna Harwell. "Legislating Jazz." *Washington History* 26 Jazz in Washington (Spring 2014): 88–97.

Célestin, Roger, and Eliane Françoise DalMolin. *France from 1851 to the Present: Universalism in Crisis.* New York: Palgrave Macmillan, 2007.

Chafer, Tony, and Emmanuel Godin. *The End of the French Exception?: Decline and Revival of the "French Model."* New York: Palgrave Macmillan, 2010.

Chalmers, David Mark. *And the Crooked Places Made Straight: The Struggle for Social Change in the 1960s* . Baltimore: Johns Hopkins University Press, 1991 .

Chambers, Jack. *Milestones: The Music and Times of Miles Davis.* Toronto: University of Toronto Press, 1990.

Chang, Edward T., and Jeannette Diaz-Veizades. *Ethnic Peace in the American City: Building Community in Los Angeles and Beyond.* New York: New York University Press, 1999.

Chavers-Wright, Madrue. *The Guarantee: P. W. Chavers, Banker, Entrepreneur, Philanthropist in Chicago's Black Belt of the Twenties.* New York: Wright-Armstead Associates, 1985.

Chenoweth, Lawrence. "The Rhetoric of Hope and Despair: A Study of the Jimi Hendrix Experience and the Jefferson Airplane." *American Quarterly* 23.1 (Spring 1971): 25–45.

Chilton, John. *Who's Who of Jazz! Storyville to Swing Street.* Philadelphia: Chilton Book Co., 1972.

_____. *The Song of the Hawk: The Life and Recordings of Coleman Hawkins* . Ann Arbor: University of Michigan Press, 1990 .

_____. *Roy Eldridge, Little Jazz Giant.* London; New York: Continuum, 2002.

Chitando, Ezra, and Nordiska Afrikainstitutet. *Singing Culture: A Study of Gospel Music in Zimbabwe.* Uppsala: Nordiska Afrikainstitutet; Somerset, NJ: Transaction Publishers (distributor), 2002.

Chong, Dennis. *Collective Action and the Civil Rights Movement.* Chicago: University of Chicago Press, 1991.

Christian, Garna L. *Black Soldiers in Jim Crow Texas, 1899-1917.* College Station: Texas A&M University Press, 1995.

Churchill, Nicholas. *Stan Getz: An Annotated Bibliography and Filmography, with Song and Session Information for Albums.* Jefferson: McFarland & Company, Inc., Publishers, 2004.

Clapham, Andrew, Paola Gaeta, Marco Sassòli, Iris van der Heijden, and Académie de droit International Humanitaire et de droits Humains à Genève. *The 1949 Geneva Conventions: A Commentary.* Oxford: Oxford University Press, 2015.

Clark, Champ. *Shuffling to Ignominy: The Tragedy of Stepin Fetchit.* New York: iUniverse, 2005.

Clarke, Cheryl. *"After Mecca": Women Poets and the Black Arts Movement.* New Brunswick, NJ: Rutgers University Press, 2005.

Clarke, John Henrik. *Marcus Garvey and the Vision of Africa.* New York, Vintage Books, 1974.

Claxton, William. *Young Chet: The Young Chet Baker.* New York: Te Neues Pub. Co., 1998.

Claxton, William, and Hitoshi Namekata. *Jazz West Coast: Artwork of Pacific Jazz Records.* Tokyo: Bijutsu Shuppan-Sha, 1992.

Cline, John, and Robert G. Weiner. *From the Arthouse to the Grindhouse: Highbrow and Lowbrow Transgression in Cinema's First Century.* Lanham, MD: Scarecrow Press, 2010.

Clinton, George, and Ben Greenman. *Brothers Be "Yo Like George, Ain't That Funkin' Kinda Hard On You?": A Memoir.* New York: Atria Books, 2014.

Coady, Christopher, and Project Muse. *John Lewis and the Challenge of "Real" Black Music.* Ann Arbor: University of Michigan Press, 2016.

Coard, Michael. "The "Black" Eye on George Washington's 'White' House." *The Pennsylvania Magazine of History and Biography* 129.4 (October 2005): 461–471.

Cobb, James C. *The Brown Decision, Jim Crow, and Southern Identity.* Athens: University of Georgia Press, 2005.

Cobussen, Marcel. *Thresholds: Rethinking Spirituality through Music.* Aldershot, Hampshire, England; Burlington, VT: Ashgate, 2008.

Cockrell, Dale. *Demons of Disorder: Early Blackface Minstrels and Their World.* Cambridge; New York: Cambridge University Press, 1997.

Coffey, Thomas M. *The Long Thirst: Prohibition in America, 1920–1933.* New York: Norton, 1975.

Cohen, Harvey G. "Duke Ellington and "Black, Brown and Beige": The Composer as Historian at Carnegie Hall." *American Quarterly* 56.4 (December 2004): 1003–1034.

Cohen, Jerry, and William S. Murphy. *Burn, Baby, Burn! The Los Angeles Race Riot, August, 1965.* New York, Dutton, 1966.

Cohen-Stratyner, Barbara. "Social Dance: Contexts and Definitions." *Dance Research Journal* 33.2, Social and Popular Dance (Winter 2001): 121–124.

Cohn, Ruby. "Black Power on Stage: Emperor Jones and King Christophe." *Yale French Studies* 46, From Stage to Street (1971): 41–47.

Coker, Joe L. *Liquor in the Land of the Lost Cause: Southern White Evangelicals and the Prohibition Movement.* Lexington: University Press of Kentucky, 2007.

Cole, Bill. *John Coltrane.* New York: Schirmer Books, 1976.

Cole, David. *No Equal Justice: Race and Class in the American Criminal Justice System.* New York: New Press: Distributed by W. W. Norton, 1999.

Cole, George. *The Last Miles: The Music of Miles Davis, 1980–1991.* London: Equinox Pub., 2005.

Colin, Sid. *Ella: The Life and Times of Ella Fitzgerald.* London: Hamish Hamilton, 1986.

Collier, Geoffrey L., and James Lincoln Collier. "An Exploration of the Use of Tempo in Jazz." *Music Perception: An Interdisciplinary Journal* 11.3 (Spring 1994): 219–242.

Collier, James Lincoln. *Duke Ellington.* New York: Oxford University Press, 1987.

――――. *Benny Goodman and the Swing Era.* New York: Oxford University Press, 1989.

――――. *Jazz: The American Theme Song.* New York: Oxford University Press, 1993.

Collins, Lisa Gail, and Margo Natalie Crawford. *New Thoughts on the Black Arts Movement.* New Brunswick, NJ: Rutgers University Press, 2006.

Collins, Michael. "'I'm Interested as a Writer in Less Exalted Persons': An Interview with Jessica Hagedorn." *Callaloo* 31.4, Cutting Down "The Wrath-Bearing Tree": The Politics Issue (Fall 2008): 1217–1228.

Coltrane, John, and Pharoah Sanders. *John Coltrane Live in Seattle Featuring Pharoah Sanders*. New York: The Verve Music Group, 2011.

Combs, C. Scott. "The Jazz Singer or the Corpse: Al Jolson, Diegetic Music, and the Moment of Death." *Music and the Moving Image* 5.3 (Fall 2012): 46–55.

Common, Dianne L. "Teacher Power and Settings for Innovation: A Response to Brown and McIntyre's 'Influences upon Teachers' Attitudes to Different Types of Innovation.'" *Curriculum Inquiry* 13.4 (Winter 1983): 435–446.

Cone, James H. *Black Theology and Black Power*. Maryknoll, NY: Orbis Books, 1997.

Connor, D. Russell. *Benny Goodman: Listen to His Legacy*. Metuchen, NJ: Scarecrow Press and the Institute of Jazz Studies, 1988.

_____. *Benny Goodman: Wrappin' It Up*. Lanham, MD: Scarecrow Press, 1996.

Conyers, James L. *African American Jazz and Rap: Social and Philosophical Examinations of Black Expressive Behavior*. Jefferson, NC: McFarland, 2001.

_____. *Engines of the Black Power Movement: Essays on the Influence of Civil Rights Actions, Arts, and Islam*. Jefferson, NC: McFarland & Co., 2007.

Cook, Richard. *It's About That Time: Miles Davis On and Off Record*. Oxford; New York: Oxford University Press, 2007.

Cooke, James J. *American Girls, Beer, and Glenn Miller: GI Morale in World War II*. Columbia: University of Missouri Press, 2012.

Cooper, Matthew J., and Michael J. Budds. *Duke Ellington as Pianist: A Study of Styles*. Missoula, Montana: The College Music Society, 2013.

Copland, Aaron. *Music and Imagination*. Cambridge: Harvard University Press, 1952.

Copland, Aaron, Elizabeth Bergman Crist, and Wayne D. Shirley. *The Selected Correspondence of Aaron Copland*. New Haven: Yale University Press, 2006.

Copland, Aaron, Richard Kostelanetz, and Steven Silverstein. *Aaron Copland: A Reader: Selected Writings 1923–1972*. New York: Routledge, 2004.

Corbett, John, Anthony Elms, Terri Kapsalis, and Hyde Park Art Center (Chicago, IL). *Pathways to Unknown Worlds: Sun-Ra, El Saturn and Chicago's Afro-Futurist Underground 1954–68*. Chicago: WhiteWalls, 2006.

Coryell, Julie, and Laura Friedman. *Jazz-Rock Fusion, The People, The Music* . Milwaukee, WI: Hal Leonard Corp., 2000 .

Cotgrove, Mark. *From Jazz Funk & Fusion to Acid Jazz: The History of the UK Jazz Dance Scene*. London: Chaser Publications; Milton Keynes [England]: AuthorHouse, 2009.

Cotkin, George. "The Photographer in the Beat-Hipster Idiom: Robert Frank's the Americans." *American Studies* 26.1 (Spring 1985): 19–33.

Cottrell, Robert C. *Sex, Drugs, and Rock 'n' Roll: The Rise of America's 1960s Counterculture* . Lanham, MD: Rowman & Littlefield, 2015 .

Cottrell, Stephen. *The Saxophone*. New Haven: Yale University Press, 2013.

Cowell, Henry, and Sidney Robertson Cowell. *Charles Ives and His Music*. New York: Oxford University Press, 1955.

Cowell, Henry, Sidney Robertson Cowell, and Paul Avrich Collection (Library of Congress). *Charles Ives and His Music*. London; New York: Oxford University Press, 1969.

Cowley, Malcolm. *A Second Flowering: Works and Days of the Lost Generation*. New York: Viking Press, 1973.

Cowley, Malcolm, and Hans Bak. *The Long Voyage: Selected Letters of Malcolm Cowley, 1915–1987*. Cambridge, Massachusetts: Harvard University Press, 2014.

Cowley, Malcolm, and Robert Cowley. *Fitzgerald and the Jazz Age*. New York: Charles Scribner's Sons, 1966.

Cox, Bette Yarbrough. *Central Avenue—Its Rise and Fall, 1890–c. 1955: Including the Musical Renaissance of Black Los Angeles*. Los Angeles: BEEM Publications, 1996.

Cox, Harvey. "Jazz and Pentecostalism." *Archives de sciences sociales des religions, 38e Année* 84, La religion aux États-Unis (October–December 1993): 181–188.

Craig, Dale A. "Trans-Cultural Composition in the 20th Century." *Tempo, New Series* 156 (March 1986): 16–18.

Crazy Horse, Kandia. *Rip It Up: The Black Experience in Rock 'n' Roll*. New York: Palgrave Macmillan, 2004.

Crease, Stephanie Stein. *Out of the Cool: The Life and Music of Gil Evans*. Chicago: A cappella, 2001.

_____. *Gil Evans: Out of the Cool: His Life and Music*. Chicago: A cappella, 2002.

Cripps, Thomas. "The Films of Spencer Williams." *Black American Literature Forum* 12.4 (Winter 1978): 128–134.

_____. *Slow Fade to Black: The Negro in American Film, 1900–1942*. Oxford; New York: Oxford University Press, 1993.

Crist, Elizabeth Bergman. *Music for the Common Man: Aaron Copland During the Depression and War*. Oxford; New York: Oxford University Press, 2005.

Crist, Stephen A. "Jazz as Democracy? Dave Brubeck and Cold War Politics." *The Journal of Musicology* 26.2 (Spring 2009): 133–174.

Cronon, Edmund David. *Black Moses: The Story of Marcus Garvey and the Universal Negro Improvement Association*. Madison: University of Wisconsin Press, 1969.

Crook, Larry. *Brazilian Music: Northeastern Traditions and the Heartbeat of a Modern Nation*. Santa Barbara, CA: ABC-CLIO, 2005.

Crouch, Stanley. *The Artificial White Man: Essays on Authenticity*. New York: Basic Civitas Books, 2004.

Crouse, Joan M. *The Homeless Transient in the Great Depression: New York State, 1929–1941*. Albany, NY: State University of New York Press, 1986.

Crowther, Bruce. *Gene Krupa, His Life and Times*. Tunbridge Wells, Kent: Spellmount Ltd.; New York: Universe Books, 1987.

Cummings, Ronald. "Jamaican Female Masculinities: Nanny of the Maroons and the Genealogy of the Man-Royal." *Journal of West Indian Literature* 21.1/2, Caribbean Masculinities (November 2012/April 2013): 129–154.

Cunningham, Lyn Driggs, and Jimmy Jones. *Sweet, Hot, and Blue: St. Louis' Musical Heritage*. Jefferson, N C: McFarland, 1989.

Cusic, Don. *The Sound of Light: A History of Gospel Music*. Bowling Green, OH: Bowling Green State University Popular Press, 1990.

Dahl, Linda. *Stormy Weather: The Music and Lives of a Century of Jazzwomen*. New York: Pantheon Books, 1984.

_____. *Morning Glory: A Biography of Mary Lou Williams*. New York: Pantheon Books, 2000.

Dance, Stanley. *The World of Earl Hines*. New York: Scribner, 1977.

_____. *The World of Count Basie*. New York: Da Capo Press, 1985.

Daniels, Douglas Henry. "Lester Young: Master of Jive." *American Music* 3.3 (Autumn 1985): 313–328.

_____. *Lester Leaps In: The Life and Times of Lester "Pres" Young*. Boston: Beacon Press, 2002.

_____. "North Side Jazz: Lester "Pres" Young in Minneapolis: The Formative Years." *Minnesota History* 59.3 (Fall 2004): 96–109.

Danielsen, Anne. *Presence and Pleasure: The Funk Grooves of James Brown and Parliament*. Middletown, CT: Wesleyan University Press, 2006.

Daulatzai, Sohail. *Black Star, Crescent Moon: The Muslim International and Black Freedom Beyond America*. Minneapolis: University of Minnesota Press 2012.

Dauncey, Hugh, and Steve Cannon, Eds. *Popular Music in France From Chanson to Techno: Culture, Identity, and Society*. Burlington, Vermont: Ashgate, 2003.

Davies, Matthew, Guy Madison, Pedro Silva, and Fabien Gouyon. "The Effect of Microtiming Deviations on the Perception of Groove in Short Rhythms." *Music Perception: An Interdisciplinary Journal* 30.5 (June 2013): 497–510.

Davis, Angela Y. *Blues Legacies and Black Feminism: Gertrude "Ma" Rainey, Bessie Smith, and Billie Holiday*. New York: Pantheon Books, 1998.

Davis, Francis. *Bebop and Nothingness: Jazz and Pop at the End of the Century*. New York: Schirmer Books, 1996.

Davis, Gregory, and Les Sussman. *Dark Magus: The Jekyll and Hyde Life of Miles Davis*. San Francisco, CA: Backbeat Books; Berkeley, CA: Distributed to the Book trade in the US and Canada by Publishers Group West, 2006.

Davis, Mary E, and Warren Zanes. *Waiting for a Train: Jimmie Rodgers's America*. Burlington, MA: Rounder Books, 2009.

Davis, Miles, and Scott Gutterman. *Miles Davis: The Collected Artwork*. San Rafael, CA: Editions, 2013.

Davis, Miles, Paul Maher, and Michael K. Dorr. *Miles on Miles: Interviews and Encounters with Miles Davis*. Chicago: Lawrence Hill Books, 2009.

Davis, Miles, and Quincy Troupe. *Miles: The Autobiography*. New York: Simon & Schuster, 1990.

Davis, Ossie, and Ruby Dee. *With Ossie and Ruby: In This Life Together*. New York: W. Morrow, 1998.

Davis, Jr., Sammy. *The Sammy Davis, Jr. Songbook: A Musical Tribute to the World's Greatest Entertainer*. Port Chester NY: Cherry Lane / IMP, 1992.

Davis, Jr., Sammy, Jane Boyar, and Burt Boyar. *Yes I Can; [The Story of Sammy Davis, Jr.]*. New York: Farrar, Straus & Giroux, 1965.

Day, Steve. *Ornette Coleman: Music Always*. Chelmsford, Essex: Soundworld, 2000. de Assis, Gilson. *Brazilian Percussion*. [Rottenburg], Germany: Advance Music, 2003.

de Barros, Paul. "'The Loud Music of Life': Representations of Jazz in the Novels of Claude McKay." *The Antioch Review* 57.3, Jazz (Summer 1999): 306–317.

_____. *Shall We Play That One Together?: The Life and Art of Jazz Piano Legend Marian McPartland*. New York: St. Martin's Press, 2012.

de Beauvoir, Simone. *The Second Sex*. New York: Knopf, 1952; James S. Williams. *Jean Cocteau*. Manchester: Manchester University Press, 2006.

DeCarava, Sherry Turner, Roy DeCarava, and Ron Carter. "Inventory: A Conversation between Roy DeCarava and Ron Carter." *MoMA* 21 (Winter–Spring 1996): 2–7.

Decker, Todd. "On the Scenic Route to Irving Berlin's *Holiday Inn* (1942)." *The Journal of Musicology* 28.4 (Fall 2011): 464–497.

DeFrantz, Thomas. *Dancing Many Drums: Excavations in African American Dance*. Madison, WI: University of Wisconsin Press, 2002.

_____. *Dancing Revelations: Alvin Ailey's Embodiment of African American Culture*. New York: Oxford University Press, 2004.

_____. "Composite Bodies of Dance: The Repertory of the Alvin Ailey American Dance Theater." *Theatre Journal* 57.4, Black Performance (December 2005): 659–678.

De Genova, Nicholas. *Working the Boundaries: Race, Space, and "Illegality" in Mexican Chicago*. Durham, NC: Duke University Press, 2005.

DeGraw, Sharon. *The Subject of Race in American Science Fiction*. New York: Routledge, 2007.

Delage, Roger, and Frayda Lindemann. "Ravel and Chabrier." *The Musical Quarterly* 61.4 (October 1975): 546–552.

Delannoy, Luc. *Pres: The Story of Lester Young*. Fayetteville: University of Arkansas Press, 1993.

Delany, Samuel R. *Silent Interviews: On Language, Race, Sex, Science Fiction, and Some Comics: A Collection of Written Interviews*. Hanover, NH: Wesleyan University Press, 1994.

Del Mar, Norman. *Richard Strauss; A Critical Commentary on His Life and Works*. Philadelphia: Chilton Book Co., 1962.

Delson, Susan. *Dudley Murphy, Hollywood Wild Card*. Minneapolis: University of Minnesota Press, 2006.

Demlinger, Sandor, and John Steiner. *Destination Chicago Jazz*. Charleston, SC: Arcadia Publishing, 2003.

Dempsey, Michael. "All the Colors: Bertrand Tavernier Talks about 'Round Midnight.'" *Film Quarterly* 40.3 (Spring 1987): 2–11.

de Nevers, Renée. "The Geneva Conventions and New Wars." *Political Science Quarterly* 121.3 (Fall 2006): 369–395.

Dennen, David. "The Third Stream: Oḍiśī Music, Regional Nationalism, and the Concept of 'Classical.'" *Asian Music* 41.2 (Summer/Fall 2010): 149–179.

Denzin, Norman K. *Reading Race: Hollywood and the Cinema of Racial Violence*. London; Thousand Oaks, CA: SAGE, 2002.

Determeyer, Eddy. *Rhythm is Our Business: Jimmie Lunceford and the Harlem Express*. Ann Arbor: University of Michigan Press, 2006.

de Valk, Jeroen. *Chet Baker: His Life and Music*. Berkeley, CA: Berkeley Hills Books: Distributed to the trade by, Publishers Group West, 2000.

_____. *Ben Webster: His Life and Music*. Berkeley, CA: Berkeley Hills Books, [United States]: Distributed by Publishers Group West, 2001.

DeVeaux, Scott. "'Black, Brown and Beige' and the Critics." *Black Music Research Journal* 13.2 (Autumn 1993): 125–146 .

_____. *The Birth of Bebop: A Social and Musical History*. Berkeley: University of California Press, 1997.

DeVeaux, Scott Knowles, and Gary Giddins. *Jazz: Essential Listening*. New York: W. W. Norton, 2011.

DeVito, Chris, and John Coltrane. *Coltrane on Coltrane: The John Coltrane Interviews*. Chicago: Chicago Review Press, 2010.

Dewberry, Jonathan. "Black Actors Unite: The Negro Actors' Guild." *The Black Scholar* 21.2, Black Cinema (March–April–May–1990): 2–11.

Diawara, Manthia. "The Song of the Griot." *Transition*, No. 74 (1997): 16–30.

Dickenson, Ben. *Hollywood's New Radicalism: War, Globalisation and the Movies from Reagan to George W. Bush*. London; New York: New York, NY: I.B. Tauris, 2006.

Dickerson, Dwight. "Jazz in Los Angeles: The Black Experience." *Black Music Research Journal* 31.1 (Spring 2011): 179–192.

Dickerson, James. *Just for a Thrill: Lil Hardin Armstrong, First Lady of Jazz*. New York: Cooper Square Press; [Lanham, MD]: Distributed by National Book Network, 2002.

Dickson, L. L. "'Keep It in the Head': Jazz Elements in Modern Black American Poetry." *Melus* 10.1, Ethnic Literature and Music (Spring 1983): 29–37.

Dietrich, Kurt. "The Role of Trombones in 'Black, Brown and Beige.'" *Black Music Research Journal* 13.2 (Autumn 1993): 111–124 .

Dines, Gail, and Jean McMahon Humez. *Gender, Race, and Class in Media: A Text-Reader*. Thousand Oaks, CA: Sage, 1995.

Diouf, Sylviane A. *Servants of Allah: African Muslims Enslaved in the Americas*. New York: New York University Press, 1998.

Distler, Jed. *Art Tatum: Transcriptions of 6 Important Solo Piano Pieces as Played by the Legendary Art Tatum*. London: Jazzwise; New York London: Amsco, 1986.

Dittmar, Linda. "Immigration Filmography for Educators." *The Radical Teacher* 84, Teaching and Immigration (Spring 2009): 61–67.

Dixon, Brenda. "Black Dance and Dancers and the White Public: A Prolegomenon to Problems of Definition." *Black American Literature Forum* 24.1 (Spring 1990): 117–123.

DJ Spooky That Subliminal Kid. *Sound Unbound: Sampling Digital Music and Culture* . Cambridge, MA: MIT Press, 2008 .

DjeDje, Jacqueline Cogdell, and Eddie S. Meadows. *California Soul: Music of African Americans in the West*. Berkeley: University of California Press, 1998.

Dobbins, Bill. "Jazz and Academia: Street Music in the Ivory Tower." *Bulletin of the Council for Research in Music Education* 96, Research in Jazz Education II (Spring 1988): 30–41.

Dobbins, Washington. *A History of Blackfaced Minstrelsy in America from 1828 to 1898*. Parker, CO: Outskirts Press, 2011.

Dobrin, Arnold. *Aaron Copland, His Life and Times*. New York: Thomas Y. Crowell Co., 1967. Doherty, Thomas Patrick. *Cold War, Cool Medium: Television, McCarthyism, and American Culture*. New York: Columbia University Press, 2003.

Dolan, Marc. *Modern Lives: A Cultural Re-Reading of "The Lost Generation."* West Lafayette, IN: Purdue University Press, 1996.

Dommett, Kenneth. "Jazz and the Composer." *Proceedings of the Royal Musical Association, 91st Sess.* (1964–1965): 11–20.

Douglas, Davison M. *Jim Crow Moves North: The Battle Over Northern School Segregation, 1865–1954.* New York: Cambridge University Press, 2005.

Driggs, Frank. *Women in Jazz: A Survey.* Brooklyn, NY: Stash Record Inc., 1977.

Driggs, Frank, and Chuck Haddix. *Kansas City Jazz: From Ragtime to Bebop—A History.* Oxford: Oxford University Press, 2005.

Drowne, Kathleen. "'Theah's Life Anywheres Theah's Booze and Jazz:' Home to Harlem and Gingertown in the Context of National Prohibition." *Callaloo* 34.3 (Summer 2011): 928–942.

Du Bois, W. E. B. *The Souls of Black Folk: Essays and Sketches.* Charlottesville, VA: University of Virginia Library, 1996.

Dudziak, Mary L. *Cold War Civil Rights: Race and the Image of American Democracy.* Princeton, NJ: Princeton University Press, 2000.

Dunn, Stephane. *"Baad Bitches" and Sassy Supermamas: Black Power Action Films.* Urbana: University of Illinois Press, 2008.

Dunning, Jennifer. *Alvin Ailey: A Life in Dance.* Reading, MA: Addison-Wesley, 1996.

Durand, Alain-Philippe. *Black, Blanc, Beur: Rap Music and Hip-Hop Culture in the Francophone World.* Lanham, MD: Scarecrow Press, 2002.

Dyson, Michael Eric. *I May Not Get There With You: The True Martin Luther King, Jr.* New York: Free Press, 2000.

_____. *Come Hell or High Water: Hurricane Katrina and the Color of Disaster.* New York: Basic Civitas Books, 2006.

_____. *April 4, 1968: Martin Luther King, Jr.'s Death and How It Changed America.* New York: Basic Civitas Books, 2008.

Dyson, Michael Eric, and Sohail Daulatzai. *Born to Use Mics: Reading Nas's Illmatic.* New York: Basic Civitas Books, 2010.

Early, Gerald. "The Passing of Jazz's Old Guard: Remembering Charles Mingus, Thelonious Monk, and Sonny Stitt." *The Kenyon Review*, New Series 7.2 (Spring 1985): 21–36.

_____. *Miles Davis and American Culture.* St. Louis: Missouri Historical Society Press, 2001.

_____. *The Sammy Davis, Jr. Reader.* New York: Farrar, Straus and Giroux, 2001.

_____. *This Is Where I Came In: Black America in the 1960s.* Lincoln: University of Nebraska Press, 2003.

Echols, Alice. "The Land of Somewhere Else: Refiguring James Brown in Seventies Disco." *Criticism* 50.1, Special Issue: Disco (Winter 2008): 19–41.

Eckland, K. O. *Jazz West, 1945-1985: The A-Z Guide to West Coast Jazz Music.* Carmel-by-the-Sea, CA: Cypress, 1986.

Edwards, Brent Hayes. "Middle Ear Recitation (A Transcription of Cecil Taylor's "Erzulie Maketh Scent")." *Callaloo* 22.4 (Autumn 1999): 771–774.

_____. "Louis Armstrong and the Syntax of Scat." *Critical Inquiry* 28.3 (Spring 2002): 618–649.

Eisler, Garrett. "Backstory as Black Story: The Cinematic Reinvention of O'Neill's 'The Emperor Jones.'" *The Eugene O'Neill Review* 32 (2010): 148–162.

Eko, Lyombe. *American Exceptionalism, The French Exception, and Digital Media Law.* Lanham, MD: Lexington Books, 2013.

Ellington, Duke. *Duke Ellington Piano Method for Blues.* New York: Robbins Music Corp., 1943.

Ellis, Abby. "Clark Terry: Ambassador of Music." *Music Educators Journal* 85.5 (March 1999): 36–38.

Ellis, Carl F. *Beyond Liberation: The Gospel in the Black American Experience.* Downers Grove, IL: InterVarsity Press, 1983.

Ellis, Trey. "The New Black Aesthetic." *Callaloo* 38 (Winter 1989): 233–243.

Ellison, Ralph. "The Art of Romare Bearden." *The Massachusetts Review* 18.4 (Winter 1977): 673–680.

Ellison, Ralph, and John F. Callahan. *The Collected Essays of Ralph Ellison*. New York: Modern Library, 1995.

Ellison, Ralph, Maryemma Graham, and Amritjit Singh. *Conversations with Ralph Ellison*. Jackson: University Press of Mississippi, 1995.

Ellison, Ralph, and Robert G. O'Meally. *Living with Music: Ralph Ellison's Jazz Writings*. New York: Modern Library, 2001.

Elsdon, Peter. *Keith Jarrett's the Köln Concert*. New York: Oxford University Press, 2013.

Emery, Lynne Fauley. *Black Dance in the United States from 1619 to 1970*. Palo Alto, CA: National Press Books, 1972.

Engelbrecht, Barbara. "Swinging at the Savoy." *Dance Research Journal* 15.2, Popular Dance in Black America (Spring 1983): 3–10.

English, Daylanne K., and Alvin Kim. "Now We Want Our Funk Cut: Janelle Monáe's Neo-Afrofuturism." *American Studies* 52.4, The Funk Issue (2013): 217–230.

Enstice, Wayne, and Paul Rubin. *Jazz Spoken Here: Conversations with Twenty-Two Musicians*. Baton Rouge: Louisiana State University Press, 1992.

Enstice, Wayne, and Janis Stockhouse. *Jazzwomen: Conversations with Twenty-One Musicians*. Bloomington: Indiana University Press, 2004.

Erenberg, Lewis A. "From New York to Middletown: Repeal and the Legitimization of Nightlife in the Great Depression." *American Quarterly* 38.5 (Winter 1986): 761–778.

_____. *Swingin' the Dream: Big Band Jazz and the Rebirth of American Culture*. Chicago: University of Chicago Press, 1999.

Escobar, Edward J. "The Dialectics of Repression: The Los Angeles Police Department and the Chicano Movement, 1968-1971." *The Journal of American History* 79.4 (March 1993): 1483–1514.

_____. *Race, Police, and the Making of a Political Identity: Mexican Americans and the Los Angeles Police Department, 1900–1945*. Berkeley: University of California Press, 1999.

Eskew, Glenn T. *Johnny Mercer: Southern Songwriter for the World*. Athens: The University of Georgia Press, 2013.

Evans, Art. "Joe Louis as a Key Functionary: White Reactions Toward a Black Champion." *Journal of Black Studies* 16.1 (September 1985): 95–111.

Evans, David. "Bessie Smith's 'Back-Water Blues': The Story Behind the Song." *Popular Music* 26.1, Special Issue on the Blues in Honour of Paul Oliver (January 2007): 97–116.

Evensmo, Jan. *The Tenor Saxophone of Ben Webster, 1931–1943*. Hosle, Norway: Jan Evensmo, 1978.

_____. *The Trumpet of Roy Eldridge, 1929–1944: With a Critical Assessment of All His Known Records and Broadcasts*. Hosle, Norway: [Jan Evensmo], 1979.

Evensmo, Jan, Per Borthen, and Ib Skovsted Thomsen. *The Alto Saxophone, Trumpet and Clarinet of Benny Carter, 1927–1946: With a Critical Assessment of All His Known Records and Broadcasts*. Hosle: Jan Evensmo, 1982.

Eversley, Shelly. *The Real Negro: The Question of Authenticity in Twentieth-Century African American Literature*. New York: Routledge, 2004 .

Fabre, Geneviève, and Michel Feith. *Temples for Tomorrow: Looking Back at the Harlem Renaissance*. Bloomington: Indiana University Press, 2001.

Fabre, Michel. *The Unfinished Quest of Richard Wright*. New York: Morrow, 1973.

_____. *The World of Richard Wright*. Jackson: University Press of Mississippi, 1985.

Fain, Kimberly. *Black Hollywood: From Butlers to Superheroes, The Changing Role of African American Men in the Movies*. Santa Barbara, CA: Praeger, an imprint of ABC-Clio, 2015.

Fair, Charles. "Poetry and Jazz." *Chicago Review* 29.1 (Summer 1977): 22–29.

Falzerano, Chet, Judith Falzerano, Brooks Tegler, and Paul Testa. *Spinnin' the Webb: Chick Webb, The Little Giant*. Anaheim Hills, CA: Centerstream Publishing LLC, [Milwaukee, WI]: Exclusively distributed by Hal Leonard, 2014.

Farnsworth, Paul R. "The Effects of Role-Taking on Artistic Achievement." *The Journal of Aesthetics and Art Criticism* 18.3 (March 1960): 345–349.

Farr, Finis. *Black Champion: The Life and Times of Jack Johnson*. London: Macmillan, 1964.

Farrington, Holly. "'I Improvised Behind Him . . . Ahead of Time": Charles Mingus, Kenneth

Patchen and Jazz/Poetry Fusion Art." *Journal of American Studies* 41.2 (August 2007): 365–374 .

Feather, Leonard. *Inside Be-bop*. New York: J. J. Robbins, 1949.

———. *The Encyclopedia of Jazz*. New York: Horizon Press, 1960.

———. *From Satchmo to Miles*. New York: Stein and Day, 1972.

———. *The Pleasures of Jazz: Leading Performers on Their Lives, Their Music, Their Contemporaries*. New York: Horizon Press, 1976.

———. *Inside Jazz*. New York: Da Capo Press, 1977.

———. *The Jazz Years: Earwitness to an Era*. New York: Da Capo Press, 1987.

Feder, Stuart. *The Life of Charles Ives*. Cambridge; New York: Cambridge University Press, 1999.

Feenberg, Andrew, and Jim Freedman. *When Poetry Ruled the Streets: The French May Events of 1968*. Albany: State University of New York Press, 2001.

Fellezs, Kevin. *Birds of Fire: Jazz, Rock, Funk, and the Creation of Fusion* . Durham [NC]: Duke University Press, 2011 .

Ferber, Jessica, and Marc Myers. *Rebirth of the Cool: Discovering the Art of Robert James Campbell*. Brooklyn, NY: PowerHouse Books, 2015.

Fidelman, Geoffrey Mark. *First Lady of Song: Ella Fitzgerald for the Record*. Secaucus, NJ: Carol Pub. Group, 1994.

Fillerup, Jessie. "Ravel, "La Valse," and the Purloined Plot." *College Music Symposium* 49/50 (2009/2010): 345–355.

———. "Ravel and Robert-Houdin, Magicians." *19th-Century Music* 37.2 (Fall 2013): 130–158.

Fine, Ruth. "Expanding the Mainstream: Romare Bearden Revisited." *Proceedings of the American Philosophical Society* 149.1 (March 2005): 40–55.

Fiofori, Tam, and Leni Sinclair. *Sun Ra: Myth, Music & Media*. London: Karnak House, 2014.

Fiol, Orlando Enrique. " Grooves and Waves: Cyclicity and Narrativity in Cuban 'Timba' Piano." *Latin American Music Review / Revista de Música Latinoamericana* 33.1 (Spring/Summer 2012): 1–26 .

Fischer-Dieskau, Dietrich. *Wagner and Nietzsche*. New York: Seabury Press, 1976.

Fišera, Vladimir Claude. *Writing on the Wall, May 1968: A Documentary Anthology*. New York: St. Martin's Press, 1979.

Fitch, Noel Riley. *Sylvia Beach and The Lost Generation: A History of Literary Paris in the Twenties and Thirties*. New York: Norton, 1983.

Fitterling, Thomas. *Thelonious Monk: His Life and Music*. Berkeley, CA: Berkeley Hills Books, 1997.

Fitzgerald, F. Scott, Jackson R. Bryer, Alan Margolies, and Ruth Prigozy. *F. Scott Fitzgerald: New Perspectives*. Athens, GA: University of Georgia Press, 2000.

Fitzgerald, Michael. "Researching Washington Jazz History." *Washington History* 26, Jazz in Washington (Spring 2014): 98–107.

Fjeldsøe, Michael. "Different Images: A Case Study on Bartók Reception in Denmark." *Studia Musicologica Academiae Scientiarum Hungaricae* 47.3/4, Bartók's Orbit. The Context and Sphere of Influence of His Work. Proceedings of the International Conference Held by the Bartók Archives, Budapest (22–24 March 2006). Part I. (September 2006): 453–465.

Flamming, Douglas. *Bound for Freedom: Black Los Angeles in Jim Crow America*. Berkeley: University of California Press, 2005.

Fleming, Colin. "Jazz: The Quiet Sideman: Tenor Saxist "Chu" Berry Emerged from the Pack at the End of His Short Life." *The American Scholar* 77.1 (Winter 2008): 110–111.

Flower, John. *Moonlight Serenade; A Bio-discography of the Glenn Miller Civilian Band*. New Rochelle, NY: Arlington House, 1972.

Floyd, Jr., Samuel A. "A Black Composer in Nineteenth-Century St. Louis." *19th-Century Music* 4.2 (Autumn 1980): 121–133.

Foertsch, Jacqueline. *American Culture in the 1940s*. Edinburgh: Edinburgh University Press, 2008.

Folmsbee, Stanley J. "The Origin of the First "Jim Crow" Law." *The Journal of Southern History* 15.2 (May 1949): 235–247.

Foner, Philip Sheldon, and Richard C. Winchester. *The Anti-Imperialist Reader: A Documentary History of Anti-Imperialism in the United States.* New York: Holmes & Meier, 1984.

Fontenot, Jr., Chester, Mary Alice Morgan, and Sarah Gardner, Eds. *W. E. B. DuBois and Race: Essays Celebrating the Centennial Publication of The Souls of Black Folk. South Atlantic Review: The Publication of the South Atlantic Modern Language Association.* 67, Part 4 (2002): 135–136.

Ford, Charlie. "The Very Best of James Brown?" *Popular Music* 21.1 (January 2002): 127–131.

Ford, Philip. "Somewhere/Nowhere: Hipness as an Aesthetic." *The Musical Quarterly* 86.1 (Spring 2002): 49–81.

Foster, Craig L. "Tarnished Angels: Prostitution in Storyville, New Orleans, 1900–1910." *Louisiana History: The Journal of the Louisiana Historical Association* 31.4 (Winter 1990): 387–397.

Foster, Frank. *In Defense of Be-bop.* Scarsdale, NY: Frank Foster Music, 1979.

Foulkes, Julia L. *Modern Bodies: Dance and American Modernism from Martha Graham to Alvin Ailey.* Chapel Hill: University of North Carolina Press, 2002.

Fox, Jo Brooks, and Jules L. Fox. *The Melody Lingers On: Scenes from the Golden Years of West Coast Jazz.* Santa Barbara, CA: Fithian Press, 1996.

Fox, Robert Elliot. "Ted Joans and the (B)reach of the African American Literary Canon." *Melus* 29.3/4, Pedagody, Canon, Context: Toward a Redefinition of Ethnic American Literary Studies (Autumn–Winter 2004): 41–58.

Foy, Anthony. "Joe Louis's Talking Fists: The Auto/Biopolitics of 'My Life Story.'" *American Literary History* 23.2 (Summer 2011): 311–336.

Frame, Gregory. *The American President in Film and Television: Myth, Politics and Representation.* Oxford; New York: Peter Lang, 2014.

Franceschina, John Charles. *Duke Ellington's Music for the Theatre.* Jefferson, NC: McFarland, 2001.

Franklin, Benjamin. *Commentaries on Jazz Musicians and Jazz Songs: A History of Jazz in Retrospect.* Lewiston, NY: E. Mellen Press, 2011.

Franklin, V. P. "Commentary: Predatory Capitalists, The New Jim Crow, and Restitutive Justice." *The Journal of African American History* 96.2 (Spring 2011): 147–150.

Freedman, Lawrence, and Efraim Karsh. *The Gulf Conflict, 1990–1991: Diplomacy and War in the New World Order.* Princeton, NJ: Princeton University Press, 1993.

Freedman, Lew. *Joe Louis: The Life of a Heavyweight.* Jefferson, NC: McFarland & Company, Inc., Publishers, 2013.

Freeman, Carla. *Entrepreneurial Selves: Neoliberal Respectability and the Making of a Caribbean Middle Class.* Durham, NC: Duke University Press, 2014.

Freeman, Phil. *Running the Voodoo Down: The Electric Music of Miles Davis.* San Francisco, CA: Backbeat Books, 2005.

Friberg, Anders, and Andreas Sundström. "Swing Ratios and Ensemble Timing in Jazz Performance: Evidence for a Common Rhythmic Pattern." *Music Perception: An Interdisciplinary Journal* 19.3 (Spring 2002): 333–349.

Friedwald, Will. *Jazz Singing: America's Great Voices from Bessie Smith to Bebop and Beyond.* New York: C. Scribner's Sons, 1990.

Fritts, Ron, and Ken Vail. *Ella Fitzgerald: The Chick Webb Years & Beyond.* Lanham, MD: Scarecrow Press, 2003.

Frontani, Michael R. *The Beatles: Image and the Media.* Jackson: University Press of Mississippi, 2007.

Fry, Andy. *Paris Blues: African American Music and French Popular Culture, 1920–1960.* Chicago: The University of Chicago Press, 2014.

Funkhouser, Christopher. "LeRoi Jones, Larry Neal, and "The Cricket": Jazz and Poets' Black Fire." *African American Review* 37.2/3 Amri Baraka Issue (Summer–Autumn 2003): 237–244.

Furia, Philip. *Skylark: The Life and Times of Johnny Mercer.* New York: St. Martin's Press, 2003.

Furia, Philip, and Graham Wood. *Irving Berlin: A Life in Song*. New York: Schirmer Books, 1998.

Furlonge, Nicole L. B. "An Instrument Blues-Tinged: Listening, Language and the Everyday in Sterling Brown's 'Ma Rainey.'" *Callaloo* 21.4, Sterling A. Brown: A Special Issue (Autumn 1998): 968–984.

Gabbard, Krin. "Signifyin(g) the Phallus: "Mo' Better Blues" and Representations of the Jazz Trumpet." *Cinema Journal* 32.1 (Autumn 1992): 43–62.

_____. *Hotter Than That: The Trumpet, Jazz, and American Culture*. New York: Faber and Faber, 2008.

_____. *Better Git It In Your Soul: An Interpretive Biography of Charles Mingus*. Oakland: University of California Press, 2016 .

Gaine, Chris, and Rosalyn George. *Gender, "Race", and Class in Schooling: A New Introduction*. London; Philadelphia, PA: Falmer Press, 1999.

Galbraith, John Kenneth. *The Great Crash, 1929*. Boston, Houghton Mifflin, 1955.

Gardner, Bettye, and Bettye Thomas. "The Cultural Impact of the Howard Theatre on the Black Community." *The Journal of Negro History* 55.4 (October 1970): 253–265.

Garvey, Marcus, and Robert Blaisdell. *Selected Writings and Speeches of Marcus Garvey*. Mineola, NY: Dover Publications, 2004.

Garvey, Marcus, and Amy Jacques Garvey. *Philosophy and Opinions of Marcus Garvey*. New York: Arno Press, 1968–69.

Garvey, Marcus, Robert A. Hill, and Universal Negro Improvement Association. *The Marcus Garvey and Universal Negro Improvement Association Papers. Vol. 10, Africa for the Africans, 1923–1945*. Berkeley, CA; London: University of California Press, 2006.

Garvey, Marcus, and Tony Martin. *The Poetical Works of Marcus Garvey*. Dover, MA: Majority Press, 1983.

Gates, Henry Louis, and Anthony Appiah. *Richard Wright: Critical Perspectives, Past and Present*. New York: Amistad, 1993.

Gauldin, Robert. "Beethoven, Tristan, and the Beatles." *College Music Symposium* 30.1 (Spring 1990): 142–152.

Gauss, Rebecca B. "O'Neill, Gruenberg and 'The Emperor Jones.'" *The Eugene O'Neill Review* 18.1/2 (Spring/Fall 1994): 38–44.

Gavin, James. *Stormy Weather: The Life of Lena Horne*. New York: Atria Books, 2009.

_____. *Deep in a Dream: The Long Night of Chet Baker*. Chicago: Chicago Review Press, 2011.

Gawronski, Donald V. *Transcendentlism: An Ideological Basis for Manifest Destiny*. Thesis/dissertation: Ann Arbor, MI: University Microfilms, 1969.

Gedo, Mary Mathews. "A Youthful Genius Confronts His Destiny: Picasso's "Old Guitarist" in The Art Institute of Chicago." *Art Institute of Chicago Museum Studies* 12.2, The Helen Birch Bartlett Memorial Collection (1986): 152–165.

Gelly, Dave. *Stan Getz: Nobody Else but Me*. San Francisco, CA: Backbeat Books, 2002.

_____. *Being Prez: The Life and Music of Lester Young*. New York: Oxford University Press, 2007.

Gennari, John. "Baraka's Bohemian Blues." *African American Review* 37.2/3, Amri Baraka Issue (Summer–Autumn 2003): 253–260.

_____. *Blowin' Hot and Cool: Jazz and its Critics*. Chicago: University of Chicago Press, 2006.

George, Luvenia A. "Duke Ellington the Man and His Music." *Music Educators Journal* 85.6 (May 1999): 15–21.

Gerdes, Louise I. *Woodstock*. Detroit: Greenhaven Press, 2012.

_____. *The 1992 Los Angeles Riots*. Detroit: Greenhaven Press, a part of Gale, Cengage Learning, 2014.

Gerrie, Ian. "Knowledge on the Horizon: A Phenomenological Inquiry into the "Framing" of Rodney King." *Human Studies* 29.3 (September 2006): 295–315.

Giddins, Gary. *Rhythm-a-ning: Jazz Tradition and Innovation in the '80s*. New York: Oxford University Press, 1985.

_____. "Coleman Hawkins, Patriarch." *The Antioch Review* 56.2, Nine Days (Spring 1998): 164–176.

_____. *Bing Crosby: A Pocketful of Dreams: The Early Years, 1903–1940*. Boston; London: Little Brown & Co., 2001.

Gilbert, Kenyatta R. *A Pursued Justice: Black Preaching from the Great Migration to Civil Rights*. Waco, TX: Baylor University Press, 2016.

Gillett, Rachel. "Jazz and the Evolution of Black American Cosmopolitanism in Interwar Paris." *Journal of World History* 21.3, Cosmopolitanism in World History (September 2010): 471–495.

Gilliam, Bryan Randolph. *Richard Strauss and His World*. Princeton, NJ: Princeton University Press, 1992.

_____. *The Life of Richard Strauss*. Cambridge, UK; New York: Cambridge University Press, 1999.

Ginell, Cary. *Mr. B.: The Life and Music of Billy Eckstine*. Montclair: Hal Leonard Books, 2013.

Ginell, Cary, and Roy Lee Brown. *Milton Brown and the Founding of Western Swing*. Urbana: University of Illinois Press, 1994.

Ginell, Cary, and Hubert Laws. *The Evolution of Mann: Herbie Mann & The Flute in Jazz*. Milwaukee, WI: Hal Leonard Books, 2014.

Gioia, Ted. *West Coast Jazz: Modern Jazz in California, 1945–1960*. New York: Oxford University Press, 1992.

Giordano, Ralph G. *Social Dancing in America: A History and Reference*. Westport, CT: Greenwood Press, 2007.

_____. *Satan in the Dance Hall: Rev. John Roach Straton, Social Dancing, and Morality in 1920s New York City*. Lanham, MD: Scarecrow Press, 2008.

Gitler, Ira. *Swing to Bop: An Oral History of the Transition in Jazz in the 1940s*. New York: Oxford University Press, USA, 1987.

Givan, Benjamin. "Swing Improvisation: A Schenkerian Perspective." *Theory and Practice* 35 (2010): 25–56.

Gjedsted, Jens Jørgen. "Electric Jazz." *Fontes Artis Musicae* 30.3 (Juli-September 1983): 132–136.

Gladney, Marvin J. "The Black Arts Movement and Hip-Hop." *African American Review* 29.2 (Summer 1995): 291–301.

Glazer, Lee Stephens. "Signifying Identity: Art and Race in Romare Bearden's Projections." *The Art Bulletin* 76.3 (September 1994): 411–426.

Gluck, Bob. *You'll Know When You Get There: Herbie Hancock and the Mwandishi Band*. Chicago; London: The University of Chicago Press, 2012.

_____. *The Miles Davis Lost Quintet: And Other Revolutionary Ensembles*. Chicago; London: University of Chicago Press, 2016.

Godin, Emmanuel, and Tony Chafer. *The French Exception*. New York: Berghahn Books, 2005.

Haskins, James. *The Cotton Club*. New York: Random House, 1977.

Gogröf-Voorhees, Andrea. *Defining Modernism: Baudelaire and Nietzsche on Romanticism, Modernity, Decadence, and Wagner*. New York: P. Lang, 1999.

Goldblatt, Burt. *Newport Jazz Festival: The Illustrated History*. New York: Dial Press, 1977.

Goldsher, Alan. *Hard Bop Academy: The Sidemen of Art Blakey and the Jazz Messengers*. Milwaukee, WI: Hal Leonard, 2002.

Gómez, Laura E. *Manifest Destinies: The Making of the Mexican American Race*. New York: New York University, 2007.

Gordon, Allan M. "The Art Ensemble of Chicago as Performance Art." *Lenox Avenue: A Journal of Interarts Inquiry* 3 (1997): 55–58.

Gordon, M. A., Robert. *Jazz West Coast: The Los Angeles Jazz Scene of the 1950s*. London; New York: Quartet Books, 1986.

Gottlieb, Robert. *Reading Jazz: A Gathering of Autobiography, Reportage, and Criticism from 1919 to Now*. New York: Pantheon Books, 1996.

Goudsouzian, Aram. *Sidney Poitier: Man, Actor, Icon*. Chapel Hill: University of North Carolina Press, 2004.

Gould, Jonathan. *Can't Buy Me Love: The Beatles, Britain, and America*. New York: Harmony Books, 2007.

Gourse, Leslie. *Unforgettable: The Life and Mystique of Nat King Cole*. New York: St. Martin's Press, 1991.

———. *Sassy: The Life of Sarah Vaughan*. New York: C. Scribner's Sons; Toronto: Collier Macmillan Canada; New York: Maxwell Macmillan International, 1993.

———. *Madame Jazz: Contemporary Women Instrumentalists*. New York: Oxford University Press, 1995.

———. *Straight, No Chaser: The Life and Genius of Thelonious Monk*. New York: Schirmer Books: Prentice Hall International, 1997.

———. *The Ella Fitzgerald Companion: Seven Decades of Commentary*. London: Schirmer Books, 1998.

———. *Timekeepers: The Great Jazz Drummers*. New York: F Watts, 1999.

———. "Playing for Keeps: Women Jazz Musicians Break the Glass Ceiling." *The Women's Review of Books* 18.3 (December 2000): 7–8.

———. *Art Blakey, Jazz Messenger*. New York: Schirmer Trade Books, 2002.

Grandt, Jürgen E. "Kinds of Blue: Toni Morrison, Hans Janowitz, and the Jazz Aesthetic Kinds of Blue: Toni Morrison, Hans Janowitz, and the Jazz Aesthetic." *African American Review* 38.2 (Summer 2004): 303–322.

Grant, M. J., and Imke Misch. *The Musical Legacy of Karlheinz Stockhausen: Looking Back and Forward*. Hofheim am Taunus: Wolke, 2016.

Gray, Herman. *Cultural Moves: African Americans and the Politics of Representation*. Berkeley: University of California Press, 2005.

Green, Sharony Andrews. *Grant Green: Rediscovering the Forgotten Genius of Jazz Guitar*. San Francisco, CA: Miller Freeman Books, 1999.

Green, Stanley. *The Rodgers and Hammerstein Story*. New York: The John Day Company, 1963.

Greenberg, Karen J., and Joshua L. Dratel. *The Torture Papers: The Road to Abu Ghraib*. New York: Cambridge University Press, 2005.

Greene, Norman N. *Jean-Paul Sartre: The Existentialist Ethic*. Ann Arbor: University of Michigan Press, 1960.

Greenspan, Charlotte. *Irving Berlin in Hollywood: The Art of Plugging a Song in Film*. *American Music*. 22.1 (Spring 2004): 40–49.

Greenwald, Jeff. "Hip-Hop Drumming: The Rhyme May Define, but the Groove Makes You Move." *Black Music Research Journal* 22.2 (Autumn 2002): 259–271.

Gregory, James N. *American Exodus: The Dust Bowl Migration and Okie Culture in California*. New York: Oxford University Press, 1989.

Grella, Jr., George. *Bitches Brew*. New York: Bloomsbury Academic, 2015.

Gridley, Mark C. *Jazz Styles: History & Analysis*. Upper Saddle River, NJ: Prentice Hall, 2000.

Griffin, Farah Jasmine. *Harlem Nocturne: Women Artists and Progressive Politics During World War II*. New York: Basic Civitas Books, 2013.

Griffin, Farah Jasmine, and Salim Washington. *Clawing at the Limits of Cool: Miles Davis, John Coltrane and the Greatest Jazz Collaboration Ever*. New York: Thomas Dunne Books, 2008.

Griffith, Jean C. "'Lita Is—Jazz': The Harlem Renaissance, Cabaret Culture, and Racial Amalgamation in Edith Wharton's 'Twilight Sleep.'" *Studies in the Novel* 38.1 (Spring 2006): 74–94.

Griffiths, David. *Hot Jazz: From Harlem to Storyville*. Lanham, MD: Scarecrow Press, 1998.

Grofman, Bernard. *Legacies of the 1964 Civil Rights Act*. Charlottesville: University Press of Virginia, 2000.

Grossman, James R. *Land of Hope: Chicago, Black Southerners, and the Great Migration*. Chicago: The University of Chicago Press, 2011.

Grove, Dick. *Modern Harmonic Relationships: An Organization of Tonal Relationships in Jazz, Rock and Popular Musical Idioms*. Studio City, CA: Dick Grove Publications, 1977.

Groves, Alan. *Bud Powell*. New York: Universe Books, 1987.

Groves, Alan, and Alyn Shipton. *The Glass Enclosure: The Life of Bud Powell*. New York: Continuum, 2001.

Grudens, Richard. *Bing Crosby: Crooner of the Century*. Stony Brook, NY: Celebrity Profiles Pub., 2003.

Grunenberg, Christoph, Jonathan Harris, and Tate Gallery Liverpool. *Summer of Love: Psychedelic Art, Social Crisis and Counterculture in the 1960s* . Liverpool: Liverpool University Press, 2005 .

Guerrero, Ed. *Framing Blackness: The African American Image in Film*. Philadelphia: Temple University Press, 1993.

Guglielmo, Thomas A. *White on Arrival: Italians, Race, Color, and Power in Chicago, 1890–1945*. New York: Oxford University Press, 2004.

Gushee, Lawrence. "A Preliminary Chronology of the Early Career of Ferd "Jelly Roll" Morton." *American Music* 3.4 (Winter 1985): 389–412.

_____. "New Orleans: Area Musicians on the West Coast, 1908–1925." *Black Music Research Journal* 22, Supplement: Best of BMRJ (2002): 5–21.

_____. *Pioneers of Jazz: The Story of the Creole Band*. New York: Oxford University Press, USA, 2010.

Gushee, Lawrence, and Harry Carr. "How the Creole Band Came to Be." *Black Music Research Journal* 8.1 (1988): 83–100.

Gussow, Adam. "'Make My Getaway': The Blues Lives of Black Minstrels in W. C. Handy's Father of the Blues." *African American Review* 35.1 (Spring 2001): 5–28.

Gysin, Fritz. "Double-Jointed Time in Nathaniel Mackey's Jazz Fiction." *Amerikastudien/ American Studies* 45.4, Time and the African-American Experience (2000): 513–518.

Haas, Ken, and Gwynne Edwards. *Flamenco!* London: Thames & Hudson, 2000.

Hae, Laam. *The Gentrification of Nightlife and the Right to the City: Regulating Spaces of Social Dancing in New York*. New York: Routledge, 2012.

Haggerty, Michael, and Kenneth ("Kenny") Spearman Clarke. "Under Paris Skies." *The Black Perspective in Music* 13.2 (Autumn 1985): 195–221.

Haines, David W., and Carol A. Mortland. *Manifest Destinies: Americanizing Immigrants and Internationalizing Americans*. Westport, CT: Praeger, 2001.

Hajdu, David. *Lush Life: A Biography of Billy Strayhorn*. New York: North Point Press, 1996.

Hall, Fred. *It's About Time: The Dave Brubeck Story*. Fayetteville: University of Arkansas Press, 1996.

Hall, George I., and Stephen A. Kramer. *Gene Krupa and His Orchestra*. Laurel, MD: Jazz Discographies Unlimited, 1975.

Hall, Gwendolyn Midlo. *Africans in Colonial Louisiana: The Development of Afro-Creole Culture in the Eighteenth Century*. Baton Rouge: Louisiana State University Press, 1992.

Halpern, Stephen C. *On the Limits of the Law: The Ironic Legacy of Title VI of the 1964 Civil Rights Act*. Baltimore, MD: Johns Hopkins University Press, 1995.

Hamer, Jennifer. *Abandoned in the Heartland: Work, Family, and Living in East St. Louis*. Berkeley: University of California Press, 2011.

Hamilton, Andy, and Lee Konitz. *Lee Konitz: Conversations on the Improviser's Art*. Ann Arbor: University of Michigan Press, 2007.

Hamm, Charles. *Irving Berlin's Early Songs as Biographical Documents. The Musical Quarterly* 77.1 (Spring 1993): 10–34.

_____. "Genre, Performance and Ideology in the Early Songs of Irving Berlin." *Popular Music* 13.2, Mellers at 80 (May 1994): 143–150.

_____. *Irving Berlin: Songs from the Melting Pot: The Formative Years, 1907–1914*. New York: Oxford University Press, 1997.

Hammond, John, and Irving Townsend. *John Hammond on Record: An Autobiography*. New York: Ridge Press, 1977.

Hampton, Lionel, James Haskins, and Vincent Pelote. *Hamp: An Autobiography*. New York: Amistad: Distributed by Penguin USA, 1993.

Hampton, Wayne. *Guerrilla Minstrels: John Lennon, Joe Hill, Woody Guthrie, Bob Dylan*. Knoxville: University of Tennessee Press, 1986.

Hancock, Black Hawk. "Put a Little Color on That!" *Sociological Perspectives* 51.4 (Winter 2008): 783–802.

————. *American Allegory: Lindy Hop and the Racial Imagination*. Chicago: The University of Chicago Press, 2013.

Hancock, Herbie, and Lisa Dickey. *Herbie Hancock: Possibilities*. New York: Viking, 2014.

Handy, D. Antoinette. *Black Women in American Bands and Orchestras*. 2nd ed. Lanham, MD: Scarecrow Press, 1998.

Handy, D. Antoinette, and Piney Woods School. *The International Sweethearts of Rhythm: The Ladies Jazz Band From Piney Woods Country Life School*. Rev. ed. Lanham, MD: Scarecrow Press, 1998.

Handy, D. Antoinette, and Mary Lou Williams. "First Lady of the Jazz Keyboard." *The Black Perspective in Music* 8.2 (Autumn 1980): 194–214.

Handy, W. C. (William Christopher), Abbe Niles, Elliott S Hurwitt, and Miguel Covarrubias. *W.C. Handy's Blues: An Anthology: Complete Words and Music of 70 Great Songs and Instrumentals*. Mineola, NY: Dover Publications, 2012.

Hankins, Sarah. "So Contagious: Hybridity and Subcultural Exchange in Hip-Hop's Use of Indian Samples." *Black Music Research Journal* 31.2 (Fall 2011): 193–208.

Hanson, Michael. "Suppose James Brown Read Fanon: The Black Arts Movement, Cultural Nationalism and the Failure of Popular Musical Praxis." *Popular Music* 27.3 (October 2008): 341–365.

Hardie, Daniel. *The Loudest Trumpet: Buddy Bolden and the Early History of Jazz*. San José: ToExcel, 2001.

Hardré, Jacques. "Jean-Paul Sartre: Literary Critic." *Studies in Philology* 55.1 (January 1958): 98–106.

Harker, Brian. "Louis Armstrong, Eccentric Dance, and the Evolution of Jazz on the Eve of Swing." *Journal of the American Musicological Society* 61.1 (Spring 2008): 67–121.

————. "In Defense of Context in Jazz History: A Response to Mark Gridley." *College Music Symposium* 48 (2008): 157–159.

————. *Louis Armstrong's Hot Five and Hot Seven Recordings*. New York City: Oxford University Press, 2011.

Harper, Colin. *Bathed in Lightning: John McLaughlin, the 60s, and the Emerald Beyond*. London: Jawbone Press: Distributed by Hal Leonard Corporation, 2014.

Harper, Michael S. "Dear Old Stockholm." *The Georgia Review* 35.1 (Spring 1981): 140–141.

Harris, Keith M. *Boys, Boyz, Bois: An Ethics of Black Masculinity in Film and Popular Media*. New York: Routledge, 2006.

Harris, Michael D. *Colored Pictures: Race and Visual Representation*. Chapel Hill: University of North Carolina Press, 2003.

Harris, Stephen L. *Harlem's Hell Fighters: The African-American 369th Infantry in World War I*. Washington, D.C.: Brassey's, Inc., 2003.

Harrison, Douglas. *Then Sings My Soul: The Culture of Southern Gospel Music*. Urbana: University of Illinois Press, 2012.

Hart House. *African Tribal Art from the Collection of Sam and Ayala Zacks, Hart House Art Gallery, March 8 to 28, 1970*. Toronto: University of Toronto Press, 1970.

Hartnett, Stephen. "Cultural Postmodernism and Bobby McFerrin: A Case Study of Musical Production as the Composition of Spectacle." *Cultural Critique* 16 (Autumn 1990): 61–85.

Harvey, Jonathan. *The Music of Stockhausen: An Introduction*. Berkeley: University of California Press, 1975.

Haskins, James, and Kathleen Benson. *Lena: A Personal and Professional Biography of Lena Horne*. New York: Stein and Day, 1984.

Haslam, Jason. *Gender, Race, and American Science Fiction: Reflections on Fantastic Identities*. Hoboken NJ: Taylor and Francis, 2015.

Hassan, Rusty. "Jazz Radio in Washington: A Personal Retrospective." *Washington History* 26, Jazz in Washington (Spring 2014): 74–87.

Hasse, John Edward. "Washington's Duke Ellington." *Washington History* 26, Jazz in Washington (Spring 2014): 36–59.

Hasse, John Edward, and Indiana Historical Society. *The Classic Hoagy Carmichael*. Indianapolis: Indiana Historical Society; Washington, D.C.: Smithsonian Collection of Recordings, 1988.

Hawkins, Coleman, Lester Young, and Ben Webster. *The Big Three Coleman Hawkins, Lester Young, Ben Webster*. New York: Doctor Jazz Records 1987.

Hawkins, Stan, and Sarah Niblock. *Prince: The Making of a Pop Music Phenomenon*. Farnham, Surrey, England; Burlington, VT: Ashgate, 2011.

Hawthorne, Julian. *Nathaniel Hawthorne and His Wife; A Biography*. Hamden, CT: Archon Books, 1968.

Hawthorne, Nathaniel. *The Complete Works of Nathaniel Hawthorne*. Boston: Houghton, Mifflin, 1882–1899.

Hayes, Michelle Heffner. *Flamenco: Conflicting Histories of the Dance*. Jefferson, NC: McFarland & Co., 2009.

Haygood, Wil. *In Black and White: The Life of Sammy Davis, Jr*. New York: A. A. Knopf: Distributed by Random House, 2003.

Heble, Ajay, and Rob Wallace. *People Get Ready: The Future of Jazz is Now!* Durham, NC: Duke University Press, 2013.

Hecht, Paul. *The Wind Cried; An American's Discovery of the World of Flamenco*. New York: Dial Press, 1968.

Hehn, Paul N. *A Low Dishonest Decade: The Great Powers, Eastern Europe, and the Economic Origins of World War II, 1930–1941*. New York: Continuum, 2002.

Heil, Alan L. *Voice of America: A History*. New York: Columbia University Press, 2003.

Heilbronner, Oded. "'Helter-Skelter'?: The Beatles, the British New Left, and the Question of Hegemony." *Interdisciplinary Literary Studies* 13.1/2 (Fall 2011): 87–107.

Heining, Duncan. *George Russell: The Story of an American Composer*. Lanham, MD: Scarecrow Press, 2010.

Heitner, Devorah. *Black Power TV*. Durham; London: Duke University Press, 2013.

Helfrich, Ronald. "'What Can a Hippie Contribute to our Community?' Culture Wars, Moral Panics, and The Woodstock Festival." *New York History* 91.3 (Summer 2010): 221–244.

Heller, Michael C. *Loft Jazz: Improvising New York in the 1970s*. Oakland: University of California Press, 2017.

Henderson, David. *Jimi Hendrix: Voodoo Child of the Aquarian Age*. Garden City, NY: Doubleday, 1978.

———. "Jimi Hendrix Deep Within the Blues and Alive Onstage at Woodstock—25 Years after Death." *African American Review* 29.2, Special Issues on The Music (Summer 1995): 213–216.

Henderson, Errol Anthony. *Afrocentrism and World Politics: Towards a New Paradigm*. Westport, CT: Praeger, 1995.

Henderson, Fletcher, and Jeffrey Magee. "Revisiting Fletcher Henderson's 'Copenhagen.'" *Journal of the American Musicological Society* 48.1 (Spring 1995): 42–66.

Hendrickson, Ryan C. *Obama at War: Congress and the Imperial Presidency*. Lexington: The University Press of Kentucky, 2015.

Hendrix, Jimi, and Steven Roby. *Hendrix on Hendrix: Interviews and Encounters with Jimi Hendrix*. Chicago: Chicago Review Press, 2012.

Hendrix, Leon, and Adam D. Mitchell. *Jimi Hendrix: A Brother's Story*. New York: Thomas Dunne Books, 2012.

Hennessey, Mike. *Klook: The Story of Kenny Clarke*. Pittsburgh, PA: University of Pittsburgh Press, 1994.

Henney, III, William H. "Le Hot: The Assimilation of American Jazz in France, 1917–1940." *American Studies* 25.1 (Spring 1984): 5–24.

Henningfeld, Diane Andrews. *Little Rock Nine*. Detroit: Greenhaven Press, a part of Gale, Cengage Learning, 2014.

Henry, Clarence Bernard. *Quincy Jones: His Life in Music*. Jackson: University Press of Mississippi, 2013.

———. *Quincy Jones: A Research and Information Guide*. New York; London: Routledge, Taylor & Francis Group, 2014.

Hentoff, Nat. "Jazz and the Intellectuals: Somebody Goofed." *Chicago Review* 9.3, Changing American Culture (Fall 1955): 110–121.
_____. *Listen to the Stories: Nat Hentoff on Jazz and Country Music*. New York: HarperCollins, 1995.
_____. *The Nat Hentoff Reader*. Cambridge, MA: Da Capo Press, 2001.
_____. *At the Jazz Band Ball: Sixty Years on the Jazz Scene*. Berkeley: University of California Press, 2010.
Herbert, Steve. "The Normative Ordering of Police Territoriality: Making and Marking Space with the Los Angeles Police Department." *Annals of the Association of American Geographers* 86. (September 1996): 567–582.
_____. "Morality in Law Enforcement: Chasing "Bad Guys" with the Los Angeles Police Department." *Law & Society Review* 30.4 (1996): 799–818.
_____. *Policing Space: Territoriality and the Los Angeles Police Department*. Minneapolis: University of Minnesota Press, 1997.
Herman, Woody. *The Woodchopper's Ball: The Autobiography of Woody Herman*. NY: Limelight, 1994.
Hersch, Charles. "Poisoning Their Coffee: Louis Armstrong and Civil Rights." *Polity* 34.3 (Spring 2002): 371–392.
Herschberg, Jacqueline. "Kansas City: The Jazz Scene." *ALA Bulletin* 62.5 (May 1968): 517–518.
Hersh, Seymour M., and Rogers D. Spotswood Collection. *Chain of Command: The Road from 9/11 to Abu Ghraib*. New York: HarperCollins, 2004.
Hewitt, Roger. "Black Through White: Hoagy Carmichael and the Cultural Reproduction of Racism." *Popular Music* 3, Producers and Markets (1983): 33–50.
Hicks, Cheryl D. *Talk With You Like a Woman: African American Women, Justice, and Reform in New York, 1890–1935*. Chapel Hill: University of North Carolina Press, 2010.
Hicock, Larry. *Castles Made of Sound: The Story of Gil Evans*. Cambridge, MA: Da Capo Press, 2002.
Hietala, Thomas R. *The Fight of the Century: Jack Johnson, Joe Louis, and the Struggle for Racial Equality*. Armonk, NY: M.E. Sharpe, 2004.
Higginbotham, Carmenita. "At the Savoy: Reginald Marsh and the Art of Slumming." *Bulletin of the Detroit Institute of Arts* 82.1/2 (2008): 16–29.
Hill, Edward Burlingame. *Maurice Ravel. The Musical Quarterly* 13.1 (January 1927): 130–146.
Hill, Lance E. *The Deacons for Defense: Armed Resistance and the Civil Rights Movement*. Chapel Hill: University of North Carolina Press, 2004.
Hiltzik, Michael A. *The New Deal: A Modern History*. New York: Free Press, 2011.
Hinant, Guy-Marc, and Michael Novy. "Artist's Notebook: TOHU BOHU: Considerations on the Nature of Noise, in 78 Fragments." *Leonardo Music Journal* 13, Groove, Pit and Wave: Recording, Transmission and Music (2003): 43–46.
Hinshaw, John H. *Steel and Steelworkers: Race and Class Struggle in Twentieth-Century Pittsburgh*. Albany: State University of New York Press, 2002.
Hirsch, Arnold R. *Making the Second Ghetto: Race and Housing in Chicago, 1940–1960*. Cambridge; New York: Cambridge University Press, 1983.
Hirsch, Arnold R, and Joseph Logsdon. *Creole New Orleans: Race and Americanization*. Baton Rouge: Louisiana State University Press, 1992.
Hischak, Thomas S. *The Rodgers and Hammerstein Encyclopedia*. Westport, CT: Greenwood Press, 2007.
Hodermarsky, Elisabeth. "The Abstractionist as Regionalist: A Young Jackson Pollock's "Stacking Hay." *Yale University Art Gallery Bulletin, Recent Acquisitions* (2014): 42–46.
Hoefsmit, Sjef, and Andrew Homzy. "Chronology of Ellington's Recordings and Performances of "Black, Brown and Beige," 1943–1973." *Black Music Research Journal* 13.2 (Autumn 1993): 161–173.
Holcomb, Gary Edward. "The Sun Also Rises in Queer Black Harlem: Hemingway and McKay's Modernist Intertext." *Journal of Modern Literature* 30.4 (Summer 2007): 61–81.

_____. *Claude McKay, Code Name Sasha: Queer Black Marxism and the Harlem Renaissance*. Gainesville: University Press of Florida, 2007.

Holiday, Billie, and William Dufty. *Lady Sings the Blues*. New York: Lancer Books, 1972.

Hollerbach, Peter. "(Re)voicing Tradition: Improvising Aesthetics and Identity on Local Jazz Scenes." *Popular Music* 23.2 (May 2004): 155–171.

Hollinrake, Roger. *Nietzsche, Wagner, and the Philosophy of Pessimism*. London; Boston: Allen and Unwin, 1982.

Holmes, Thom, and Terence M. Pender. *Electronic and Experimental Music: Technology, Music, and Culture*. New York: Routledge, 2012.

Homzy, Andrew. "'Black, Brown and Beige' in Duke Ellington's Repertoire, 1943-1973." *Black Music Research Journal* 13.2 (Autumn 1993): 87–110.

hooks, bell. *Reel to Real: Race, Sex, and Class at the Movies*. New York: Routledge, 1996.

Horn, David. "The Sound World of Art Tatum." *Black Music Research Journal* 20.2, European Perspectives on Black Music (Autumn 2000): 237–257.

Horne, Gerald. *Fire This Time: The Watts Uprising and the 1960s*. Charlottesville: University Press of Virginia, 1995.

Horne, Jed. *Breach of Faith: Hurricane Katrina and the Near Death of a Great American City*. New York: Random House, 2006.

Horne, Lena, Helen Arstein, and Carlton Moss. *In Person, Lena Horne: As Told to Helen Arstein and Carlton Moss*. New York: Greenberg, 1950.

Horne, Lena, and Richard Schickel. *Lena*. Garden City, NY: Doubleday, 1965.

Horricks, Raymond. *Count Basie and His Orchestra, Its Music and Its Musicians*. Westport, CT: Negro Universities Press, 1975.

_____. *The Importance of Being Eric Dolphy*. Tunbridge Wells: Costello, 1988.

Horsman, Reginald. *Race and Manifest Destiny: The Origins of American Racial Anglo-Saxonism*. Cambridge: Harvard University Press, 1981.

Howard, Leon. *Herman Melville*. Minneapolis: University of Minnesota Press, 1961.

Howland, John. "Jazz Rhapsodies in Black and White: James P. Johnson's 'Yamekraw.'" *American Music* 24.4 (Winter 2006): 445–509.

_____. "'The Blues Get Glorified': Harlem Entertainment, Negro Nuances, and Black Symphonic Jazz." *The Musical Quarterly* 90.3/4 (Fall–Winter 2007): 319–370.

Huang, Hao. "Enter the Blues: Jazz Poems by Langston Hughes and Sterling Brown." *Hungarian Journal of English and American Studies* (HJEAS) 17.1 (Spring 2011): 9–44.

Hughes, Langston, Evelyn Louise Crawford, and MaryLouise Patterson. *Letters from Langston: from the Harlem Renaissance to the Red Scare and Beyond*. Oakland: University of California Press, 2016.

Hughes, Langston, and Susan Duffy. *The Political Plays of Langston Hughes*. Carbondale: Southern Illinois University Press, 2000.

Hunt, Darnell M., and Ana-Christina Ramón. *Black Los Angeles: American Dreams and Racial Realities*. New York: New York University Press, 2010.

Huret, Romain, and Randy J. Sparks. *Hurricane Katrina in Transatlantic Perspective*. Baton Rouge: Louisiana State University Press, 2014.

Hurston, Zora Neale, Jean Lee Cole, and Charles Mitchell. *Zora Neale Hurston: Collected Plays*. New Brunswick, NJ: Rutgers University Press, 2008.

Hurston, Zora Neale, and Carla Kaplan. *Zora Neale Hurston: A Life in Letters*. New York: Doubleday, 2002.

Hurston, Zora Neale, and Alice Walker. *I Love Myself When I Am Laughing . . . And Then Again When I Am Looking Mean and Impressive: A Zora Neale Hurston Reader*. Old Westbury, NY: Feminist Press, 1979.

Hutchinson, George. *The Cambridge Companion to the Harlem Renaissance*. New York: Cambridge University Press, 2007.

Hutchinson, Ron. "The Vitaphone Project. Answering Harry Warner's Question: 'Who the Hell Wants to Hear Actors Talk?'" *Film History* 14.1, Film/Music (2002): 40–46.

Iddon, Martin. *New Music at Darmstadt: Nono, Stockhausen, Cage, and Boulez*. New York: Cambridge University Press, 2013.

Ikard, David, and Martell L. Teasley. *Nation of Cowards: Black Activism in Barack Obama's Post-Racial America*. Bloomington: Indiana University Press, 2012.

Imbert, Claude. "The End of French Exceptionalism." *Foreign Affairs* 68.4 (Fall 1989): 48–60.

Ind, Peter. *Jazz Visions: Lennie Tristano and His Legacy*. London: Equinox, 2007.

Inglis, Ian. "Ideology, Trajectory & Stardom: Elvis Presley & The Beatles." *International Review of the Aesthetics and Sociology of Music* 27.1 (June 1996): 53–78.

_____. *Performance and Popular Music: History, Place and Time*. Aldershot, Hants, England; Burlington, VT: Ashgate, 2006.

Isaac, Larry, and Lars Christiansen. "How the Civil Rights Movement Revitalized Labor Militancy." *American Sociological Review* 67.5 (October 2002): 722–746.

Isaacs, Arnold R, and Rogers D. Spotswood Collection. *Vietnam Shadows: The War, its Ghosts, and its Legacy*. Baltimore: Johns Hopkins University Press, 1997.

Iseminger, Gary. "Sonicism and Jazz Improvisation." *The Journal of Aesthetics and Art Criticism* 68.3 (Summer 2010): 297–299.

Isoardi, Steven Louis. *The Dark Tree: Jazz and the Community Arts in Los Angeles*. Berkeley: University of California Press, 2006.

Israels, Chuck. "Bill Evans (1929-1980): A Musical Memoir." *The Musical Quarterly* 71.2 (1985): 109–115.

Ives, Charles, and Thomas Clarke Owens. *Selected Correspondence of Charles Ives*. Berkeley: University of California Press, 2007.

Iyer, Vijay. "Embodied Mind, Situated Cognition, and Expressive Microtiming in African-American Music." *Music Perception: An Interdisciplinary Journal* 19.3 (Spring 2002): 387–414.

Izzo, David Garrett. *Movies in the Age of Obama: The Era of Post Racial and Neo-Racist Cinema*. Lanham, MD: Rowman & Littlefield, 2015.

Jablonski, Edward. *Irving Berlin: American Troubadour*. New York: Henry Holt, 1999.

Jackson, Jeffrey H. *Making Jazz French: Music & Modern Life in Interwar Paris*. Durham, NC: Duke University Press, 2003.

Jackson, Jonathan David. "Improvisation in African-American Vernacular Dancing." *Dance Research Journal* 33.2, Social and Popular Dance (Winter 2001): 40–53.

Jackson, Travis A. *Blowin' the Blues Away: Performance and Meaning on the New York Jazz Scene*. Berkeley: Chicago: University of California Press, 2012.

Jackson, Jr., John L. *Harlem World: Doing Race and Class in Contemporary Black America*. Chicago: University of Chicago Press, 2001.

_____. *Real Black: Adventures in Racial Sincerity* . Chicago: University of Chicago Press, 2005 .

Jacobs, Ronald N. "Civil Society and Crisis: Culture, Discourse, and the Rodney King Beating." *American Journal of Sociology* 101.5 (March 1996): 1238–1272.

_____. *Race, Media and the Crisis of Civil Society: From the Watts Riots to Rodney King*. Cambridge: Cambridge University Press, 2000.

Jacobs, Wilbur R. *Dispossessing the American Indian: Indians and Whites on the Colonial Frontier*. New York: Scribner, 1972.

Jacoway, Elizabeth, and C. Fred Williams. *Understanding the Little Rock Crisis: An Exercise in Remembrance and Reconciliation*. Fayetteville: University of Arkansas Press, 1999.

Jaffee, Barbara. "Jackson Pollock's Industrial Expressionism." *Art Journal* 63.4 (Winter 2004): 68–79.

James, Martin. *French Connections: From Discothèque to Discovery*. London: Sanctuary, 2003.

Japtok, Martin, and Rafiki Jenkins. *Authentic Blackness/"Real" Blackness: Essays on the Meaning of Blackness in Literature and Culture* . New York: Peter Lang, 2011 .

Jarrett, Gene. "Entirely Black Verse From Him Would Succeed." *Nineteenth-Century Literature* 59.4 (March 2005): 494–525 .

Jeffords, Susan. *Hard Bodies: Hollywood Masculinity in the Reagan Era*. New Brunswick, NJ: Rutgers University Press, 1994.

Jeffords, Susan, and Lauren Rabinovitz. *Seeing Through the Media: The Persian Gulf War*. New Brunwick, NJ: Rutgers University Press, 1994.

Jeffries, J. L. *Black Power in the Belly of the Beast*. Urbana: University of Illinois, 2006.

Jenkins, Candice M. "Decoding Essentialism: Cultural Authenticity and the Black Bourgeoisie in Nella Larsen's *Passing* ." *Melus* 30.3, Personal and Political (Fall 2005): 129–154 .

Jessup, Lynne, and Isaac Hirt-Manheimer. *All Hands On!: An Introduction to West African Percussion Ensembles*. Danbury, CT: World Music Press, 1997.

Johnson, Howard Eugene, and Wendy Johnson. *A Dancer in the Revolution: Stretch Johnson, Harlem Communist at the Cotton Club*. New York: Empire State Editions, 2014.

Johnson, Jack. *Jack Johnson in the Ring and Out*. Chicago: National Sports Pub. Co., 1927.

_____. *Jack Johnson Is a Dandy: An Autobiography*. New York: Chelsea House, 1969.

Johnson, Michael K. *Black Masculinity and the Frontier Myth in American Literature*. Norman: University of Oklahoma Press, 2002.

Johnson, Phylis. *KJLH-FM and the Los Angeles Riots of 1992: Compton's Neighborhood Station in the Aftermath of the Rodney King Verdict*. Jefferson, NC: McFarland & Co., Publishers, 2009.

Jones, Jeannette Eileen. *In Search of Brightest Africa: Reimagining the Dark Continent in American Culture, 1884–1936*. Athens: University of Georgia Press, 2010.

Jones, Max. *Jazz Talking: Profiles, Interviews, and other Riffs on Jazz Musicians*. Boulder, CO: Da Capo Press, 2000.

Jones, Max, and John Chilton. *Louis: The Louis Armstrong Story, 1900–1971*. Boston: Little, Brown, 1971.

Jones, Meta DuEwa. *The Muse is Music: Jazz Poetry from the Harlem Renaissance to Spoken Word*. Urbana: University of Illinois Press, 2011.

Jones, Patricia Spears. "Sly and the Family Stone under the Big Tit, Atlanta, 1973." *The Kenyon Review, New Series* 15.4 (Autumn 1993): 66–68.

Jones, Quincy. *Q: The Autobiography of Quincy Jones*. New York: Doubleday, 2001.

Jones, Stacy Linn Holman. *Torch Singing: Performing Resistance and Desire from Billie Holiday to Edith Piaf*. Lanham, MD: AltaMira Press, 2007.

Jordan, Matthew. *Le Jazz: Jazz and French Cultural Identity*. Urbana: University of Illinois Press, 2010.

Jordan-Lake, Joy. *Whitewashing Uncle Tom's Cabin: Nineteenth-Century Women Novelists Respond to Stowe*. Nashville, TN: Vanderbilt University Press, 2005.

Joseph, Peniel E. *Waiting 'til the Midnight Hour: A Narrative History of Black Power in America*. New York: Henry Holt and Co., 2006.

_____. *The Black Power Movement: Rethinking the Civil Rights-Black Power Era*. New York: Routledge, 2006.

Joyce, James. *Selected Letters of James Joyce*. New York: Viking Press, 1975.

Joyce, James, and Stuart Gilbert. *Letters of James Joyce*. New York: Viking Press, 1957.

Joyce, James, Michael Groden, Hans Walter Gabler, David Hayman, A Walton Litz, and Danis Rose. *The James Joyce Archive*. New York: Garland, 1977–1979.

Joyce, James, and Harry Levin. *The Essential James Joyce*. Harmondsworth, Middlesex: Penguin Books, 1948.

Joyce, James, Ellsworth Mason, and Richard Ellmann. *The Critical Writings of James Joyce*. New York: Viking Press, 1959.

Judaken, Jonathan. *Jean-Paul Sartre and the Jewish Question: Anti-Antisemitism and the Politics of the French Intellectual*. Lincoln: University of Nebraska Press, 2006.

Julien, Patricia. "'Sakeena's Vision': The Trifocal Organization of Harmonic Relations in One of Wayne Shorter's Early Compositions." *Theory and Practice* 34 (2009): 107–140 .

Kahn, Ashley. *A Love Supreme: The Story of John Coltrane's Signature Album*. New York: Viking, 2002.

Kahn, Ashley, and Jimmy Cobb. *Kind of Blue: The Making of the Miles Davis Masterpiece*. Cambridge, MA: Da Capo Press, 2007.

Kajanová, Yvetta. "The Rock, Pop and Jazz in Contemporary Musicological Studies." *International Review of the Aesthetics and Sociology of Music* 44.2 (December 2013): 343–359 .

Kaliss, Jeff. *I Want to Take You Higher: The Life and Times of Sly & the Family Stone*. New York: Backbeat Books, 2008.

Kamin, Ben. "Harry Belafonte, Janet Levison, and a Totally Different 'Kennedy.'" *Dangerous Friendship: Stanley Levison, Martin Luther King Jr., and the Kennedy Brothers.* East Lansing: Michigan State University Press, 2014, 67–82.

Kamin, Jonathan. "Parallels in the Social Reactions to Jazz and Rock." *The Black Perspective in Music* 3.3 (Autumn 1975): 278–298.

Kandelhart, Alex. *Montreux Jazz Festival Portraits—Live at Montreux.* Hamburg: Edel Germany GmbH, cop. 2012.

Kania, Andrew. "All Play and No Work: An Ontology of Jazz." *The Journal of Aesthetics and Art Criticism* 69.4 (Fall 2011): 391–403.

Kaplan, Temma. *Red City, Blue Period: Social Movements in Picasso's Barcelona.* Berkeley: University of California Press, 1992.

Keister, Jay. "Seeking Authentic Experience: Spirituality in the Western Appropriation of Asian Music." *The World of Music* 47.3, The Music of "Others" in the Western World (2005): 35–53.

Keizer, Arlene R. *Black Subjects: Identity Formation in the Contemporary Narrative of Slavery.* Ithaca, NY: Cornell University Press, 2004.

Keller, Susan L. "The Riviera's Golden Boy: Fitzgerald, Cosmopolitan Tanning, and Racial Commodities in 'Tender Is the Night.'" *The F. Scott Fitzgerald Review* 8 (2010): 130–159.

Kelley, Robin D. G. *Race Rebels: Culture, Politics, and the Black Working Class.* New York: Free Press; Toronto: Maxwell Macmillan Canada; New York: Maxwell Macmillan International, 1994.

_____. "New Monastery: Monk and the Jazz Avant-Garde." *Black Music Research Journal* 19.2, New Perspectives on Thelonious Monk (Autumn 1999): 135–168.

_____. *Thelonious Monk: The Life and Times of an American Original.* New York: Free Press, 2009.

Kelly, Robert, and Erin Cook. "Martin Luther King, Jr., and Malcolm X: A Common Solution." *OAH Magazine of History* 19.1, Martin Luther King, Jr. (January 2005): 37–40.

Kennedy, Michael. *Richard Strauss: Man, Musician, Enigma.* Cambridge, UK; New York: Cambridge University Press, 1999.

Kennedy, Rick, and Ted Gioia. *Jelly Roll, Bix, and Hoagy: Gennett Records and the Rise of America's Musical Grassroots.* Bloomington; Indianapolis: Indiana University Press, 2013.

Kenney III, William Howland. "Jazz and the Concert Halls: The Eddie Condon Concerts, 1942–48." *American Music* 1.2 (Summer 1983): 60–72.

_____. "James Scott and the Culture of Classic Ragtime." *American Music* 9.2 (Summer 1991): 149–182.

_____. *Chicago Jazz: A Cultural History, 1904-1930.* New York: Oxford University Press, 1993.

Kern, Edith. *Sartre, A Collection of Critical Essays.* Englewood Cliffs, NJ, Prentice-Hall, 1962.

Kernodle, Tammy Lynn. "This Is My Story, This Is My Song: The Historiography of Vatican II, Black Catholic Identity, Jazz, and the Religious Compositions of Mary Lou Williams." *U.S. Catholic Historian* 19.2, African American Spirituality and Liturgical Renewal (Spring 2001): 83–94.

_____. *Soul on Soul: The Life and Music of Mary Lou Williams.* Boston: Northeastern University Press, 2004.

_____. "Diggin' You Like Those Ol' Soul Records: Meshell Ndegeocello and the Expanding Definition of Funk in Postsoul America." *American Studies* 52.4, The Funk Issue (2013): 181–204.

Kerr, George. "Belfast, Home of Amazing Jazz." *Fortnight* 410 (January 2003): 19 .

Keyes, Cheryl L. "'She Was Too Black for Rock and Too Hard for Soul': (Re)discovering the Musical Career of Betty Mabry Davis." *American Studies* 52.4, The Funk Issue (2013): 35–55.

Khan, Chaka, and Tonya Bolden. *Chaka!: Through the Fire.* Emmaus, Pa.: Rodale; [New York]: Distributed to the Book trade by St. Martin's Press, 2003.

Kidd, Hayward, and Jack Ernest Shalom. *Fragmented France: Two Centuries of Disputed Identity.* Oxford; New York: Oxford University Press, 2007.

Kidd, William, and Sian Reynolds. *Contemporary French Cultural Studies*. Hoboken: Taylor and Francis, 2014.

Kienzle, Richard. *Southwest Shuffle: Pioneers of Honky Tonk, Western Swing, and Country Jazz*. New York: Routledge, 2003.

Kilpatrick, Emily. "Into the Woods: Retelling the Wartime Fairytales of Maurice Ravel." *The Musical Times* 149.1902 (Spring 2008): 57–66.

Kimble, Jr., Lionel. *A New Deal for Bronzeville: Housing, Employment, & Civil Rights in Black Chicago, 1935-1955*. Carbondale: Southern Illinois University Press, 2015.

King, Jr., Martin Luther, and Clayborne Carson. *The Autobiography of Martin Luther King, Jr.* New York: Intellectual Properties Management in association with Warner Books, 1998.

King, Jr., Martin Luther, Clayborne Carson, Peter Holloran, Ralph E. Luker, and Penny A. Russell. *The Papers of Martin Luther King, Jr.* Berkeley: University of California Press, 1992.

King, Jr., Martin Luther, and Coretta Scott King. *The Words of Martin Luther King, Jr.* New York: Newmarket Press, 1983.

King, Jr., Martin Luther, and Cornel West. *The Radical King*. Boston: Beacon Press, 2014.

Kinnamon, Keneth. *Richard Wright: An Annotated Bibliography of Criticism and Commentary, 1983–2003*. Jefferson, NC: McFarland & Co., 2006.

Kirkeby, Ed, Duncan P. Schiedt, and Sinclair Traill. *Ain't Misbehavin'; The Story of Fats Waller*. New York, Dodd, Mead, 1966.

Kisseloff, Jeff. *Generation on Fire: Voices of Protest from the 1960s: An Oral History* . Lexington, KY: University Press of Kentucky, 2007 .

Klare, Michael T. *Beyond the "Vietnam Syndrome": U.S. Interventionism in the 1980s*. Washington, D.C.: Institute for Policy Studies, 1981.

Klarman, Michael J. *From Jim Crow to Civil Rights: The Supreme Court and the Struggle for Racial Equality*. Oxford; New York: Oxford University Press, 2004.

Klatch, Rebecca E. *A Generation Divided: The New Left, The New Right, and the 1960s* . Berkeley: University of California Press, 1999.

Klauber, Bruce H. *World of Gene Krupa: That Legendary Drummin' Man*. Ventura, CA: Pathfinder Pub., 1990.

Klein, Maury. *Rainbow's End: The Crash of 1929*. Oxford; New York: Oxford University Press, 2001.

Klinkowitz, Jerome. *Listen, Gerry Mulligan: An Aural Narrative in Jazz*. New York: Schirmer Books, 1991.

Knapp, Jeffrey. "Sacred Songs Popular Prices": Secularization in The Jazz Singer," *Critical Inquiry* 34.2 (Winter 2008): 313–335.

Knauer, Wolfram. "'Simulated Improvisation' in Duke Ellington's 'Black, Brown and Beige.'" *The Black Perspective in Music* 18.1/2 (1990): 20–38.

Knight, Alfred H. *The Life of the Law: The People and Cases That Have Shaped our Society, from King Alfred to Rodney King*. Oxford; New York: Oxford University Press, 1998.

Knight, Arthur. *Disintegrating the Musical: Black Performance and American Musical Film*. Durham, NC: Duke University Press, 2002.

Kofsky, Frank. "The State of Jazz." The Black Perspective in Music 5.1 (Spring 1977): 44–66.

_____. "Indecent Coverage." *The Threepenny Review* 1 (Winter - Spring 1980): 21–22.

_____. *John Coltrane and the Jazz Revolution of the 1960s*. New York: Pathfinder Press, 1998.

Koger, Terry S., Mark Martin, Gary Richardson, Hassan Sabree, Anthony Wade, and Dominique-René de Lerma. "Fifty Years of "Down Beat" Solo Jazz Transcriptions: A Register." *Black Music Research Journal* 5 (1985): 43–79.

Köhler, Joachim, and Ronald Taylor. *Nietzsche and Wagner: A Lesson in Subjugation*. New Haven, CT: Yale University Press, 1998.

Kolosky, Walter. *Follow Your Heart: John McLaughlin Song by Song: A Listener's Guide*. Cary, NC: Abstract Logix Books, 2010.

Konkobo, Christophe. "Dark Continent, Dark Stage: Body Performance in Colonial Theatre and Cinema." *Journal of Black Studies* 40.6 (July 2010): 1094–1106.

Korall, Burt. *Drummin' Men: The Heartbeat of Jazz, The Swing Years.* New York: Schirmer Books; Toronto: Collier Macmillan Canada; New York: Maxwell Macmillan International, 1990.

_____. *Drummin' Men: The Heartbeat of Jazz: The Bebop Years.* Oxford; New York: Oxford University Press, 2002.

Koven, Mikel J. *Blaxploitation Films.* Harpenden [Hertfordshire]: Kamera, 2010.

Kreiss, Daniel. "Performing the Past to Claim the Future: Sun Ra and the Afro-Future Underground, 1954–1968." *African American Review* 45.1/2 (Spring/Summer 2012): 197–203.

Krims, Adam. *Music and Urban Geography.* New York: Routledge, 2007.

Kroll, Andy. "The African American Jobs Crisis and the New Jim Crow." *Race, Poverty & the Environment* 18.2, Autumn Awakening: From Civil Rights to Economic Justice (2011): 49–52.

Krugler, David F. *The Voice of America and the Domestic Propa`ganda Battles, 1945–1953.* Columbia: University of Missouri Press, 2000.

Kun, Josh, and Laura Pulido. *Black and Brown in Los Angeles: Beyond Conflict and Coalition.* Berkeley: University of California Press, 2013.

Kuru, Ahmet T. "Secularism, State Policies, and Muslims in Europe: Analyzing French Exceptionalism." *Comparative Politics* 41.1 (October 2008): 1–19.

Lajoie, Steve. *Gil Evans & Miles Davis: Historic Collaborations: An Analysis of Selected Gil Evans Works, 1957-1962.* [Rottenburg am Neckar]: Advance Music, 2003.

Lambert, Philip. *The Music of Charles Ives.* New Haven: Yale University Press, 1997.

Landau, Emily Epstein. *Spectacular Wickedness: Sex, Race, and Memory in Storyville, New Orleans.* Baton Rouge: Louisiana State University Press, 2013.

Landy, Elliott. *Woodstock Vision: The Spirit of a Generation.* New York: Backbeat Books, 2009. Lang, Michael, and Holly George-Warren. *The Road to Woodstock.* New York: Ecco, 2009.

LaNier, Carlotta Walls, and Lisa Frazier Page. *A Mighty Long Way: My Journey to Justice at Little Rock Central High School.* New York: One World Trade Paperbacks, 2010.

Laplace, Michel. *Roger Guerin, or The Jazz Trumpet: 1946-1988.* Menden: Jazzfreund, 1993.

Larson, Steve. "Musical Forces, Melodic Expectation, and Jazz Melody." *Music Perception: An Interdisciplinary Journal* 19.3 (Spring 2002): 351–385.

_____. "Composition versus Improvisation?" *Journal of Music Theory* 49.2 (Fall 2005): 241–275.

Laubich, Arnold, and Ray Spencer. *Art Tatum, A Guide to His Recorded Music.* [Newark, NJ]: Institute of Jazz Studies, Rutgers University; Metuchen, NJ: Scarecrow Press, 1982.

Lavender, III, Isiah. *Race in American Science Fiction.* Bloomington: Indiana University Press, 2011.

_____. *Black and Brown Planets: The Politics of Race in Science Fiction.* Jackson: University Press of Mississippi, 2014.

Lawlor, William. *Beat Culture: Icons, Lifestyles, and Impact.* Santa Barbara, CA: ABC-CLIO, 2005.

Lawrence, A. H. *Duke Ellington and His World: A Biography.* New York: Routledge, 2001.

Lawrence, Novotny. *Blaxploitation Films of the 1970s: Blackness and Genre.* New York: Routledge, 2008.

Leblon, Bernard, and Centre de recherches tsiganes (Université René Descartes). *Gypsies and Flamenco: The Emergence of the Art of Flamenco in Andalusia.* Hatfield: University of Hertfordshire Press, 2003.

Lee, Benjamin. "Avant-Garde Poetry as Subcultural Practice: Mailer and Di Prima's Hipsters." *New Literary History* 41.4, What Is an Avant-Garde? (Autumn 2010): 775–794.

Lee, Christopher J. *Making a World After Empire: The Bandung Moment and its Political Afterlives.* Athens: Ohio University Press, 2010.

Lee, David. *The Battle of the Five Spot: Ornette Coleman and the New York Jazz Field.* Toronto, ON: Mercury Press, 2006.

Lee, William F. *Jazz Saxophone Players: A Biographical Handbook.* Silver Spring, MD: Beckham Publications Group, 2010.

Lees, Gene. *Cats of Any Color: Jazz Black and White*. New York: Oxford University Press, 1994.

_____. *Leader of the Band: The Life of Woody Herman*. Bridgewater, NJ: Replica Books, 2000.

_____. *Portrait of Johnny: The Life of John Herndon Mercer*. New York: Pantheon Books, 2004.

Leininger-Miller, Theresa A. *New Negro Artists in Paris: African American Painters and Sculptors in the City of Light, 1922–1934*. New Brunswick, NJ: Rutgers University Press, 2001.

Leonard, Herman, and Philippe Carles. *The Eye of Jazz*. London; New York: Viking, 1989.

Leonard, Herman, David Wallace Houston, and Jenny Bagert. *Jazz, Giants, and Journeys: The Photography of Herman Leonard*. London: Scala; Easthampton, MA: Distributed in USA by Antique Collectors' Club, 2006.

Leonard, Neil. "The Worlds of Andre Hodeir." *American Quarterly* 15.2, Part 1 (Summer 1963): 210–213.

_____. *Jazz: Myth and Religion*. New York: Oxford University Press, 1987.

Lerfeldt, Hans Henrik, and Thorbjørn Sjøgren. *Chet: The Discography of Chesney Henry Baker*. Copenhagen, Denmark: Distribution, Tiderne Skifter Publishers, 1985.

Lester, James. *Too Marvelous for Words: The Life and Genius of Art Tatum*. New York: Oxford University Press, 1994.

Leuchtenburg, William E. *Franklin D. Roosevelt and the New Deal, 1932–1940*. New York: Harper & Row, 1963.

_____. *The New Deal: A Documentary History*. Columbia: University of South Carolina Press, 1968.

Levering Lewis, David. "Failing to Know Martin Luther King, Jr." *The Journal of American History* 78.1 (June 1991): 81–85.

Levine, Andrea. "'The (Jewish) White Negro': Norman Mailer's Racial Bodies." *Melus* 28.2, Haunted by History (Summer 2003): 59–81.

Levine, Lawrence W. *Highbrow/Lowbrow: The Emergence of Cultural Hierarchy in America*. Cambridge, MA: Harvard University Press, 1988.

_____. "Jazz and American Culture." *The Journal of American Folklore* 102.403 (January–March 1989): 6–22.

Levinson, Peter J. *Trumpet Blues: The Life of Harry James*. New York: Oxford University Press, 1999.

Levitt, Jeremy I., & Matthew C. Whitaker. *Hurricane Katrina: America's Unnatural Disaster*. Lincoln: University of Nebraska Press, 2009.

Levy, Alan Howard. *Tackling Jim Crow: Racial Segregation in Professional Football*. Jefferson, NC: McFarland & Co, 2003.

Lewis, Barbara Brewster. "Women Crossing Boundaries: A Field Report on the Paris Conference 'African Americans and Europe.'" *African American Review* 26.3, Fiction Issue (Autumn 1992): 515–519.

Lewis, Catherine M, and J. Richard Lewis. *Jim Crow America: A Documentary History*. Fayetteville: University of Arkansas Press, 2009.

Lewis, George. *A Power Stronger Than Itself: The AACM and American Experimental Music*. Chicago: University of Chicago Press, 2008.

Lewis, Mark W. *The Diffusion of Black Gospel Music in Postmodern Denmark: How Mission and Music are Combining to Affect Christian Renewal*. Lexington, KY: Emeth Press, 2010.

Lewis, Robert M. *From Traveling Show to Vaudeville: Theatrical Spectacle in America, 1830–1910*. Baltimore, MD: Johns Hopkins University Press, 2003.

Liberman, Peter. "Punitiveness and U.S. Elite Support for the 1991 Persian Gulf War." *The Journal of Conflict Resolution* 51.1 (February 2007): 3–32.

Lieb, Sandra R. *Mother of the Blues: A Study of Ma Rainey*. Amherst: University of Massachusetts Press, 1981.

Lincoln, Bruce. *Religion, Empire, and Torture: The Case of Achaemenian Persia, With a Postscript on Abu Ghraib*. Chicago: University of Chicago Press, 2007.

Lindsey, Treva B . " If You Look in My Life: Love, Hip-Hop Soul, and Contemporary African American Womanhood." *African American Review* 46.1, Special issue: Hip Hop and the Literary (Spring 2013): 87–99 .

Ling, Huping. *Chinese Chicago: Race, Transnational Migration, and Community Since 1870.* Stanford, CA: Stanford University Press, 2012.

Ling, Peter J, and Sharon Monteith. *Gender and the Civil Rights Movement.* New Brunswick, NJ: Rutgers University Press, 2004.

Lion, Jean Pierre. *Bix: The Definitive Biography of a Jazz Legend: Leon "Bix" Beiderbecke (1903–1931).* New York: Continuum, 2005.

Lipset, Seymour Martin. *American Exceptionalism: A Double-edged Sword.* New York: W. W. Norton, 1996.

Litweiler, John. *The Freedom Principle: Jazz after 1958.* New York: W. Morrow, 1984.

_____. *Ornette Coleman: A Critical Biography.* London: Quartet, 1990.

_____. *Ornette Coleman: A Harmolodic Life.* New York: W. Morrow, 1992.

Livingston, Carolyn, and Dawn Elizabeth Smith. *Rhode Island's Musical Heritage: An Exploration.* Sterling Heights, MI: Harmonie Park Press, 2008.

Lock, Graham. *Blutopia: Visions of the Future and Revisions of the Past in the Work of Sun Ra, Duke Ellington, and Anthony Braxton.* Durham: Duke University Press, 1999.

Loevy, Robert D. *To End All Segregation: The Politics of the Passage of the Civil Rights Act of 1964.* Lanham, MD: University Press of America, 1990.

_____. *The Civil Rights Act of 1964: The Passage of the Law That Ended Racial Segregation.* Albany, NY: State University of New York Press, 1997.

Lomax, Alan. *Mister Jelly Roll: The Fortunes of Jelly Roll Morton, New Orleans Creole and "Inventor of Jazz."* Berkeley: University of California Press, 2001.

Long, Alecia P. *The Great Southern Babylon: Sex, Race, and Respectability in New Orleans, 1865–1920.* Baton Rouge: LSU Press, 2005.

_____. "Poverty Is the New Prostitution: Race, Poverty, and Public Housing in Post-Katrina New Orleans." *The Journal of American History* 94.3, Through the Eye of Katrina: The Past as Prologue? (December 2007): 795–803.

Longstreet, Stephen. *Storyville to Harlem: Fifty Years in the Jazz Scene.* New Brunswick: Rutgers University Press, 1986.

Looker, Benjamin. *BAG: "Point from Which Creation Begins": The Black Artists' Group of St. Louis.* St. Louis: Missouri Historical Society Press, [Columbia, MO]: Distributed by University of Missouri Press, 2004.

Lopes, Paul. "Diffusion and Syncretism: The Modern Jazz Tradition." *The Annals of the American Academy of Political and Social Science* 566, The Social Diffusion of Ideas and Things (November 1999): 25–36.

Lorch, Catrin. "Drawings of Removal." *Afterall: A Journal of Art, Context and Enquiry* 10 (Autumn/Winter 2004): 76–80.

Los Angeles (CA). Grand Avenue Committee. *Reimagining Grand Avenue: Creating a Center for Los Angeles.* Los Angeles: Grand Avenue Committee, 2005.

Los Angeles Times (Firm). *Understanding the Riots: Los Angeles before and after the Rodney King Case.* Los Angeles: Los Angeles Times, 1992.

Louis, Joe, Edna Rust, and Art Rust. *Joe Louis: My Life.* Hopewell, NJ: Ecco Press, 1997.

Loukides, Paul, and Linda K. Fuller. *Beyond the Stars: Stock Characters in American Popular Film.* Bowling Green, OH: Bowling Green University Popular Press, 1990.

Love, Monifa. "Listening to Jimi Hendrix Near Lafayette Park." *The Massachusetts Review* 43.4 (Winter 2002/2003): 616–617.

Lumpkins, Charles L. *American Pogrom: The East St. Louis Race Riot and Black Politics.* Athens, OH: Ohio University Press, 2008.

Lusane, Clarence. *The Black History of the White House.* San Francisco, CA: City Lights Books, 2011.

Lyne, Bill. "God's Black Revolutionary Mouth: James Baldwin's Black Radicalism." *Science & Society* 74.1 (January 2010): 12–36.

Lyons, Leonard. *The Great Jazz Pianists: Speaking of their Lives and Music.* New York: W. Morrow, 1983.

Macdonald, Marie-Paule. *Jimi Hendrix: Soundscapes*. London, UK: Reaktion Books, 2016.

Machlin, Paul S. *Stride, The Music of Fats Waller*. Boston, MA: Twayne Publishers, 1985.

Macías, Anthony. "California's Composer Laureate: Gerald Wilson, Jazz Music, and Black-Mexican Connections." *Boom: A Journal of California* 3.2 (Summer 2013): 34–51.

Mackey, Nathaniel. "Some Thoughts on 'Fusion.'" *The Threepenny Review* 1 (Winter–Spring 1980): 23–24.

MacKinnon, Kenneth. *The Politics of Popular Representation: Reagan, Thatcher, AIDS, and the Movies*. Rutherford: London; Cranbury, NJ: Fairleigh Dickinson University Press, 1992.

Macksey, Richard, and Frank E. Moorer. *Richard Wright, A Collection of Critical Essays*. Englewood Cliffs, NJ: Prentice-Hall, 1984.

Maconie, Robin. *The Works of Karlheinz Stockhausen*. London; New York: Oxford University Press, 1976.

_____. *Other Planets: The Music of Karlheinz Stockhausen*. Lanham, MD: Scarecrow Press, 2005.

Madhubuti, Haki R. *Why L.A. Happened: Implications of the '92 Los Angeles Rebellion*. Chicago: Third World Press, 1993.

Madura Ward-Steinman, Patrice. "Musical Training and Compensation in the Big Band Era: A Case Study of Madura's Danceland from 1930-1950." *Journal of Historical Research in Music Education* 24.2 (April 2003): 164–177.

Magee, Gayle Sherwood. *Charles Ives Reconsidered*. Urbana: University of Illinois Press, 2008.

Magee, Jeffrey. "Fletcher Henderson, Composer: A Counter-Entry to the 'International Dictionary of Black Composers.'" *Black Music Research Journal* 19.1 (Spring 1999): 61–70.

_____. "Before Louis: When Fletcher Henderson Was the 'Paul Whiteman of the Race.'" *American Music* 18.4 (Winter 2000): 391–425.

_____. "Irving Berlin's "Blue Skies": Ethnic Affiliations and Musical Transformations." *The Musical Quarterly* 84.4 (Winter 2000): 537–580.

_____. "'Everybody Step': Irving Berlin, Jazz, and Broadway in the 1920s." *Journal of the American Musicological Society* 59.3 (Fall 2006): 697–732.

_____. *The Uncrowned King of Swing: Fletcher Henderson and Big Band Jazz*. Oxford: Oxford University Press, 2010.

Magee, Michael. *Emancipating Pragmatism: Emerson, Jazz, and Experimental Writing*. Tuscaloosa: University of Alabama Press, 2004.

Maggin, Donald L. *Stan Getz: A Life in Jazz*. New York: W. Morrow & Co., 1996.

Majer, Gerald. *The Velvet Lounge: On Late Chicago Jazz*. New York: Columbia University Press, 2005.

Malcolm, Douglas. "'Jazz America': Jazz and African American Culture in Jack Kerouac's 'On the Road.'" *Contemporary Literature* 40.1 (Spring 1999): 85–110.

Mandel, Howard. *Future Jazz*. Oxford; New York: Oxford University Press, 1999.

_____. *Miles, Ornette, Cecil: Jazz Beyond Jazz: How Miles Davis, Ornette Coleman, and Cecil Taylor Revolutionized the World of Jazz*. London [u.a.]: Routledge, 2008.

Manganelli, Kimberly Snyder, and American Literatures Initiative. *Transatlantic Spectacles of Race: The Tragic Mulatta and the Tragic Muse*. New Brunswick, NJ: Rutgers University Press, 2012.

Manning, Frankie, and Cynthia R. Millman. *Frankie Manning: Ambassador of Lindy Hop*. Philadelphia: Temple University Press, 2007.

Manuel, Carme. "A Ghost in the Expressionist Jungle of O'Neill's 'The Emperor Jones.'" *African American Review* 39.1/2 (Spring–Summer 2005): 67–85.

Marable, Lawrance, Steven Louis Isoardi, and University of California, Los Angeles. Oral History Program. *Central Avenue Sounds Oral History Transcript, 1996: Lawrance Marable*. Los Angeles: Oral History Program, University of California, Los Angeles, 2001.

Marable, Manning. *Black America: Multicultural Democracy in the Age of Clarence Thomas, David Duke and LA Uprisings*. Westfield, NJ: Open Media, 1992.

Marcus, Kenneth H. "Living the Los Angeles Renaissance: A Tale of Two Black Composers." *The Journal of African American History* 91.1, The African American Experience in the Western States (Winter 2006): 55–72.

Marcy, Kirk. "Vocal Jazz: "What's in Your Folder?" Balanced Programming for Vocal Jazz Ensembles." *The Choral Journal* 51.10 (May 2011): 56–59.

Marek, George R. *Richard Strauss: The Life of a Non-Hero*. New York: Simon and Schuster, 1967.

Margolick, David. *Beyond Glory: Joe Louis vs. Max Schmeling and a World on the Brink*. New York: Vintage Books, 2006.

_____. *Elizabeth and Hazel: Two Women of Little Rock*. New Haven, CT: Yale University Press, 2011.

Margolies, Edward. *The Art of Richard Wright*. Carbondale: Southern Illinois University Press, 1969.

Marmorstein, Gary. "Central Avenue Jazz: Los Angeles Black Music of the Forties." *Southern California Quarterly* 70.4 (Winter 1988): 415–426.

Marovich, Robert M. *A City Called Heaven: Chicago and the Birth of Gospel Music*. Urbana: University of Illinois Press, 2015.

Marquis, Donald M. *In Search of Buddy Bolden: First Man of Jazz*. Baton Rouge: Louisiana State University Press, 1978.

Marsh, Graham, Glyn Callingham, and Felix Cromey. *Blue Note: The Album Cover Art*. San Francisco, CA: Chronicle Books, 1991.

Marszalek, John F. *A Black Congressman in the Age of Jim Crow: South Carolina's George Washington Murray*. Gainesville: University Press of Florida, 2006.

Martin, Henry. "Balancing Composition and Improvisation in James P. Johnson's 'Carolina Shout.'" *Journal of Music Theory* 49.2 (Fall 2005): 277–299.

_____. *"Ellington Uptown": Duke Ellington, James P. Johnson, & The Birth of Concert Jazz*. Ann Arbor: University of Michigan Press, 2009.

Marvin, Elizabeth West, and Richard Hermann. *Concert Music, Rock, and Jazz since 1945: Essays and Analytical Studies*. Rochester, NY: University of Rochester Press, 1995.

Marvin, Thomas F. "'Preachin' the Blues': Bessie Smith's Secular Religion and Alice Walker's The Color Purple." *African American Review* 28.3 (Autumn 1994): 411–421.

Massing, Paul W. "Communist References to the Voice of America." *The Public Opinion Quarterly* 16.4, Special Issue on International Communications Research (Winter 1952–1953): 618–622.

Mathieson, Kenny. *Cookin': Hard Bop and Soul Jazz, 1954-65*. Edinburgh: Canongate, 2002.

Matory, James Lorand. *Black Atlantic Religion: Tradition, Transnationalism, and Matriarchy in the Afro-Brazilian Candomblé*. Princeton, NJ: Princeton University Press, 2005.

Matus, Jill L. *Toni Morrison*. Manchester; New York: Manchester University Press, 1998.

Matviko, John W. *The American President in Popular Culture*. Westport, CT: Greenwood Press, 2005.

Mawer, Deborah. *Darius Milhaud: Modality & Structure in Music of the 1920s*. Aldershot, England: Scolar Press; Brookfield, Vt.: Ashgate Pub. Co., 1997.

_____. *French Music and Jazz in Conversation: From Debussy to Brubeck*. Cambridge; New York: Cambridge University Press, 2014.

Maxile, Jr., Horace J. "Extensions on a Black Musical Tropology: From Trains to the Mothership (and Beyond)." *Journal of Black Studies* 42.4 (May 2011): 593–608.

Mazor, Barry. *Meeting Jimmie Rodgers: How America's Original Roots Music Hero Changed the Pop Sounds of a Century*. Oxford; New York: Oxford University Press, 2009.

McAlister, Melani. "One Black Allah: The Middle East in the Cultural Politics of African American Liberation, 1955–1970." *American Quarterly* 51.3 (September 1999): 622–656.

McBride, Dwight A. *James Baldwin Now*. New York: New York University Press, 1999.

McBride, James. *Kill 'Em and Leave: Searching for James Brown and the American Soul*. New York: Spiegel & Grau, 2016.

McCaffrey, Enda. *The Gay Republic: Sexuality, Citizenship and Subversion in France*. Aldershot, England; Burlington, VT: Ashgate, 2005.

McCann, Paul. *Race, Music, and National Identity: Images of Jazz in American Fiction, 1920-1960*. Madison, NJ: Fairleigh Dickinson University Press, 2008.

McCarren, Felicia M. *French Moves: The Cultural Politics of Le Hip Hop*. New York: Oxford University Press, 2012.

Bibliography

McCarthy, Albert J. *The Trumpet in Jazz*. London: Citizen Press, 1945.

McCartney, John T. *Black Power Ideologies: An Essay in African-American Political Thought*. Philadelphia: Temple University Press, 1992.

McClellan, Lawrence. *The Later Swing Era, 1942 to 1955*. Westport, Connecticut: Greenwood, 2004.

McClendon, William H. "Black Music: Sound and Feeling for Black Liberation." *The Black Scholar* 7.5 Black Popular Culture (January–February 1976): 20–25.

McCrisken, Trevor B. *American Exceptionalism and the Legacy of Vietnam: US Foreign Policy Since 1974*. Basingstoke, Hampshire; New York: Palgrave Macmillan, 2003.

McDonald, Michael Bruce. "Traning the Nineties, or the Present Relevance of John Coltrane's Music of Theophany and Negation." *African American Review* 29.2, Special Issues on The Music (Summer 1995): 275–282.

McDonnell, Janet A. *The Dispossession of the American Indian, 1887-1934*. Bloomington: Indiana University Press, 1991.

McElvaine, Robert S. *The Depression and New Deal: A History in Documents*. New York: Oxford University Press, 2000.

McEvoy-Levy, Siobhán. *American Exceptionalism and US Foreign Policy: Public Diplomacy at the End of the Cold War*. Houndmills, Basingstoke, Hampshire; New York: Palgrave, 2001.

McGee, Kristin A. *Some Liked It Hot: Jazz Women in Film and Television, 1928–1959*. Middletown, CT: Wesleyan University Press, 2009.

McGuire, Danielle L. *At the Dark End of the Street: Black Women, Rape, and Resistance- A New History of the Civil Rights Movement from Rosa Parks to the Rise of Black Power*. New York: Alfred A. Knopf, 2010.

McIlwain, Charlton D, and Stephen M. Caliendo. "Black Messages, White Messages: The Differential Use of Racial Appeals by Black and White Candidates." *Journal of Black Studies* 39.5 (May 2009): 732–743 .

McKeown, Adam. *Chinese Migrant Networks and Cultural Change: Peru, Chicago, Hawaii, 1900–1936*. Chicago: University of Chicago Press, 2001.

McKinney, Devin. *Magic Circles: The Beatles in Dream and History*. Cambridge, MA: Harvard University Press, 2003.

McLaughlin, Malcolm. *Power, Community, and Racial Killing in East St. Louis*. New York: Palgrave Macmillan, 2005.

McMahon, Eileen M. *What Parish Are You From?: A Chicago Irish Community and Race Relations*. Lexington: University Press of Kentucky, 1995.

McMahon, Joseph H. *Humans Being: The World of Jean-Paul Sartre*. Chicago: University of Chicago Press, 1971.

McMichael, Robert K. "'We Insist-Freedom Now!': Black Moral Authority, Jazz, and the Changeable Shape of Whiteness." *American Music* 16.4 (Winter 1998): 375–416.

McNally, Karen. "'Where's the Spinning Wheel?' Frank Sinatra and Working-Class Alienation in 'Young at Heart.'" *Journal of American Studies* 41.1 (April 2007): 115–133.

_____. *When Frankie Went to Hollywood: Frank Sinatra and American Male Identity*. Urbana: University of Illinois Press, 2008.

McNeil, John. The Art of Jazz Trumpet. Brooklyn, NY: Gerard & Sarzin, 1999.

McRae, Donald. *In Black & White: The Untold Story of Joe Louis and Jesse Owens*. London: Simon & Schuster, 2014.

McShane, Larry. "In Memoriam: Max Roach (1924-2007): Jazz Master Max Roach Dies at Eighty-Three." *The Black Scholar* 37.3, Black Social Agenda (Fall 2007): 50–51.

Meadows, Eddie S. *Bebop to Cool: Context, Ideology, and Musical Identity*. Westport, CT: Greenwood Press, 2003.

_____. "Clifford Brown in Los Angeles." *Black Music Research Journal* 31.1 (Spring 2011): 45–63.

Meeder, Christopher. *Jazz: The Basics*. New York: Routledge, 2008.

Megill, Donald, and Richard S. Demory. *Introduction to Jazz History*. Englewood Cliffs, New Jersey: Prentice-Hall, 1984.

Meier, Marco. *All That Funk James Brown, Herbie Hancock, George Clinton.* Zürich TA-Media AG 1999.

Mellow, James R. *Nathaniel Hawthorne in His Times.* Boston: Houghton Mifflin, 1980.

Melville, Herman. *The Letters of Herman Melville.* New Haven: Yale University Press, 1960.

Melville, Herman, and Douglas Robillard. *The Poems of Herman Melville.* Kent, OH: Kent State University Press, 2000.

Mercer, Johnny. *Too Marvelous For Words: The Magic of Johnny Mercer.* Miami, Florida: Warner Bros., 1985.

Mercer, Johnny, Bob Bach, and Ginger Mercer. *Johnny Mercer: The Life, Times, and Song Lyrics of Our Huckleberry Friend.* Atlanta, GA: Cherokee Pub., 2009.

Mercer, Michelle. *Footprints: The Life and Work of Wayne Shorter .* New York: J. P. Tarcher/ Penguin, 2004 .

Merk, Frederick, and Lois Bannister Merk. *Manifest Destiny and Mission in American History: A Reinterpretation.* Cambridge, MA: Harvard University Press, 1995.

Merod, Jim, and Frank Strazzeri. "Paint Another Picture: An Interview with Frank Strazzeri." *Boundary 2* 22.2, Jazz as a Cultural Archive (Summer 1995): 191–206.

Meron, Theodor. "The Geneva Conventions as Customary Law." *The American Journal of International Law* 81.2 (April 1987): 348–370.

Metzer, David. "'Spurned Love': Eroticism and Abstraction in the Early Works of Aaron Copland." *The Journal of Musicology* 15.4 (Autumn 1997): 417–443 .

Meyer, Gerald. "Frank Sinatra: The Popular Front and an American Icon." *Science & Society* 66.3 (Fall 2002): 311–335.

Meyer, Marshall W. "Police Shootings at Minorities: The Case of Los Angeles." *The Annals of the American Academy of Political and Social Science* 452, The Police and Violence (November 1980): 98–110.

Meyerowitz, Joanne J. *Not June Cleaver: Women and Gender in Postwar America, 1945–1960.* Philadelphia: Temple University Press, 1994.

Mielke, Randall G. *Road to Box Office: The Seven Film Comedies of Bing Crosby, Bob Hope, and Dorothy Lamour, 1940-1962.* Jefferson, NC: McFarland & Co., 1997.

Miller, Doug. "The Moan within the Tone: African Retentions in Rhythm and Blues Saxophone Style in Afro-American Popular Music." *Popular Music* 14.2 (May 1995): 155–174.

Miller, Keith D. "Composing Martin Luther King, Jr." *PMLA* 105.1, Special Topic: African and African American Literature (January 1990): 70–82.

Miller, Marc H., Donald Bogle, and Queens Museum of Art, Eds. *Louis Armstrong: A Cultural Legacy.* Seattle: Queens Museum of Art, New York in association with University of Washington Press, 1994.

Miller, Monica L. *Slaves to Fashion: Black Dandyism and the Styling of Black Diasporic Identity.* Durham, NC: Duke University Press, 2009.

Miller, Terry E., and Andrew C. Shahriari. *World Music: A Global Journey.* New York: Routledge, 2009.

Mills, David, and Dave Marsh. *George Clinton and P-Funk: An Oral History.* New York: Avon Books, 1998.

Mingo, Anne Marie, and Gwendolyn Zoharah Simmons. "Expanding the Narrative: Exploring New Aspects of the Civil Rights Movement Fifty Years Later." *Fire!!!,* 2.2, (2013): 1–4.

Mingus, Charles. *Beneath the Underdog; His World as Composed by Mingus .* New York, Knopf, 1971 .

Mitchell, Broadus. *Depression Decade; From New Era through New Deal, 1929–1941.* New York, Rinehart, 1947.

Mitchell, Greg. *Tricky Dick and the Pink Lady: Richard Nixon vs. Helen Gahagan Douglas—Sexual Politics and the Red Scare, 1950.* New York: Random House, 1998.

Moehn, Frederick. "A Carioca Blade Runner, or How Percussionist Marcos Suzano Turned the Brazilian Tambourine into a Drum Kit, and Other Matters of (Politically) Correct Music Making." *Ethnomusicology* 53.2 (Spring/Summer 2009): 277–307.

Mokhtari, Shadi. *After Abu Ghraib: Exploring Human Rights in America and the Middle East.* Cambridge [UK]; New York: Cambridge University Press, 2009.

Monk, Craig. *Writing the Lost Generation: Expatriate Autobiography and American Modernism*. Iowa City: University of Iowa Press, 2008.

Monson, Ingrid. "Monk Meets SNCC." *Black Music Research Journal* 19.2, New Perspectives on Thelonious Monk (Autumn 1999): 187–200.

————. *Freedom Sounds: Civil Rights Call Out to Jazz and Africa*. Oxford; New York: Oxford University Press, 2007.

Montell, William Lynwood. *Singing the Glory Down: Amateur Gospel Music in South Central Kentucky, 1900–1990*. Lexington: University Press of Kentucky, 1991.

Moon, Krystyn R. *Yellowface: Creating the Chinese in American Popular Music and Performance, 1850s–1920s*. New Brunswick, NJ: Rutgers University Press, 2005.

Mooney, Amy M. "Representing Race: Disjunctures in the Work of Archibald J. Motley, Jr." *Art Institute of Chicago Museum Studies* 24.2, African Americans in Art: Selections from The Art Institute of Chicago (1999): 162–179+262–265.

Moore, John. "'The Hieroglyphics of Love': The Torch Singers and Interpretation." *Popular Music* 8.1, *Performance* (January 1989): 31–58.

Morales, Donald M. "The Pervasive Force of Music in African, Caribbean, and African American Drama." *Research in African Literatures* 34.2 (Summer 2003): 145–154.

Morant, Kesha M. "Language in Action: Funk Music as the Critical Voice of a Post-Civil Rights Movement Counterculture." *Journal of Black Studies* 42.1 (January 2011): 71–82.

Moreno, Jairo. "Body 'n' Soul?: Voice and Movement in Keith Jarrett's Pianism." *The Musical Quarterly* 83.1 (Spring 1999): 75–92.

Morgan, Dan. *Rising in the West: The True Story of an "Okie" Family from the Great Depression through the Reagan Years*. New York: Knopf: Distributed by Random House, 1992.

Morgan, Edmund S., and Oscar Handlin. *The Puritan Dilemma: The Story of John Winthrop*. Boston: Little, Brown, and Company, 1958.

Morgan, Elmo. "Noise/Funk: Fo' Real Black Theatre on 'Da Great White Way.'" *African American Review* 31.4, Contemporary Theatre Issue (Winter 1997): 677–686.

Morgan, Francesca. *Women and Patriotism in Jim Crow America*. Chapel Hill: University of North Carolina Press, 2005.

Morgan, Jo-Ann. *Uncle Tom's Cabin as Visual Culture*. Columbia: University of Missouri Press, 2007.

Morrill, Dexter. *Woody Herman: A Guide to the Big Band Recordings, 1936–1987*. New York; London: Greenwood, 1991.

Morrison, Toni. *Playing in the Dark: Whiteness and the Literary Imagination*. Cambridge, MA: Harvard University Press, 1992.

————. *Jazz*. London: Vintage Digital, 2014.

Morrison, Toni, and Danille Kathleen Taylor-Guthrie. *Conversations with Toni Morrison*. Jackson: University Press of Mississippi, 1994.

Morton, Jelly Roll, and James Dapogny. *Ferdinand "Jelly Roll" Morton: The Collected Piano Music*. Washington, D.C.: Smithsonian Institution, 1982.

Morton, John Fass. *Backstory in Blue: Ellington at Newport '56*. New Brunswick, NJ: Rutgers University Press, 2008.

Moskowitz, David V. *The Words and Music of Jimi Hendrix*. Santa Barbara: Praeger, 2010.

Moten, Fred. *In the Break: The Aesthetics of the Black Radical Tradition*. Minneapolis: University of Minnesota Press, 2003.

Motley, Jr., Archibald John, Richard J. Powell, Nasher Museum of Art at Duke University, Amon Carter Museum of American Art, Los Angeles County Museum of Art, Chicago Cultural Center, and Whitney Museum of American Art. *Archibald Motley: Jazz Age Modernist*. Durham, NC: Nasher Museum of Art at Duke University, 2014.

Muir, Peter C. *Long Lost Blues: Popular Blues in America, 1850–1920*. Urbana: University of Illinois Press, 2010.

Murchison, Gayle. "Mary Lou Williams's Hymn "Black Christ of the Andes (St. Martin de Porres):" Vatican II, Civil Rights, and Jazz as Sacred Music." *The Musical Quarterly* 86.4 (Winter 2002): 591–629.

Murphy, Brenda. "McTeague's Dream and 'The Emperor Jones': O'Neill's Move from Naturalism to Modernism." *The Eugene O'Neill Review* 17.1/2 (Spring/Fall 1993): 21–29.

Murray, Charles A. *American Exceptionalism: An Experiment in History*. Washington, D.C.: AEI Press, 2013.

Murray, Charles Shaar. *Crosstown Traffic: Jimi Hendrix and Post-War Pop*. London: Faber, 1989.

Musser, Charles. "Why Did Negroes Love Al Jolson and The Jazz Singer?: Melodrama, Blackface and Cosmopolitan Theatrical Culture." *Film History* 23.2, Black Representations (2011): 196–222.

Myler, Patrick. *Ring of Hate: The Brown Bomber and Hitler's Hero, Joe Louis v. Max Schmeling and the Bitter Propaganda War*. Edinburgh: Mainstream, 2006.

Nabokov, Peter. *Native American Testimony: A Chronicle of Indian-White Relations from Prophecy to the Present, 1492–1992*. New York: Viking, 1991.

Nadel, Alan. *Invisible Criticism: Ralph Ellison and the American Canon*. Iowa City: University of Iowa Press, 1988.

––––––––. *Flatlining on the Field of Dreams: Cultural Narratives in the Films of President Reagan's America*. New Brunswick, NJ: Rutgers University Press, 1997.

Nama, Adilifu. *Black Space: Imagining Race in Science Fiction Film*. Austin: University of Texas Press, 2008.

Nanry, Charles. *American Music: From Storyville to Woodstock*. New Brunswick, NJ, Transaction Books; distributed by E.P. Dutton, 1972.

Naremore, James. *"Uptown Folk: Blackness and Entertainment in Cabin in the Sky." An Invention Without a Future: Essays on Cinema*. Berkeley: University of California Press, 2014.

Nathan, David. *The Soulful Divas: Personal Portraits of Over a Dozen Divine Divas, from Nina Simone, Aretha Franklin & Diana Ross to Patti LaBelle, Whitney Houston & Janet Jackson*. New York: Billboard Books, 1999.

Neal, Jocelyn R. *The Songs of Jimmie Rodgers: A Legacy in Country Music*. Bloomington: Indiana University Press, 2009.

Neal, Larry, Amiri Baraka, and Michael Schwartz. *Visions of a Liberated Future: Black Arts Movement Writings*. New York: Thunder's Mouth Press; St. Paul, MN: Distributed by Consortium Book Sales and Distribution, 1989.

Needs, Kris. *George Clinton & The Cosmic Odyssey of the P-Funk Empire*. London: Omnibus Press, 2014.

Nelson, Marilyn, and Jerry Pinkney. *Sweethearts of Rhythm: The Story of the Greatest All-girl Swing Band in the World*. New York: Dial Books, 2009.

Neto, Luiz Costa-Lima, Laura Coimbra, and Tom Moore. *The Experimental Music of Hermeto Pascoal and Group (1981–1993): Conception and Language*. Hillsdale, NY: Pendragon Press, 2015.

Nettl, Bruno. *The Western Impact on World Music: Change, Adaptation, and Survival*. New York: Schirmer Books; London: Collier Macmillan, 1985.

––––––––. *Excursions in World Music*. Upper Saddle River, NJ: Prentice Hall, 1997.

Nettl, Bruno, and Melinda Russell. *In the Course of Performance: Studies in the World of Musical Improvisation*. Chicago: University of Chicago Press, 1998.

Nettl, Bruno, Ruth M. Stone, James Porter, and Timothy Rice. *The Garland Encyclopedia of World Music*. New York: Garland Pub., 1998–2002.

Netto, Alberto. *Brazilian Rhythms for Drum Set and Percussion*. Boston, MA: Berklee Press, 2003.

Nevader, Arun. "John Coltrane: Music and Metaphysics." *The Threepenny Review* 10 (Summer 1982): 26–27.

Nichols, Roger. *Stravinsky*. Milton Keynes: Open University Press, 1978.

Nicholson, Stuart. *Ella Fitzgerald: A Biography of the First Lady of Jazz*. New York: Da Capo Press, 1995.

––––––––. *Jazz Rock: A History* . New York: Schirmer Books, 1998 .

––––––––. *Reminiscing in Tempo: A Portrait of Duke Ellington*. Boston: Northeastern University Press, 1999.

Nicole, Sabine, and S. T. Wagner. *On Stage, Backstage: Montreux Jazz Festival*. Lausanne: Editions Illustré, 1986.

Nidel, Richard. *World Music: The Basics*. New York: Routledge, 2005.
Nielsen, Aldon L. "Clark Coolidge and a Jazz Aesthetic." *Pacific Coast Philology* 28.1 (September 1993): 94–112.
_____. *Black Chant: Languages of African-American Postmodernism*. Cambridge; New York: Cambridge University Press, 1997.
Nietzsche, Friedrich Wilhelm. *The Case of Wagner: Nietzsche contra Wagner. The Twilight of the Idols. The Antichrist*. London: Fisher Unwin, 1899.
_____. *The Birth of Tragedy, and the Case of Wagner*. New York: Vintage Books, 1967.
Nietzsche, Friedrich Wilhelm, Anthony M. Ludovici, and John McFarland Kennedy. *I. The Case of Wagner; II. Nietzsche Contra Wagner; III. Selected Aphorisms*. Edinburgh: T.N. Foulis, 1911. Nietzsche, Friedrich Wilhelm, Richard Wagner, Elisabeth Förster-Nietzsche, Caroline V. Kerr, and H. L. Mencken. *The Nietzsche-Wagner Correspondence*. New York: Boni and Liveright, 1921.
Nilsen, Per. *Dance Music Sex Romance: Prince: The First Decade*. London: Firefly, 1999.
Nisenson, Eric. *'Round About Midnight: A Portrait of Miles Davis*. New York: Dial Press, 1982.
_____. *Ascension: John Coltrane and His Quest*. New York: Da Capo Press, 1995.
_____. *Open Sky: Sonny Rollins and His World of Improvisation*. New York: St. Martin's Press, 2000.
_____. *The Making of Kind of Blue: Miles Davis and His Masterpiece*. New York: St. Martin's Press, 2000.
Njoroge, Njoroge. "Dedicated to the Struggle: Black Music, Transculturation, and the Aural Making and Unmaking of the Third World." *Black Music Research Journal* 28.2 (Fall 2008): 85–104.
Nobs, Claude, and Perry Richardson. *Live from Montreux: "Unbeveevable": 40 Years of Music from the Montreux Jazz Festival*. London; New York: A Publishing Company Limited, 2007.
Nolan, Frederick W. *The Sound of Their Music: The Story of Rodgers and Hammerstein*. New York: Walker, 1978.
Nolan, Tom. *Three Chords for Beauty's Sake: The Life of Artie Shaw*. New York: W. W. Norton, 2010.
_____. *Artie Shaw, King of the Clarinet: His Life and Times*. New York: W. W. Norton & Co., 2011.
Nollen, Scott Allen. *Louis Armstrong: The Life, Music, and Screen Career*. Jefferson, NC: McFarland, 2010.
_____. *Paul Robeson: Film Pioneer*. Jefferson, NC: McFarland, 2010.
Norman, Brian, and Piper Kendrix Williams. *Representing Segregation: Toward an Aesthetics of Living Jim Crow, and other Forms of Racial Division*. Albany: State University of New York Press, 2010.
Oakley, Giles. *The Devil's Music: A History of the Blues*. London: British Broadcasting Corp., 1983.
O'Connell, Sean J. *Los Angeles's Central Avenue Jazz*. Charleston, SC: Arcadia Publishing, 2014.
O'Daniel, Therman B. *James Baldwin, A Critical Evaluation*. Washington, D.C.: Howard University Press, 1977.
O'Grady, Terence J. "The Ballad Style in the Early Music of the Beatles." *College Music Symposium* 19.1 (Spring 1979): 221–230.
_____. *The Beatles: A Musical Evolution*. Boston: Twayne, 1983.
Oja, Carol J., and Judith Tick. *Aaron Copland and His World*. Princeton, NJ; Woodstock, Oxfordshire: Princeton University Press, 2005.
Okrent, Daniel. *Last Call: The Rise and Fall of Prohibition*. New York: Scribner, 2010.
Oliphant, Dave. *The Early Swing Era, 1930 to 1941*. Westport, CT: Greenwood Press, 2002.
Oliphant, Dave, et al. *The Bebop Revolution in Words and Music*. Austin, TX: Harry Ransom Humanities Research Center, University of Texas at Austin, 1994.
Olson, Ted, and Charles K. Wolfe. *The Bristol Sessions: Writings about the Big Bang of Country Music*. Jefferson, NC: McFarland, 2005.

Olsson, Göran Hugo, and Goran Olsson. *The Black Power Mixtape: 1967–1975*. Chicago: Haymarket Books, 2013.

Omry, Keren. "Literary Free Jazz? "Mumbo Jumbo" and "Paradise": Language and Meaning." *African American Review* 41.1 (Spring 2007): 127–141.

———. *Cross-Rhythms: Jazz Aesthetics in African-American Literature*. London; New York: Continuum, 2008.

O'Neal, Hank. *The Ghosts of Harlem: Sessions with Jazz Legends*. Nashville: Vanderbilt University Press, 2009.

O'Neill, Eugene. *The Emperor Jones, The Straw, and Diff'rent: Three Plays*. London: J. Cape, 1922.

O'Neill, John. *The Jazz Method for Saxophone*. London: Schott Educational, 1992.

Ongiri, Amy Abugo. "We Are Family: Black Nationalism, Black Masculinity, and the Black Gay Cultural Imagination." *College Literature* 24.1, Queer Utilities: Textual Studies, Theory, Pedagogy, Praxis (February 1997): 280–294.

———. *Spectacular Blackness: The Cultural Politics of the Black Power Movement and the Search for a Black Aesthetic*. Charlottesville: University of Virginia Press, 2010.

Orenstein, Arbie. "Maurice Ravel's Creative Process." *The Musical Quarterly* 53.4 (October 1967): 467–481.

———. *Ravel: Man and Musician*. New York: Columbia University Press, 1975.

Ostendorf, Berndt. "The Afro-American Musical Avant-Garde: Bebop Jazz." *Angol Filológiai Tanulmányok / Hungarian Studies in English* 21 (1990): 45–57.

Otis, Johnny. *Upside Your Head!: Rhythm and Blues on Central Avenue*. Hanover, N.H.: University Press of New England, 1993.

Ottenheimer, Harriet. "The Blues Tradition in St. Louis." *Black Music Research Journal* 9.2, Papers of the 1989 National Conference on Black Music Research (Autumn 1989): 135–151.

Ouellette, Dan, and Nat Hentoff. *Ron Carter: Finding the Right Notes*. New York: Retrac Productions, 2014.

Owens, Thomas. *Bebop: The Music and Its Players*. New York: Oxford University Press, 1995.

Owsley, Dennis, Clark Terry, and Sheldon Art Galleries. *City of Gabriels: The History of Jazz in St. Louis, 1895–1973*. St. Louis, MO: Reedy Press, 2006.

Pakay, Sedat. *James Baldwin in Turkey: Bearing Witness from Another Place*. Seattle: Northwest African American Museum: Distributed by the University of Washington Press, 2012.

Palmer, Richard. *Stan Getz*. London: Apollo, 1988.

———. *Sonny Rollins: The Cutting Edge*. New York: Continuum, 2004.

Pappas, George D. *The Literary and Legal Genealogy of Native American Dispossession: The Marshall Trilogy Cases*. Abingdon, Oxon; New York: Routledge, Taylor & Francis Group, 2017.

Parini, Jay. "'The Souls of Black Folk': A Book That Changed America. *The Journal of Blacks in Higher Education* 62 (Winter 2008/2009): 72–80.

Paris, Mike, and Chris Comber. *Jimmie the Kid: The Life of Jimmie Rodgers*. New York: Da Capo Press, 1977.

Pastras, Philip. *Dead Man Blues: Jelly Roll Morton Way Out West*. Berkeley: University of California Press; [Chicago]: Center for Black Music Research, Columbia College Chicago, 2001.

Pattillo, Mary E. *Black on the Block: The Politics of Race and Class in the City*. Chicago: University of Chicago Press, 2007.

Paudras, Francis. *Dance of the Infidels: A Portrait of Bud Powell*. New York: Da Capo Press, 1998.

Paul, David C. *Charles Ives in the Mirror: American Histories of an Iconic Composer*. Urbana; Chicago; Springfield: University of Illinois Press, 2013.

Peabody, Rebecca. "African American Avant-Gardes, 1965–1990." *Getty Research Journal* 1 (2009): 211–217.

Pearson, Hugh. *The Shadow of the Panther: Huey Newton and the Price of Black Power in America*. Reading, MA: Addison-Wesley Pub. Co., 1994.

Pearson, Nathan W. *Goin' to Kansas City*. Urbana: University of Illinois Press, 1987.

_____. "Political and Musical Forces That Influenced the Development of Kansas City Jazz." *Black Music Research Journal* 9.2, Papers of the 1989 National Conference on Black Music Research (Autumn 1989): 181–192.

Pease, Donald E. *The New American Exceptionalism*. Minneapolis: University of Minnesota Press, 2009.

Peck, Garrett. *The Prohibition Hangover: Alcohol in America from Demon Rum to Cult Cabernet*. New Brunswick, NJ: Rutgers University Press, 2009.

Peddie, Ian. *Popular Music and Human Rights. Vol. 2: World Music*. Farnham, Surrey, England; Burlington, VT: Ashgate, 2011.

Pelote, Vincent. "The Institute of Jazz Studies." *Fontes Artis Musicae* 36.3 (July–September 1989): 177–181.

Pepin, Elizabeth, and Lewis Watts. *Harlem of the West: The San Francisco Fillmore Jazz Era*. San Francisco, CA: Chronicle Books, 2006.

Perchard, Tom. "Hip Hop Samples Jazz: Dynamics of Cultural Memory and Musical Tradition in the African American 1990s." *American Music* 29.3 (Fall 2011): 277–307.

Pereira, Malin. *Rita Dove's Cosmopolitanism*. Urbana: University of Illinois, 2003.

Peress, Maurice. "My Life with 'Black, Brown and Beige.'" *Black Music Research Journal* 13.2 (Autumn 1993): 147–160 .

Perkins, William Eric. *Droppin' Science: Critical Essays on Rap Music and Hip Hop Culture*. Philadelphia: Temple University Press, 1996.

Perkiömäki, Jari, and Sibelius-Akatemia (Helsinki, Finland). *Lennie and Ornette: Searching for Freedom in Improvisation: Observations on the Music of Lennie Tristano and Ornette Coleman*. Helsinki: Sibelius Academy Jazz Department, 2009.

Perle, George. *Serial Composition and Atonality; An Introduction to the Music of Schoenberg, Berg, and Webern*. Berkeley: University of California Press, 1962.

Perlis, Vivian. *Charles Ives Remembered: An Oral History*. New Haven, CT: Yale University Press, 1974.

Perone, James E. *Woodstock: An Encyclopedia of the Music and Art Fair*. Westport, CT: Greenwood Press, 2005.

_____. *The Sound of Stevie Wonder: His Words and Music*. Westport, CT: Praeger, 2006.

_____. *The Words and Music of Prince*. Westport, CT: Praeger Publishers, 2008.

Perrigo, Sarah, and Jim Whitman. *The Geneva Conventions Under Assault*. London; New York: Pluto Press, 2010.

Perrone, Charles A., and Christopher Dunn. *Brazilian Popular Music and Globalization*. Gainesville: University Presses of Florida, 2001.

Perry, Jeffrey Babcock. *Hubert Harrison: The Voice of Harlem Radicalism, 1883–1918*. New York: Columbia University Press, 2009.

Perry, Rosalie Sandra. *Charles Ives and the American Mind*. Kent, OH: Kent State University Press, 1974.

Perucci, Tony. *Paul Robeson and the Cold War Performance Complex: Race, Madness, Activism*. Ann Arbor: University of Michigan Press, 2012.

Peterson, Dale. *Storyville, USA*. Athens: University of Georgia Press, 1999.

Peterson, Lloyd. *Music and the Creative Spirit: Innovators in Jazz, Improvisation, and the Avant Garde*. Lanham, MD: Scarecrow Press, 2006.

Petkov, Steven, and Leonard Mustazza. *The Frank Sinatra Reader*. New York: Oxford University Press, 1995.

Pettinger, Peter. *Bill Evans: How My Heart Sings*. New Haven: Yale University Press, 1998.

Pettit, Alexander, James Baird, and Jacqueline Vanhoutte. "Bob Dylan and The Emperor Jones Revisited." *The Eugene O'Neill Review* 33.2 (2012): 273–274.

Petty, Miriam J. *Stealing the Show: African American Performers and Audiences in 1930s Hollywood*. Oakland: University of California Press, 2016.

Phelps, Carmen L. *Visionary Women Writers of Chicago's Black Arts Movement*. Jackson: University Press of Mississippi, 2013.

Piazza, Tom. *The Guide to Classic Recorded Jazz*. Iowa City, IA: University of Iowa Press,1995.

Picasso, Pablo, and Laszlo Glozer. *Picasso: Masterpieces of the Blue Period: 38 Paintings.* New York: W. W. Norton, 1988.

Piekut, Benjamin. "New Thing? Gender and Sexuality in the Jazz Composers Guild." *American Quarterly* 62.1 (March 2010): 25–48.

Pinckney, Warren R. "Toward a History of Jazz in Bermuda." *The Musical Quarterly* 84.3 (Autumn 2000): 333–371.

Pinder, Kymberly N. "'Our Father, God; our Brother, Christ; or are We Bastard Kin?': Images of Christ in African American Painting." *African American Review* 31.2 (Summer 1997): 223–233.

Pinson, K. Heather. *The Jazz Image: Seeing Music Through Herman Leonard's Photography.* Jackson: University Press of Mississippi, 2010.

Pinto, Samantha. *Difficult Diasporas: The Transnational Feminist Aesthetic of the Black Atlantic.* New York: New York University Press, 2013.

Pipes, Kasey S. *Ike's Final Battle: The Road to Little Rock and the Challenge of Equality.* Los Angeles: World Ahead Pub., 2007.

Placksin, Sally. *American Women in Jazz: 1900 to the Present: Their Words, Lives, and Music.* New York: Wideview Books, 1982.

Pleasants, Henry. "Jazz and the Movies / Jazz et Cinéma / Jazz und Film." *The World of Music* 10.3 (1968): 38–47.

Pohren, D. E. *Lives and Legends of Flamenco; A Biographical History.* Madrid: Society of Spanish Studies; [distribution: H. Howell, La Mesa, CA], 1964.

Polic, Edward F. *The Glenn Miller Army Air Force Band: Sustineo Alas = I Sustain the Wings.* Metuchen, NJ: Scarecrow Press; [New Brunswick, NJ]: Institute of Jazz Studies, Rutgers University, 1989.

Polišenský, Josef V. *Aristocrats and the Crowd in the Revolutionary Year 1848: A Contribution to the History of Revolution and Counter-Revolution in Austria.* Albany: State University of New York Press, 1980.

Polka, Brayton. *Modernity Between Wagner and Nietzsche.* Lanham; Boulder; New York; London: Lexington Books, 2015.

Pollack, Howard. *Aaron Copland: The Life and Work of an Uncommon Man.* New York: Henry Holt, 1999.

Pollard, Sidney. *Wealth & Poverty: An Economic History of the Twentieth Century.* Oxford; New York: Oxford University Press, 1990.

Pollock, Mary S., and Susanne Vincenza. "Feminist Aesthetics in Jazz: An Interview with Susanne Vincenza of Alive!" *Frontiers: A Journal of Women Studies* 8.1 (1984): 60–63.

Pond, Steven F. "'Chameleon' Meets 'Soul Train': Herbie, James, Michael, Damita Jo, and Jazz-Funk." *American Studies* 52.4, The Funk Issue (2013): 125–140.

Porter, Horace A. *Jazz Country: Ralph Ellison in America.* Iowa City: University of Iowa Press, 2001.

Porter, Lewis. "Lester Leaps in: The Early Style of Lester Young." *The Black Perspective in Music* 9.1 (Spring 1981): 3–24.

———. "'You Can't Get up There Timidly': Jazzwomen: Part II." *Music Educators Journal* 71.2 (October 1984): 42–51.

———. *A Lester Young Reader.* Washington; London: Smithsonian Institution Press, United States of America, 1991.

———. *John Coltrane: His Life and Music.* Ann Arbor: University of Michigan Press, 1998.

Porterfield, Nolan. *Jimmie Rodgers: The Life and Times of America's Blue Yodeler.* Jackson: University Press of Mississippi, 2007.

Potter, Keith. *Four Musical Minimalists: La Monte Young, Terry Riley, Steve Reich, Philip Glass.* Cambridge; New York: Cambridge University Press, 2000.

Powell, Eric A. "Tales from Storyville." *Archaeology* 55.6 (November/December 2002): 26–31.

Powers, Peter Kerry. "Gods of Physical Violence, Stopping at Nothing: Masculinity, Religion, and Art in the Work of Zora Neale Hurston." *Religion and American Culture: A Journal of Interpretation*, 12.2 (Summer 2002): 229–247.

Prange, Martine. *Nietzsche, Wagner, Europe.* Berlin; Boston: De Gruyter, 2013.

Prashad, Vijay. *The Karma of Brown Folk*. Minneapolis: University of Minnesota Press, 2000.

Prévos, André J. M. "The Evolution of French Rap Music and Hip Hop Culture in the 1980s and 1990s." *The French Review* 69.5 (April 1996): 713–725.

Prial, Dunstan. *The Producer: John Hammond and the Soul of American Music*. New York: Farrar, Straus and Giroux, 2006.

Price, Charles Gower. "Sources of American Styles in the Music of the Beatles." *American Music* 15.2 (Summer 1997): 208–232.

Price, Sally, Richard Price, and Romare Bearden. *Romare Bearden: The Caribbean Dimension*. Philadelphia: University of Pennsylvania Press, 2006.

Priestley, Brian. *Mingus, A Critical Biography*. London; New York: Quartet Books, 1982 .

Prigozy, Ruth, and Walter Raubicheck. *Going My Way: Bing Crosby and American Culture*. Rochester, NY: University of Rochester Press, 2007.

Prince, Stephen, and American Council of Learned Societies. *American Cinema of the 1980s: Themes and Variations*. New Brunswick, NJ: Rutgers University Press, 2007.

Puddington, Arch. *Broadcasting Freedom: The Cold War Triumph of Radio Free Europe and Radio Liberty*. Lexington: University Press of Kentucky, 2000.

Puffett, Derrick. *Richard Strauss, Elektra*. Cambridge [Cambridgeshire]; New York: Cambridge University Press, 1989.

Pulido, Laura. *Black, Brown, Yellow, and Left: Radical Activism in Los Angeles*. Berkeley: University of California Press, 2006.

Pullman, Peter. *Wail: The Life of Bud Powell*. New York: Peter Pullman LLC, 2012 .

Purdum, Todd S. *An Idea Whose Time Has Come: Two Presidents, Two Parties, and the Battle for the Civil Rights Act of 1964*. New York: Henry Holt and Company, 2014.

Quigley, Maeve. "Block Rockin' Beats." *Fortnight* 386 (June 2000): 22-23; David Glen Such. *Avant-Garde Jazz Musicians: Performing "Out There."* Iowa City: University of Iowa Press, 1993.

Quinn, Kate. *Black Power in the Caribbean*. Gainesville: University Press of Florida, 2014.

Ra, Sun. *The Immeasurable Equation: The Collected Poetry and Prose*. Wartaweil: Waitawhile, 2005.

Ra, Sun, and John Corbett. *The Wisdom of Sun-Ra: Sun Ra's Polemical Broadsheets and Streetcorner Leaflets*. Chicago: WhiteWalls, 2006.

Raeburn, Bruce Boyd. "'They're Tryin' to Wash Us Away': New Orleans Musicians Surviving Katrina." *The Journal of American History* 94.3, Through the Eye of Katrina: The Past as Prologue? (December 2007): 812–819.

Rambsy II, Howard. *Beyond Keeping It Real: OutKast, the Funk Connection, and Afrofuturism*. *American Studies* 52.4, The Funk Issue (2013): 205-216.

Ramírez, Leonard G., and Yenelli Flores. *Chicanas of 18th Street: Narratives of a Movement from Latino Chicago*. Urbana: University of Illinois Press, 2011.

Rampersad, Arnold. *Richard Wright: A Collection of Critical Essays*. Englewood Cliffs, NJ: Prentice Hall, 1995.

_____. *Ralph Ellison: A Biography*. New York: Alfred A. Knopf, 2007.

Ramsey, Guthrie P. *The Amazing Bud Powell: Black Genius, Jazz History, and the Challenge of Bebop*. Berkeley: Chicago: University of California Press, 2013.

Rasmussen, Anne. "An Evening in the Orient": The Middle Eastern Nightclub in America." *Asian Music* 23.2 (Spring–Summer 1992): 63–88.

Ratliff, Ben. *Coltrane: The Story of a Sound*. New York: Farrar, Straus and Giroux, 2007.

_____. *The Jazz Ear: Conversations Over Music*. New York: Times Books, 2008.

Rattenbury, Ken. *Duke Ellington, Jazz Composer*. London; New Haven, CT: Yale University Press, 1990.

Ravel, Maurice, and Arbie Orenstein. *A Ravel Reader: Correspondence, Articles, Interviews*. New York: Columbia University Press, 1990.

Ravel, Maurice, Vlado Perlemuter, Hélène Jourdan-Morhange, and Harold Taylor. *Ravel According to Ravel*. London: Kahn & Averill, 1988.

Reed, Christopher Robert. *Knock at the Door of Opportunity: Black Migration to Chicago, 1900-1919*. Carbondale: Southern Illinois University Press, 2014.

Reed, Joseph W. *Three American Originals: John Ford, William Faulkner & Charles Ives.* Middletown, CT: Wesleyan University Press; Scranton, PA: Distributed by Harper & Row, 1984.

Reeves-Ellington, Barbara, Kathryn Kish Sklar, and Connie Anne Shemo. *Competing Kingdoms: Women, Mission, Nation, and the American Protestant Empire, 1812–1960.* Durham, NC: Duke University Press, 2010.

Regester, Charlene B. *African American Actresses: The Struggle for Visibility, 1900–1960.* Bloomington: Indiana University Press, 2010.

Regis, Helen A. "Second Lines, Minstrelsy, and the Contested Landscapes of New Orleans Afro-Creole Festivals." *Cultural Anthropology* 14.4 (November 1999): 472–504.

Reich, Howard, and William Gaines. *Jelly's Blues: The Life, Music, and Redemption of Jelly Roll Morton.* Cambridge, MA: Da Capo, 2003.

Reich, Steve, and Paul Hillier. *Writings on Music, 1965–2000.* Oxford; New York: Oxford University Press, 2002.

Reilly, Jack. *The Harmony of Bill Evans.* Brooklyn, NY: Unichrom; Milwaukee, WI: H. Leonard [distributor], 1993.

———. *The Harmony of Dave Brubeck.* New York: Music Sales America, 2013.

Reilly, Maureen. *Swing Style: Fashions of the 1930s–1950s.* Atglen, PA: Schiffer, 1999.

Retman, Sonnet. "Langston Hughes's 'Rejuvenation Through Joy': Passing, Racial Performance, and the Marketplace." *African American Review* 45.4 (Winter 2012): 593–602 .

Ribowsky, Mark. *Signed, Sealed, and Delivered: The Soulful Journey of Stevie Wonder.* Hoboken, NJ: John Wiley & Sons, 2010.

Riccardi, Ricky. *What a Wonderful World: The Magic of Louis Armstrong's Later Years.* New York: Pantheon Books, 2011.

Rice, Alan J. *Creating Memorials, Building Identities: The Politics of Memory in the Black Atlantic.* Liverpool: Liverpool University Press, 2010.

Rice, Marc. "Break o' Day Blues: The 1923 Recordings of the Bennie Moten Orchestra." *The Musical Quarterly* 86.2 (Summer 2002): 282–306.

Richards, Jason. "Imitation Nation: Blackface Minstrelsy and the Making of African American Selfhood in 'Uncle Tom's Cabin.'" *Novel: A Forum on Fiction* 39.2, Postcolonial Disjunctions (Spring 2006): 204–220.

Ringgold, Gene, and Clifford McCarty. *The Films of Frank Sinatra.* New York: Citadel Press, 1971.

Risen, Clay. *The Bill of the Century: The Epic Battle for the Civil Rights Act.* New York: Bloomsbury Press, 2014.

Rizzo, Gene. *The Fifty Greatest Jazz Piano Players of all Time: Ranking, Analysis & Photos.* Milwaukee, WI: Hal Leonard Corporation, 2005.

Ro, Ronin. *Prince: Inside the Music and the Masks.* New York: St. Martin's Press, 2011.

Roberts, Kodi A. *Voodoo and Power: The Politics of Religion in New Orleans, 1881–1940.* Baton Rouge: Louisiana State University Press, 2015.

Roberts, Michael. "A Working-Class Hero Is Something to Be: The American Musicians' Union's Attempt to Ban the Beatles, 1964." *Popular Music* 29.1 (January 2010): 1–16.

Roberts, Randy. *Papa Jack: Jack Johnson and the Era of White Hopes.* New York: London: Free Press, 1983.

———. *Joe Louis: Hard Times Man.* New Haven, CT: Yale University Press, 2010.

Roberts, Timothy Mason. *Distant Revolutions: 1848 and the Challenge to American Exceptionalism.* Charlottesville: University of Virginia Press, 2009.

Robertson, David. *W.C. Handy: The Life and Times of the Man Who Made the Blues.* New York: Alfred A. Knopf, 2009.

Robertson, Pamela. *Guilty Pleasures: Feminist Camp from Mae West to Madonna.* Durham, NC: Duke University Press, 1996.

Robertson, Priscilla Smith. *Revolutions of 1848, A Social History.* Princeton: Princeton University Press, 1952.

Robeson, Paul. *The Negro People and the Soviet Union.* New York: New Century Publishers, 1950.

Rodgers, Carrie. *My Husband, Jimmie Rodgers*. Nashville, TN: Country Music Foundation Press, 1995.

Rodgers, Richard, and Oscar Hammerstein, II. *6 Plays by Rodgers and Hammerstein*. New York: Random House, 1955.

Roger, Philippe. "Global Anti-Americanism and the Lessons of the 'French Exception.'" *The Journal of American History* 93.2 (September 2006): 448–451.

Rogin, Michael Paul. *Ronald Reagan, the Movie and Other Episodes in Political Demonology*. Berkeley: University of California Press, 1987.

_____. "Blackface, White Noise: The Jewish Jazz Singer Finds His Voice." *Critical Inquiry* 18.3 (Spring 1992): 417–453.

_____. "Making America Home: Racial Masquerade and Ethnic Assimilation in the Transition to Talking Pictures." *The Journal of American History* 79.3, Discovering America: A Special Issue (December 1992): 1050–1077.

_____. "'Democracy and Burnt Cork': The End of Blackface, the Beginning of Civil Rights." *Representations* 46 (Spring 1994): 1–34.

_____. *Blackface, White Noise: Jewish Immigrants in the Hollywood Melting Pot*. Berkeley: University of California Press, 1996.

Rohan, Marc. *Paris '68: Graffiti, Posters, Newspapers and Poems of the May 1968 Events*. London: Impact, 1988.

Rojas, Fabio. *From Black Power to Black Studies: How a Radical Social Movement Became an Academic Discipline*. Baltimore: Johns Hopkins University Press, 2007.

Rojek, Chris. *Frank Sinatra*. Cambridge; Malden, MA: Polity, 2004.

Rollefson, J. Griffith. "The "Robot Voodoo Power" Thesis: Afrofuturism and Anti-Anti-Essentialism from Sun Ra to Kool Keith." *Black Music Research Journal* 28.1, Becoming: Blackness and the Musical Imagination (Spring 2008): 83–109.

Rommen, Timothy. *"Mek Some Noise": Gospel Music and the Ethics of Style in Trinidad*. Berkeley: University of California Press; Chicago: Center for Black Music Research, Columbia College, 2007.

Rose, Al. *Storyville, New Orleans, Being an Authentic, Illustrated Account of the Notorious Red-light District*. Tuscaloosa: University of Alabama Press, 1974.

Rose, Cynthia. *Living in America: The Soul Saga of James Brown*. London: Serpent's Tail, 1990.

Rosenbaum, Art, and Johann S. Buis. *Shout Because You're Free: The African American Ring Shout Tradition in Coastal Georgia*. Athens: University of Georgia Press, 1998.

Rosenberg, Joel. "What You Ain't Heard Yet: The Languages of The Jazz Singer." *Prooftexts* 22.1–2, Special Issue: The Cinema of Jewish Experience (Winter/Spring 2002): 11–54.

Rosenthal, David H. "Jazz in the Ghetto: 1950–70." *Popular Music* 7.1 (January 1988): 51–56.

_____. "Hard Bop and Its Critics." *The Black Perspective in Music* 16.1 (Spring 1988): 21–29.

_____. *Hard Bop: Jazz and Black Music, 1955–1965*. New York: Oxford University Press, 1992.

Rouse, Carolyn Moxley. *Engaged Surrender: African American Women and Islam*. Berkeley: University of California Press, 2004.

Rowden, Terry. *The Songs of Blind Folk: African American Musicians and the Cultures of Blindness*. Ann Arbor: University of Michigan Press, 2009.

Rowley, Hazel. *Richard Wright: The Life and Times*. New York: Henry Holt and Co., 2001.

Rozell, Mark J., and Gleaves Whitney. *Testing the Limits: George W. Bush and the Imperial Presidency*. Lanham, MD: Rowman & Littlefield, 2009.

Rubin, William. *"Primitivism" in 20th Century Art: Affinity of the Tribal and the Modern*. New York: Museum of Modern Art, 1994.

Rudalevige, Andrew. *The New Imperial Presidency: Renewing Presidential Power After Watergate*. Ann Arbor: University of Michigan Press, 2006.

Rudwick, Elliott M. *Race Riot at East St. Louis, July 2, 1917*. Carbondale, Illinois: Southern Illinois University Press, 1964.

Rudwick, Elliott M., and Mike Acquiviva. *The East St. Louis Race Riot of 1917*. Frederick, MD: University Publications of America, 1985.

Runstedtler, Theresa. *Jack Johnson, Rebel Sojourner: Boxing in the Shadow of the Global Color Line*. Berkeley: University of California Press, 2012.

Russell, Bill. *"Oh, Mister Jelly": A Jelly Roll Morton Scrapbook*. Copenhagen: JazzMedia, 1999.

Russell, George. *George Russell's Lydian Chromatic Concept of Tonal Organization*. Brookline, MA: Concept Pub. Co., 2001.

Russell, Ross. *Jazz Style in Kansas City and the Southwest*. Berkeley: University of California Press, 1971.

Rustin, Nichole T., and Sherrie Tucker. *Big Ears: Listening for Gender in Jazz Studies*. Durham, NC: Duke University Press, 2008.

Rutkoff, Peter, and William Scott. "Bebop: Modern New York Jazz." *The Kenyon Review* , New Series 18.2 (Spring 1996): 91–121 .

Rye, Howard, and Jeffrey Green. "Black Musical Internationalism in England in the 1920s." *Black Music Research Journal* 15.1 (Spring 1995): 93–107.

Sagee, Alona. "Bessie Smith: 'Down Hearted Blues' and 'Gulf Coast Blues' Revisited." *Popular Music* 26.1, Special Issue on the Blues in Honour of Paul Oliver (January 2007): 117–127.

Saito, Natsu Taylor. *Meeting the Enemy: American Exceptionalism and International Law*. New York: New York University Press, 2010.

Sakai, Machie. *The Newport Jazz Festival Story, 1953–1960: A Profile of the Newport Jazz Festival Founder, Elaine Lorillard*. Larchmont, NY: Machie Sakai, 1998.

Salazar, Dixie. *Flamenco Hips and Red Mud Feet*. Tucson: University of Arizona Press, 2010.

Salenius, Sirpa. *An Abolitionist Abroad: Sarah Parker Remond in Cosmopolitan Europe*. Amherst: University of Massachusetts Press, 2016.

Sanders, Cheryl Jeanne. *Living the Intersection: Womanism and Afrocentrism in Theology*. Minneapolis, MN: Fortress Press, 1995.

Santoro, Gene. *Dancing in Your Head: Jazz, Blues, Rock, and Beyond*. New York: Oxford University Press, 1995.

_____. "Myself When I Am Real: The Life and Music of Charles Mingus." New York; Oxford: Oxford University Press, 2001 .

_____. "Jazz: The Edgy Optimist: At 76, Saxist Sonny Rollins Is Still On Top Of His Game." *The American Scholar* 76.1 (Winter 2007): 125–129.

Saraswati, L. Ayu. "Cosmopolitan Whiteness: The Effects and Affects of Skin-Whitening Advertisements in a Transnational Women's Magazine in Indonesia." *Meridians* 10.2 (2010): 15–41.

Sartre, Jean-Paul, and Robert Denoon Cumming. *The Philosophy of Jean-Paul Sartre*. New York: Random House, 1965.

Sarzin, Evan, and Charley Gerard. *Hard Bop Piano Jazz Compositions of the 50s and 60s*. New York: Gerard & Sarzin 1992.

Saul, Scott. "Outrageous Freedom: Charles Mingus and the Invention of the Jazz Workshop." *American Quarterly* 53.3 (September 2001): 387–419.

Sautman, Francesca Canadé. "Hip-Hop/Scotch: "Sounding Francophone" in French and United States Cultures." *Yale French Studies* 100, France/USA: The Cultural Wars (2001): 119–144.

Saxton, Alexander. "Blackface Minstrelsy and Jacksonian Ideology." *American Quarterly* 27.1 (March 1975): 3–28.

Schiedt, Duncan P. *Jazz in Black & White: The Photographs of Duncan Schiedt*. Bloomington: Indiana University Press, 2004.

Schlabach, Elizabeth Schroeder. *Along the Streets of Bronzeville: Black Chicago's Literary Landscape*. Urbana: University of Illinois Press, 2013.

Schlosser, Joel Alden. "Socrates in a Different Key: James Baldwin and Race in America." *Political Research Quarterly*, 66.3 (September 2013): 487–499.

Schmid, Mark-Daniel. *The Richard Strauss Companion*. Westport, CT: Praeger, 2003.

Schneider, Mark R. *We Return Fighting: The Civil Rights Movement in the Jazz Age*. Boston, MA: Northeastern University Press, 2002.

Schreiner, Claus, Madeleine Claus, and Reinhard G. Pauly. *Flamenco: Gypsy Dance and Music from Andalusia*. Portland, OR: Amadeus Press, 1990.

Schroeder, David. "Four Approaches to Jazz Improvisation Instruction." *Philosophy of Music Education Review* 10.1 (Spring 2002): 36–40.

Schubart, Rikke. *Super Bitches and Action Babes: The Female Hero in Popular Cinema, 1970–2006*. Jefferson, NC: McFarland & Co., 2007.

Schuller, Gunther. *Early Jazz: Its Roots and Musical Development*. New York: Oxford University Press, 1968.

Schultz, Debra L. *Going South: Jewish Women in the Civil Rights Movement*. New York: New York University Press, 2001.

Schwartz, Jeff. "Writing Jimi: Rock Guitar Pedagogy as Postmodern Folkloric Practice." *Popular Music* 12.3 (October 1993): 281–288.

Schwarz, A. B. Christa. *Gay Voices of the Harlem Renaissance*. Bloomington: Indiana University Press, 2003.

Schweitzer, Kenneth George. *The Artistry of Afro-Cuban Batá Drumming: Aesthetics, Transmission, Bonding, and Creativity*. Jackson: University Press of Mississippi, 2013.

Scoates, Christopher. *Brian Eno: Visual Music* . San Francisco, CA: Chronicle Books, 2013 .

Scott, Joan Wallach. *Parité!: Sexual Equality and the Crisis of French Universalism*. Chicago: University of Chicago Press, 2005.

Scott, Jonathan. "Advanced, Repressed, and Popular: Langston Hughes during the Cold War." *College Literature* 33.2 (Spring 2006): 30–51.

Scott, Michelle R. *Blues Empress in Black Chattanooga: Bessie Smith and the Emerging Urban South*. Urbana: University of Illinois Press, 2008.

Sears, Benjamin. *The Irving Berlin Reader*. New York: Oxford University Press, 2012.

Sears, David O., and John B. McConahay. *The Politics of Violence; The New Urban Blacks and the Watts Riot*. Boston, MA: Houghton Mifflin, 1973.

Secrest, Meryle. *Leonard Bernstein: A Life*. New York: A. A. Knopf, 1994.

Seewood, André. *Slave Cinema: The Crisis of the African-American in Film*. Philadelphia: Xlibris Corp., 2008.

Segell, Michael. *The Devil's Horn: The Story of the Saxophone, From Noisy Novelty to the King of Cool*. New York: Farrar, Straus and Giroux, 2005.

Seldes, Barry. *Leonard Bernstein: The Political Life of an American Musician*. Berkeley; London: University of California Press, 2009.

Sell, Mike. *Avant-Garde Performance & the Limits of Criticism: Approaching the Living Theatre, Happenings/Fluxus, and the Black Arts Movement*. Ann Arbor: University of Michigan Press, 2005.

Selvin, Joel, and Dave Marsh. *Sly and the Family Stone: An Oral History*. New York: Avon Books, 1998.

Selzer, Linda F. "Barack Obama, the 2008 Presidential Election, and the New Cosmopolitanism: Figuring the Black Body." *Melus* 35.4, The Bodies of Black Folk (Winter 2010): 15–37.

Seung, T. K. *Goethe, Nietzsche, and Wagner: Their Spinozan Epics of Love and Power*. Lanham, MD: Lexington Books, 2006.

Shabazz, Rashad. *Spatializing Blackness: Architectures of Confinement and Black Masculinity in Chicago*. Urbana: University of Illinois Press, 2015.

Shack, William. *Harlem in Montmartre: A Paris Jazz Story Between the Great Wars*. Berkeley: University of California Press, 2001.

Shadwick, Keith. *Bill Evans: Everything Happens to Me, A Musical Biography*. San Francisco, CA: Backbeat Books, 2002.

Shahriari, Andrew C. *Popular World Music*. Upper Saddle River, NJ: Prentice Hall/Pearson, 2011.

Shapiro, Harry, and Caesar Glebbeek. *Jimi Hendrix, Electric Gypsy*. New York: St. Martin's Press, 1991, 1990.

Shapiro, Nat, and Nat Hentoff. *Hear Me Talkin' To Ya: The Story of Jazz by the Men Who Made It*. New York: Rinehart, 1955.

Sharpley-Whiting, T. Denean. *Bricktop's Paris: African American Women in Paris Between the Two World Wars*. Albany: State University of New York Press, 2015.

Shaw, Arnold. *The Street That Never Slept: New York's Fabled 52nd St*. New York: Coward, McCann & Geoghegan, 1971.

———. *Honkers and Shouters: The Golden Years of Rhythm and Blues*. New York: Macmillan, 1978.

———. *Black Popular Music in America: The Singers, Songwriters, and Musicians Who Pioneered the Sounds of American Music*. New York: Schirmer Books, 1986.

Shaw, Arnold, and Abel Green. *52nd Street: The Street of Jazz*. New York: Da Capo Press, 1971.

Shaw, Artie. *Artie Shaw And His Orchestra*. Santa Monica, CA: Flashback Records, 1998.

Shaw, John. *This Land That I Love: Irving Berlin, Woody Guthrie, and the Story of Two American Anthems*. New York: PublicAffairs, 2013.

Shaw, Stephanie J. *What a Woman Ought To Be and To Do: Black Professional Women Workers During the Jim Crow Era*. Chicago: University of Chicago Press, 1996.

Shaw-Miller, Simon. *Visible Deeds of Music: Art and Music from Wagner to Cage*. New Haven, CT: Yale University Press, 2002.

Shelby, Tommie, and Paul Gilroy. "Cosmopolitanism, Blackness, and Utopia." *Transition* 98 (2008): 116–135.

Sheppard, David. *On Some Faraway Beach: The Life and Times of Brian Eno* . London: Orion, 2015.

Sheridan, Chris. *Count Basie: A Bio-Discography*. London: Greenwood/Eurospan, 1986.

Shim, Eunmi. *Lennie Tristano: His Life in Music*. Ann Arbor: University of Michigan Press, 2007.

Shindo, Charles J. *Dust Bowl Migrants in the American Imagination*. Lawrence: University Press of Kansas, 1997.

Shipton, Alyn. *Fats Waller: The Cheerful Little Earful*. London; New York: Continuum, 2002.

———. *Jazz Makers: Vanguards of Sound*. Oxford; New York: Oxford University Press, 2002.

———. *Hi-de-ho: The Life of Cab Calloway*. Oxford; New York: Oxford University Press, 2010.

Sicko, Dan. *Techno Rebels: The Renegades of Electronic Funk*. Detroit, MI: Wayne State University Press, 2010.

Sidbury, James. *Becoming African in America: Race and Nation in the Early Black Atlantic*. Oxford; New York: Oxford University Press, 2007.

Sidran, Ben. *Talking Jazz: An Oral History*. New York: Da Capo Press, 1995.

Sieving, Christopher. *Soul Searching: Black-themed Cinema From the March On Washington to the Rise of Blaxploitation*. Middletown, CT: Wesleyan University Press, 2011.

Silver, Horace. *Horace Silver: The Art of Small Combo Jazz Playing, Composing and Arranging*. Milwaukee, WI: Hal Leonard Corp., 1995.

Silver, Horace, and Philip Pastras. *Let's Get to the Nitty Gritty: The Autobiography of Horace Silver*. Berkeley, CA: University of California Press, 2006.

Silverlight, Terry, Felipe Orozco, and Adrian Hopkins. *Jazz, Funk & Fusion: Over 60 Classic Grooves in Standard Notation*. London: Wise, 2011.

Silverman, Debra B. "Nella Larsen's Quicksand: Untangling the Webs of Exoticism." *African American Review* 27.4 (Winter 1993): 599–614.

Silverman, Julian. "What Theory Says and What Musicians Do: Some Thoughts on the George Russell Event." *Tempo* 57.226 (October 2003): 32–39.

———. "Prelude to Swing: The 1920s Recordings of the Bennie Moten Orchestra." *American Music* 25.3 (Fall 2007): 259–281.

Simawe, Saadi. *Black Orpheus: Music in African American Fiction from the Harlem Renaissance to Toni Morrison*. New York: Garland Pub., 2000.

Simmons, Martha J., and Frank A. Thomas. *Preaching with Sacred Fire: An Anthology of African American Sermons, 1750 to the Present*. New York: W. W. Norton, 2010.

Simon, George Thomas. *Glenn Miller and His Orchestra*. New York: Da Capo Press, 1980.

Simons, G. L. *Vietnam Syndrome: Impact on US Foreign Policy*. New York: St. Martin's Press, 1998.

Simosko, Vladimir. *Artie Shaw: A Musical Biography and Discography*. Lanham, MD: Scarecrow Press, 2000.

Simosko, Vladimir, and Barry Tepperman. *Eric Dolphy: A Musical Biography and Discography*. Washington: Smithsonian Institution Press; [distributed in the U.S. and Canada by G. Braziller, New York, 1971.

Simpson, Anne Key. "Those Everlasting Blues: The Best of Clarence Williams." *Louisiana History: The Journal of the Louisiana Historical Association* 40.2 (Spring 1999): 179–195.

Sims, Yvonne D. *Women of Blaxploitation: How the Black Action Film Heroine Changed American Popular Culture*. Jefferson, NC: McFarland, 2006.

Sjøgren, Thorbjørn. *Long Tall Dexter: The Discography of Dexter Gordon*. Copenhagen: Thorbjørn Sjøgren, 1986.

Sklaroff, Lauren Rebecca. "Constructing G.I. Joe Louis: Cultural Solutions to the "Negro Problem" during World War II." *The Journal of American History* 89.3 (December 2002): 958–983.

Slate, Nico. *Black Power Beyond Borders: The Global Dimensions of the Black Power Movement*. New York: Palgrave Macmillan, 2012.

Small, Mark, Andrew Taylor, Jonathan Feist, and Berklee College of Music. *Masters of Music: Conversations with Berklee Greats*. Boston, MA: Berklee Press; Milwaukee, WI: Distributed by H. Leonard, 1999.

Smethurst, James. "'Pat Your Foot and Turn the Corner': Amiri Baraka, the Black Arts Movement, and the Poetics of a Popular Avant-Garde." *African American Review* 37.2/3, Amri Baraka Issue (Summer –Autumn 2003): 261–270.

_____. *The Black Arts Movement: Literary Nationalism in the 1960s and 1970s*. Chapel Hill: University of North Carolina Press, 2005.

Smethurst, James Edward, Sonia Sanchez, and John H. Bracey. *SOS/Calling All Black People: A Black Arts Movement Reader*. Amherst: University of Massachusetts Press, 2014.

Smith, Carl, and Chick Corea. *Bouncing with Bud: All the Recordings of Bud Powell*. Brunswick, ME: Biddle Pub. Co., 1997.

Smith, Christopher. "A Sense of the Possible: Miles Davis and the Semiotics of Improvised Performance." *TDR* (1988–) 39.3 (Autumn 1995): 41–55.

Smith, Valerie. *Representing Blackness: Issues in Film and Video*. New Brunswick, NJ: Rutgers University Press, 1997.

Smith, Larry David. *Elvis Costello, Joni Mitchell, and the Torch Song Tradition*. Westport, CT: Praeger, 2004.

Smith, Michael P. "Behind the Lines: The Black Mardi Gras Indians and the New Orleans Second Line." *Black Music Research Journal* 14.1 (Spring 1994): 43–73.

Smith, R. J. *The One: The Life and Music of James Brown*. New York: Gotham Books, 2012.

Smith, Wendy. "Recording: The Man Who Got His Way: John Hammond, Scion of White Privilege, Helped Integrate Popular Music." *The American Scholar* 75.3 (Summer 2006): 110–114.

Sneed, Paul. "Bandidos de Cristo: Representations of the Power of Criminal Factions in Rio's Proibidão Funk." *Latin American Music Review / Revista de Música Latinoamericana* 28.2 (Autumn–Winter 2007): 220–241.

_____. "Favela Utopias: The "Bailes Funk" in Rio's Crisis of Social Exclusion and Violence." *Latin American Research Review* 43.2 (2008): 57–79.

Snitzer, Herb, and Lewis Porter. "'Such Sweet Thunder': A Visual Journey." *The Georgia Review* 46.4 (Winter 1992): 663–680.

Solis, Gabriel. *Monk's Music: Thelonious Monk and Jazz History in the Making*. Berkeley: University of California Press, 2008.

_____. *Thelonious Monk Quartet Featuring John Coltrane at Carnegie Hall*. New York: Oxford University Press, 2014.

Solís, Ted. *Performing Ethnomusicology: Teaching and Representation in World Music Ensembles*. Berkeley: University of California Press, 2004.

Solomon, William L., and William S. Solomon. "Images of Rebellion: News Coverage of Rodney King." *Race, Gender & Class* 11.1, Race, Gender, Class and the 1992 L.A. "Riots" (2004): 23–38.

Solymosi, Emőke Tari. "'Bartók Always Called Me Latin': The Influence of Béla Bartók on László Lajtha's Life and Art." *Studia Musicologica* 48.1/2 (March 2007): 215–223.

Sotiropoulos, Karen. *Staging Race: Black Performers in Turn of the Century America.* Cambridge, MA; London: Harvard University Press, 2008.

Soussloff, Catherine M. "Jackson Pollock's Post-Ritual Performance: Memories Arrested in Space." *TDR* (1988–) 48.1 (Spring 2004): 60–78.

Southern, Eileen, and William Clarence ("Billy") Eckstine. "'Mr. B' of Ballad and Bop." *The Black Perspective in Music* 8.1 (Spring 1980): 54–64.

Spanos, William V. *Redeemer Nation in the Interregnum: An Untimely Meditation on the American Vocation.* New York: Fordham University Press, 2015.

Spaulding, Carina, and Josephine Metcalf. *African American Culture and Society after Rodney King: Provocations and Protests, Progression and "Post-Racialism."* Aldershot, Hampshire: Ashgate Publishing 2015.

Spellman, A. B. *Four Lives in the Bebop Business.* [London]: Macgibbon & Kee, 1967.

———. *Four Jazz Lives.* Ann Arbor, MI: University of Michigan Press, 2004.

Spencer, Michael T. "Jazz Education at the Westlake College of Music, 1945–61." *Journal of Historical Research in Music Education* 35.1 (October 2013): 50–65.

Sperber, Jonathan. *The European Revolutions, 1848–1851.* Cambridge [England]; New York: Cambridge University Press, 1994.

Spitz, Bob. *Barefoot in Babylon: The Creation of the Woodstock Music Festival, 1969.* New York: Viking Press, 1979.

———. *The Beatles: The Biography.* New York: Little Brown, 2005.

Spring, Howard. "Swing and the Lindy Hop: Dance, Venue, Media, and Tradition." *American Music* 15.2 (Summer 1997): 183–207.

Stanfield, Peter. "An Excursion into the Lower Depths: Hollywood, Urban Primitivism, and "St. Louis Blues," 1929–1937." *Cinema Journal* 41.2 (Winter 2002): 84–108.

———. *Body and Soul: Jazz and Blues in American Film, 1927-63.* Urbana: University of Illinois Press, 2005.

———. "Crossover: Sam Katzman's "Switchblade Calypso Bop Reefer Madness Swamp Girl" or 'Bad Jazz,' Calypso, Beatniks and Rock 'n' Roll in 1950s Teenpix." *Popular Music* 29.3 (October 2010): 437–455.

Stange, Maren, and International Center of Photography. *Bronzeville: Black Chicago in Pictures, 1941–1943.* New York: New Press: Distributed by Norton, 2003.

Starr, Kevin. *Golden Dreams: California in an Age of Abundance, 1950–1963.* Oxford; New York: Oxford University Press, 2009.

Starr, Larry. *A Union of Diversities: Style in the Music of Charles Ives.* New York: Schirmer Books; Toronto: Maxwell Macmillan Canada; New York: Maxwell Macmillan International, 1992.

State Council of Defense of Illinois. Labor Committee. *Report to the Illinois State Council of Defense on the Race Riots at East St. Louis.* Chicago: Illinois State Council of Defense, 1917.

Steed, Janna Tull. *Duke Ellington: A Spiritual Biography.* New York: Crossroad Pub. Co., 1999.

Steen, Shannon. "Melancholy Bodies: Racial Subjectivity and Whiteness in O'Neill's "The Emperor Jones." *Theatre Journal* 52.3 (October 2000): 339–359.

Stein, Daniel. "Hearing, Seeing, and Writing Thelonious Monk: Toward a Theory of Changing Iconotexts." *Amerikastudien / American Studies* 50.4 (2005): 603–627.

Stein, Gertrude, F. W. Dupee, and Carl Van Vechten. *Selected Writings of Gertrude Stein.* New York: Modern Library, 1962.

Stein, Walter J. *California and the Dust Bowl Migration.* Westport, CT: Greenwood Press, 1973.

Steindl, Frank G. *Understanding Economic Recovery in the 1930s: Endogenous Propagation in the Great Depression.* Ann Arbor: University of Michigan Press, 2004.

Stephens, Michelle. "The First Negro Matinee Idol: Harry Belafonte and American Culture in the 1950s." *Left of the Color Line: Race, Radicalism, and Twentieth-Century Literature of the United States*, edited by Bill Mullen and James Edward Smethurst. Chapel Hill: University of North Carolina Press, 2003, 223–238.

Stephens, Vincent. "Pop Goes the Rapper: A Close Reading of Eminem's Genderphobia." *Popular Music* 24.1 (January 2005): 21–36.

Stevens, Errol Wayne. *Radical L.A.: from Coxey's Army to the Watts Riots, 1894-1965*. Norman: University of Oklahoma Press, 2009.

Stewart, Alexander. "Make It Funky: Fela Kuti, James Brown and the Invention of Afrobeat." *American Studies* 52.4, The Funk Issue (2013): 99–118.

Stewart, Jacqueline Najuma. *Migrating to the Movies: Cinema and Black Urban Modernity*. Berkeley: University of California Press, 2005.

Stockhausen, Karlheinz. *Towards a Cosmic Music*. Longmead, Shaftesbury, Dorset: Element, 1989.

Stockhausen, Karlheinz, and Robin Maconie. *Stockhausen on Music: Lectures and Interviews*. London; New York: M. Boyars; New York: Distributed in the U.S. by Kampmann, 1989.

Stockhausen, Karlheinz, and Mya Tannenbaum. *Conversations with Stockhausen*. Oxford [Oxfordshire]: Clarendon Press; Oxford [Oxfordshire]; New York: Oxford University Press, 1987.

Stockton, Sharon. "'Blacks vs. Browns': Questioning the White Ground." *College English* 57.2 (February 1995): 166–181 .

Stokes, W. Royal, Charles Peterson, and Don Peterson. *Swing Era New York: The Jazz Photographs of Charles Peterson*. Philadelphia: Temple University Press, 1994.

Stone, Chris. "'My Beliefs Are in My Song': Engaging Black Politics through Popular Music." *OAH Magazine of History* 20.5, Social Movements in the 1960s (October 2006): 28–32.

Stone, Sonja H. "An Ethno/Youth Perspective for Teaching Afro-American Culture." *The High School Journal* 60.2, Cultural Diversity (November 1976): 77–85.

Storb, Ilse, and Klaus-Gotthard Fischer. *Dave Brubeck, Improvisations and Compositions: The Idea of Cultural Exchange: With Discography*. New York: P. Lang, 1994.

Stowe, David W. "Jazz in the West: Cultural Frontier and Region during the Swing Era." *The Western Historical Quarterly* 23.1 (February 1992): 53–73.

———. *Swing Changes: Big-Band Jazz in New Deal America*. Cambridge: Harvard University Press, 1996.

Strachan, Ian G., and Mia Mask. *Poitier Revisited: Reconsidering a Black Icon in the Obama Age*. New York: Bloomsbury Academic, 2014.

Stratemann, Klaus. *Louis Armstrong on the Screen*. Copenhagen, Denmark: JazzMedia, 1996.

Strauss, Richard, and Beaumont Glass. *Richard Strauss' Complete Song Texts: In One Volume Containing All Solo Songs Including Those Not Published During the Composer's Lifetime*. Mt. Morris, NY: Leyerle, 2004.

Strauss, Richard, and Stefan Zweig. *A Confidential Matter: The Letters of Richard Strauss and Stefan Zweig, 1931–1935*. Berkeley: University of California Press, 1977.

Stravinsky, Igor. *Igor Stravinsky, An Autobiography*. New York: W. W. Norton & Company, Inc., 1962.

Stravinsky, Igor, and Robert Craft. *Conversations with Igor Stravinsky*. Garden City, NY: Doubleday, 1959.

Stravinsky, Vera, Robert Craft, and Otto Klemperer Archive (Library of Congress). *Stravinsky in Pictures and Documents*. New York: Simon and Schuster, 1978.

Stricklin, David. *Louis Armstrong: The Soundtrack of the American Experience*. Chicago: Ivan R. Dee, 2010.

Strunk, Steven. "Chick Corea's 1984 Performance of 'Night and Day.'" *Journal of Music Theory* 43.2 (Autumn 1999): 257–281.

———. "Notes on Harmony in Wayne Shorter's Compositions, 1964–67." *Journal of Music Theory* 49.2 (Fall 2005): 301–332.

Stump, Paul. *Go Ahead John: The Music of John McLaughlin*. London: SAF Publishing Ltd, 1999.

Sturm, Douglas. "Martin Luther King, Jr., as Democratic Socialist." *The Journal of Religious Ethics* 18.2 (Fall 1990): 79–105.

Sudhalter, Richard M. *Stardust Melody: The Life and Music of Hoagy Carmichael.* Oxford; New York: Oxford University Press, 2002.

Sudhalter, Richard M., and Philip R. Evans. *Bix: Man & Legend.* New Rochelle, NY: Arlington House 1974.

Sullivan, Denise. *Keep on Pushing: Black Power Music from Blues to Hip-Hop.* Chicago: Lawrence Hill Books, 2011.

Svorinich, Victor. *Listen to This: Miles Davis and Bitches Brew.* Jackson: University Press of Mississippi, 2015.

Swafford, Jan. *Charles Ives: A Life With Music.* New York: W. W. Norton, 1996. Sweeney, Carole. *From Fetish to Subject: Race, Modernism, and Primitivism, 1919–1935.* Westport, CT: Praeger Publishers, 2004.

Sweeney, Don. *Backstage at The Tonight Show: From Johnny Carson to Jay Leno.* Lanham, MD: Taylor Trade Pub., 2006.

Szwed, John F. *Space is the Place: The Lives and Times of Sun Ra.* New York: Pantheon Books, 1997.

———. *So What: The Life of Miles Davis.* New York: Simon & Schuster, 2002.

Tang, Patricia. *Masters of the Sabar: Wolof Griot Percussionists of Senegal.* Philadelphia: Temple University Press, 2007.

Tankel, Jonathan D. "The Impact of *The Jazz Singer* on the Conversion to Sound." *Journal of the University Film Association* 30.1, Topics in American Film History (Winter 1978): 21–25.

Tannenbaum, Allan, Peter Occhiogrosso, and Debbie Harry. *Grit and Glamour: The Street Style, High Fashion, and Legendary Music of the 1970s.* San Rafael, CA: Insight Editions, 2016.

Tari, Lujza. "Bartók's Collection of Hungarian Instrumental Folk Music and Its System." *Studia Musicologica Academiae Scientiarum Hungaricae* 47.2 (June 2006): 141–166.

Taruskin, Richard. "Why You Cannot Leave Bartók Out." *Studia Musicologica Academiae Scientiarum Hungaricae* 47.3/4, Bartók's Orbit. The Context and Sphere of Influence of His Work. Proceedings of the International Conference Held by the Bartók Archives, Budapest (22–24 March 2006). Part I. (September 2006): 265–277.

Tate, Greg. *Midnight Lightning: Jimi Hendrix and the Black Experience.* Chicago: Lawrence Hill Books, 2003.

Taylor, Dennis. *Jazz Saxophone: An In-Depth Look at the Styles of the Tenor Masters.* Milwaukee, WI: Hal Leonard Corp., 2004.

Taylor, Jeffrey J. "Earl Hines's Piano Style in the 1920s: A Historical and Analytical Perspective." *Black Music Research Journal* 12.1 (Spring 1992): 57–77.

———. "Louis Armstrong, Earl Hines, and 'Weather Bird.'" *The Musical Quarterly* 82.1 (Spring 1998): 1–40 .

Taylor, Shawn. *Tribe Called Quest's People's Instinctive Travels and the Paths of Rhythm.* London: Continuum International Pub., 2007.

Taylor, Stephen. *Fats Waller on the Air: The Radio Broadcasts and Discography.* Lanham, MD: Scarecrow Press, 2006.

Taylor, Timothy Dean. *Global Pop: World Music, World Markets.* New York: Routledge, 1997.

Taylor, William "Billy". "Jazz: America's Classical Music." *The Black Perspective in Music* 14.1, Special Issue: Black American Music Symposium 1985 (Winter 1986): 21–25.

Taylor, Yuval, and Jake Austen. *Darkest America: Black Minstrelsy From Slavery to Hip-Hop.* New York: W. W. Norton, 2012.

Teachout, Terry. *Duke: A Life of Duke Ellington.* New York: Gotham Books, 2013.

Teal, Kimberly Hannon. "Posthumously Live: Canon Formation at Jazz at Lincoln Center through the Case of Mary Lou Williams." *American Music* 32.4 (Winter 2014): 400–422.

Tenzer, Michael. *Analytical Studies in World Music.* Oxford; New York: Oxford University Press, 2006.

Terefenko, Dariusz. *Keith Jarrett's Transformation of Standard Tunes: Theory, Analysis, and Pedagogy*. Saarbrücken, Germany: VDM Verlag Dr. Müller, 2009.

_____. "Keith Jarrett's Art of Solo Introduction: "Stella by Starlight"—A Case Study." *Intégral* 24, Special Issue in Honor of Robert Wason (2010): 81–114.

Terry, Clark, and Gwen Terry. *Clark: The Autobiography of Clark Terry*. Berkeley: University of California Press, 2011.

Thomas, Gerald Lamont. *African American Preaching: The Contribution of Dr. Gardner C. Taylor*. New York: Peter Lang, 2004.

Thomas, Lorenzo, and Aldon Lynn Nielsen. *Don't Deny My Name: Words and Music and the Black Intellectual Tradition*. Ann Arbor: University of Michigan Press, 2008.

Thompson, Shirley Elizabeth. *Exiles At Home: The Struggle to Become American in Creole New Orleans*. Cambridge, MA: Harvard University Press, 2009.

Thomson, Guy P. C. *The European Revolutions of 1848 and the Americas*. London: Institute of Latin American Studies, 2002.

Thorne, Matt. *Prince: The Man and His Music*. Chicago: Bolden, 2016.

Thurman, Wallace. *Marcus Garvey*. New Brunswick, NJ: Rutgers University Press, 2003.

Thurman, Wallace, Amritjit Singh, and Daniel M. Scott. *The Collected Writings of Wallace Thurman: A Harlem Renaissance Reader*. New Brunswick, NJ: Rutgers University Press, 2003.

Timner, W. E. *Ellingtonia: The Recorded Music of Duke Ellington and his Sidemen*. Metuchen, NJ: Institute of Jazz Studies: Scarecrow Press, 1988.

Tingen, Paul. *Miles Beyond: The Electric Explorations of Miles Davis, 1967–1991*. New York: Billboard Books, 2001.

Tiongson, Antonio T. *Filipinos Represent: DJs, Racial Authenticity, and the Hip-Hop Nation*. Minneapolis: University of Minnesota Press, 2013 .

Tischauser, Leslie Vincent. *Jim Crow Laws*. Santa Barbara, CA: Greenwood, 2012.

Tkweme, W. S. "Blues in Stereo: The Texts of Langston Hughes in Jazz Music Ellison's Hemingways." *African American Review* 42.3/4 (Fall– Winter 2008): 503–512.

Tomko, Linda J. *Dancing Class: Gender, Ethnicity, and Social Divides in American Dance, 1890–1920*. Bloomington: Indiana University Press, 1999.

Tompkins, E. Berkeley. *Anti-Imperialism in the United States: The Great Debate, 1890–1920*. Philadelphia: University of Pennsylvania Press, 1970.

Tormé, Mel. *Traps, The Drum Wonder: The Life of Buddy Rich*. New York: Oxford University Press, 1991.

Totton, Robin. *Song of the Outcasts: An Introduction to Flamenco*. Portland, OR: Amadeus Press, 2003.

Tracy, Steven C. *Writers of the Black Chicago Renaissance*. Urbana: University of Illinois Press, 2011.

Travis, Dempsey J. "Chicago's Jazz Trail, 1893-1950." *Black Music Research Journal* 10.1 (Spring 1990): 82–85.

_____. *Billy Eckstine: The Ballad Singer of the Century*. Chicago: Urban Research Press, 1994.

_____. *The Louis Armstrong Odyssey: From Jane Alley to America's Jazz Ambassador*. Chicago: Urban Research Press, 1997.

Trethewey, Ken. *John McLaughlin: The Emerald Beyond*. Jazz-Fusion Books, 2013.

Tucker, Bruce. "Living Metaphors: Recent Black Music Biography." *Black Music Research Journal* 3 (1983): 58–69.

Tucker, Mark. "Count Basie and the Piano That Swings the Band." *Popular Music* 5, Continuity and Change (1985): 45–79.

_____. "In Search of Will Vodery." *Black Music Research Journal* 16.1 (Spring 1996): 123–182.

_____. "The Genesis of 'Black, Brown and Beige.'" *Black Music Research Journal* 22 Supplement: Best of BMRJ (2002): 131–150.

Tucker, Sherrie. "'Where the Blues and the Truth Lay Hiding': Rememory of Jazz in Black Women's Fiction." *Frontiers: A Journal of Women Studies* 13.2 (1993): 26–44.

_____. "Telling Performances: Jazz History Remembered and Remade by the Women in the Band." *The Oral History Review* 26.1 (1999): 67–84.

_____. *Swing Shift: "All-Girl" Bands of the 1940s*. Durham, NC: Duke University Press, 2000.

Tumpak, John R. *When Swing Was the Thing: Personality Profiles of the Big Band Era*. Milwaukee, WI: Marquette University Press, 2008.

Turley, Alan C. "The Ecological and Social Determinants of the Production of Dixieland Jazz in New Orleans." *International Review of the Aesthetics and Sociology of Music* 26.1 (June 1995): 107–121.

Turner, Richard Brent. *Jazz Religion, the Second Line, and Black New Orleans*. Bloomington: Indiana University Press, 2009.

Turner, Sarah E., and Sarah Nilsen. *The Colorblind Screen: Television in Post-Racial America*. New York: NYU Press, 2014.

Tuveson, Ernest Lee. *Redeemer Nation: The Idea of America's Millennial Role*. Chicago: University of Chicago Press, 1968.

Ulanov, Barry. "Jazz: Issues of Identity." *The Musical Quarterly* 65.2 (April 1979): 245–256.

Ulrich, Thomas, and Jayne Obst. *Stockhausen: A Theological Interpretation*. Kürten, Germany: Stockhausen-Stiftung für Musik, 2012.

United States. Congress. House. Special Committee to Investigate the East St. Louis Riots. *East St. Louis Riots: Report of the Special Committee Authorized by Congress to Investigate the East St. Louis Riots*. Washington, D.C.: [U.S. G.P.O.], 1918.

University of California, Los Angeles. Asian American Studies Center. *Los Angeles Since 1992: Commemorating the 20th Anniversary of the Uprisings*. Los Angeles: Asian American Studies Center, University of California, Los Angeles, 2012.

Uribe, Ed. *The Essence of Brazilian Percussion and Drum Set: With Rhythm Section Parts: Rhythms, Songstyles, Techniques, Applications*. Van Nuys, CA: Alfred Publishing, 2006.

Vacca, Richard. *The Boston Jazz Chronicles: Faces, Places, and Nightlife, 1937-1962*. Belmont, MA: Troy Street Publishing, 2012.

Vacher, Peter. *Swingin' on Central Avenue: African American Jazz in Los Angeles* . Lanham, MD: Rowman & Littlefield, 2015.

Vail, Ken. *Count Basie: Swingin' the Blues, 1936-1950*. Lanham, MD: Scarecrow Press, 2003.

Van Deburg, William L. *New Day in Babylon: The Black Power Movement and American Culture, 1965–1975*. Chicago: University of Chicago Press, 1992.

van de Leur, Walter. *Something To Live For: The Music of Billy Strayhorn*. New York: Oxford University Press, 2002.

van der Tuuk, Alex. *Out of Anonymity: The Paramount and Broadway Territory Bands*. Glenwood Springs, CO: Rustbooks Publishing, 2014.

van Ginneken, Jaap. *Screening Difference: How Hollywood's Blockbuster Films Imagine Race, Ethnicity, and Culture*. Lanham, MD: Rowman & Littlefield, 2007.

Van Wormer, Katherine S., David W. Jackson, and Charletta Sudduth. *The Maid Narratives: Black Domestic and White Families in the Jim Crow South*. Baton Rouge: Louisiana State University Press, 2012.

Vincent, Rickey. *Funk: The Music, The People, and the Rhythm of the One*. New York: St. Martin's Griffin, 1996.

Vlad, Roman, Frederick Fuller, and Ann Fuller. *Stravinsky*. London; New York Oxford University Press, 1967.

Vogel, Shane. "Closing Time: Langston Hughes and the Queer Poetics of Harlem Nightlife." *Criticism* 48.3 (Summer 2006): 397–425.

_____. "Performing "Stormy Weather": Ethel Waters, Lena Horne, and Katherine Dunham." *South Central Review* 25.1, Staging Modernism (Spring 2008): 93–113.

_____. *The Scene of Harlem Cabaret: Race, Sexuality, Performance*. Chicago: The University of Chicago Press, 2009.

von Kruedener, Jürgen. *Economic Crisis and Political Collapse: The Weimar Republic 1924–1933*. New York: Berg, 1990.

von Lintig, Bettina, and Hughes Dubois. *African Impressions: Tribal Art and Currents of Life*. Milan, Italy: 5 Continents Editions, 2011.

Wager, Gregg. *Symbolism as a Compositional Method in the Works of Karlheinz Stockhausen.* College Park, MD: G. Wager, 1998.

Wagner, Naphtali. "'Domestication' of Blue Notes in the Beatles' Songs." *Music Theory Spectrum*, 25.2 (Fall 2003): 353–365.

Wald, Elijah. *Global Minstrels: Voices of World Music.* New York: Routledge, 2007.

Wald, Sarah D. *The Nature of California: Race, Citizenship, and Farming since the Dust Bowl.* Seattle: University of Washington Press, 2016.

Walden, Daniel. "Black Music and Cultural Nationalism: The Maturation of Archie Shepp." *Negro American Literature Forum* 5.4 (Winter 1971): 150–154.

Waldman, Tom. *We All Want to Change the World: Rock and Politics from Elvis to Eminem.* Lanham, MD: Taylor Trade Pub., 2003.

Walker, Travis T. J. *Western Swing Music: A Complete Reference Guide.* Charleston, SC: [CreateSpace Independent Publishing Platform], 2016.

Wall, Cheryl A. "Passing for what? Aspects of Identity in Nella Larsen's Novels." *Black American Literature Forum* 20.1/2 (Spring–Summer 1986): 97–111.

_____. *Women of the Harlem Renaissance.* Bloomington: Indiana University Press, 1995.

Wallace, John, and Alexander McGrattan. *The Trumpet.* New Haven, CT: Yale University Press, 2011.

Wallach, Jennifer Jensen. *Richard Wright: From Black Boy to World Citizen.* Chicago: Ivan R. Dee, 2010.

Waller, Maurice, and Anthony Calabrese. *Fats Waller.* New York: Schirmer Books, 1977.

Wang, Richard. "Researching the New Orleans-Chicago Jazz Connection: Tools and Methods." *Black Music Research Journal* 8.1 (1988): 101–112.

Ward, Brian. "Civil Rights and Rock and Roll: Revisiting the Nat King Cole Attack of 1956." *OAH Magazine of History* 24.2 (April 2010): 21–24.

Warren, Sandy. *Art Blakey Cookin' and Jammin': Recipes and Remembrances from a Jazz Life.* Donaldsonville, LA: Margaret Media, 2010.

Washabaugh, William. *Flamenco: Passion, Politics, and Popular Culture.* Oxford; Washington, D.C.: Berg, 1996.

_____. *Flamenco Music and National Identity in Spain.* Farnham, Surrey; Burlington, VT: Ashgate, 2012.

Washington, Sylvia Hood. *Packing Them In: An Archaeology of Environmental Racism in Chicago, 1865–1954.* Lanham, MD: Lexington Books, 2005.

Waters, Keith. "Modes, Scales, Functional Harmony, and Nonfunctional Harmony in the Compositions of Herbie Hancock." *Journal of Music Theory* 49.2 (Fall 2005): 333–357.

_____. *The Studio Recordings of the Miles Davis Quintet, 1965–68.* New York: Oxford University Press, 2011.

Watkins, Mel. *Stepin Fetchit: The Life and Times of Lincoln Perry.* New York: Pantheon Books, 2005. Llc, 2015.

Webb, Constance. *Richard Wright; a Biography.* New York: Putnam, 1968.

Webster, Jason. *Duende: A Journey in Search of Flamenco.* London: Doubleday, 2003.

Weheliye, Alexander. "In the Mix: Hearing the Souls of Black Folk." *Amerikastudien / American Studies* 45.4, Time and the African-American Experience (2000): 535–554.

Weiner, Howard T., Rutgers University. Institute of Jazz Studies, and Historic Brass Society. *Early Twentieth-Century Brass Idioms: Art, Jazz, and Other Popular Traditions: Proceedings of the International Conference Presented by the Institute of Jazz Studies of Rutgers University and the Historic Brass Society, November 4–5, 2005.* Lanham, MD: Scarecrow Press, 2009.

Weisenfeld, Judith. "'On Not Being Jewish . . . and Other Lies': Reflections on Racial Fever." *Soundings: An Interdisciplinary Journal* 96.1 (2013): 3–11.

Welburn, Ron. "Jazz Magazines of the 1930s: An Overview of Their Provocative Journalism." *American Music* 5.3 (Autumn 1987): 255–270.

Welch, Allison. "Meetings along the Edge: Svara and Tāla in American Minimal Music." *American Music* 17.2 (Summer 1999): 179–199.

Werbner, Pnina, and Muhammad Anwar. *Black and Ethnic Leaderships in Britain: The Cultural Dimensions of Political Action.* London; New York: Routledge, 2003.

Werner, Craig Hansen. *Playing the Changes: From Afro-modernism to the Jazz Impulse*. Urbana: University of Illinois Press, 1994.

_____. *Higher Ground: Stevie Wonder, Aretha Franklin, Curtis Mayfield, and the Rise and Fall of American Soul*. New York: Crown Publishers, 2004.

Westendorf, Lynette. "Cecil Taylor: Indent—'Second Layer.'" *Perspectives of New Music* 33.1/2 (Winter–Summer 1995): 294–326.

Westerberg, Hans. *Boy from New Orleans: Louis "Satchmo" Armstrong: On Records, Films, Radio, and Television*. Copenhagen: Jazzmedia, 1981.

Weston, Ollie. *Exploring Jazz Saxophone: An Introduction to Jazz Harmony, Technique and Improvisation*. London: Schott, 2009.

Whalen, Charles W., and Barbara Whalen. *The Longest Debate: A Legislative History of the 1964 Civil Rights Act*. Cabin John, MD; Washington, D.C.: Seven Locks Press, 1985.

Wheeler, Geoffrey. *Dial Records: West Coast Jazz and the Be-Bop Era*. Ft. Wayne, IN: Hillbrook Press, 2009.

Whidden, Seth. "French Rap Music Going Global: IAM, They Were, We Are." *The French Review* 80.5 (April 2007): 1008–1023.

Whitcomb, Ian. *Irving Berlin and Ragtime America*. New York: Limelight Editions, 1987.

White, E. Frances. *Dark Continent of Our Bodies: Black Feminism and the Politics of Respectability*. Philadelphia: Temple University Press, 2001.

White, John. *Artie Shaw: His Life and Music*. New York: Continuum, 2004.

Whiteley, Sheila. "Progressive Rock and Psychedelic Coding in the Work of Jimi Hendrix." *Popular Music* 9.1 (January 1990): 37–60.

Whyton, Tony. *Beyond A Love Supreme: John Coltrane and the Legacy of an Album*. New York: Oxford University Press, 2013.

Widener, Daniel. *Black Arts West: Culture and Struggle in Postwar Los Angeles*. Durham, NC: Duke University Press, 2010.

Widick, B. J. *Detroit: City of Race and Class Violence*. Detroit, MI: Wayne State University Press, 1989.

Wilk, Max. *Overture and Finale: Rodgers & Hammerstein and the Creation of Their Two Greatest Hits*. New York: Back Stage Books, 1999.

Wilkinson, Christopher. "A National Band from the Southwest: The Don Albert Orchestra." *American Music* 14.3 (Autumn 1996): 313–351.

_____. *Jazz on the Road: Don Albert's Musical Life*. Berkeley: University of California Press; [Chicago]: Center for Black Music Research Columbia College, Chicago, 2001.

_____. "Hot and Sweet: Big Band Music in Black West Virginia before the Swing Era." *American Music* 21.2 (Summer 2003): 159–179.

Willey, Ann. "A Bridge over Troubled Waters: Jazz, Diaspora Discourse, and E. B. Dongala's 'Jazz and Palm Wine' as Response to Amiri Baraka's 'Answers in Progress.'" *Research in African Literatures* 44.3 (Fall 2013): 138–151.

Williams, Justin A. *Rhymin' and Stealin': Musical Borrowing in Hip-Hop*. Ann Arbor: The University of Michigan Press, 2014.

Williams, Linda. *Playing the Race Card: Melodramas of Black and White from Uncle Tom to O.J. Simpson*. Princeton, NJ: Princeton University Press, 2001.

Williams, Martin. "Art Tatum: Not for the Left Hand Alone." *American Music* 1.1 (Spring 1983): 36–40.

_____. "Jazz: What Happened in Kansas City?" *American Music* 3.2 (Summer 1985): 171–179.

Williams, Megan E. "The "Crisis" Cover Girl: Lena Horne, the NAACP, and Representations of African American Femininity, 1941–1945." *American Periodicals* 16.2 (2006): 200–18.

_____. "'Meet the Real Lena Horne': Representations of Lena Horne in "Ebony" Magazine, 1945–1949." *Journal of American Studies* 43.1 (2009): 117–30.

Williams, Richard. *Miles Davis: The Man in the Green Shirt*. New York: H. Holt, 1993.

_____. *The Blue Moment: Miles Davis' Kind of Blue and the Remaking of Modern Music*. London: Faber, 2009.

Williamson, Joel. *New People: Miscegenation and Mulattoes in the United States*. New York: Free Press, 1980.

Willis, Sharon. *The Poitier Effect: Racial Melodrama and Fantasies of Reconciliation*. Minneapolis: University of Minnesota Press, 2015.

Wilson, James F. *Bulldaggers, Pansies, and Chocolate Babies: Performance, Race, and Sexuality in the Harlem Renaissance*. Ann Arbor: University of Michigan Press, 2010.

Wilson, Peter Niklas. *Ornette Coleman: His Life and Music*. Berkeley, CA: Berkeley Hills Books, 1999.

———. "Living Time: Ancient to the Future. Concepts and Fantasies of Micro- and Macro-Time in Contemporary Jazz." *Amerikastudien / American Studies* 45.4, Time and the African-American Experience (2000): 567–574.

———. *Sonny Rollins: The Definitive Musical Guide*. Berkeley, CA: Berkeley Hills Books, 2001.

Wilson, Teddy, Arie Ligthart, and Humphrey Van Loo. *Teddy Wilson Talks Jazz*. New York: Continuum, 2001.

Winthrop, John, Richard S. Dunn, James Savage, and Laetitia Yeandle. *The Journal of John Winthrop, 1630–1649*. Cambridge, MA: Harvard University Press, 1996.

Winthrop, John, and James K. Hosmer. *Winthrop's Journal, "History of New England," 1630–1649*. New York: C. Scribner's Sons, 1908.

Winthrop, Robert C. *Life and Letters of John Winthrop: Governor of the Massachusetts-Bay Company at Their Emigration to New England, 1630*. Boston: Little, Brown, 1869.

Wise, Tim J. *Colorblind: The Rise of Post-Racial Politics and the Retreat from Racial Equity*. San Francisco, CA: City Lights Books, 2010.

Witkovsky, Matthew S. "Experience vs. Theory: Romare Bearden and Abstract Expressionism." *Black American Literature Forum* 23.2, Fiction Issue (Summer 1989): 257–282.

Witmer, Robert, and James Robbins. "A Historical and Critical Survey of Recent Pedagogical Materials for the Teaching and Learning of Jazz." *Bulletin of the Council for Research in Music Education* 96, Research in Jazz Education II (Spring 1988): 7–29.

Wolcott, Victoria W. *Remaking Respectability: African American Women in Interwar Detroit*. Chapel Hill: University of North Carolina Press, 2001.

Wolfenstein, E. Victor. *A Gift of the Spirit: Reading The Souls of Black Folk*. Ithaca, NY: Cornell University Press, 2007.

Wölfer, Jürgen. *Anita O'Day: An Exploratory Discography*. Zephyrhills, FL: Joyce Record Club Publication, 1990.

Wolff, Francis, Michael Cuscuna, Charlie Lourie, Oscar Schnider, and Blue Note (Firm). *The Blue Note Years: The Jazz Photography of Francis Wolff*. New York: Rizzoli, 1995.

Wolfskill, Phoebe. "Caricature and the New Negro in the Work of Archibald Motley Jr. and Palmer Hayden." *The Art Bulletin* 91.3 (September 2009): 343–365.

Womack, Kenneth. "Authorship and the Beatles." *College Literature* 34.3 (Summer 2007): 161–182.

Won-gu Kim, Daniel. "'In the Tradition': Amiri Baraka, Black Liberation, and Avant-Garde Praxis in the U.S." *African American Review* 37.2/3, Amri Baraka Issue (Summer–Autumn 2003): 345–363.

Woodward, C. Vann. *The Strange Career of Jim Crow*. New York: Oxford University Press, 1974.

Woodward, Walter William, and Omohundro Institute of Early American History & Culture. *Prospero's America: John Winthrop, Jr., Alchemy, and the Creation of New England Culture, 1606–1676*. Chapel Hill: Published for the Omohundro Institute of Early American History and Culture by the University of North Carolina Press, 2010.

Woodworth, Griffin. "Prince, Miles, and Maceo: Horns, Masculinity, and the Anxiety of Influence." *Black Music Research Journal* 33.2 (Fall 2013): 117–150.

Wörner, Karl H., and Bill Hopkins. *Stockhausen; Life and Work*. Berkeley: University of California Press, 1973.

Wriggle, John. "Chappie Willet, Frank Fairfax, and Phil Edwards' Collegians: From West Virginia to Philadelphia." *Black Music Research Journal* 27.1 (Spring 2007): 1–22.

Wright, Amy Nathan. "Exploring the Funkadelic Aesthetic: Intertextuality and Cosmic Philosophizing in Funkadelic's Album Covers and Liner Notes." *American Studies* 52.4, The Funk Issue (2013): 141–169.

Wright, Ellicott. "The Souls of Black Folk and My Larger Education." *The Journal of Negro Education* 30.4 (Autumn 1961): 440–444.

Wright, John S. *Shadowing Ralph Ellison*. Jackson: University Press of Mississippi, 2006.

Wright, Josephine R. B., and John Birks "Dizzy" Gillespie. "Conversation with John Birks "Dizzy" Gillespie, Pioneer of Jazz." *The Black Perspective in Music* 4.1 (Spring 1976): 82–89.

Wright, Richard, and Earle V. Bryant. *Byline, Richard Wright: Articles from the Daily Worker and New Masses*. Columbia: University of Missouri Press, 2015.

Wright, Richard, Keneth Kinnamon, and Michel Fabre. *Conversations with Richard Wright*. Jackson: University Press of Mississippi, 1993.

Wright, Richard, Ellen Wright, and Michel Fabre. *Richard Wright Reader*. New York: Harper & Row, 1978.

Wynn, Linda T. "William Edward Burghardt Du Bois: The Tennessee Connections to "The Souls of Black Folk.'" *Tennessee Historical Quarterly* 63.1 (Spring 2004): 18–33.

Wynne, Ben. *In Tune: Charley Patton, Jimmie Rodgers, and the Roots of American Music*. Baton Rouge: Louisiana State University Press, 2014.

Yanow, Scott. *The Trumpet Kings: The Players Who Shaped the Sound of Jazz Trumpet*. San Francisco, CA: Backbeat Books, 2001.

———. *Jazz on Film: The Complete Story of the Musicians & Music Onscreen*. San Francisco, CA: Backbeat Books, 2004.

———. *Jazz: A Regional Exploration*. Westport, CT: Greenwood Press, 2005.

Yong, Amos, and Estrelda Alexander. *Afro-Pentecostalism: Black Pentecostal and Charismatic Christianity in History and Culture*. New York: New York University Press, 2011.

Young, Lola. *Fear of the Dark: 'Race', Gender, and Sexuality in the Cinema*. London; New York: Routledge, 1996.

Youngquist, Paul. *A Pure Solar World: Sun Ra and the Birth of Afrofuturism*. Austin: University of Texas Press, 2016.

Yu, Timothy. *Race and the Avant-Garde: Experimental and Asian American Poetry since 1965*. Stanford, CA: Stanford University Press, 2009.

Yudkin, Jeremy. *Miles Davis, Miles Smiles, and the Invention of Post Bop*. Bloomington: Indiana University Press, 2008.

Zaborowska, Magdalena. *James Baldwin's Turkish Decade: Erotics of Exile*. Durham, NC: Duke University Press, 2009.

Zak III, Albin J. "Bob Dylan and Jimi Hendrix: Juxtaposition and Transformation 'All along the Watchtower.'" *Journal of the American Musicological Society* 57.3 (Fall 2004): 599–644.

Zielenziger, Michael. *Shutting Out the Sun: How Japan Created Its Own Lost Generation*. New York: Nan A. Talese, 2006.

Index

About the Author

Dr. Aaron E. Lefkovitz received his American Studies PhD from the University at Buffalo (SUNY) and Master in Contemporary Music Studies from Goldsmiths College, University of London. He teaches US History at Harold Washington College, The City Colleges of Chicago, and DePaul University.

CPSIA information can be obtained
at www.ICGtesting.com
Printed in the USA
LVHW091930160721
692904LV00003B/48